# STATISTICS IN PSYCHOLOGICAL RESEARCH

THE MACMILLAN COMPANY
NEW YORK • CHICAGO
DALLAS • ATLANTA • SAN FRANCISCO
LONDON • MANILA
IN CANADA
BRETT-MACMILLAN LTD.
GALT, ONTARIO

# STATISTICS IN PSYCHOLOGICAL RESEARCH

WILLIAM S. RAY

The Macmillan Company New York

First Printing

Library of Congress catalog card number: 62-7083

The Macmillan Company, New York
Brett-Macmillan Ltd., Galt, Ontario

Printed in the United States of America

# PREFACE

The plan for *Statistics in Psychological Research* was developed, in outline and detail, over a six-year period, during which the author was a member of the faculty of the Department of Psychology at Pennsylvania State University. In twelve semesters, nearly five hundred advanced undergraduate students and graduate students were enrolled in a statistics course which was taught by the author and which served as the testing ground for the methods and materials of the text. The students were primarily majors in psychology, but students from education, speech, home economics, civil engineering, physical education, mathematics, and mineralogy constituted a substantial proportion of the enrollment. In addition, numerous members of the faculty from various departments of the University audited the course.

The text is intended for a one-semester course in psychological statistics. It may be used as an introductory text for advanced undergraduates and graduate students. It may also be used as a second- or intermediate-level text for psychology majors in general. It covers the standard topics, but concentrates on critical issues rather than some minor or peripheral matters. Emphasis is given to the distinction between descriptive and inferential statistics, between experimental and non-experimental research, and between testing significance and estimating parameters.

Considerable space is devoted to developing the concept of psychological statistics as an important part of the language of the research psychologist. To assist the reader in developing this concept, chapters are identified as referring to syntactics, semantics, or pragmatics. Thus an attempt has been made throughout the text to organize the discussion of statistical issues around certain fundamental notions about the study of language. This language approach to the study of psychological statistics assists the student in recognizing the nature of a given issue and its resolution without introducing any additional assumptions into the discussion or placing any restrictions on the standard treatment of the subject.

Dr. Kendon R. Smith and Dr. Lewis R. Aiken, Jr., presently my colleagues at The Woman's College of the University of North Carolina, made many helpful criticisms and suggestions.

I am indebted to the authors and to the publishers, Oliver & Boyd Ltd., Edinburgh, for permission to reprint Table No. III from *Statistical Methods for Research Workers* by Professor Sir Ronald A. Fisher, and Table No. III from *Statistical Tables for Biological, Agricultural, and Medical Research* by Professor Sir Ronald A. Fisher and Dr. Frank Yates.

Finally, I must give credit to my students whose expressions of interest and enthusiasm over the past six years were a constant source of encouragement in bringing this project to completion.

W. S. R.

*Greensboro, North Carolina*

# CONTENTS

# STATISTICS IN PSYCHOLOGICAL RESEARCH

# LANGUAGE, SCIENCE, AND STATISTICS

# 1

We shall begin with a definition.

A *language* is a system of interrelated signs employed by the members of a social group for purposes of communication.

In the totality of human language, one can discern numerous overlapping systems and subsystems which vary considerably in size and complexity, and which are combined in various ways to suit the purposes of their users. The familiar, extensive sign systems of everyday life, such as English, French, German, and Russian, are often called *natural languages* to distinguish them from certain specialized and restricted languages. One specialized and restricted system of signs which is of interest to us here is what might be called the *language of empirical science*. The language of empirical science can be described, in general terms, as consisting of technical language of various sorts along with some parts of one or more natural languages.

Progress in empirical science, as the modern world has known it, would have been impossible without language. To achieve new additions to one's knowledge of natural phenomena, observation, a basic component of empirical research, must be converted to data which can be accumulated, analyzed, and reported. Language is necessary in recording and storing data, in organizing and systematizing data, in describing and predicting natural processes and events represented by the observations, and in generalizing and communicating the final results.

Although mathematics is a language in itself, it also constitutes an important part of the more complex language system of empirical science. Mathematical language is a system of signs whose interrelations are unambiguously and completely determined. It is a language remarkably adapted to the formation of relations among signs and the transformation of these relations. As a vehicle for logic and deduction it is unequaled by any other language system. In mathematics very complex and extended operations upon certain initial sets of signs will yield numerous other sets without error or controversy. It is, finally, the language in which the scientist sets forth his propositions with the greatest precision.

Mathematical statistics, a branch of mathematics, is also a language. (The suffix " -ics " of the word " statistics," as the term is employed at this point, indicates a branch of systematized knowledge and the term is construed as singular in number.) Mathematical statistics is a system of interrelated signs which includes certain special symbols in addition to the common symbols of arithmetic, algebra, geometry, calculus, and probability theory. It shares in the deductive perfection of mathematics.

Mathematical statistics has developed rapidly and extensively in the present century. It has become an important part of the language of the biological and behavioral sciences. The significance of this development is indicated by the fact that the formal design and analysis of research in these sciences are now largely guided and determined by statistical theory. Psychology and education share this concern with and dependence on statistics.

## The Study of Language

There are numerous ways of analyzing and describing language, but the approach which seems particularly appropriate and valuable to the present discussion is that of Rudolf Carnap and Charles W. Morris, whose scholarly contributions in this area are widely known. (Selected writings by these authors are listed at the end of Chapter 1 as suggested readings.) We wish to indicate that the discussion which follows is based to a considerable extent, but not entirely, upon the writings of Carnap and Morris. In our very brief and introductory treatment of language analysis, we shall make no pretense of being highly technical and complete, and we shall not try to preserve certain fine distinctions which can be made between the views of various authorities in this area.

Three points of reference can be employed in the analysis of any language. They are the sign, what is referred to by the sign, and the response of an interpreter made directly to the sign and indirectly to the sign's referent.

The sign is the unit of language. Signs may be letters, numbers, words, or marks such as " ? ", " / ", and " + ". Signs may be combined, arranged in sequence to form expressions, and composed into sentences.

In general, what is referred to is an object,[1] a property of an object, a relation between properties, a function involving relations, or a complex

[1]When we say " object," we intend " object or event."

situation involving objects, properties, relations, and functions.[2] What is referred to is said to be *designated* by the sign and, in consequence, is called the *designatum* of the sign.

In responding to a sign, an interpreter takes account of the designatum. Any attempt at a complete explanation or understanding of the response to a sign would have to include, as possible factors, the personality of the interpreter and the nature of his group. Making the response of an interpreter a point of reference for the analysis of language has the effect of assigning a place of central importance in that analysis to the interpreter's personal characteristics and the social context within which he operates.

A comprehensive investigation of a language would deal with signs and their interrelations; the designation of objects, properties, relations, functions, and situations by signs, expressions, and sentences; and the interpreter of the signs with the totality of his personal and social behavior associated with the use of the signs. Studies of language can, of course, vary in their comprehensiveness. The terms " syntactics," " semantics," and " pragmatics " are employed to distinguish three levels of comprehensiveness in language analyses. *Syntactics* is the study of language in which only the signs and their interrelations are abstracted and analyzed. *Semantics* refers to language analysis in which signs and their designata are abstracted and investigated without reference to the interpreter or user. *Pragmatics* is the language study in which extensive reference is made to the interpreter or user of the language.

Taking the sign, the designatum, and the response of the interpreter as three points of reference, we can characterize the three kinds or levels of language study by three simple relations. In syntactics the abstracted relations of signs to signs are analyzed. In semantics the relation between the sign and its designatum is the main object of study. In pragmatics the relation of principal interest is that between sign and user.

Syntactics has to do with what one would ordinarily think of as the fashioning of letters, spelling, constructing sentences, and reasoning logically. In mathematics, formulas and equations are sentences; proofs and derivations are examples of deductive reasoning. Calculation is a special form of deduction applied to numerical expressions.

A well-developed language has three sets of syntactical rules: rules which provide the means of introducing new signs; rules which indicate how signs can be combined, placed in sequence, and composed into sentences; and rules which guide deduction, the obtaining of a sentence from one or more other sentences. When expressions or sentences conform to these three kinds of

[2]For example, the object might be a ten-year-old child, the behavioral event might be his reading of several pages of test material. The property of interest to a psychologist might be the child's speed of reading. A relation between properties might be shown by comparing the reading speed of one child with the speed of another. A function might be established for predicting differences in reading speed from differences in spelling accuracy for a large number of children.

syntactical rules, they are considered to be correct. When they do not conform in some respect, they are considered to be incorrect in that respect.

Semantics is concerned primarily with designation. Several levels of designation can be distinguished. The lowest level is the relation between an object and a sign which simply directs attention to or points to the object.

At a higher level, properties of objects, relations between properties, and functions are designated by signs or combinations of signs. Sentences which designate relations, functions, or situations are called *propositions*.

At the lowest level of designation the assignment of signs to designata is often arbitrary.[3] These semantical definitions pose no special problem and, at the same time, add nothing to empirical knowledge. Although certain designations may be arbitrary, expressions and propositions which incorporate them may be true or false.[4] Qualities of truth and falsity can be determined only by experience and observation. Success in acquiring empirical knowledge is largely a matter of formulating true propositions. (Later we shall prefer using " confirmable," a relative term, in place of " true," an absolute term.)

At the higher and more complex levels of designation, the meaningful assignment of signs, expressions, and sentences to designata such as properties, relations, functions, and situations is seldom, if ever, arbitrary.[5] The designation presupposes some kind of correspondence or isomorphism between signs and their designata. Verification of the correspondence is again only the yield of experience and observation. In particular we wish to emphasize that the development of an elaborate syntax, which may be entirely correct within itself, has no necessary consequence for semantical verification.

There are other special signs which connect or indicate relations between signs but do not themselves designate objects, properties, relations, or functions. Examples of these special signs are the English words: " all," " and," " any," " are," " every," " if," " is," and " not." There are still other signs which indicate the reaction of the user to the situation being described. In the following sentence, " unfortunately " indicates the reaction of the author of the sentence. " Unfortunately, everyone agrees that statistics

[3]Given three distinguishable objects and the three labels—RIL, ZUP, and NEM, the labels could be assigned as names for the objects in any arbitrary fashion as long as these labels were then used consistently in later communications.

[4]The words, " farmers," " milk," and " cows," may have been assigned to their designata arbitrarily, but in our everyday experience only one order of these words produces a true proposition.

[5]Scoring a set of test papers may yield a set of numbers, each of which is assigned to a student. Students may then be compared with respect to these scores. Furthermore, the scores might be employed in a specific mathematical equation for predicting other measures of performance. No part of this procedure would be considered meaningful by a psychologist if the assignment of numbers was arbitrary. Nor would the prediction be considered of any value if the choice of the equation was completely arbitrary.

is misused, but few can agree on what specific practices actually constitute misuse." We shall not attempt here a discussion of the designata of these special signs which either connect other signs or indicate the user's reaction. Our reason is that the discussion would go beyond the reasonable scope of these brief, introductory considerations and would not be especially profitable for the student of psychological statistics.

We have already stated that success in acquiring empirical knowledge is largely a matter of formulating true semantical relations but that verification itself depends on experience and not on the logical manipulation of signs. What is the nature of the extremely important and critical process of verification?

The question does not have a simple answer. We can say, in general, that one must observe the semantical rules of the language in question. A semantical rule is one which determines the conditions under which a sign or an expression is applicable to a designatum. In other words, a semantical rule provides the means of establishing correspondence between signs and what they refer to. The problem of correspondence in the case of attention-directing signs is not difficult. The semantical rule is that the sign designates what is pointed to. Much more difficult is the problem of correspondence for signs, expressions, or sentences which designate properties, relations, functions, or situations.

In the development of logical empiricism, three views on the problem of verifying propositions have been prominent.[6] One view is that scientific statements are verified by means of immediate experiences. That is to say, propositions can be reduced to so-called *primitive sentences* about which there can be no question. A second view is that a proposition is checked only by incorporating it in a system with other propositions. These criterion propositions have been called *protocol sentences* and are defined as direct statements of observations as typically employed by natural scientists. A third view is that the base of all empirical knowledge is the ultimate reduction of all propositions to attention-directing and pointing, a process called *substantiation.*

Carnap has tried to synthesize these three views. He stressed the importance of distinguishing between the terms " truth " and " confirmation " as applied to propositions. Carnap maintained that truth is an absolute concept and that confirmation is a relative one, degrees of which vary with the progress of any science. He also distinguished between directly and indirectly testable propositions. A directly testable proposition is one which, on the basis of observation, can be regarded as confirmed or disconfirmed. An indirectly testable proposition is one which is tested by directly testing other propositions which are related to it. The testing operations include checking a proposition against observation and checking a proposition against other propositions which have already been confirmed.

[6]See Joergensen (6).

Pragmatics, the study of the relation between signs and the user of signs, includes and depends on syntactics and semantics but goes beyond them. A language cannot be adequately described, nor can its functions be completely explained, on the basis of its syntax and its semantical relations. Language as behavior is intimately involved with the attitudes, values, and judgments of the users. Usages may develop because of their convenience for the user, their effectiveness in communication, or their demonstrated practical benefits.

Common-sense considerations enter pragmatics in the supposedly sound and valid judgments underlying the thinking, reasoning, and argument which play very important roles in the practical affairs of men. It is certainly true that some of what passes for common sense is not sound and valid. It is possible, too, that part or all of what is actually sound and valid judgment could be shown to be so by syntactical analysis with respect to the deductive processes of the language. Although common sense conclusions might, in theory, be reducible to formal deduction, it is quite impractical to do so as a general thing. In everyday life there is insufficient time to reduce all of one's judgments to the syntactical level of evaluation. Furthermore, only a few highly specialized scholars could do the logical analyses in those instances in which they are possible. Most of us believe that many important problems can be solved and their solutions communicated satisfactorily in language by an application of sound judgment on the part of one or more individuals without recourse to a formal analysis; and we act accordingly. Consequently, it seems appropriate to study, in pragmatics, the important role of common sense as it is exercised by the user of the language.

Convention and habit are also important factors in language behavior. At any given point in time in any social group, certain ways of speaking and writing are taken for granted and used uncritically. If a member of the group does question a specific construction or idiom, he is often at a loss to explain it or account for it except as a convention. Even so, it would not be justifiable to conclude that conventional and habitual usages have completely arbitrary origins. They may have originated in the attitudes, values, and judgments of members of the social group of an earlier period.

Corresponding to the sentence of syntactics and the proposition of semantics is the expectation of pragmatics. An *expectation* is the response of an interpreter to a proposition initiated by himself or another person. Expectations are fulfilled or not fulfilled in the experience of the user.

# Psychological Statistics

Psychological statistics, as we wish to consider it here, is a language consisting of mathematics, psychological terms and other technical English words, and words employed in formal English for speaking and writing. It is a language employed by psychologists in research, the objective of which is the acquisition of knowledge about the behavior of organisms.[7] The signs of psychological statistics include numbers, the letters of the Latin and Greek alphabets, mathematical symbols, and words. The designata of psychological statistics are behavioral events or products, their properties and relations, taken singly and in groups produced by sampling. The interpreter in psychological statistics is the research psychologist as he responds to and makes use of the signs.

Our problem is to give an account of a specialized language by means of a natural language. The specialized language is psychological statistics. The natural language is English. We must employ English to introduce and describe psychological statistics. The fact that the two languages overlap somewhat has both advantages and disadvantages. Common features of the two will sometimes facilitate our efforts at communication. On the other hand, important discriminations in psychological statistics are occasionally made difficult by the relatively loose usage which characterizes the ordinary, natural language.

We shall not make a great fuss about this distinction between the specialized language and the natural language. It may be sufficient to say simply that we hope to proceed from everyday, classroom and textbook English, by a kind of process of successive approximation, to the statistical language of the research psychologist. The transition from the one to the other will be gradual and the dividing line between the two will often be imperceptible. We take it for granted that the transition will not be without discontinuities and that much backtracking will be necessary.

We propose dividing the study of psychological statistics into three parts: syntactics, semantics, and pragmatics. This proposal deserves amplification and explanation in a number of respects.

Syntactics, semantics, and pragmatics as studies of different dimensions of the same language are the results of abstraction. In no instance does the process of abstraction yield three perfectly discriminable disciplines. There is some natural and unavoidable overlap and interdependence. Furthermore, one does not have to try very hard to make this overlap and interdependence the cause for confusion. For example, treating as semantical problems those designations for which the designata are themselves linguistic abstractions is

[7]Behavior is defined here as meaning a movement, an action, or a vocalization on the part of a living organism. Behavior is public, not private; that is, it is open to objective study.

not a profitable line of activity for our purposes. It is true that signs themselves might be taken as designata, or the syntactical relations among signs might be so considered, or states of the user, or pragmatical issues, or semantical issues, or properties of properties. But enough of this proliferation of abstract designata. Common sense tells us that, if we continued, we could soon reach a level of complete absurdity.

How the study of psychological statistics can be divided into syntactics, semantics, and pragmatics is not immediately obvious upon first consideration of the subject, a circumstance which will very likely provoke in the student some skepticism as to the desirability of doing so. Our previous experience indicates that, at many points, the distinctions among the three separate studies can be made and maintained with ease and confidence on the part of the student. At a few points the distinctions may be difficult and may appear to be arbitrary. The advantage which derives from the many relatively clear distinctions far outweighs the disadvantage of the few unclear ones.

What is the advantage of dividing psychological statistics into three separate studies? We can answer this question by considering the kinds of problems encountered in the general study of the subject and how these problems can be grouped under the three headings: syntactics, semantics, and pragmatics. We shall see that these three groups of problems possess clearly distinguishable features and require for their solutions quite different approaches. The important advantage of the analysis, then, is that it brings into sharp focus the different kinds of problems and the peculiar nature of the solution appropriate to each kind of problem.

## EXAMPLES OF SYNTACTICAL PROBLEMS

Recall that syntactics is the study of the relations of signs to signs. Although in psychological statistics we have problems of English syntax as well as mathematical syntax, we shall assume that students possess an acceptable level of competence in the former and that it will, therefore, be profitable to focus upon problems in the latter. Listed below are examples of problems which belong in syntactics. In these examples no attempt has been made to stay within the prior experience of the student, a circumstance which should not alarm him for issues of this kind will be dealt with in later chapters as it becomes necessary and appropriate to do so.

1. Perform the arithmetic operations indicated below.

$$42 \times 21 + 31 \times 56 + 29 \times 38$$

2. Given the equations,

$$\begin{aligned} \beta_1 \quad + \beta_2 r_{12} &= r_{13}, \\ \beta_1 r_{12} + \beta_2 \quad &= r_{23}, \end{aligned}$$

solve for $\beta_1$ and $\beta_2$ in terms of $r_{12}$, $r_{13}$, and $r_{23}$.

3. Transform the equation,

$$Y' = b_{yx}X + (\overline{Y} - b_{yx}\overline{X}),$$

by translating the axes so that the origin is at the point, $(\overline{X}, \overline{Y})$.

4. Find the value of $M_x$ which minimizes the value of the expression

$$\sum_{i=1}^{n} (X_i - M_x)^2.$$

5. Given a discrete population distribution for the variable $X$, find the mean of the sampling distribution of means of random samples of two values when the sampling involves replacement.

The five problems given above are entirely devoid of empirical content. One has only to know the rules for handling the symbols and the solutions can be readily obtained.

No doubt some of the five syntactical problems given above will be difficult for individuals who have a limited background in mathematics. In the face of such difficulties, beginning students in psychological statistics often imagine that they would be helped if they were given examples of applications. The fact is that applications almost always introduce new issues and complexities without resolving any of the original ones. Students who have difficulty with any of these problems will only overcome that difficulty by applying themselves diligently and with concentration to the syntactical rules involved in the solutions. It is possible, of course, that they need a review of mathematics or further training in that subject.

## EXAMPLES OF SEMANTICAL PROBLEMS

Consider next the area of semantics in psychological statistics. Recall that semantics is the study of sign-object relations in terms of the confirmability of the designations. Again we must acknowledge that the nontechnical verbal portions of statistical language give rise to semantical problems but, as in the case of syntactics, we shall assume that students use everyday English with reasonable regard for the semantical rules and that the important matter here is sign-designatum correspondence in two areas: measurement and statistical inference.

While a number of different levels of sign-designatum relations can be conceptualized, we shall limit our consideration here to one of these levels. In our discussion, what is designated is not itself a sign, a combination of signs, or a property of signs. The designatum is, rather, some physical, biological, psychological, or social attribute of an individual or a group. That is to say, what is designated is some aspect of behavior and not language or any part of language, formally so considered.

For the behavioral scientist, two important kinds of designations can be distinguished. First there are the designations implied by measurement, the process of quantifying observation. Psychological measurement is the designation of the properties of behavioral events by means of numbers. Second there is the designation of the error variability in measurements. For example, specification of the sampling variability in measures of behavioral events is the designation of an empirical sampling distribution by means of a mathematical function.

These two kinds of semantical relations, measurement and the specification of error variability, should be preeminent in the study of psychological statistics because the confirmability of these designations is of critical importance for the ultimate use of statistics in research. The behavioral scientist's chances of success in acquiring knowledge through his research are increased considerably if the research is carried out under conditions of confirmed measurement and confirmable specification of error variation. One could, of course, extend the notion of confirmability to the final results of research. Since an account of the use of statistics and the interpretation of results in research involves to a considerable extent comment on the users, we shall not treat the problems of confirming research results as semantical problems. Instead, we shall limit our concern with confirmability in semantics to the two intermediate issues: measurement and the specification of error variation.

Listed below are five problems in psychological measurement.

1. A student participates in the javelin throw in the track and field events at his school. His best throw under the standard conditions for the event is a distance of 35.45 meters. Opposite his name in the record of the meet there is written, as a measure of his performance on that occasion, " 35.45 m." Can this method of assigning numbers to behavioral events be justified?

2. A candidate for pilot training is given a test of visual acuity. Two parallel black lines drawn to standard dimensions and located on a white background are presented as visual stimuli by means of a device which makes it possible to vary and measure, in millimeters, the separation between the lines. The candidate is instructed to report, on each presentation of the stimulus, whether or not the lines appear to be separated. The examiner determines the size of the separation which is detected correctly in 50 per cent of presentations. The result is that the candidate is given a measure of visual acuity of 11 millimeters. Does this procedure qualify as measurement?

3. An arithmetic test is administered to the pupils in the fifth grade of an elementary school. The test consists of 25 problems. The answers given by each pupil are classified as right or wrong and his correct answers are then counted. The number of correct answers is the score given to the pupil. Do the properties of the numbers correspond to the properties of the test performances?

4. Ten applicants for a supervisory position are interviewed by three personnel psychologists. Each psychologist then rates every applicant on four

scales. The four scales are intended to measure important dimensions of the applicants' behavior. A scale is represented by a horizontal line on which are located five, equally spaced points, numbered " one " to " five " from left to right. Each point is also labeled with one or two words intended to assist the rater in making his judgment. The twelve ratings from four scales and three judges are summed for each applicant. The sum constitutes the applicant's combined rating. Does this sum qualify as a measure of the characteristics of an applicant, as intended by the interviewers?

5. A clinical psychologist obtains 100 items, each item consisting of a statement which may be used by a mother in describing her behavior with respect to an infant son. He instructs a client to order these items in terms of the way they describe her relations with her son, the order running from those " most like " herself to those " least like " herself. He then asks her to order the items a second time as an ideal mother would have performed the task. The two orderings are then correlated. The product-moment coefficient of correlation for this particular client is 0.55. The psychologist reports the coefficient as a measure of agreement between the client's self-concept and her ideal self-concept. Is this measure of agreement confirmable?

The five semantical problems posed above all have to do with the observation of behavior and ways of quantifying observation. In each example numbers are assigned to behavioral events. The purpose of the assignment is to characterize and record properties of the events. One certainly cannot assume that the assignment of numbers by any arbitrary system whatever will automatically achieve the goal of characterizing the properties of the events. Furthermore, there is nothing in mathematics or any other language which makes it possible to deduce evidence of confirmation or disconfirmation. Confirmation can only be achieved by experience.

A comprehensive treatment of psychological measurement would go far outside the scope of a single text and would overlap the content of numerous courses in the conventional course offerings of a department of psychology. What we shall attempt in this book is a brief outline of the fundamentals of measurement. This discussion of the objective conditions under which the degree of correspondence between properties of numbers and properties of events designated by the numbers can be determined will be given in Chapter 5. For the immediate present, we shall say only that these conditions have to do with the reproducibility and predictiveness of the assigned numbers.

We have not yet finished with our examples of semantical problems. There is the other important class involving the specification of error variability, of which three examples are given below.

1. A student has 10 coins. The two sides of each coin can be readily identified as " head " and " tail." He tosses the 10 coins, then counts and records the number of heads. He repeats the tossing and counting procedure until he has 1,200 counts. He notes and records the number of times he

counted zero heads, one head, two heads, and so on. He then converts these frequencies to proportions of the total number of counts.

He is then told by his teacher that the terms in the expansion of the binomial,

$$(p + q)^{10},$$

when $p = q = 0.50$, will approximate the proportions he obtained.

What justification is there for this prediction?

2. A machinist's apprentice is tested for his accuracy and precision in measuring the diameter of a standard metal rod using a micrometer. He is required to make a lengthy series of measurements in which the standard is alternated with other rods whose diameters vary somewhat but not enough to be detected by a visual inspection. His results for the standard rod are summarized in a frequency distribution. It is observed that this distribution is roughly symmetrical around a central value with relatively few values at either extreme and a relatively large concentration of values in and near the middle. A statistician sees the data and tries to fit a normal curve to them. The fit is considered quite good. He makes note of the fact that the apprentice's variation in performance is " normally distributed." Is this correspondence an accident or is it evidence of the operation of some general law of behavior?

3. A teacher of statistics makes up a frequency distribution of 100,000 numbers. The frequency distribution has the form of a normal curve except that it possesses a finite number of class or score intervals. The teacher then assigns students in his class a sampling exercise. He instructs them in the use of a device called a *table of random numbers* to draw a sample from the artificial frequency distribution. The students, working together, obtain 1,000 samples, each one consisting of 10 values. The mean of each sample is computed and a new frequency distribution of the 1,000 means is constructed. The instructor predicts in advance that the form of the distribution of means will be approximately that of a normal curve. How does he know what the outcome will be?

The semantical problem of specifying the form of sampling distributions will be discussed at some length in Chapter 13. In this preliminary consideration, we shall say only that confirmation of the correspondence between a mathematical function and an actual distribution cannot be deduced. We must look to experience for the verdict.

## EXAMPLES OF PRAGMATICAL PROBLEMS

Let us turn now to pragmatics. The term " pragmatics " probably suggests to most students the study of practical applications. Although this interpretation of the study of sign-user relations is not irrelevant, it has the fault of being an oversimplification and might hinder the development of more meaningful notions if we did not at once caution the student regarding this possibility.

The danger is that a student, when he comes to pragmatics, may think that all he has to do is memorize a list of statistical methods and corresponding applications. At a very low level of sophistication and understanding his task might be so construed. But there is much more than imitation in employing statistics in research and consequently much more than memorizing in pragmatics.

Let us illustrate with three issues.

1. Summarization of data is one application of psychological statistics. One might look upon this summarizing process as a condensing of the original data to a form which makes them more convenient to handle but which lacks the original detail. There are, of course, degrees of condensation. One could reduce a mass of data—let us say 10,000 observations—to a single value, or to two values, or three, or one hundred, or whatever number one chose. And what does one choose? What degree of condensation is desirable? How much detail can one afford to lose? The answers to these questions will depend on a complex of considerations arising out of the practical situation and relating to current practices among research psychologists.

2. A common problem for a research psychologist is the choice of an equation to express a relation between two variables. Equations vary from simple to complex. Ideally an investigator would want to use the equation which was correct or best, in some sense, regardless of complexity. Practically he must take account of the inconvenience and expense involved and he will, therefore, often accept a simple equation as an approximation and reject an intractable, but possibly more exact, one. Unfortunately there is no simple rule for comparing a loss in predictiveness with gains in convenience and economy. Consequently, there is a fair amount of disagreement among psychologists in the choice of approximations of various kinds. Although one may justifiably deplore this state of affairs, there is no point in insisting on perfection in these matters. It is in the very nature of research that one must be willing to employ approximations even when they are subject to somewhat arbitrary selection.

3. In examining the results of an experiment, we recognize that error may have produced the result. We agree to a standard evaluation procedure which will ensure our being misled by error on no more than one in twenty occasions, in the long run. Why do we resign ourselves to being mistaken in our evaluations? Why do we choose one-in-twenty as the ratio and not some other? What uncertainty is revealed in this final projection into the future—" in the long run "? The answers to these questions involve a mixture of common sense, convention, and experience. They will be amplified in later discussions.

A reference was made earlier to the correlatives: the sentence of syntactics, the proposition of semantics, and the expectation of pragmatics. We say that a sentence is correct or incorrect, a proposition is confirmed or disconfirmed, and an expectation is fulfilled or not fulfilled. What constitutes the fulfilment of an expectation? The most direct answer is that, if the researcher employs correct syntax and confirmed semantical relations, his immediate expectations are fulfilled in the acquisition of empirical knowledge.

Although the acquiring of knowledge is a prime goal of the researcher, there is more to be said about the user of statistics and his expectations, in a broader sense. Students are confronted with what they often perceive as a burdensome chore in studying psychological statistics. What are the concomitants and products of this learning experience, in addition to the very fundamental development of research skills?

The first important outcome of studying and mastering psychological statistics is that one comes to understand research issues and to know that one understands them. Understanding and knowing that one understands these issues are necessary preconditions for intellectual independence and authority, for successful self-direction, and for a personally healthy and socially acceptable degree of confidence in one's work.

The second important outcome is that one comes to be understood by one's colleagues and to command agreement and assent, on an intellectual level, in the resolving of research issues.

The third important outcome is that one becomes a better teacher of psychology and psychological research methods in the classroom, the laboratory, and the field.

## Looking Ahead

In anticipation of what lies ahead, let us consider some of the prominent features of the plan for dividing psychological statistics into syntactics, semantics, and pragmatics.

The plan does not involve a simple division of the subject matter into three parts, to be presented in three successive sections of the book. There is some appropriate and necessary alternation of the three approaches. Furthermore, they do not receive equal emphasis and elaboration.

Since the syntax of arithmetic and algebra is very important in psychological statistics, exercises and suggestions for review of these elementary mathematical subjects are given in Chapter 2.

Another syntactical topic, the symbolism of sums, is given a fairly detailed treatment in Chapter 3.

Before we can continue with the outline, we must introduce a few terms. It was pointed out earlier that the word "statistics," construed as singular, indicates a branch of knowledge. The meaning of the word "statistic," construed as singular, deserves comment. We shall not use the word " statistic " without a qualifying prefix. Any value computed from a set of measures will be called a " *d*-statistic " because it is, to some degree, descriptive of the set. By definition, a *d*-statistic does not involve the notion of error and, in a formal sense, nothing can be said about its error. The plural form of *d*-statistic is obtained by adding " s."

Any value computed from a set of measures subject to random variation, as in computing from the measures in a sample drawn from a population, will be called an " *i*-statistic " because certain inferences may possibly be based on that value. An *i*-statistic has descriptive value with respect to its sample; a *d*-statistic does not have inferential value for a population. The plural of *i*-statistic is obtained by adding " s."

While the qualifications represented by the prefixes, " *d*- " and " *i*-," are widely known and understood, these prefixes are not in general use. The distinction between two corresponding branches of systematized knowledge, descriptive statistics and inferential statistics, is, however, frequently made by statisticians.

The thirteen chapters from 4 through 16 are classifiable, as follows:

| | *Chapter* | *Topic* |
|---|---|---|
| *Syntactics* | 4 | A class of values called *moments* |
| | 7 | A class of values called *product-moments* |
| | 8 | Partial and multiple correlation |
| | 10 | The analysis of variability in classifications of numbers |
| | 11 | Sampling theory |
| | 12 | Sampling distributions |
| *Semantics* | 5 | Measurement |
| | 13 | Practical random sampling |
| *Pragmatics* | 6 | Descriptive uses of moments |
| | 9 | Descriptive uses of product-moments |
| | 14 | Statistical inference in research |
| | 15 | Tests of significance in experimental research |
| | 16 | Tests of significance and estimates of parameters in non-experimental research |

Chapter 17 deals with syntactical and pragmatical issues relating to the application of statistical inference to frequency classifications.

Note that two chapters, 6 and 9, are devoted to descriptive statistics, while four chapters, 14 through 17, deal with inferential statistics.

Because we believe that learning is facilitated if the student keeps in mind the division of the subject into syntactics, semantics, and pragmatics, each chapter or section devoted solely to one of the three kinds of study is so designated by an appropriate sub-heading.

**SUGGESTED READINGS**

Carnap, Rudolf, *The Logical Syntax of Language* (London: Paul, Trench, Trubner, 1937).

———, " Foundations of Logic and Mathematics," *International Encyclopedia of Unified Science* (Chicago: The University of Chicago Press, 1938), Vol. I, No. 2.

———, " Testability and Meaning," in Feigl, Herbert & Broadbeck, May, *Readings in the Philosophy of Science* (New York: Appleton-Century-Crofts, 1953), pp. 47–92.

———, *Introduction to Symbolic Logic and Its Applications* (New York: Dover, 1958).

———, *Introduction to Semantics and Formalization of Logic* (Cambridge: Harvard University Press, 1959).

Joergensen, Joergen, " The Development of Logical Empiricism," *International Encyclopedia of Unified Science* (Chicago: The University of Chicago Press, 1951), Vol. II, No. 9.

Morris, Charles W., " Foundations of the Theory of Signs," *International Encyclopedia of Unified Science* (Chicago: The University of Chicago Press, 1938), Vol. I, No. 2.

# ARITHMETIC AND ALGEBRA

## Syntactics | 2

Students are sometimes handicapped in statistics by their failure to recall, or to grasp the significance of, certain very elementary principles or rules in arithmetic and algebra. It is our purpose here to provide a brief review of arithmetic and algebra with focus upon those principles and rules which have the most direct bearing on the work to be undertaken later. It is not our intention to present a course in arithmetic and algebra. Students who have had no previous training in algebra should either set out upon a course of self-directed study using a standard text or enroll in a first course in college algebra.[1]

Exercises will be provided at appropriate points in the review. The student should make full use of these exercises for the evaluation of his progress and the diagnosis of his difficulties. Answers will be given to the exercises bearing odd numbers but not to those bearing even numbers.

## On Arithmetic Operations

Addition is indicated by the sign, " + ".

$$8 + 9$$

Subtraction is indicated by the sign, " − ".

$$7 - 5$$

[1]One algebra text which students might find helpful is J. B. Rosenbach, E. A. Whitman, B. E. Meserve, and P. M. Whitman, *College Algebra* (Boston: Ginn, 1958). A book in which many psychology and education students have done their reviewing of the fundamentals of mathematics is Helen M. Walker, *Mathematics Essential for Elementary Statistics*, rev. ed. (New York: Holt, 1951).

Multiplication can be indicated in three different ways.

$$5 \times 3 \text{ or } 5(3) \text{ or } 5 \cdot 3$$

Division can be indicated by either a slant, " / ", or a bar, " — ".

$$9/2 \text{ or } \frac{9}{2}$$

The order in which numbers are added does not affect the sum. For example, the summation,

$$3 + 4 + 8 + 6,$$

is usually performed in the following steps which, under ordinary circumstances, would not be written out:

$$3 + 4 \text{ is equal to } 7,$$
$$7 + 8 \text{ is equal to } 15,$$
$$15 + 6 \text{ is equal to } 21.$$

Note that the numbers were accumulated from left to right. Arranging the same numbers in a different order, we have

$$8 + 4 + 6 + 3.$$

Accumulating, as before, from left to right, we take the following steps:

$$8 + 4 \text{ is equal to } 12,$$
$$12 + 6 \text{ is equal to } 18,$$
$$18 + 3 \text{ is equal to } 21$$

which is the same sum obtained from the original order. Any other order of accumulating the same numbers would give the same answer.

Grouping of numbers in addition does not affect the sum. If we use parentheses to indicate arbitrary groups whose sums are to be obtained before the final summation takes place, we can write:

$$8 + 11 + 16 + 5$$

as

$$(8 + 11) + (16 + 5)$$

which is equal to

$$19 + 21$$

which is equal to

$$40.$$

We can write the same summation as:

$$(8 + 16) + (11 + 5)$$

which is equal to

$$24 + 16$$

which again is equal to

$$40.$$

The order in which numbers are multiplied does not affect the product. Given the problem,

$$5 \times 8 \times 3 \times 4,$$

we can multiply from left to right.

$5 \times 8$ is equal to 40,

$40 \times 3$ is equal to 120,

$120 \times 4$ is equal to 480.

These same numbers can be written and multiplied in a different order, as below,

$$3 \times 8 \times 4 \times 5,$$

but the final product is the same.

$3 \times 8$ is equal to 24,

$24 \times 4$ is equal to 96,

$96 \times 5$ is equal to 480.

Grouping of numbers in multiplication does not affect the final product. Again we can use parentheses to indicate the operations which are to be performed first.

$$3 \times 8 \times 10 \times 6$$

is equal to

$$(3 \times 8) \times (10 \times 6)$$

is equal to

$$24 \times 60$$

is equal to

$$1{,}440$$

which is the same result we would get if the numbers were grouped as

$$(3 \times 10) \times (8 \times 6)$$

which is equal to

$$30 \times 48$$

is equal to

$$1{,}440.$$

When addition and multiplication occur in the same expression, it is necessary to have rules regarding which is performed first. In the following sum of products, the multiplications are performed before the addition:

$$3 \times 5 + 8 \times 6 + 7 \times 7$$

is equal to

$$15 + 48 + 49$$

is equal to

$$112.$$

With respect to the expression,

$$5(9 + 7),$$

which contains addition and multiplication, there are two correct solutions. In the first solution the addition within the parentheses is performed before the multiplication. That is,

$$5(9 + 7)$$

is equal to

$$5(16)$$

is equal to

$$80.$$

In the second solution each number within the parentheses is multiplied by five and the products are then added. This procedure is an example of *distribution of multiplication.* Thus

$$5(9 + 7)$$

is equal to

$$5 \times 9 + 5 \times 7$$

is equal to

$$45 + 35$$

is equal to

$$80.$$

There are also two correct solutions for the problem,

$$(2 + 8)(6 + 5)$$

In the first solution the additions within parentheses are performed before multiplication. Thus

$$(2 + 8)(6 + 5)$$

is equal to

$$(10)(11)$$

is equal to

$$110.$$

In the second solution multiplication is distributed and then addition is performed. That is,

$$(2 + 8)(6 + 5)$$

is equal to

$$2 \times 6 + 2 \times 5 + 8 \times 6 + 8 \times 5$$

is equal to

$$12 + 10 + 48 + 40$$

is equal to

$$110,$$

which is the answer obtained in the first solution.

The order and grouping rules for addition apply also to subtraction and to combinations of both operations.

The order, grouping, and distribution rules for multiplication apply to division when the division is expressed as equivalent multiplication by employing the reciprocal of the divisor. (The reciprocal of a number is " one " divided by the number.)

Examples of division expressed as equivalent multiplication:

$$\frac{3}{4} \text{ is equal to } \frac{1}{4}(3),$$

$$\frac{(4+5)}{3} \text{ is equal to } \frac{1}{3}(4+5),$$

$$\frac{(3+6)}{(5+2)} \text{ is equal to } \frac{1}{(5+2)}(3+6).$$

*Caution:* The use of the sign, " $\div$ ", to indicate division can yield ambiguous expressions where more than one division is to be performed or where both multiplication and division occur. We shall not use the symbol.

Note that the position of the bar or the slant is critical in expressing division. Observe that

$$\frac{3/4}{5/6} \text{ is equal to } \frac{1}{5/6} \times \frac{3}{4} \text{ is equal to } \frac{6}{5} \times \frac{3}{4} \text{ is equal to } \frac{18}{20}$$

whereas

$$\frac{(3/4)/5}{6} \text{ is equal to } \frac{1}{6} \times \frac{3/4}{5} \text{ is equal to } \frac{1}{6} \times \frac{1}{5} \times \frac{3}{4} \text{ is equal to } \frac{3}{120}.$$

## Signed Numbers

A signed number is a number with a sign, either " + " or " − ", preceding it. A number preceded by " + " is a positive number; a number preceded by " − " is a negative number. Signed numbers are also called *directed numbers* or *algebraic numbers.*

In working with signed numbers, we sometimes wish to disregard the signs and consider only the so-called *absolute values* of the signed numbers. To do so we drop the signs and perform operations with the numbers as if they were unsigned. Thus the absolute value of +9 is 9; the absolute value of −4 is 4. The absolute value is also called the *arithmetic value* or the *numerical value*. The symbol for absolute value is two vertical, parallel bars written as

$|-6|$, which is equal to 6, and

$|+8|$, which is equal to 8.

An expression involving numbers and signs, such as

$$+3-1+2-4-2+6,$$

can be interpreted correctly in any one of three ways. The signs can be taken as referring to the operations of addition and subtraction involving unsigned numbers, or to the operations of addition and subtraction involving all positive numbers, as indicated below,

$$(+3)-(+1)+(+2)-(+4)-(+2)+(+6),$$

or to the addition of positive and negative numbers, that is, as

$$(+3)+(-1)+(+2)+(-4)+(-2)+(+6).$$

Rules have been established for the addition and subtraction of signed numbers. They are listed below.

1. To add numbers with like signs, add the absolute values and prefix the sum with the common sign.

2. To add numbers with unlike signs, add the absolute values of those with positive signs, add the absolute values of those with negative signs, subtract the smaller of these two sums from the larger, and finally prefix to the difference the common sign of the numbers in the larger sum.

3. To subtract one signed number from another, change the sign of the number to be subtracted and proceed as in addition.

Rules have also been established for the multiplication and division of signed numbers. They are given below.

1. The product or quotient of two numbers with like signs is positive.

2. The product or quotient of two numbers with unlike signs is negative.

In writing expressions involving signed numbers, the signs of positive numbers are often omitted but understood to be in effect.

In multiplication, when the two signs are positive, the product may be interpreted as the repeated addition of a positive number. That is,

$6(3)$ is equal to $3+3+3+3+3+3$.

When one sign is positive and the other is negative, the product may be interpreted as repeated addition of a negative number. Thus:

$7(-4)$ is equal to $(-4)+(-4)+(-4)+(-4)+(-4)+(-4)+(-4)$.

When both signs are negative, the product is defined as positive, thereby maintaining consistency in the distribution of multiplication. Consider the problem,

$$-3(7 - 2).$$

There should be two correct solutions. In one we subtract within the parentheses before multiplying. Subtraction gives us

$$-3(5) \text{ which is equal to } -15.$$

In the other solution, we distribute the multiplication by $-3$ over both numbers within parentheses, obtaining

$$(-3)(7) + (-3)(-2).$$

The first product has factors with unlike signs and is, therefore, negative. The second product has two factors with negative signs. This second product must be given a positive sign to yield a final answer of $-15$ and be consistent with the first solution. That is,

$$(-21) + (+6) \text{ is equal to } -15.$$

The sign rules for division are justified by expressing the division as equivalent multiplication and applying the sign rules for multiplication.

## Geometric Interpretation of Signed Numbers

A signed number is interpreted as a distance on a scale measured in one of two directions. Consider the scale represented below by the horizontal line marked off in equal segments.

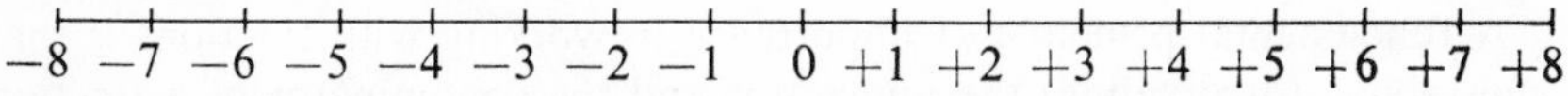


Notice there is a point labeled " 0 " and other points numbered consecutively in each direction, that is, to the left and to the right of the zero point. The point labeled with zero is called the *origin.* Points to the right of the origin are labeled with positive numbers which increase in value as one reads the scale from left to right; points to the left of the origin are labeled with negative numbers which decrease in value as one reads from right to left. A signed number expresses a distance in either the positive or the negative direction and locates a point on the scale. The correspondence between a signed number, $X$, and a point on the scale, $P$, is acknowledged by calling the number the *coordinate* of the point and the point, the *graph* of the number.

The length of a segment of the scale between the origin and point $P$, disregarding the direction, corresponds to the absolute value of $X$.

## Geometric Interpretation of the Combining of Signed Numbers

An expression containing positive and negative numbers can be referred to the scale given above and interpreted as locating a point on the scale. For example, the expression,

$$+3 - 1 + 2 - 4 + 1 + 2,$$

is interpreted, as follows.

Start at zero on the scale and measure three units in a positive direction, then one unit in the negative direction, then two positive, four negative, one positive, and finally two positive. Movements along the scale are diagrammed below. They stop at the point, +3, which corresponds to the value of the expression after all the operations have been carried out.

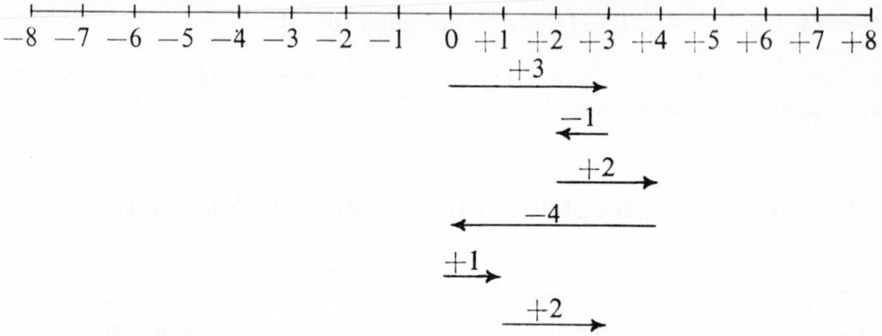


## Fractions

A fundamental principle of importance in working with fractions is that multiplying (or dividing) the numerator and the denominator of a fraction by the same quantity does not change the value of the fraction.

*Example:*

$$\frac{3}{7} \text{ is equal to } \frac{5(3)}{5(7)} \text{ is equal to } \frac{8(3)}{8(7)}$$

*Caution:* Adding or subtracting the same quantity in the numerator and the denominator does change the value of a fraction.

In adding and subtracting fractions we obtain a common denominator and then add the numerators.

*Example:*

$$\frac{1}{3} + \frac{2}{5} \text{ is equal to } \frac{5}{15} + \frac{6}{15} \text{ is equal to } \frac{11}{15}$$

In multiplying fractions we obtain the product of the numerators and the product of the denominators, and write the former over the latter.

*Example:*

$$\frac{2}{5} \times \frac{3}{7} \text{ is equal to } \frac{6}{35}$$

In dividing fractions we invert the divisor and multiply.

*Example:*

$$\frac{1/3}{3/5} \text{ is equal to } \frac{1}{3} \times \frac{5}{3} \text{ is equal to } \frac{5}{9}$$

## Algebraic Symbolism

Students of psychological statistics soon discover, and are often exasperated by, the fact that practices in writing symbolism vary considerably from one author or teacher to another. The brief description of writing practices given below should not be taken as a universal, invariant standard. It is well for students to develop, at the very beginning, an attitude of adaptability and flexibility where symbolism is concerned. One of the chores a statistician takes for granted as part of his lot in life is the constant adjustment and readjustment of his frame of reference for the interpretation of symbols as he goes from one text or article to another.

With these cautions a matter of record, we shall proceed to describe certain rather general but not necessarily fixed practices in writing symbolism.

Letters are used, in a variety of ways, to represent numbers.

*Example:* Let $X$ represent any number in a set or class of numbers.

We use different letters for different sets or classes.

*Example:* Let $X$ represent any number in one set; let $Y$ represent any number in another set.

Numerical subscripts are attached to letters to permit identification of particular numbers within a set.

*Examples:* $X_3$ refers to the third number in a set; $Y_7$ refers to the seventh number in another set. The assignment of numerical subscripts may be arbitrary.

Letter subscripts also are employed for purposes of identification.

*Examples:* $X_i$ refers to the $i^{\text{th}}$ number in a set, where $i$ is any integer from " 1 " to " $n$." $S_x$ refers to a number computed, by means of a certain formula, from the numbers in the $X$ set. The symbol, $r_{xy}$, refers to a number computed, by means of a certain formula, from the numbers in the $X$ set and the $Y$ set.

Identification is also achieved by means of superscripts.

*Example:* We might let $Y'$ (read " $Y$-prime ") represent any number in one set and $Y$ represent any number in another related set, as when each value of $Y'$ is computed from a corresponding value of $Y$ by means of a stated rule.

We sometimes need seconds, such as $X''$ and $Y''$, as well as primes.

Capital letters and small letters serve different purposes.

*Example:* We might let $X$ represent any number in one set and $x$ represent any number in another set obtained by applying a transformation to each $X$.

Small letters from the first part of the alphabet often represent constants while letters, capital or small, near the end of the alphabet often represent numbers in sets as indicated earlier.

*Examples:* We might let $a$ represent a particular number whose value remains unspecified and $X$ represent any number in a set of numbers whose values may vary but also remain unspecified.

On occasion a letter is selected by an author or a teacher because it is the first letter of some descriptive word or term in a problem but this practice is not always possible or desirable.

Thus far we have referred only to letters of the familiar Latin alphabet. The demands of our statistical language force us to go to the Greek alphabet for additional symbols. The Greek alphabet is given below. Capitals are on the left; small letters are on the right.

| *Letters* | *Names* | *Letters* | *Names* | *Letters* | *Names* |
|---|---|---|---|---|---|
| $A, \alpha$ | Alpha | $I, \iota$ | Iota | $P, \rho$ | Rho |
| $B, \beta$ | Beta | $K, \kappa$ | Kappa | $\Sigma, \sigma$ | Sigma |
| $\Gamma, \gamma$ | Gamma | $\Lambda, \lambda$ | Lambda | $T, \tau$ | Tau |
| $\Delta, \delta$ | Delta | $M, \mu$ | Mu | $\Upsilon, \upsilon$ | Upsilon |
| $E, \epsilon$ | Epsilon | $N, \nu$ | Nu | $\Phi, \phi$ | Phi |
| $Z, \zeta$ | Zeta | $\Xi, \xi$ | Xi | $X, \chi$ | Chi |
| $H, \eta$ | Eta | $O, o$ | Omicron | $\Psi, \psi$ | Psi |
| $\Theta, \theta$ | Theta | $\Pi, \pi$ | Pi | $\Omega, \omega$ | Omega |

The Greek capital letter, $\Sigma$, is a very important statistical symbol but it is not used to represent a number. As we shall use it here, it will always be written before at least one other numerical or literal symbol to indicate an operation of summation to be performed with reference to that other symbol. The symbol, $\Sigma$, when it indicates a summation, is called an *operator*. Common practices and rules in summational notation are discussed at length in Chapter 3.

As revealed by the examples given below, the operations of arithmetic can be indicated with letters representing numbers.

| | |
|---|---|
| *Addition:* | $X + Y + Z$ |
| | $p + q$ |
| | $n + 1$ |
| | $X + a$ |
| *Subtraction:* | $x - y$ |
| | $N - 1$ |
| | $Y - c$ |
| | $a + b - c - d$ |
| *Multiplication:* | $XY$ (read " $X$ times $Y$") |
| | $aX$ |
| | $3XY$ |
| | $a(X + Y)$ |
| *Division:* | $X/Y$ (read " $X$ divided by $Y$") |
| | $a/X$ |
| | $(X + Y)/N$ |
| | $(X - a)/5$ |

It is important to keep in mind that an indicated sum, difference, product, or quotient, no matter how complex it may be, represents a number which can be employed in further operations.

## Equality and Inequality

The symbol of equality, =, is read " is equal to." It is used in stating that two expressions represent the same number.

One kind of equality statement is the identity. An example is given below.

$$3(x - 2) = 3x - 6$$

This statement qualifies as an identity because the equality holds for all values of $x$.

A second kind of equality statement is the equation, an example of which is

$$3X + 5 = 29.$$

This equation is distinguished from an identity because there are values for $X$ for which the statement of equality does not hold.

A third kind of equality statement is the formula, which states that the number represented by one symbol is the same as the number represented by an expression involving one or more other symbols. The following statement is an example of a formula:

$$Z_x = (X - M_x)/S_x.$$

The symbols of inequality are " $<$ ", which is read " is less than," and " $>$ ", which is read " is greater than." An inequality symbol appears in a statement that the number represented by one expression is less than (or greater than, as the case may be) the number represented by another expression.

*Examples* (with interpretations):

| | |
|---|---|
| $m < n$ | $m$ is less than $n$ |
| $P < 0.05$ | $P$ is less than five hundredths |
| $a > b$ | $a$ is greater than $b$ |
| $F > F_{.95}$ | $F$ is greater than $F_{.95}$ |
| $0.01 < P < 0.05$ | 0.01 is less than $P$ which is less than 0.05 |

The symbol for nonequality, $\neq$, is read " is not equal to." It is employed in stating that the number represented by one expression is not the number represented by another expression.

*Example:* In general,

$$X_1Y_1 + X_2Y_2 \neq (X_1 + X_2)(Y_1 + Y_2).$$

The following exercises are provided to give opportunity for practice in writing algebraic symbolism.

**Exercise 2.1**

Let $a$ represent a particular number. Write the expression for

1. twice the number
2. the number minus 5
3. the product of the number and itself
4. the number divided by 10
5. the reciprocal of the number
6. 8 divided by the number
7. the number multiplied by its reciprocal
8. the quantity, $a$ plus 5, divided by the quantity, $a$ minus 4
9. the quantity, $a$ minus 3, multiplied by the quantity, $a$ plus 8
10. the quantity, $a$ divided by 2, multiplied by 9

**Answers to Exercise 2.1**

1. $2a$
2. $a - 5$
3. $a \cdot a$
4. $a/10$
5. $1/a$
6. $8/a$
7. $a(1/a) = 1$
8. $(a + 5)/(a - 4)$
9. $(a - 3)(a + 8)$
10. $9(a/2)$

**Exercise 2.2**

Let $c$ represent a particular number. Write the expression for

1. the product of the number and 5
2. the number plus 10
3. the number multiplied by itself
4. the ratio of the number to 100
5. one divided by the number
6. the number divided by 10
7. the reciprocal of the number multiplied by twice the number
8. the quantity, $c$ minus 3, divided by the reciprocal of $c$
9. the quantity, $c$ plus 3, multiplied by the quantity, $c$ minus 3
10. 20 times the reciprocal of the number

**Exercise 2.3**

Let $a$ represent a particular number and let $X_1$, $X_2$, $X_3$, and $X_4$ be four numbers in a set. Also let $X_i$ represent any number in the set where $i$ may be any integer from "1" to "4."

Write:

1. the sum of the numbers in the set
2. $a$ times any number in the set
3. the product of $a$ and the first number
4. the product of $a$ and the second number
5. the third number multiplied by $a$
6. $a$ times the fourth number
7. the sum of the products written in (3), (4), (5), and (6)
8. $a$ times the sum of the four numbers
9. the sum of the four numbers divided by 4
10. any number in the set minus $a$
11. any number in the set divided by $a$
12. any number in the set multiplied by the reciprocal of $a$.

**Answers to Exercise 2.3**

1. $X_1 + X_2 + X_3 + X_4$
2. $aX_i$
3. $aX_1$
4. $aX_2$
5. $aX_3$
6. $aX_4$
7. $aX_1 + aX_2 + aX_3 + aX_4$
8. $a(X_1 + X_2 + X_3 + X_4)$
9. $(X_1 + X_2 + X_3 + X_4)/4$
10. $X_i - a$
11. $X_i/a$
12. $(1/a)X_i$

**Exercise 2.4**

Let $c$ represent a particular number and let $Y_1$, $Y_2$, $Y_3$, $Y_4$, and $Y_5$ be five numbers in a set. Also let $Y_i$ be any number in that set. We define $i$ as taking any integral value from "1" to "5" inclusive.

Write:

1. the sum of the numbers in the set
2. the sum of the products obtained by multiplying each number in the set by $c$

3. $c$ times the sum of the numbers
4. the sum of the numbers divided by 5
5. any number in the set minus the reciprocal of $c$
6. any number in the set divided by $c$
7. any number in the set multiplied by the reciprocal of $c$
8. the sum of the quotients obtained by dividing each number in the set by 5
9. the sum of the products obtained by multiplying each number in the set by the reciprocal of 5
10. any number in the set minus the quantity, 3 times $c$
11. any number in the set minus the quotient obtained by dividing the sum of the numbers by 5
12. the sum of the five numbers multiplied by itself.

**Exercise 2.5**

Let $a$ represent a particular number. Let $X_1$ and $Y_1$ be a pair of numbers, $X_2$ and $Y_2$ be a second pair, $X_3$ and $Y_3$ a third pair, and $X_4$ and $Y_4$ a fourth pair. Also let $X_i$ be the $i^{th}$ number in the $X$ set and $Y_i$ be the corresponding number in the $Y$ set.

Write:

1. the product of $X$-sub-one and $Y$-sub-one
2. $X$-sub-two times $Y$-sub-two
3. $Y$-sub-three multiplied by $X$-sub-three
4. the product of the members of the fourth pair of numbers
5. the sum of the four products obtained in (1), (2), (3), and (4)
6. $a$ times each of the four products
7. $a$ times the sum of the four products
8. the sum of $X$
9. the sum of $Y$
10. the product of the sum of $X$ and the sum of $Y$

Compare your answer to (10) with your answer to (5). Are they equal?

11. the product of the members of the $i^{th}$ pair of numbers
12. $a$ times the product of the members of the $i^{th}$ pair of numbers.

**Answers to Exercise 2.5**

1. $X_1Y_1$
2. $X_2Y_2$
3. $X_3Y_3$
4. $X_4Y_4$
5. $X_1Y_1 + X_2Y_2 + X_3Y_3 + X_4Y_4$
6. $aX_1Y_1$<br>$aX_2Y_2$<br>$aX_3Y_3$<br>$aX_4Y_4$
7. $a(X_1Y_1 + X_2Y_2 + X_3Y_3 + X_4Y_4)$
8. $X_1 + X_2 + X_3 + X_4$
9. $Y_1 + Y_2 + Y_3 + Y_4$
10. $(X_1 + X_2 + X_3 + X_4)$<br>$(Y_1 + Y_2 + Y_3 + Y_4)$ ; No
11. $X_iY_i$
12. $aX_iY_i$

**Exercise 2.6**

Let $c$ be a particular number. Let $X_i$ be the $i^{th}$ number in a set of five numbers; let $Y_i$ be the corresponding number in another set.

Write:

1. the product of the numbers in each pair
2. the sum of the five products obtained in (1)
3. $c$ times each of the five products obtained in (1)
4. the sum of the five products obtained in (3)
5. $c$ times the sum obtained in (2)

Compare your answer to (5) with your answer to (4). Are they equal?

6. the sum of $X$
7. the sum of $Y$
8. the sum of $X$ divided by the sum of $Y$
9. the ratio of $X$ to $Y$ for each of the five pairs
10. the sum of the five quotients obtained in (9)

Compare your answer to (10) with your answer to (8). Are they equal?

11. the sum of the five products obtained in (1), divided by 5
12. the difference between the members of each of the five pairs
13. the sum of the five differences obtained in (12)
14. the sum of the five differences obtained in (12), divided by 5

# Exponents

When two quantities are multiplied together, each is called a *factor* of the product. When more than two quantities are multiplied together, each one or the product of any number of them is also called a factor.

An exponent is a number or a literal number symbol written as a superscript to a given quantity to express a product of identical factors. The exponent indicates the number of identical factors in the product, where each factor is the given quantity. That is, by definition,

$$\begin{aligned} X^1 &= X && \text{(one factor } X\text{)} \\ X^2 &= X \cdot X && \text{(two factors } X\text{)} \\ X^3 &= X \cdot X \cdot X && \text{(threes factor } X\text{)} \\ X^m &= X \cdot X \cdot X \cdots X && \text{(}m\text{ factors } X\text{)} \\ X^n &= X \cdot X \cdot X \cdots X && \text{(}n\text{ factors } X\text{)} \end{aligned}$$

$X^1$ is read " $X$ to the first power "; $X^2$ is read " $X$ to the second power " or simply " $X$ square "; $X^3$ is read " $X$ to the third power " or " $X$ cube "; $X^m$ is read " $X$ to the $m^{th}$ power "; and $X^n$ is read " $X$ to the $n^{th}$ power."

Products expressed by means of exponents may themselves be factors in another product. For example, the product of two powers of $X$,

$$X^2 \cdot X^3,$$

has two factors, $X^2$ and $X^3$, each of which is a product. By definition

$$X^2 = X \cdot X$$

and

$$X^3 = X \cdot X \cdot X.$$

Therefore

$$X^2 \cdot X^3 = X \cdot X \cdot X \cdot X \cdot X = X^5,$$

from which we see that we could have added the exponents " 2 " and " 3 " to obtain the exponent " 5 " of the final product. In general, then,

$$X^m \cdot X^n = X^{m+n}.$$

Again, by definition,

$$(X^2)^3 = X^2 \cdot X^2 \cdot X^2 = X^6,$$

from which we see that the power of a power can be obtained by multiplying exponents. In general,

$$(X^n)^m = X^{mn}.$$

Division involving two powers of the same quantity is performed by subtracting the exponent of the divisor from that of the dividend, as in the example,

$$\frac{X^3}{X^2} = \frac{X \cdot X \cdot X}{X \cdot X} = X = X^{3-2},$$

or, in general, as

$$\frac{X^m}{X^n} = X^{m-n},$$

when $m > n > 0$.

If we extend this practice of subtracting exponents to situations in which $m = n$, we find that

$$X^0 = 1.$$

Given

$$\frac{X^m}{X^m},$$

we divide the numerator and the denominator by $X^m$. Thus:

$$\frac{X^m}{X^m} = \frac{1}{1} = 1.$$

If we subtract the exponent of the divisor from that of the dividend, we obtain

$$\frac{X^m}{X^m} = X^{m-m} = X^0.$$

Therefore,

$$1 = \frac{X^m}{X^m} = X^0.$$

By a similar extension to cases in which $n > m > 0$, we can show that

$$\frac{X^m}{X^n} = \frac{1}{X^{n-m}} = X^{-(n-m)}$$

where $(n - m)$ is positive and $-(n - m)$ is negative. Given

$$\frac{X^m}{X^n}$$

with $n > m > 0$, we can divide the numerator and denominator by $X^m$, obtaining

$$\frac{1}{X^{n-m}}$$

where $(n - m)$ is positive. But if we subtract the exponent of the divisor from that of the dividend in the original fraction, we obtain

$$X^{m-n}$$

which can be written

$$X^{-(n-m)}$$

where $(m - n)$ is negative and equal to $-(n - m)$.

We can also show that

$$\frac{1}{X} = X^{-1},$$

$$\frac{1}{X^2} = X^{-2},$$

and, in general where $n > 0$,

$$\frac{1}{X^n} = X^{-n}.$$

Recall that

$$X^0 = 1.$$

It follows that we can write

$$\frac{1}{X^n} = \frac{X^0}{X^n}.$$

Dividing by subtracting exponents yields

$$\frac{1}{X^n} = \frac{X^0}{X^n} = X^{0-n} = X^{-n}.$$

Logarithms are special cases of exponents. It is possible to take a given number and express it as a power of 10. Thus

$$100 = 10^2,$$
$$1{,}000 = 10^3,$$
$$10{,}000 = 10^4,$$

$$0.01 = \frac{1}{10^2} = 10^{-2},$$

and

$$0.001 = \frac{1}{10^3} = 10^{-3}.$$

Also it can be determined that

$$345 = 10^{2.53782},$$

$$6{,}581 = 10^{3.81829}$$

and

$$0.125 = 10^{-.90309}.$$

The exponent in the right member of each of the equality statements given above is a *logarithm*. The quantity 10 is referred to as the *base*. The number which is given expression as a power of 10, that is, the quantity in the left member of each equality statement, is called the *antilog*.

Examine the relations among the antilogs and the relations among the logarithms or exponents. Note that

$$100 < 345 < 1{,}000 \text{ and } 2 < 2.53782 < 3;$$

$$1{,}000 < 6{,}581 < 10{,}000 \text{ and } 3 < 3.81829 < 4;$$

$$0.100 < 0.125 < 1.000 \text{ and } -1 < -0.90309 < 0.$$

Logarithms employing 10 as a base are called *common* logarithms. Another system, the so-called *natural* logarithms, employs as a base the constant $e$ whose value is approximately 2.71828. We shall confine references in the following discussion to the common system of logarithms.

If one keeps in mind that logarithms are exponents, it is not so difficult to see that two quantities can be multiplied by expressing each as a power of 10 and then adding the logarithms (exponents), that division can be performed by expressing the dividend and the divisor as powers of 10 and then subtracting logarithms (exponents), and that a power of a given quantity can be obtained by multiplying the logarithm (exponent) of that quantity by the specified power. These operations are usually put in a form in which the base does not appear and one works only with the logarithms (exponents), understanding that the base is implied. In each operation, after the computation has been performed on the logarithms (exponents), the antilog (the quantity expressed as a power of 10) must be read from a table in which the argument is the value computed from the logarithms (exponents).

Students who wish to review logarithms and the use of logarithmic tables in computing should consult Hodgman (**1**, 1–9), Rosenbach *et al.* (**2**, 369–415), or Walker (**3**, 234–249).

## Roots and Radicals

Consider the following definition: The $n^{\text{th}}$ root of a given number $A$ is the value of each of $n$ equal factors whose product is equal to $A$. The $n^{\text{th}}$ root of $A$ is written

$$\sqrt[n]{A}.$$

Then $X$ is the $n^{\text{th}}$ root of $A$ or $X = \sqrt[n]{A}$ if

$$A = X \cdot X \cdot X \cdots X \ (n \text{ factors } X).$$

In the radical,

$$\sqrt[n]{A},$$

$n$ is the *index*, $\sqrt{\ }$ is the *radical sign*, and $A$ is the *radicand.*

*Examples:*

The second or square root of $A$ is the value of each of two equal factors whose product is $A$. Then $X$ is the square root of $A$ if

$$X \cdot X = A.$$

We also observe that the square root of $A$ is $A^{1/2}$ since

$$A^{1/2} \cdot A^{1/2} = A.$$

Note that the square root of $A$ is usually written as $\sqrt{A}$ with the index implied.

The third or cube root of $A$ is the value of each of three equal factors whose product is $A$. Then $X$ is the cube root of $A$ if

$$X \cdot X \cdot X = A.$$

And $A^{1/3}$ is also the cube root of $A$ since

$$A^{1/3} \cdot A^{1/3} \cdot A^{1/3} = A.$$

Roots are in some instances positive, in some instances negative, and in others either positive or negative. By convention $\sqrt{9}$ is assumed to refer to the positive root, $+3$; $-\sqrt{9}$ refers to the negative root, $-3$.

Radicals having the same index and the same radicand can be added or subtracted. For example,

$$\sqrt{2X} + 3\sqrt{2X} = 4\sqrt{2X}.$$

The product of two radicals with the same index is obtained by taking the product of the radicands and employing one radical sign. For example,

$$\sqrt[3]{5} \cdot \sqrt[3]{6} = \sqrt[3]{30}.$$

The product of two radicals with the same radicand and different indices is obtained by changing the expressions to a form involving fractional exponents and then adding exponents. For example,

$$\sqrt{3} \cdot \sqrt[3]{3} = 3^{1/2} \cdot 3^{1/3} = 3^{3/6} \cdot 3^{2/6} = 3^{5/6} = \sqrt[6]{3^5}.$$

It is sometimes convenient to rewrite a radical in factored form as

$$128 = \sqrt{2}\sqrt{64}.$$

The root of 64 can then be obtained by inspection and the entire quantity rewritten as

$$8\sqrt{2}.$$

## Factorial Notation

The product of all the positive integers from 1 to 5 inclusive,

$$1 \times 2 \times 3 \times 4 \times 5,$$

can be written in a more concise form by means of the following conventional notation:

$$5! \text{ (read " five factorial ").}$$

In general, the product of all the positive integers from 1 to $n$ inclusive,

$$(1)(2)(3)\cdots(n-3)(n-2)(n-1)(n),$$

is written

$$n! \text{ (read " } n \text{ factorial ").}$$

## The Term in Algebraic Symbolism

An algebraic expression is made up of one or more terms, a *term* being the product of a number and one or more literal number symbols. The product has a prefixed sign. Thus a term is a signed quantity. When the sign is not written, it is understood to be positive.

The numerical factor in a term is called the *numerical coefficient*. When a factor of a term is an unknown or a variable, the other part, which is also a factor, is called simply the *coefficient* of the term. When no number appears in the term, the numerical coefficient is understood to be " 1."

An expression involving a single term is called a *monomial*. An expression consisting of two terms is a *binomial*. An expression of two or more terms is a *multinomial*. Here are some examples of each.

| | |
|---|---|
| *Monomials:* | $NX$, $-nY^2$, $aX$, $-3XY$ |
| *Binomials:* | $X + Y$, $x - y$, $NX^2 - aXY$, $3X^3 - 2X^2$ |
| *Multinomials:* | $X^2 - 2XY + Y^2$ |
| | $a + bX + cX^2 + dX^3$ |
| | $X^3 + 3X^2Y + 3XY^2 + Y^3$ |
| | $p^3 - 3p^2q + 3pq^2 - q^3$ |

Technically these expressions are also *polynomials* but no attempt will be made here to distinguish between the two terms, "multinomial" and "polynomial."

Terms may be combined when the literal factors are identical. The numerical coefficients are combined and written with the literal factor, as shown in the examples below:

$$3X + 2X - 4X = X,$$
$$2X^2 - 3X^2 + 5X^2 = 4X^2,$$
$$2XY - 3XY - 2XY = -3XY.$$

**Exercise 2.7**

Combine terms wherever possible in each of the following expressions:

1. $3X^2 - X^2 + 4X^2$
2. $4XY - 5XY + 2XY$
3. $3aX + 2X - 5aX$
4. $X + aX - 3XY$
5. $X^2 - XY - XY + Y^2$
6. $nX - 2nX + 3X$
7. $X^2 - 3X^2 - 2X^2$
8. $X^2 + Y^2 + 2X^2 - bY^2$
9. $3X^3 - Y + X^3 + 5Y$
10. $3X^3Y - 3XY^3$

**Answers to Exercise 2.7**

1. $6X^2$
2. $XY$
3. $2X - 2aX$
4. $X + aX - 3XY$
5. $X^2 - 2XY + Y^2$
6. $3X - nX$
7. $-4X^2$
8. $3X^2 + Y^2 - bY^2$
9. $4X^3 + 4Y$
10. $3X^3Y - 3XY^3$

**Exercise 2.8**

Combine terms wherever possible in each of the following expressions:

1. $3X + 3X^2 + 3X^3$
2. $2XYZ - 3XY + XYZ$
3. $4cY + cY - 9cY$
4. $aX + cY + 4XY$
5. $X^2 + XY - XY - Y^2$
6. $mX + b - 5mX$
7. $2Y^2 + 3Y^2 + 4Y^2$
8. $4X^2 + 4Y^2 + 4Z^2$
9. $X^3 - X^2Y - X^2Y + XY^2 - X^2Y + XY^2 + XY^2 - Y^3$
10. $p^3 + p^2q + p^2q + pq^2 + p^2q + pq^2 pq^2 + q^3$

Terms are multiplied by multiplying the numerical coefficients, taking account of signs, of course, and applying rules for exponents to the literal factors.

**Exercise 2.9**

Perform the indicated multiplication.

1. $(4a)(3a)$
2. $(NX)(NY)$
3. $(NX^2)(nX)$
4. $(aX)(aY)$
5. $(3aX)(4aX)$
6. $(5a)(4XY)$
7. $(5aX)(3bX)$
8. $(abX^2)(3acXY^2)$
9. $(-5X^2)(4X^3)$
10. $(-4Y)(-3Y)$

**Answers to Exercise 2.9**

1. $12a^2$
2. $N^2XY$
3. $NnX^3$
4. $a^2XY$
5. $12a^2X^2$
6. $20aXY$
7. $15abX^2$
8. $3a^2bcX^3Y^2$
9. $-20X^5$
10. $12Y^2$

**Exercise 2.10**

Perform the indicated multiplication.

1. $(-5b)(6b^2)$
2. $(nX)(nY)$
3. $(mX^2)(nX^2)$
4. $(-a)(-b)$
5. $(-5aX)(+5aX)$
6. $(8c)(cXY)$
7. $(6b)(-5c)$
8. $(-5a)(-5b)(-5c)$
9. $(2x)(3x)(4x)$
10. $(6X)(6X^2)(6X^3)$

One term is divided by another by dividing the numerical coefficients, taking account of the signs, and applying the rules for exponents to the literal factors.

**Exercise 2.11**

Perform the indicated division.

1. $10X^2/aX$
2. $6Y/3$
3. $3XY/X$
4. $10aX^2/2aX$
5. $NX^2/N$
6. $N^2XY/NX$
7. $n^2X^2Y/nY$
8. $fX^2/f$
9. $fXY/XY$
10. $fXY/NXY$

**Answers to Exercise 2.11**

1. $10X/a$
2. $2Y$
3. $3Y$
4. $5X$
5. $X^2$
6. $NY$
7. $nX^2$
8. $X^2$
9. $f$
10. $f/N$

**Exercise 2.12**

Perform the indicated division,

1. $15aX^3/5b$
2. $30XY/20$
3. $aXY/bXY$
4. $2bX^2/2aX$
5. $NXY/N$
6. $n^2/n^3$
7. $fX/fXY$
8. $fX/N$
9. $fX/fX^2$
10. $fXY/fX$

In multiplying a binomial (or a multinomial) by a monomial, multiplication by the single term is distributed over the two terms of the binomial (or all terms of the multinomial).

**Exercise 2.13**

Perform the indicated multiplication.

1. $a(X - Y)$
2. $a(X - a)$
3. $a(aX - bY)$
4. $a(X + Y)$
5. $a(X + b)$
6. $c(Y - 2a)$
7. $cX(X - Y)$
8. $bY(X^2 - Y^2)$
9. $ac(X^2 + a)$
10. $(a - c)XY$

**Answers to Exercise 2.13**

1. $aX - aY$
2. $aX - a^2$
3. $a^2X - abY$
4. $aX + aY$
5. $aX + ab$
6. $cY - 2ac$
7. $cX^2 - cXY$
8. $bX^2Y - bY^3$
9. $acX^2 + a^2c$
10. $aXY - cXY$

**Exercise 2.14**

Perform the indicated multiplication.

1. $3(X + Y)$
2. $P(a + b)$
3. $\alpha(x - y)$
4. $\beta(n - 1)$
5. $\delta(\alpha - \beta)$
6. $N(N - 1)$
7. $N(X^2 - X^2/N)$
8. $(\sigma^2/n)(n - 1)$
9. $p(p - q)$
10. $p(1 - p)$

Notice that each of the answers to Exercises 2.13 and 2.14 can be viewed as a problem in *factoring* which means resolving a product into the factors which when multiplied together yield the product. For example, given the expression,

$$aX - aY,$$

and instructed to factor it, we would examine the expression, note a factor common to each term, and write the expression in factored form as

$$a(X - Y).$$

The student should practice finding the common factor in each of the answers to Exercises 2.13 and 2.14.

Dividing a binomial (or a multinomial) by a monomial follows the pattern of multiplication. Using the monomial as the divisor, the division is distributed over each term of the dividend.

**Exercise 2.15**

Perform the indicated division.

1. $(aX^2 - aX)/aX$
2. $(3X^3 + 6X^2)/3X^2$
3. $(4aX^2 + 6aY^2)/2a$
4. $(2X + 3X^2 + 4X^3)/3X$

**Answers to Exercise 2.15**

1. $X - 1$
2. $X + 2$
3. $2X^2 + 3Y^2$
4. $(2 + 3X + 4X^2)/3$

**Exercise 2.16**

1. $(15aX - 30aY + 45aZ)/15a$
2. $(X^3 + X^2 + X)/5X$
3. $(X^2Y + XY + XY^2)/aXY$
4. $(2X^3 + 2X^2 + 2X)/2X^{-1}$

The product of two binomial expressions can be obtained by distributing the multiplication by one binomial over each term of the other. Thus

$$(X + Y)(X + Y)$$

can be rewritten, after distribution, as

$$X(X + Y) + Y(X + Y)$$

which expression now involves two simple problems in the distribution of multiplication. The final answer is

$$X^2 + XY + XY + Y^2 = X^2 + 2XY + Y^2.$$

By the same operations

$$(Y + a)^2 = Y^2 + 2aY + a^2$$
$$(X - Y)^2 = X^2 - 2XY + Y^2$$

and

$$(X + Y)(X - Y) = X^2 - XY + XY - Y^2 = X^2 - Y^2.$$

Notice the form of each product and consider the reverse process, that is, resolving these answers into the binomial factors which produce them.

**Exercise 2.17**

Perform the indicated multiplication.

1. $(x + y)^2$
2. $(\alpha - 1)(\beta - 1)$
3. $(n - 1)^2$
4. $(X - M_x)^2$
5. $(X - a)(X + a)$
6. $(a - d)(b - c)$
7. $(Y + c)^2$
8. $(3X - 2)^2$
9. $(Y - a)(Y + b)$
10. $N(N - 1)(N - 2)$

**Answers to Exercise 2.17**

1. $x^2 + 2xy + y^2$
2. $\alpha\beta - \alpha - \beta + 1$
3. $n^2 - 2n + 1$
4. $X^2 - 2M_xX + M_x^2$
5. $X^2 - a^2$
6. $ab - ac - bd + cd$
7. $Y^2 + 2cY + c^2$
8. $9X^2 - 12X + 4$
9. $Y^2 - aY + bY - ab$
10. $N^3 - 3N^2 + 2N$

**Exercise 2.18**

Perform the indicated multiplication.

1. $(\alpha - \beta)(\delta - 1)$
2. $(a - \alpha)(b - \beta)$
3. $(n - 1)(m - 1)$
4. $(X - M_x)(Y - M_y)$
5. $(\mu + \alpha)^2$
6. $(1 + r_{xy})(1 - r_{xy})$
7. $(X + Y)^2$
8. $(X_1 + X_2)^2$
9. $(X_1 + X_2)(Y_1 + Y_2)$
10. $(X + \delta)^2$

**Exercise 2.19**

You are given two sets of paired numbers, $X$ and $Y$, with four numbers in each set. Write:

1. the sum of $X$
2. the sum of $Y$
3. the sum of the sum of $X$ and the sum of $Y$
4. the sum of the four pair sums

Compare your answers to (3) and (4).

5. the sum of the squares of $X$
6. the sum of the squares of $Y$
7. the square of the sum of $X$
8. the square of the sum of $Y$

Compare your answers to (5) and (7); to (6) and (8).

9. the difference between $X$ and $Y$ for any pair
10. the sum of the four pair differences
11. the difference between the sum of $X$ and the sum of $Y$

Compare the answers to (10) and (11).

12. the sum of the squares of the four pair differences.

**Answers to Exercise 2.19**

1. $X_1 + X_2 + X_3 + X_4$
2. $Y_1 + Y_2 + Y_3 + Y_4$
3. $(X_1 + X_2 + X_3 + X_4) + (Y_1 + Y_2 + Y_3 + Y_4)$
4. $(X_1 + Y_1) + (X_2 + Y_2) + (X_3 + Y_3) + (X_4 + Y_4)$
5. $X_1^2 + X_2^2 + X_3^2 + X_4^2$
6. $Y_1^2 + Y_2^2 + Y_3^2 + Y_4^2$
7. $(X_1 + X_2 + X_3 + X_4)^2$
8. $(Y_1 + Y_2 + Y_3 + Y_4)^2$
9. $X_i - Y_i$ or $X - Y$
10. $(X_1 - Y_1) + (X_2 - Y_2) + (X_3 - Y_3) + (X_4 - Y_4)$
11. $(X_1 + X_2 + X_3 + X_4) - (Y_1 + Y_2 + Y_3 + Y_4)$
12. $(X_1 - Y_1)^2 + (X_2 - Y_2)^2 + (X_3 - Y_3)^2 + (X_4 - Y_4)^2$

**Exercise 2.20**

We are given two sets of paired numbers. Let $u_1$, $u_2$, and $u_3$ be the three numbers in one set. Let $v_1$, $v_2$, and $v_3$ be the three numbers in the second set. We shall add a constant value, $\alpha$, to each number in the $u$ set. We shall also add a constant value, $\beta$, to each number in the $v$ set. The three numbers in the $u$ set are now transformed to $u_1 + \alpha$, $u_2 + \alpha$, and $u_3 + \alpha$. The three numbers in the $v$ set are now $v_1 + \beta$, $v_2 + \beta$, and $v_3 + \beta$. Let us refer to the numbers in the new sets as $u'$ and $v'$.

Write, in terms of the original numbers and the constants,

1. the sum of $u'$
2. the sum of $v'$
3. the sum of the sum of $u'$ and the sum of $v'$
4. the sum of the three pair sums
5. the sum of the squares of $u'$
6. the sum of the squares of $v'$

7. the square of the sum of $u'$
8. the square of the sum of $v'$
9. the difference between $u'$ and $v'$ for any pair
10. the sum of the three pair differences
11. the difference between the sum of $u'$ and the sum of $v'$
12. the sum of the squares of the three pair differences.

## Equations

An equation is the statement of an equality which does not hold for some values which might be assigned to the literal symbol(s) in the statement. When an equation involves one literal number symbol, it is said to be an equation in one unknown and the number represented by the letter can be determined. When an equation involves two different literal number symbols, it is said to be an equation in two unknowns and it is possible to determine the number represented by one of the letters if a value is given to the other. Thus an equation in two unknowns expresses a relation between two literal symbols. When an equation involves three unknowns, the number represented by any one letter can be determined if values are assigned to the other two.

**Exercise 2.21**

Write the following as equations.

1. $X$ is equal to 7.
2. The product of 5 and $X$ is equal to 15.
3. $X$ plus 3 is equal to 5.
4. Six times $Y$ is equal to 18 plus 3 times $Y$.
5. Three less than the product of 5 and $X$ is equal to 32.
6. $X$ minus 10 is equal to $X'$.
7. The difference, $Y$ minus 10, divided by 5 is equal to $Y'$.
8. The difference, $X$ minus $M_x$, divided by $S_x$, is equal to $Z_x$.
9. $Y$ is equal to the square of $X$.
10. $Y$ is equal to 20 plus the product of 5 and $X$.

**Answers to Exercise 2.21**

1. $X = 7$
2. $5X = 15$
3. $X + 3 = 5$
4. $6Y = 18 + 3Y$
5. $5X - 3 = 32$
6. $X - 10 = X'$
7. $(Y - 10)/5 = Y'$
8. $(X - M_x)/S_x = Z_x$
9. $Y = X^2$
10. $Y = 20 + 5X$

**Exercise 2.22**

Write the following as equations.

1. Two more than 5 times an unknown value, $X$, is equal to 42.
2. Five less than the reciprocal of the unknown, $Y$, is equal to 15.

3. Twenty-eight times the quotient, $N$ divided by the quantity, $N$ minus 1, is equal to 30.
4. The sum of the four numbers in the $X$ set is equal to 10.
5. The quotient obtained by dividing the sum of five numbers in the $Y$ set by 5 is equal to 4.
6. The sum of the squares of the four numbers in the $X$ set is equal to 30.
7. The sum of the squares of the five numbers in the $Y$ set is equal to 90.
8. The sum of the third powers of the four numbers in the $X$ set is equal to 100.
9. The sum of the fourth powers of the four numbers in the $X$ set is equal to 354.
10. The square of the difference between two unknowns, $X$ and $Y$, is equal to 25.

## SOLVING SIMPLE EQUATIONS

In an equation containing a single, literal number symbol, that symbol is called an *unknown* and determining the number(s) represented by the symbol is called *solving* the equation. Each such number is called a *solution* of the equation and is said to *satisfy* the equation.

The fundamental principle in solving an equation in one unknown is that certain arithmetic operations can be performed on both sides of the equation yielding a new equation in which the literal symbol represents the same number(s) as it did in the original equation. That is to say, given an equation in one unknown, we can

(1) add the same number or expression to both sides,
(2) subtract the same number or expression from both sides,
(3) multiply each side by the same number, or
(4) divide each side by the same number

and the new equation will have the same solution as the original.

*Caution:* There are other operations which must be employed with discretion. Multiplying both members by an expression containing the unknown may yield an equation in which the literal symbol represents numbers, one or more of which will not satisfy the original equation. For this reason, all solutions should be checked in the original equation. Dividing both members by an expression containing the unknown may result in a loss of a solution. Raising both sides to a power poses the same problem as does multiplication by the unknown. Extracting the same root on both sides presents the same problem as dividing by the unknown.

An equation in which the exponent of the unknown is " one " is a *linear equation.* To solve a linear equation in one unknown:

1. Clear the equation of fractions by multiplying both sides by the least common denominator of the fractions.
2. By addition and subtraction, obtain an equation with all terms containing the unknown on one side and all other terms on the other side.
3. Combine terms containing the unknown.
4. Divide both sides by the coefficient of the unknown.

Here is an example of the solution of a linear equation in one unknown. Given the equation,

$$\frac{2x - 4}{7} = 4,$$

we multiply both sides by 7. The new equation is

$$2x - 4 = 28.$$

We now add 4 to both sides. The equation becomes

$$2x = 32.$$

Finally we divide both sides by 2 and obtain the solution,

$$x = 16.$$

The solution can be checked by substitution in the original equation.

Given an equation in two unknowns, one can solve for one unknown in terms of the other. Given the linear equation,

$$2x + 3y = 7,$$

one can solve for $y$ in terms of $x$. First, subtract $2x$ from each side, thereby obtaining a new equation,

$$3y = 7 - 2x.$$

Next, divide both sides by 3 and find the solution for $y$ to be

$$y = \frac{7 - 2x}{3}.$$

An equation in two unknowns has an unlimited number of solutions, by which we mean pairs of numbers which will satisfy the equation.

**Exercise 2.23**

Solve each equation for the unknown appearing in it.

1. $X - 5 = 10$
2. $6Y = 18$
3. $\frac{X + 3}{2} = 12$
4. $\frac{3Y - 8}{8} = 5$
5. $X^2 + 3 = 19$
6. $2X^2 - 8 = 42$
7. $(X - 3)^2 = 25$
8. $X^2 - 6X + 9 = 25$
9. $\sqrt{Y + 6} = 3$
10. $\sqrt{Y + 6} = \sqrt{2Y}$

**Answers to Exercise 2.23**

1. $X = 15$
2. $Y = 3$
3. $X = 21$
4. $Y = 16$
5. $X = \pm 4$
6. $X = \pm 5$
7. $X = 8$ or $-2$
8. $X = 8$ or $-2$
9. $Y = 3$
10. $Y = 6$

**Exercise 2.24**

Solve each equation for the unknown appearing in it.

1. $5X = 15$
2. $X + 3 = 5$
3. $6Y = 3Y + 18$
4. $5X - 3 = 32$
5. $5X + 2 = 42$
6. $\frac{1}{Y} - 5 = 15$
7. $\frac{28\ N}{N - 1} = 30$
8. $1 - r^2_{xy} = 0.36$
9. $\frac{40 - M_x}{4} = 3$
10. $(X + 2)^2 = 25X^2$

**Exercise 2.25**

In each problem solve for the indicated unknown in terms of the other unknowns.

1. $X + 2 = 5Y$
   $Y =$
2. $m + 1 = 9(n + 1)$
   $n =$
3. $2X + 7Y = 18$
   $X =$
4. $p + q = 1$
   $p =$
5. $3(X - Y) = 24$
   $X =$
6. $(x - y)^2 = 36$
   $x =$
7. $Y = a + bX$
   $X =$
8. $X' = (X - 50)/10$
   $X =$
9. $x = X - M_x$
   $X =$
10. $Z_x = (X - M_x)/S_x$
    $M_x =$

**Answers to Exercise 2.25**

1. $Y = (X + 2)/5$
2. $n = (m + 1)/9 - 1$
3. $X = (18 - 7Y)/2$
4. $p = 1 - q$
5. $X = Y + 8$
6. $x = y \pm 6$
7. $X = (Y - a)/b$
8. $X = 10X' + 50$
9. $X = x + M_x$
10. $M_x = X - Z_xS_x$

**Exercise 2.26**

In each problem solve for the indicated unknown in terms of the other unknowns.

1. $X + \alpha = \beta Y$
   $Y =$
2. $\alpha - 1 = n(\beta - 1)$
   $\beta =$
3. $3\alpha + 5\beta = \delta$
   $\alpha =$
4. $3M_x = X_1 + X_2 + X_3$
   $M_x =$
5. $a(X - Y) = b^2$
   $X =$
6. $(X - a)^2 = (Y + b)^2$
   $X =$
7. $Y' = (Y - a)/b$
   $Y =$
8. $y - x = (Y - M_y) - (X - M_x)$
   $X =$
9. $y = Y - M_y$
   $M_y =$
10. $y' = b_{yx}x$
    $b_{yx} =$

## SYSTEMS OF EQUATIONS

Suppose that we have two linear equations, each involving the same two unknowns. It is possible that a pair of numbers which satisfies the one equation will also satisfy the other. It is also possible that only one pair of numbers will satisfy both equations. When two linear equations are satisfied by one and only one pair of numbers, they constitute a *system of simultaneous linear equations* and we can solve for the numbers represented by the letters.

Here is an example of a system of two simultaneous equations:

$$x + y = 6$$
$$5x - y = 18.$$

One way to solve this system of equations is to perform an arithmetic operation which will yield a new equation in only one unknown. Examine the two equations given above. If we add the left numbers and then add the right members, we obtain

$$(5x - y) + (x + y) = 24,$$

or

$$6x = 24.$$

We can then divide by 6, obtaining the solution:

$$x = 4.$$

We can now find the value represented by $y$, by substituting 4 for $x$ in either of the original equations and solving for $y$. Substituting in the first equation and solving for $y$ gives

$$4 + y = 6$$

and

$$y = 2.$$

We can check these values, $x = 4$ and $y = 2$, by substituting them in the original equations to see if each equation is satisfied. Substituting in the first equation gives

$$4 + 2 = 6.$$

Substituting in the second equation yields

$$5(4) - 2 = 18.$$

We observe that the original equations are satisfied by the solutions.

Given below are three sets of simultaneous equations in two unknowns. Note the varied operations which can be employed to eliminate one of the unknowns.

1. a. $2x + y = 5$

   b. $x + y = 3$

   Subtract (b) from (a) to eliminate $y$ in (c).

   c. $x = 2$

Substitute for $x$ in (a) or (b) and solve for $y$.

$$y = 1$$

Check by substituting the two solutions in (a) and (b).

2. a. $5x - 3y = 21$
   b. $x + y = 1$
   Multiply (b) by three to obtain (c).
   c. $3x + 3y = 3$
   Add (a) and (c) to eliminate $y$ in (d).
   d. $8x = 24$
   Solve for $x$.
   $$x = 3$$
   Substitute for $x$ in (a) or (b) and solve for $y$.
   $$y = -2$$
   Check by substituting the two solutions in (a) and (b).
3. a. $7x + 2y = 38$
   b. $4x + 3y = 31$
   Multiply (a) by three to obtain (c). Multiply (b) by two to obtain (d).
   c. $21x + 6y = 114$
   d. $8x + 6y = 62$
   Subtract (d) from (c) to eliminate $y$ in (e).
   e. $13x = 52$
   Solve for $x$.
   $$x = 4$$
   Substitute for $x$ in either (a) and (b) and solve for $y$.
   $$y = 5$$
   Check by substituting the two solutions in (a) and (b).

Systems of simultaneous equations in more than two unknowns can be solved by similar procedures. With three equations in three unknowns, operations are chosen which will yield two equations in two unknowns; then further operations are performed to produce one equation in one unknown. After solving for this single unknown, we go back, substitute in an equation with two unknowns and solve for a second. Then we go back to one of the original equations in three unknowns to obtain the value of the third. Checking is accomplished by substitution in all three of the original equations.

Here is a demonstration of the solving of a set of three simultaneous linear equations in three unknowns.

a. $3x - 2y + z = 2$
b. $x - 2y + 3z = 6$

c. $2x - y - z = -3$
Subtract (b) from (a) to eliminate $y$ in (d).
d. $2x - 2z = -4$
Multiply (c) by two to obtain (e).
e. $4x - 2y - 2z = -6$
Subtract (e) from (b) to eliminate $y$ in (f).
f. $-3x + 5z = 12$
Multiply (d) by five to obtain (g).
g. $10x - 10z = -20$
Multiply (f) by two to obtain (h).
h. $-6x + 10z = 24$
Add (g), and (h), to eliminate $z$ in (i).
i. $4x = 4$
Solve for $x$.

$$x = 1$$

Substitute for $x$ in (d) and solve for $z$.

$$z = 3$$

Substitute for $x$ and $z$ in (a) and solve for $y$.

$$y = 2$$

Check by substituting all three values in (a), (b), and (c).

**Exercise 2.27**

Solve each set of equations for the unknowns appearing in them.

1. $b_1(5) + b_2(3) = 25$
   $b_1(3) + b_2(2) = 16$

2. $a_1(20) + a_2(16) + a_3(30) = 208$
   $a_1(16) + a_2(10) + a_3(10) = 102$
   $a_1(30) + a_2(10) + a_3(8) = 122$

**Answers to Exercise 2.27**

1. $b_1 = 2; b_2 = 5$
2. $a_1 = 2; a_2 = 3; a_3 = 4$

**Exercise 2.28**

Solve each set of equations for the unknowns appearing in them.

1. $c_1(16) + c_2(24) = 520$
   $c_1(10) + c_2(4) = 160$

2. $a(10) + b(12) + c(15) = 116$
   $a(12) + b(8) + c(20) = 128$
   $a(15) + b(20) + c(16) = 154$

# Functions and Graphs

A function is a specification of the relation between two or more sets of numbers. The relation is usually expressed in terms of the dependence of one set on the other(s). When a letter symbol represents any number in a set of numbers, the letter symbol is said to be a *variable*. There are two principal ways of incorporating variables in the writing of functions. In the one way, the number represented by an algebraic expression is shown to depend on the number or numbers represented by one or more variables. The number represented by the expression is called the *value* of the function. The variable on which the value of the function depends is called the *argument*. Two examples of this first way of writing functions are given below.

1. The expression,

$$(3X + 2),$$

is a "function of $X$"; that is, the number represented by the expression depends on the number represented by $X$. The number represented by $(3X + 2)$ is the value of the function; $X$ is the argument.

2. The expression,

$$(X_1 + X_2 + X_3),$$

is a function of $X_1$, $X_2$, and $X_3$. The number represented by $(X_1 + X_2 + X_3)$, is the value of the function. There are three arguments: $X_1$, $X_2$, and $X_3$.

The other principal way of writing a function is to employ an equality statement and specify the relation between the number represented by one variable and the number or numbers represented by one or more other variables. If $y$ is said to depend on $x$, then $y$ is the value of the function and $x$ is the argument. Two examples are given below.

1. The variable $y$ is expressed as a function of the variable $x$ by the equality statement:

$$y = 3x^2 + 2x + 5.$$

Here $y$ is the value of the function and $x$ is the argument.

2. The variable $M_x$ is expressed as a function of the variables $X_1$, $X_2$, $X_3$, and $X_4$ by the equality statement:

$$M_x = \frac{X_1 + X_2 + X_3 + X_4}{4}.$$

$M_x$ is the value of the function; $X_1$, $X_2$, $X_3$, and $X_4$ are the arguments.

Recall that a literal number symbol sometimes refers to a particular number of unspecified value rather than to any number in a set. Such literal symbols are said to be *constants*. Numbers themselves are, of course, constants.

A function involving only one argument lends itself quite readily to graphical representation. Let us suppose that we have a function involving $x$ and $y$, where $x$ is the argument and $y$ is the value of the function. For a graphical representation we employ two intersecting straight lines, a horizontal line for the scale of $x$ and a vertical line for the scale of $y$. The horizontal line is called the $x$-axis. The vertical line is called the $y$-axis. The lines form a right angle at their intersection. The point of intersection is called the *origin*. The two lines are called the *coordinate axes*.

Each scale is marked off in equal intervals and numbered from zero at the origin. The $x$-axis is numbered from the origin to the right with positive numbers and to the left with negative numbers. The $y$-axis is numbered from the origin upward with positive numbers and downward with negative numbers.

Given an equality statement showing the relation between $y$ and $x$, a value of $y$ can be computed for any value assigned to $x$. These two values constitute a pair which can be represented as a point located in the two-dimensional space in which the coordinate axes are located. The two values are called the *coordinates* of that point. The point is located by the intersection of two lines, one drawn perpendicular to each axis at a point on the scale corresponding to the value of that coordinate. The coordinate which locates the line drawn perpendicular to the horizontal axis is called the *abscissa*. The coordinate which locates the line drawn perpendicular to the vertical axis is called the *ordinate*. The coordinates of a point are written $(x, y)$ with the abscissa first and the ordinate second.

For a given function we might locate a number of points and draw a continuous line which would indicate the locus of points whose coordinates would satisfy the equation.

The linear function

$$Y = 0.5X + 1$$

yields a straight line when it is plotted. This line intersects the vertical axis at the point (0, 1), in which case we say that the $Y$ intercept is one. The $X$ intercept, at the point $(-2, 0)$ on the horizontal axis, is $-2$. The coefficient of $X$, $+0.5$, indicates the *slope* of the line, the distance the line moves vertically per unit change horizontally.

The function given above, $Y = 0.5X + 1$, can be plotted by assigning several values to $X$, computing the corresponding values of $Y$, and drawing a line through the points located by these several pairs of values. Listed below are three arbitrarily chosen values of $X$ and the corresponding values of $Y$. These three pairs of values have been employed, in Fig. 2.1, to locate three points through which a straight line has been drawn.

| $X$ | $Y$ |
|---|---|
| $-3$ | $-0.5$ |
| 0 | 1 |
| 2 | 2 |

The following quadratic equation is an example of a function whose plot is a curved line:

$$Y = 2X^2 - 4X + 4.$$

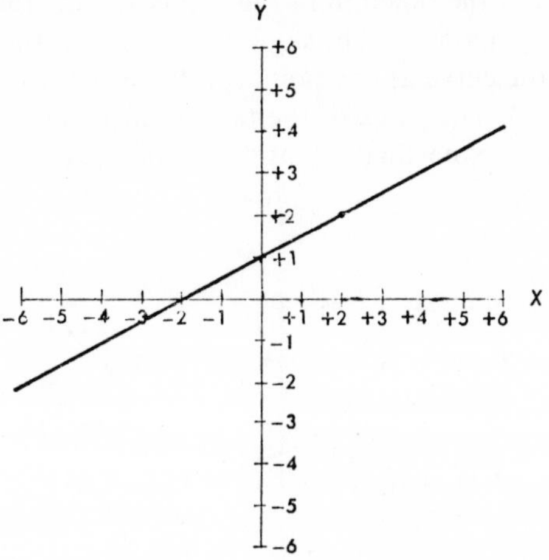


**Fig. 2.1** Plot of the linear function, $Y = 0.5X + 1$.

Listed below are paired values of $X$ and $Y$. These paired values have been plotted in Fig. 2.2. A smooth curve has been drawn through the points.

| $X$ | $Y$ |
|---|---|
| −4 | 52 |
| −3 | 34 |
| −2 | 20 |
| −1 | 10 |
| 0 | 4 |
| 1 | 2 |
| 2 | 4 |
| 3 | 10 |
| 4 | 20 |
| 5 | 34 |
| 6 | 52 |

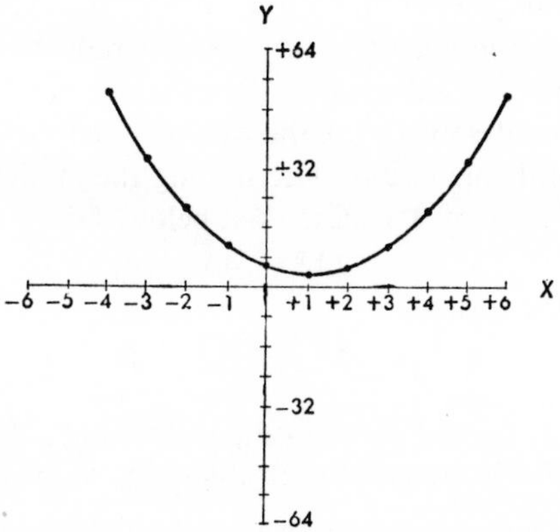

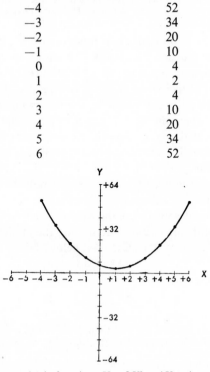

**Fig. 2.2** Plot of the quadratic function, $Y = 2X^2 - 4X + 4$.

The $Y$ intercept of the function in Fig. 2.2 is 4. Note that the slope of this curve varies, depending on $X$. The slope can be shown graphically by drawing a line tangent to the curve at any point. A tangent has been drawn at point $P$ (4, 20) in Fig. 2.3. The slope of the tangent at point $P$ is the slope of the curve at that point. Note that a tangent at any other point would have a different slope.

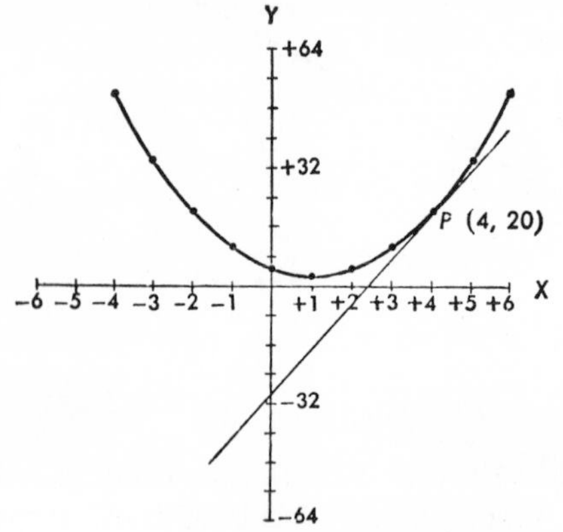


**Fig. 2.3** A straight line has been drawn tangent to the curve of Fig. 2.2 at point $P$ (4, 20). The function is $Y = 2X^2 - 4X + 4$. The slope of the tangent, $4X - 4$, at the point $P$ is equal to 12.

The slope can be expressed as a function of $X$. It is determined by differentiating the expression $2X^2 - 4X + 4$ with respect to $X$.[2] The derivative—that is, the slope—is equal to $(4X - 4)$. Notice that the slope is negative when $X < 1$ and positive when $X > 1$. Notice also that the slope is zero when $X = 1$. In this particular example, the minimum value of the function occurs at the point where the slope is equal to zero. That is, the lowest point on the curve is located where $X = 1$. An important method of statistics involves the determination of the number represented by a literal symbol, a number which would give the minimum value of the expression in which the symbol occurs. The minimizing value can generally be obtained by a procedure commonly used in calculus: finding the derivative, setting the derivative equal to zero, and solving for the quantity represented by the symbol.

A simpler, algebraic method of determining the minimum value of $Y$ and the corresponding value of $X$ is described below. Given the equation,

$$Y = 2X^2 - 4X + 4,$$

we can write it in the form

$$Y = \frac{4X^2 - 8X + 8}{2}$$

obtained by multiplying and dividing the right-hand side of the equation by the coefficient of $X^2$. The numerator on the right can be rewritten as follows:

[2]Differentiation is a major topic of calculus and is beyond the scope of the present review.

$$Y = \frac{(4X^2 - 8X + 4) + 4}{2}$$

or

$$Y = \frac{(2X - 2)^2 + 4}{2}.$$

Since $(2X - 2)^2$ cannot be negative and must be equal to or greater than zero, we observe that $Y$ will have its minimum value when

$$(2X - 2)^2 = 0,$$

in which case

$$(2X - 2) = 0,$$
$$2X = 2,$$

and

$$X = 1.$$

The minimum value of $Y$ can be determined by substituting this value of $X$ in the original equation,

$$Y = 2X^2 - 4X + 4.$$

Substituting, we find that

$$Y = 2(1)^2 - 4(1) + 4$$

or

$$Y = 2.$$

## Functions of Angles

Imagine a set of coordinate axes and a line which coincides with the positive segment of the $X$ axis and which, like the hand of a clock, is free to rotate clockwise or counterclockwise. In Fig. 2.4, the line $OQ$ is shown

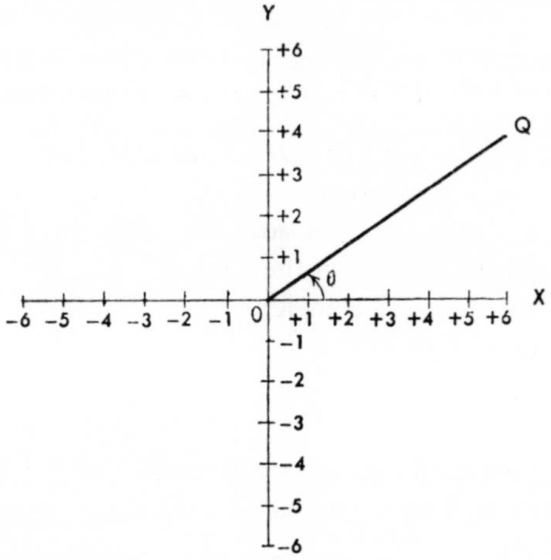


**Fig. 2.4** The angle $\theta$ generated by the counterclockwise rotation of the line $OQ$.

rotated counterclockwise from its initial position to the terminal position indicated.

In trigonometry, an angle is the amount of rotation required to move a line from its initial position to a terminal position. The amount of rotation can be measured in terms of degrees, minutes, and seconds.

If we let $O$ be the point of origin, $P$ be any point on a rotated line, and $MP$ be a perpendicular erected on the horizontal axis at point $M$ and projected through $P$, we can identify a triangle, $OPM$. An example of a triangle determined in this fashion is shown in Fig. 2.5. We can also identify three values corresponding to the three sides of the triangle. $OP$ is the length of the hypotenuse of the right triangle; $OM$ is the distance of $M$ from the origin, one of the coordinates of the point $P$; $MP$ is the distance of $P$ from the horizontal axis, the other coordinate of $P$.

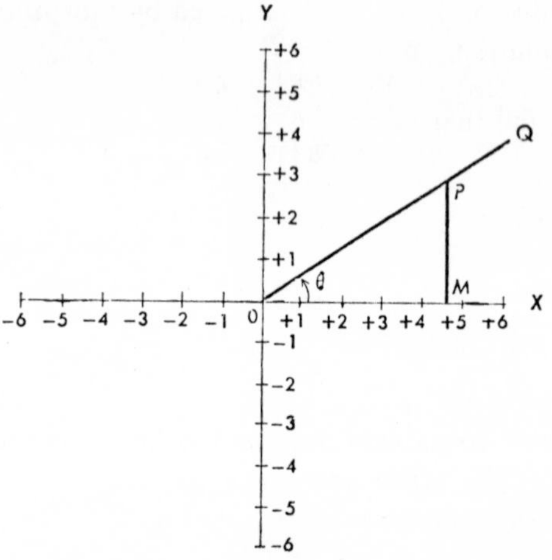


**Fig 2.5** Determination of the right triangle $OPM$. $P$ is an arbitrarily chosen point on line $OQ$. The line from $M$ to $P$ is perpendicular to the $X$ axis.

For convenience, let us use $r$ for $OP$, $X$ for $OM$, and $Y$ for $MP$, and $\theta$ for the amount of rotation. Functions of the angle $\theta$ are defined by certain ratios involving $r$, $X$ and $Y$. We shall consider here only three of these ratios: the sine, the cosine, and the tangent of the angle $\theta$.

Sin $\theta$ is read " the sine of the angle theta " or simply " sine theta " and is defined as the ratio of $Y$ to $r$. That is,

$$\sin \theta = \frac{Y}{r}.$$

Cos $\theta$ is read " the cosine of the angle theta " or " cosine theta " and is defined as the ratio of $X$ to $r$. That is,

$$\cos \theta = \frac{X}{r}.$$

Tan $\theta$ is read " the tangent of the angle theta " or " tangent theta " and is the ratio of $Y$ to $X$. Thus

$$\tan \theta = \frac{Y}{X}.$$

Values of sin $\theta$, cos $\theta$, and tan $\theta$, as well as the other trigonometric functions not given above, depend on the amount of rotation of the line and not on the distance $OP = r$ which locates the point $P$ on the line $OQ$. In other words, for any given amount of rotation, the sine, cosine, and tangent are fixed values.

The student should try to integrate these ideas about the functions of angles with his ideas about functions in general. A trigonometric function involves two variables: the value of the function (a ratio) and the argument (the angular amount of rotation). Values of these functions are widely available in tabular form. See, for example, Hodgman (1, pp. 87-110) and Walker (3, pp. 330-331).

## REFERENCES

1. Hodgman, C. D., *Mathematical Tables from Handbook of Chemistry and Physics* (Cleveland: Chemical Rubber Publishing Co., 1946).
2. Rosenbach, J. B., Whitman, E. A., Meserve, B. E., and Whitman, P. M., *College Algebra* (Boston: Ginn, 1958).
3. Walker, H. M., *Mathematics Essential for Elementary Statistics*, rev. ed. (New York: Holt, 1951).

# THE SIGN OF SUMMATION

## Syntactics | 3

In psychological statistics, the Greek capital letter "sigma," formed $\Sigma$, is not a literal number symbol, that is, it does not represent a number. It is an *operator* and serves a very useful purpose, that of indicating the arithmetic operation of summing. If it were necessary to write every term in the sums with which one works in statistics, the symbolism would be excessively burdensome. Because the operation of summing can be indicated conveniently and efficiently by a single letter, statistical symbolism can be condensed and one's facility with it is increased immeasurably.

In this introductory discussion of the sign of summation, we shall let $X$ represent any number in one set, there being $N$ numbers in that set. We shall let $Y$ represent any number in a second set and $Z$ any number in a third set, each of these sets also having $N$ numbers. We require that $X_1$, $Y_1$, and $Z_1$ be classified together, that $X_2$, $Y_2$, and $Z_2$ be classified together, and so on, and that there are, in all, $N$ such triplets, the members of each triplet bearing identical subscripts.

The classification of the $3N$ numbers represented by $X$, $Y$, and $Z$ is shown in Table 3.1. Columns of the table correspond to the letters $X$, $Y$, and $Z$.

**Table 3.1**

**A CLASSIFICATION OF NUMBERS**

| | | Columns | | |
|---|---|---|---|---|
| | | $X$ | $Y$ | $Z$ |
| | 1 | $X_1$ | $Y_1$ | $Z_1$ |
| | 2 | $X_2$ | $Y_2$ | $Z_2$ |
| | 3 | $X_3$ | $Y_3$ | $Z_3$ |
| Rows | . | . | . | . |
| | . | . | . | . |
| | . | . | . | . |
| | $N$ | $X_N$ | $Y_N$ | $Z_N$ |

Rows of the table correspond to the triplets and can be identified by the common subscript of the three letters representing the numbers in a particular row. The table is rectangular and possesses as many columns as there are sets of numbers and as many rows as there are numbers in each set.

In the discussion that follows, the letters $a$, $b$, and $c$ are constants, that is, particular numbers of unspecified value.

Here are the definitions of some fundamental expressions in which " $\Sigma$ " occurs.

1. $\Sigma X = X_1 + X_2 + X_3 + \ldots + X_N$
   $\Sigma X$ is read " sum of $X$."

The operation is equivalent to summing the numbers in the first column of Table 3.1.

2. $\Sigma Y = Y_1 + Y_2 + Y_3 + \ldots + Y_N$
   $\Sigma Y$ is read " sum of $Y$."

The operation is the summing of numbers in the second column of Table 3.1.

3. $\Sigma Z = Z_1 + Z_2 + Z_3 + \ldots + Z_N$
   $\Sigma Z$ is read " sum of $Z$."

The summation involves the numbers in the third column of Table 3.1.

Notice that each of the summations given above has $N$ terms.

4. $(\Sigma X)^2 = (X_1 + X_2 + X_3 + \ldots + X_N)^2$
   $(\Sigma X)^2$ is read " the square of the sum of $X$."

The operation involves adding the $N$ numbers in the first column of Table 3.1 and squaring the resulting sum. Similar expressions could be written for the square of the sum of $Y$ and the square of the sum of $Z$.

5. $\Sigma X^2 = X_1^2 + X_2^2 + X_3^2 + \ldots + X_N^2$
   $\Sigma X^2$ is read " the sum of squares of $X$."

The operation requires computation of the square of each number in the first column of Table 3.1, followed by the summation of these squares. $\Sigma Y^2$ and $\Sigma Z^2$ are defined in a similar fashion. Notice that

$$\Sigma X^2 \neq (\Sigma X)^2.$$

The sum of squares of $X$ is not equal to the square of the sum of $X$, since

$$\Sigma X^2 = X_1^2 + X_2^2 + X_3^2 + \ldots + X_N^2 \neq$$
$$(X_1 + X_2 + X_3 + \ldots + X_N)^2 = (\Sigma X)^2.$$

The quantity, $(\Sigma X)^2$, involves product terms like $2X_1X_2$; these product terms do not appear in the quantity, $\Sigma X^2$. A numerical example is given below.

$$2^2 + 3^2 + 4^2 \neq (2 + 3 + 4)^2$$
$$29 \neq 81.$$

6. $\Sigma(X + Y) = (X_1 + Y_1) + (X_2 + Y_2) + \ldots + (X_N + Y_N)$
   $\Sigma(X + Y)$ is read " the sum of the pair sums of $X$ and $Y$."

This operation involves two summations. Referred to Table 3.1., it involves adding the two values in the first and second columns of each row. Then these row or pair sums are added. Notice the pairing of $X$ and $Y$.

7. $\Sigma aX = aX_1 + aX_2 + aX_3 + \ldots + aX_N$

$\Sigma aX$ is read " the sum of products of the constant $a$ and the variable $X$."

To perform this operation on Table 3.1, one would multiply each value in the first column by $a$ and then sum the resulting products.

8. $\Sigma a = a + a + a + \ldots + a$ ($N$ terms $a$)

$\Sigma a$ is read " sum of $a$ " and implies the repeated addition of the constant. Similar expressions could be written for $b$ and $c$, and for other constants.

9. $\Sigma XY = X_1Y_1 + X_2Y_2 + X_3Y_3 + \ldots + X_NY_N$

$\Sigma XY$ is read " the sum of products of variables $X$ and $Y$."

Referred to Table 3.1, this set of operations involves multiplying the values in the first and second columns of each row and then summing the resulting products. Notice the pairing of $X$ and $Y$.

**Exercise 3.1**

Write, in symbols, the definition of each of the expressions listed below. $X$ and $Y$ are variables; $a$, $b$, and $c$ are constants.

1. $\Sigma X$
2. $\Sigma(X + Y)$
3. $\Sigma aX$
4. $\Sigma c$
5. $\Sigma XY$
6. $\Sigma Y^2$
7. $\Sigma bcY$
8. $\Sigma b^2$
9. $\Sigma(X + Y)^2$
10. $\Sigma(X/Y)$
11. $(\Sigma Y)^2$
12. $\Sigma aX^2$

**Answers to Exercise 3.1**

1. $X_1 + X_2 + X_3 + \ldots + X_N$
2. $(X_1 + Y_1) + (X_2 + Y_2) + \ldots + (X_N + Y_N)$
3. $aX_1 + aX_2 + aX_3 + \ldots + aX_N$
4. $c + c + c + \ldots + c$ ($N$ terms $c$)
5. $X_1Y_1 + X_2Y_2 + X_3Y_3 + \ldots + X_NY_N$
6. $Y_1^2 + Y_2^2 + Y_3^2 + \ldots + Y_N^2$
7. $bcY_1 + bcY_2 + bcY_3 + \ldots + bcY_N$
8. $b^2 + b^2 + b^2 + \ldots + b^2$
9. $(X_1 + Y_1)^2 + (X_2 + Y_2)^2 + \ldots + (X_N + Y_N)^2$
10. $X_1/Y_1 + X_2/Y_2 + X_3/Y_3 + \ldots + X_N/Y_N$
11. $(Y_1 + Y_2 + Y_3 + \ldots + Y_N)^2$
12. $aX_1^2 + aX_2^2 + aX_3^2 + \ldots + aX_N^2$

**Exercise 3.2**

Write, in symbols, the definition of each of the following expressions. Only $a$, $b$, and $c$ are constants; all other letters are variables.

1. $\Sigma Z$
2. $\Sigma(X + Y + Z)$
3. $a\,\Sigma X$
4. $\Sigma xyz$
5. $\Sigma x^2$
6. $\Sigma abX$
7. $\Sigma X + \Sigma Y$
8. $\Sigma c^2$
9. $\Sigma(X - Y)^2$
10. $\Sigma(X/Z)$
11. $(\Sigma Z)^2$
12. $\Sigma a(X - Y)$

**Exercise 3.3**

Translate the following verbal expressions into algebraic expressions involving "$\Sigma$":

1. the sum of $X$
2. the sum of the pair sums of $X$ and $Y$
3. the sum of products of $X$ and $Y$
4. the sum of squares of $Y$
5. the square of the sum of $X$
6. the product of the sum of $X$ and the sum of $Y$
7. the square of the sum of products of $X$ and $Y$
8. the sum of products of a constant, $a$, and a variable, $X$
9. the sum of products of a constant, $a$, and two variables, $X$ and $Y$
10. the sum of $N$ numbers, each of which has the constant value, $a$
11. the sum of the ratios of $Y$ to $X$
12. the ratio of the sum of $Y$ to the sum of $X$.

**Answers to Exercise 3.3**

1. $\Sigma X$
2. $\Sigma(X + Y)$
3. $\Sigma XY$
4. $\Sigma Y^2$
5. $(\Sigma X)^2$
6. $\Sigma X \Sigma Y$
7. $(\Sigma XY)^2$
8. $\Sigma aX$
9. $\Sigma aXY$
10. $\Sigma a$
11. $\Sigma(Y/X)$
12. $\Sigma Y/\Sigma X$

**Exercise 3.4**

Translate the following verbal expressions into algebraic expressions involving "$\Sigma$":

1. the sum of the $N$ numbers in the $Y$ set
2. the sum of the $Y$-and-$Z$ pair sums
3. the sum of the $N$ products of $X$ and $Z$
4. the sum of the cubes of $X$
5. the square root of the sum of $X$
6. the product of the sum of $X$ and the sum of $Z$
7. the square root of the sum of products of $X$ and $Y$
8. the square of the sum of products of $a$ and $X$
9. the sum of products of the constant $a$ and the variable, the reciprocal of $X$
10. the repeated addition of the constant $a$
11. the sum of products of the reciprocals of $X$ and $Y$
12. the sum of the ratios of the constant $a$ to the variable $X$.

## Simplification Rules

Certain expressions involving " $\Sigma$ " can be rewritten in forms which are more convenient for computation and which may be necessary for other reasons to be discussed later. The rewriting of these expressions is called *simplification.* There are four rules which can be applied singly and in various combinations to effect these simplifications. The four rules are listed and explained below.

RULE I. $\Sigma(X + Y) = \Sigma X + \Sigma Y.$

The sum of the $X$-and-$Y$ pair sums is equal to the sum of the sum of $X$ and the sum of $Y$.

*Proof:* By definition,

$$\Sigma(X + Y) = (X_1 + Y_1) + (X_2 + Y_2) + (X_3 + Y_3) + \ldots + (X_N + Y_N).$$

The terms in the right member of the equality statement can be regrouped as

$$(X_1 + X_2 + X_3 + \ldots + X_N) + (Y_1 + Y_2 + Y_3 + \ldots + Y_N),$$

which expression can then be written as

$$\Sigma X + \Sigma Y.$$

The rule is based upon the fact that the sum of the values of $X$ and $Y$ is not affected by the grouping of those values or the order of adding them.

Referred to Table 3.1, the expression, $\Sigma(X + Y)$, gives the instruction to obtain the sum of the two numbers, $X$ and $Y$, in each row and then to combine the $N$ row sums. Referred to the same Table, the expression, $\Sigma X + \Sigma Y$, implies adding the $N$ numbers in the $X$ column, adding the $N$ numbers in the $Y$ column, and then adding the two column sums.

*Caution:* Rewriting $\Sigma(X + Y)$ as $\Sigma X + \Sigma Y$ looks superficially like the distribution of multiplication by " $\Sigma$ ", but this interpretation is not correct. As the symbol " $\Sigma$ " is employed in this book, it does not represent a number, and, taken alone, is never a factor in multiplication.

RULE II. $\Sigma aX = a\Sigma X.$

The sum of the products of a constant and a variable is equal to the product of the constant and the sum of the variable.

*Proof:* By definition,

$$\Sigma aX = aX_1 + aX_2 + aX_3 + \ldots + aX_N.$$

We observe that $a$ is a factor common to each term in the right member of the equality. We can remove this common factor and write the expression as

$$a(X_1 + X_2 + X_3 + \ldots + X_N),$$

which can then be rewritten as

$$a\Sigma X.$$

RULE III. $\Sigma a = Na$.

The repeated addition of a constant, when there are $N$ terms in the summation, is equal to the product of $N$ and the constant.

*Proof:* By definition,

$$\Sigma a = a + a + a + \ldots + a \qquad (N \text{ terms } a),$$

but recall that, in arithmetic, the multiplication, $N \times a$, is defined in the same way. That is, $N \times a$ is defined as the repeated addition of $a$, there being $N$ terms in the addition. It follows that

$$\Sigma a = Na.$$

RULE IV. $\Sigma XY$ cannot be rewritten in any form which simplifies computation. By definition,

$$\Sigma XY = X_1Y_1 + X_2Y_2 + X_3Y_3 + \ldots + X_NY_N$$

and, with respect to the multiplication and the addition, there is only one correct order of operations, multiplication before addition.

*Caution:* The sum of products of two variables is not equal to the product of the sums of the two variables. That is,

$$\Sigma XY \neq \Sigma X \Sigma Y$$

or

$$X_1Y_1 + X_2Y_2 + \ldots + X_NY_N \neq (X_1 + X_2 + \ldots + X_N)(Y_1 + Y_2 + \ldots + Y_N).$$

A numerical example in which the sum of products for two variables does not equal the product of the sums of the two variables is given below.

$$2 \times 3 + 4 \times 5 + 6 \times 7 \neq (2 + 4 + 6)(3 + 5 + 7)$$
$$68 \neq 180$$

**Exercise 3.5**

Rewrite the following expressions in simplified form by applying the rules given above. In addition to $a$, $b$, and $c$, $N$ and numerals are constants. All other letters are to be considered variables.

1. $\Sigma(x - y)$
2. $\Sigma bY$
3. $\Sigma N$
4. $\Sigma(X/Y)$
5. $\Sigma(Y + a)$
6. $\Sigma abX$
7. $\Sigma ac$
8. $\Sigma X \Sigma Y$
9. $\Sigma(aX - c)$
10. $\Sigma cXY$
11. $\Sigma b^2N$
12. $\sum \dfrac{X + Y}{Z}$
13. $\Sigma(bX - cY)$
14. $\Sigma aX^2$
15. $\Sigma(a - b)$
16. $\Sigma(X - Y)^2$
17. $\Sigma(X/a)$
18. $\Sigma(a/c)$
19. $\Sigma X/\Sigma Y$
20. $\Sigma(Y - c)^2$

21. $\Sigma(a/Y)$
22. $\sum \frac{X+Y}{a}$
23. $\Sigma(a/N)$
24. $\Sigma(X - a/N)$
25. $\Sigma 3X^2Y$
26. $\Sigma 4aY$
27. $\Sigma(X - 2)$
28. $\Sigma Y^2$
29. $\Sigma X \Sigma X$
30. $\Sigma(a - X)$

**Answers to Exercise 3.5**

1. $\Sigma x - \Sigma y$
2. $b\,\Sigma Y$
3. $N^2$
4. $\Sigma(X/Y)$
5. $\Sigma Y + Na$
6. $ab\,\Sigma X$
7. $Nac$
8. $\Sigma X \Sigma Y$
9. $a\,\Sigma X - Nc$
10. $c\,\Sigma XY$
11. $b^2N^2$
12. $\sum \frac{X+Y}{Z}$ *
13. $b\,\Sigma X - c\,\Sigma Y$
14. $a\,\Sigma X^2$
15. $N(a - b)$
16. $\Sigma X^2 - 2\,\Sigma XY + \Sigma Y^2$
17. $(1/a)\,\Sigma X$
18. $Na/c$
19. $\Sigma X/\Sigma Y$
20. $\Sigma Y^2 - 2c\,\Sigma Y + Nc^2$
21. $a\,\Sigma(1/Y)$
22. $(1/a)(\Sigma X + \Sigma Y)$
23. $a$
24. $\Sigma X - a$
25. $3\,\Sigma X^2Y$
26. $4a\,\Sigma Y$
27. $\Sigma X - 2N$
28. $\Sigma Y^2$
29. $\Sigma X \Sigma X$ or $(\Sigma X)^2$
30. $Na - \Sigma X$

* $\sum \frac{X}{Z} + \sum \frac{Y}{Z}$ is also correct but would not be considered a simplification of computation.

**Exercise 3.6**

Rewrite the following expressions in simplified form by applying the four simplification rules. In addition to $a$, $b$, $c$, $N$, and numerals, Greek letters are constants. All other letters are variables.

1. $\Sigma(X + Y + Z)$
2. $\Sigma a^2X$
3. $\Sigma abc$
4. $\Sigma XYZ$
5. $\Sigma(a + bX)$
6. $\Sigma a^2X^2$
7. $\Sigma N^2$
8. $\Sigma X \Sigma Y \Sigma Z$
9. $\Sigma(aX - bY)$
10. $\Sigma aX^2Y$
11. $\Sigma c$
12. $\sum \frac{a}{X+Y}$
13. $\Sigma(\alpha X + \delta)$
14. $\Sigma aX^3$
15. $\Sigma(\alpha + \beta)$
16. $\Sigma(X + a)^2$
17. $\Sigma(Y/c)$
18. $\Sigma(ab/c)$
19. $(\Sigma X \Sigma Y)/\Sigma Z$
20. $\Sigma(Y - \delta)^2$
21. $\Sigma(\alpha/X)$
22. $\sum \frac{X+Y+Z}{a}$
23. $\Sigma(\alpha/\beta)$
24. $\Sigma(X/N)$

25. $\Sigma 5$
26. $\Sigma 5N$
27. $\Sigma(X^2 - 10)$
28. $\Sigma X^2 Y^2$
29. $(\Sigma X)^2$
30. $\Sigma(a - X/a)$

## The Summation Sign in Equations

We have been employing literal number symbols as constants and variables, and we have been writing the Greek capital letter "$\Sigma$" to indicate the operation of summing. To indicate a summation, "$\Sigma$" will always be written with one or more other symbols; it will not be written alone. When "$\Sigma$" is written with another letter, number, or combination of letters and numbers, the entire expression represents a number or a quantity which can be used in further arithmetic operations or computation. In solving a single equation or a system of simultaneous equations, a factor or a term involving the summation sign is treated as a literal symbol representing a number. On occasion, the solution of an equation for some specified unknown may require application of the rules of simplification.

Given below are some examples of operations performed on equations containing one or more summation signs.

1. *The problem:* Given $M_x = \Sigma X/N$, solve for $\Sigma X$.

   *The solution:* Multiply both sides of the equation by $N$ and obtain

$$\Sigma X = NM_x.$$

2. *The problem:* Given $S_x = \sqrt{(\Sigma x^2/N)}$, solve for $\Sigma x^2$.

   *The solution:* Square both sides of the equation to obtain

$$S_x^2 = \Sigma x^2/N.$$

Multiply both sides by $N$ to obtain

$$\Sigma x^2 = NS_x^2.$$

3. *The problem:* Given

$$r_{xy}NS_xS_y = \Sigma xy,$$

solve for $r_{xy}$.

   *The solution:* Divide both sides of the equation by $NS_xS_y$ and obtain

$$r_{xy} = \frac{\Sigma xy}{NS_xS_y}.$$

4. *The problem:* Given

$$S_x' = \sqrt{\frac{\Sigma x^2}{N - 1}},$$

solve for the quantity, $N - 1$.

*The solution:* Square both sides of the equation to obtain

$$S_x'^2 = \frac{\Sigma x^2}{N - 1}.$$

Multiply both sides by $(N - 1)$ and then divide both sides by $S_x'^2$ to obtain the answer,

$$N - 1 = \frac{\Sigma x^2}{S_x'^2}.$$

5. *The problem:* Given

$$\Sigma(X - M_x) = 0,$$

where $M_x$ is a constant, solve for $M_x$.

*The solution:* Apply the first and third simplification rules and obtain the equation,

$$\Sigma X - NM_x = 0.$$

Add $NM_x$ to both sides and then divide both sides by $N$ to obtain the solution,

$$M_x = \frac{\Sigma X}{N}.$$

6. *The problem:* Given

$$\Sigma X' = \sum \frac{X - a}{b},$$

where $a$ and $b$ are constants, solve for $\Sigma X$.

*The solution:* Apply the first, second, and third simplification rules to the expression on the right side to obtain

$$\Sigma X' = \frac{1}{b}(\Sigma X - Na).$$

Multiply both sides by $b$ and then add $Na$ to both sides to obtain the solution,

$$\Sigma X = b\Sigma X' + Na.$$

7. *The problem:* Given the simultaneous equations:

$$(1) \qquad a\Sigma x^2 + b\Sigma xy = \Sigma xz,$$

$$(2) \qquad a\Sigma xy + b\Sigma y^2 = \Sigma yz,$$

solve for $a$ and $b$.

*The solution:* Divide (1) by $\Sigma x^2$ to obtain

$$(3) \qquad a + b\Sigma xy/\Sigma x^2 = \Sigma xz/\Sigma x^2.$$

Divide (2) by $\Sigma xy$ to obtain

$$(4) \qquad a + b\Sigma y^2/\Sigma xy = \Sigma yz/\Sigma xy.$$

Subtract (4) from (3) to obtain

$$(5) \qquad b\Sigma xy/\Sigma x^2 - b\Sigma y^2/\Sigma xy = \Sigma xz/\Sigma x^2 - \Sigma yz/\Sigma xy.$$

Remove the common factor, $b$, on the left side in (5) and write

$$b(\Sigma xy/\Sigma x^2 - \Sigma y^2/\Sigma xy) = \Sigma xz/\Sigma x^2 - \Sigma yz/\Sigma xy.$$

Divide both sides by the coefficient of $b$ to obtain the solution,

$$b = \frac{\Sigma xz/\Sigma x^2 - \Sigma yz/\Sigma xy}{\Sigma xy/\Sigma x^2 - \Sigma y^2/\Sigma xy}.$$

Note that the final solution for $b$ can be written in a different form. If we multiply the numerator and the denominator (above and below the bar) by $\Sigma x^2 \Sigma xy$, we obtain

$$b = \frac{\Sigma xy\Sigma xz - \Sigma x^2\Sigma yz}{(\Sigma xy)^2 - \Sigma x^2\Sigma y^2}.$$

By a similar procedure, which will not be presented here, we could solve for $a$. We would find that

$$a = \frac{\Sigma yz/\Sigma y^2 - \Sigma xz/\Sigma xy}{\Sigma xy/\Sigma y^2 - \Sigma x^2/\Sigma xy},$$

which can be rewritten as

$$a = \frac{\Sigma xy\Sigma yz - \Sigma y^2\Sigma xz}{(\Sigma xy)^2 - \Sigma x^2\Sigma y^2}.$$

We could compute the values of $a$ and $b$, by the formulas derived above, if we were given the actual numbers represented by the various sums of squares and products: $\Sigma x^2$, $\Sigma y^2$, $\Sigma xy$, $\Sigma xz$, and $\Sigma yz$.

## Limits and Indices

As the summational notation was described above, the number of terms in the summation was understood to be $N$ and the summation was understood to involve all terms from the first to the $N^{\text{th}}$, but other possibilities must be taken into account. There is a conventional way of making explicit the number of values in the entire set to which the summation applies, and the last term in the series of terms. A number is written above the summation sign. The number is called the *upper limit* of the summation. Several examples are listed below.

In the expression, $\overset{N}{\Sigma} X$, the limit, $N$, indicates that there are $N$ values of $X$ and that the summation ends with the $N^{\text{th}}$ value. It is understood that the summation begins with the first term and includes all $N$ terms.

In the expression, $\overset{n}{\Sigma} Z$, the limit, $n$, indicates there are $n$ values of $Z$ and the summation ends with the $n^{\text{th}}$ value. It is implied that the summation begins with the first term and involves all $n$ values of $Z$.

In $\overset{c}{\Sigma}\, Y$, the limit, $c$, indicates there are $c$ values of $Y$ and the summation ends with the $c^{\text{th}}$ value. It is understood that the summation begins with the first term and includes all $c$ values.

In $\overset{8}{\Sigma}\, X^2$, the limit indicates there are eight values of $X$ and, consequently eight values of $X^2$. It also indicates that the summation ends with the eighth value. It is implied that the summation begins with the first term and includes all eight terms.

In each of the expressions given above, the summation begins with the first term but it is possible to begin with some term other than the first. There is a conventional way of writing a summation to make explicit where in the series of terms it begins. A number is written below the summation sign. It is referred to as the *lower limit*. The lower limit indicates the number of the term with which the summation begins and the summation is then understood to include all succeeding terms including the last as indicated by the upper limit. Examples of expressions in which both limits are made explicit, are given below, with their definitions.

$$\sum_{1}^{N} X = X_1 + X_2 + X_3 + \ldots + X_N$$

$$\sum_{3}^{n} X = X_3 + X_4 + X_5 + \ldots + X_n$$

$$\sum_{p}^{m} X = X_p + X_{p+1} + X_{p+2} + \ldots + X_m$$

Since, in our work, the summation will always begin with the first term, there will be no need to write the lower limit. On occasion, it will be necessary, however, to make the upper limit explicit. Where no limits are written, the intended lower limit is 1 and the intended upper limit is either $N$ or a value which is clearly given by the context in which the expression appears.

There is another feature of summational notation which should be mentioned. A letter can be placed under the summation sign and written at the same time as a subscript to one or more variables indicating that the subscripted variables are to be summated and that quantities with different subscripts or no subscripts at all are to be considered constants.

*Examples:*

In the expression, $\sum_{i}^{N} aX_i$, $X_i$ is a variable, $a$ is a constant, the lower limit is understood to be 1, and the number of values of the variable is $N$. The symbol, $i$, is called the *index of summation*.

In the expression, $\sum_{j}^{n} aX_j$, $X_j$ is the variable in the summation, $a$ is a constant, a lower limit of 1 is implied, the number of values of the variable is $n$, and $j$ is the index of summation.

In the expression, $\sum_{i=1}^{m} a_j Y_i$, $Y_i$ is the variable in the summation, $a_j$ may vary but in this summation is a constant, the lower limit is 1 and is made explicit, the number of values of the variable is $m$, and $i$ is the index of summation.

In the expression, $\sum_{i}^{n} aX_i Y_i$, there are two sets of paired values, $X_i$ and $Y_i$. The index of summation is $i$. There is a constant, $a$. There are $n$ terms in the summation.

When a set of numbers is classified into subsets, the succession of terms in a summation can be formed in more than one way and it becomes necessary to specify the particular group or series of terms intended by the summation. This specification is also made possible by the adoption of an index of summation for each way of summing. In a later chapter dealing with the analysis of variability for classifications of numbers, limits and indices will be discussed more fully and it will be shown how they considerably extend the range of application of summational notation.

When there is no need for limits and indices, we shall omit them.

# MOMENTS

## Syntactics 4

Moments constitute a class of values which may be computed for any set of numbers by the application of a general formula. To compute a moment for a set of $N$ numbers, one raises each number in the set to a specified power, sums these powers, and divides this sum by $N$. Particular moments are identified and named by reference to the power to which the numbers are raised, that is, by reference to the exponent employed. Thus the $m^{\text{th}}$ moment in the class of moments is defined as follows:

*The $m^{\text{th}}$ moment of a set of $N$ numbers is the sum of the $m^{\text{th}}$ powers of the $N$ numbers, divided by $N$.*

### Moments of $X$

In summational notation, the $m^{\text{th}}$ moment of $X$ is written

$$\frac{\Sigma X^m}{N},$$

the first moment of $X$ is written

$$\frac{\Sigma X}{N},$$

the second moment is

$$\frac{\Sigma X^2}{N},$$

the third moment is

$$\frac{\Sigma X^3}{N},$$

and the fourth moment is

$$\frac{\Sigma X^4}{N}.$$

We could, of course, continue indefinitely in the writing of higher moments.

Notice that the zeroth moment is

$$\frac{\Sigma X^0}{N},$$

which can be written

$$\frac{\Sigma(1)}{N} = \frac{N}{N} = 1.$$

### THE MEAN

The first moment of $X$ is called the *mean of X*. We shall employ $M_x$ as the symbol representing the mean. ($\bar{X}$ is employed by many authors for this purpose.) Thus

$$M_x = \frac{\Sigma X}{N}. \tag{4.1}$$

$M_x$ is computed as indicated by formula (4.1), that is, by summing the $N$ numbers in a set and dividing the sum by $N$.

*Example:* Given the numbers: 4, 4, 6, 6, 6, and 10, we let $X$ represent any value in the set and $N$, the number of values in the set. Then

$$\Sigma X = 36$$

and

$$M_x = \frac{\Sigma X}{N} = \frac{36}{6} = 6.$$

## Moments of $x$

We propose transforming $X$ to $x$ by the formula:

$$x = X - M_x.$$

In the formula, $X$ refers to any number in the original set; $M_x$ is the mean or first moment of the original values; $x$ is any number in the new set which results from the transformation and is called a *deviation from the mean.*

Consider now the first four moments of $x$. In summational notation, the first moment of $x$ is written

$$\frac{\Sigma x}{N},$$

the second moment of $x$ is

$$\frac{\Sigma x^2}{N},$$

the third moment is

$$\frac{\Sigma x^3}{N},$$

and the fourth moment is

$$\frac{\Sigma x^4}{N}.$$

Notice that the zeroth moment of $x$ is

$$\frac{\Sigma x^0}{N},$$

which can be written

$$\frac{\Sigma(1)}{N} = \frac{N}{N} = 1.$$

Notice also that the first moment of $x$,

$$\frac{\Sigma x}{N},$$

can be written

$$\frac{\Sigma(X - M_x)}{N},$$

an expression which can be simplified, as follows:

$$\frac{\Sigma X - \Sigma M_x}{N} = \frac{\Sigma X - NM_x}{N} = \frac{\Sigma X}{N} - \frac{NM_x}{N} = M_x - M_x = 0.$$

## THE VARIANCE

The second moment of $x$ is called the *variance*. We shall employ $V_x$ as the symbol for the variance. $\sqrt{V_x}$ is called the *standard deviation* and will be represented symbolically as $S_x$. It is evident that $V_x = S_x^2$.

*Example:* Given the numbers: 4, 4, 6, 6, 6, and 10, we found the mean to be 6. Transforming the original numbers by the formula,

$$x = X - M_x,$$

yields a new set which consists of $-2$, $-2$, 0, 0, 0, and 4. Then

$$\Sigma x^2 = (-2)^2 + (-2)^2 + 0^2 + 0^2 + 0^2 + 4^2 = 24$$

and

$$V_x = \frac{\Sigma x^2}{N} = \frac{24}{6} = 4.$$

Note that $S_x = \sqrt{V_x} = \sqrt{4} = 2$.

The formula used above,

$$V_x = \frac{\Sigma x^2}{N},$$

is not generally convenient for computing. We can rewrite it and apply the rules of simplification to obtain a computing formula which is especially well suited to machine computation.

The expression,

$$\frac{\Sigma x^2}{N},$$

can be written as

$$\frac{\Sigma(X - M_x)^2}{N}.$$

It should be evident that, if we obtain a computing formula for the numerator, $\Sigma(X - M_x)^2$, which is the sum of squares of deviations from the mean, the final computation of $V_x$ will require only division by $N$.

Since $M_x$ is a constant for any given set of numbers, simplification of the numerator proceeds, as follows:

$$\Sigma(X - M_x)^2 = \Sigma(X^2 - 2M_xX + M_x^2) = \Sigma X^2 - 2M_x\Sigma X + NM_x^2$$

We can now substitute $\Sigma X/N$ for $M_x$ and obtain

$$\Sigma X^2 - 2\frac{\Sigma X}{N}\Sigma X + N\frac{(\Sigma X)^2}{N^2} = \Sigma X^2 - 2\frac{(\Sigma X)^2}{N} + \frac{(\Sigma X)^2}{N}.$$

Combining the second and third terms on the right yields a computing formula for $\Sigma(X - M_x)^2$,

$$\Sigma X^2 - \frac{(\Sigma X)^2}{N}. \tag{4.2}$$

Keep in mind that formula (4.2) gives $\Sigma x^2$ which must be divided by $N$ to obtain $V_x$. That is,

$$V_x = \frac{\Sigma x^2}{N} = \frac{\Sigma X^2 - \dfrac{(\Sigma X)^2}{N}}{N}$$

To compute the standard deviation, $S_x$, one finds the square root of the variance, $V_x$.

*Example:* For the numbers: 4, 4, 6, 6, 6, and 10, $\Sigma X = 36$, $\Sigma X^2 = 240$, and $N = 6$. Substituting these values in formula (4.2) yields

$$240 - \frac{36^2}{6} = 24.$$

Then $V_x = 24/6 = 4$ and $S_x = 2$.

# Moments of $Z_x$

Consider next a transformation of $x$ to $Z_x$ by the formula,

$$Z_x = \frac{x}{\sqrt{V_x}} = \frac{x}{S_x}.$$

In mathematical statistics, $Z_x$ is called a *standardized variable*. In psychological statistics, $Z_x$ is usually called a *standard score* or simply a "$z$-score."

The first moment of $Z_x$ is written

$$\frac{\Sigma Z_x}{N}.$$

The second moment of $Z_x$ is

$$\frac{\Sigma Z_x^2}{N}.$$

The third moment is

$$\frac{\Sigma Z_x^3}{N}.$$

The fourth moment is

$$\frac{\Sigma Z_x^4}{N}.$$

Notice that the zeroth moment of $Z_x$,

$$\frac{\Sigma Z_x^0}{N},$$

can be written

$$\frac{\Sigma(1)}{N} = \frac{N}{N} = 1,$$

and that the first moment of $Z_x$,

$$\frac{\Sigma Z_x}{N},$$

can be written

$$\frac{\Sigma(x/S_x)}{N} = \frac{(1/S_x)\Sigma x}{N} = \frac{(1/S_x)(0)}{N} = 0.$$

Notice also that the second moment of $Z_x$,

$$\frac{\Sigma Z_x^2}{N},$$

can be written

$$\frac{\Sigma(x/S_x)^2}{N} = \frac{\Sigma(x^2/S_x^2)}{N} = \frac{(1/S_x^2)\Sigma x^2}{N} = \frac{1}{V_x}(V_x) = 1.$$

## THE INDEX OF SKEWNESS

The third moment of $Z_x$ is called the *index of skewness*. It will be represented here by the symbol, $S$.[1] (The symbol, $\beta_1$, was suggested by Karl Pearson and is widely employed.)

[1]The student should not confuse $S$, the index of skewness, with $S_x$, the standard deviation of the variable $X$. The subscript, $x$, distinguishes the standard deviation.

*Example:* Given the numbers

4, 4, 6, 6, 6, and 10,

for which $M_x = 6$, $V_x = 4$, and $S_x = 2$, the numbers can be transformed to the deviations:

−2, −2, 0, 0, 0, and 4.

The deviations can be transformed to standard scores by the formula,

$$Z_x = \frac{x}{S_x}.$$

The standard scores produced by the transformation are

−1, −1, 0, 0, 0, and 2.

Then

$$\Sigma Z_x^3 = (-1)^3 + (-1)^3 + 0^3 + 0^3 + 0^3 + 2^3 = 6$$

and

$$S = \frac{\Sigma Z_x^3}{N} = \frac{6}{6} = 1.$$

The formula for $S$ employed above is seldom convenient for computing because the standard scores are usually troublesome to obtain. A computing formula can be derived by substituting

$$\frac{(X - M_x)}{S_x}$$

for $Z_x$ in $\Sigma Z_x^3/N$ producing

$$S = \frac{\Sigma(X - M_x)^3}{NS_x^3}.$$

The numerator can be rewritten as

$$\Sigma(X^3 - 3X^2M_x + 3XM_x^2 - M_x^3),$$

and rewritten again as

$$\Sigma X^3 - 3M_x\Sigma X^2 + 3M_x^2\Sigma X - NM_x^3,$$

and finally as

$$\Sigma X^3 - 3M_x\Sigma X^2 + 3NM_x^3 - NM_x^3 = \Sigma X^3 - 3M_x\Sigma X^2 + 2NM_x^3.$$

The formula for the index of skewness now becomes

$$S = \frac{\Sigma X^3 - 3M_x\Sigma X^2 + 2NM_x^3}{NS_x^3} \tag{4.3}$$

Although formula (4.3) is more convenient for computing the index of skewness than is the defining formula, $S = \Sigma Z_x^3/N$, it still represents a forbidding task on a desk calculator even when $N$ is only moderately large. Fortunately, programs are now available for computing the higher moments on electronic machines, which can do the task with speed and accuracy.

### THE INDEX OF KURTOSIS

The fourth moment of $Z_x$ is called the *index of kurtosis*. It will be represented by the letter, $K$. (Karl Pearson used $\beta_2$ for this value.)

An example: The numbers

$$4, 4, 6, 6, 6, \text{ and } 10,$$

were transformed to standard scores in the preceding section. The standard scores which were produced by the transformation are

$$-1, -1, 0, 0, 0, \text{ and } 2.$$

Then

$$\Sigma Z_x^4 = (-1)^4 + (-1)^4 + 0^4 + 0^4 + 0^4 + 2^4 = 18$$

and

$$K = \frac{\Sigma Z_x^4}{N} = \frac{18}{6} = 3.$$

As is true of the index of skewness, the index of kurtosis is not, in general, easy to compute. The formula employed above can be rewritten, as follows:

$$K = \frac{\Sigma Z_x^4}{N} = \frac{\Sigma(x/S_x)^4}{N} = \frac{\Sigma(x^4/S_x^4)}{N} = \frac{\Sigma x^4}{NS_x^4} = \frac{\Sigma(X - M_x)^4}{NV_x^2}.$$

The simplification rules can then be applied to the numerator to produce

$$\Sigma(X^4 - 4X^3M_x + 6X^2M_x^2 - 4XM_x^3 + M_x^4)$$

which is equal to

$$\Sigma X^4 - 4M_x\Sigma X^3 + 6M_x^2\Sigma X^2 - 4M_x^3\Sigma X + NM_x^4.$$

After the last two terms are combined, the final computing formula for the index of kurtosis is

$$K = \frac{\Sigma X^4 - 4M_x\Sigma X^3 + 6M_x^2\Sigma X^2 - 3NM_x^4}{NV_x^2}. \qquad (4.4)$$

Computation of $K$ is possible on an automatic desk calculator but can be done with much greater speed and accuracy on an electronic computer.

## The Descriptive Moments

The student has probably noticed that we have paid special attention to the first moment of $X$, the second moment of $x$, the third moment of $Z_x$, and the fourth moment of $Z_x$. For reasons which will become clear later on, we shall refer to these four moments as the *descriptive moments*. It will be profitable to examine certain logical properties of the four descriptive moments. The logical properties of these moments with reference to a set of numbers will be considered first. Their properties with reference to a frequency distribution of those numbers will be considered second. At this point in our discussion, those logical properties having to do with error will be disregarded. Later on, in the discussion of random variation, logical properties having to do with error will be considered.

## PROPERTIES OF $M_x$

Listed below are five logical properties of the first moment, or mean, of $X$.

1. Inspection of the formula,

$$M_x = \frac{\Sigma X}{N},$$

and the equation,

$$\Sigma X = NM_x,$$

which is easily derived from the formula, reveals that the mean of a set of numbers is the constant value which results when the sum of the set is divided into $N$ equal quantities.

2. The formula,

$$M_x = \frac{\Sigma X}{N},$$

can be rewritten as

$$M_x = \frac{1}{N} \cdot X_1 + \frac{1}{N} \cdot X_2 + \frac{1}{N} \cdot X_3 + \ldots + \frac{1}{N} \cdot X_N.$$

If we let $p = 1/N$ and substitute, the preceding statement becomes

$$M_x = pX_1 + pX_2 + pX_3 + \ldots + pX_N$$

and can be interpreted, as follows: The mean is a number constituted by combining equal proportions of the numbers in the set. Because the mean has this property, one might think of it as a *representative value*. (It should be noted that $p$ is a constant and that it is the proportion contributed to the value of the mean by each number in the set.) " Representative," as used here, does not mean typical or most frequently occurring.

3. Given the numbers:

$$X_1, X_2, X_3, \ldots, X_N,$$

where $X_1 < X_N$ and there is no lower algebraic value than $X_1$ and no higher algebraic value than $X_N$, then it can be shown that

$$X_1 < M_x < X_N.$$

When the numbers in a set vary in value, the mean will lie between the lowest value and the highest. That is, the mean can be said to be an *interjacent value*. (A proof will not be given here.)

*Caution:* The mean will not necessarily lie midway between the two extreme values on the scale of $X$ and will not necessarily lie in the middle of the distribution of values, with as many values above it as below.

4. We observe that

$$\frac{\Sigma x}{N} = 0,$$

for the reason that

$$\Sigma(X - M_x) = 0.$$

That is, we showed that

$$\Sigma(X - M_x) = \Sigma X - \Sigma M_x = \Sigma X - NM_x = \Sigma X - \Sigma X = 0.$$

Thus we can say that the sum of deviations from the mean is zero, which statement implies that the absolute value of the sum of negative deviations is equal to the absolute value of the sum of positive deviations.

*Caution:* The fact that the sum of deviations from the mean is zero does not imply that for every positive deviation there is necessarily a corresponding negative deviation of equal absolute value, although such correspondence is possible.

5. It can be shown that

$$\Sigma(X - M_x)^2 < \Sigma(X - a)^2$$

when $a \neq M_x$. In words, we can state that the sum of squares of deviations from the mean is less than the sum of squares of deviations from any other reference value. That the mean has this property can be proved, as follows: Consider the expression,

$$\Sigma(X - c)^2;$$

it can be viewed as being a function of $c$. We may ask what value $c$ must have for the value of the function to be a minimum for any set of numbers. The expression can be simplified and rewritten as indicated below.

$$\begin{aligned}\Sigma(X - c)^2 &= \Sigma(X^2 - 2cX + c^2) = \Sigma X^2 - 2c\Sigma X + Nc^2\\ &= Nc^2 - 2c\Sigma X + \Sigma X^2\\ &= \frac{N^2c^2 - 2cN\Sigma X + N\Sigma X^2}{N}\\ &= \frac{(Nc - \Sigma X)^2 - (\Sigma X)^2 + N\Sigma X^2}{N},\end{aligned}$$

from which we see that, if $N$, $\Sigma X$, and $\Sigma X^2$ are treated as constants, which they would be for any given set of numbers, then the value of the function depends only on $c$.

We know that

$$(Nc - \Sigma X)^2 \geqq 0$$

and that the value of the function will be a minimum when

$$(Nc - \Sigma X)^2 = 0,$$

in which case

$$Nc - \Sigma X = 0$$

and

$$c = \frac{\Sigma X}{N} = M_x.$$

Therefore, the value of the function,

$$\frac{\Sigma(X - c)^2}{N},$$

is a minimum only when $c = M_x$.

Summary of the properties of the mean:

1. The mean is a value which results when the sum of a set of numbers is divided into $N$ equal parts.
2. The mean is a representative value, constituted by combining equal proportions of all $N$ numbers in a set. (It is not necessarily a typical value or the most-frequently-occurring value.)
3. The mean is an interjacent value, with respect to the extreme values in a set of numbers.
4. The sum of deviations from the mean is zero.
5. The sum of squares of deviations from the mean is smaller than the sum of squares of deviations from any other reference value.

## PROPERTIES OF $V_x$

Two properties of the second moment of $x$, or the variance, are presented next.

1. Let $(X_1 - X)$ be the difference between a particular number and any number in the set including itself. The mean of these $N$ differences,

$$\frac{\Sigma(X_1 - X)}{N},$$

is equal to

$$\frac{\Sigma X_1 - \Sigma X}{N} = \frac{NX_1}{N} - \frac{\Sigma X}{N} = X_1 - M_x = x_1.$$

Thus a particular deviation, $x_1$, can be said to be a function of the differences between $X_1$ and the $N$ numbers in the set. That is,

$$x_1 = \frac{\Sigma(X_1 - X)}{N}.$$

Now the variance is a function of deviations from the mean as indicated by the formula,

$$V_x = \frac{\Sigma x^2}{N}.$$

Since each deviation is a function of a set of differences and the variance is a function of all of the deviations, the variance can be said to be a function of the differences among the numbers themselves. That is, the magnitude of the variance depends on the magnitude of the differences among the numbers.

2. Recall that the value of the function,

$$\Sigma(X - c)^2,$$

is a minimum for any set of numbers when $c = M_x$. It follows that the second moment of $(X - c)$ is a minimum when $c = M_x$, that is, when the second moment is

$$\frac{\Sigma(X - M_x)^2}{N} = \frac{\Sigma x^2}{N}$$

which is the variance as we have defined it. Thus the variance is the minimum value of the second moment of $(X - c)$ where $c$ is a constant that is to be subtracted from each value of $X$.

## PROPERTIES OF $S$

The logical properties of the index of skewness will be discussed next. The index of skewness has been defined as

$$S = \frac{\Sigma Z_x^3}{N}.$$

Note that $S$ is a pure or abstract number in that it is not expressed in the units of the original scale of $X$, as are $M_x$ and $V_x$. The units of the original scale cancel in

$$Z_x = \frac{x}{S_x}$$

and the units of the new scale of $Z_x$ are actually standard deviations. Thus $S$ is said to be dimensionless.

Recall that $\Sigma x/N = 0$. That is, the first moment of $x$, an odd moment, is always equal to zero, in which case the absolute value of the sum of negative deviations is equal to the absolute value of the sum of positive deviations. Recall also that $\Sigma Z_x/N = 0$. The first moment of $Z_x$ is always zero, in which case the absolute value of the sum of negative values of $Z_x$ is equal to the absolute value of the sum of positive values. With neither of these first moments, however, does the cancelling imply that there is a positive number of absolute value equal to the absolute value of each negative number, although that situation could occur.

Now $S$, the third moment of $Z_x$, is also an odd moment. When values of $Z_x$ are positive, the corresponding values of $Z_x^3$ will be positive. When values of $Z_x$ are negative, the corresponding values of $Z_x^3$ will be negative. Thus it could happen that positive cubes would cancel negative cubes completely in $\Sigma Z_x^3$, resulting in a value of $S$ equal to zero. This cancelling will not necessarily take place in every case as it does with $\Sigma x/N$ and $\Sigma Z_x/N$.

One situation in which the cancelling is complete and $S$ is equal to zero is that in which there is a positive $Z_x$ of absolute value equal to the absolute value of each negative $Z_x$. There are other situations in which this correspondence does not obtain but the cancelling *is* complete and $S$ *is* equal to zero.

When the absolute value of the sum of the positive values of $Z_x^3$ exceeds the absolute value of the sum of the negative values of $Z_x^3$, then $S$ is positive. That is, $S > 0$. When the absolute value of the sum of positive values of $Z_x^3$ is less than the absolute value of the sum of negative values of $Z_x^3$, then $S$ is negative. That is, $S < 0$. There is, in general, no upper or lower limit on the value of $S$.

## PROPERTIES OF *K*

The logical properties of the index of kurtosis will be considered next. The index of kurtosis has been defined as

$$K = \frac{\Sigma Z^4}{N}.$$

As is true of $S$, $K$ is a dimensionless value, a pure or abstract number. It can be shown that

$$K \geqq S^2 + 1.$$

It should be apparent that the lowest value, $K = 1$, can occur only when $S = 0$. $K$ has no upper limit. It can also be shown that

$$K = S^2 + 1$$

only when there are two distinct values of $Z_x$ and that

$$K = 1$$

(which means that $\Sigma Z_x^4/N = \Sigma Z_x^2/N = 1$) only when the two distinct values of $Z_x$ are $+1$ and $-1$, in which case the two values occur with equal frequency in the set of numbers.

Given a set of numbers in which there is a positive $Z_x$ of absolute value equal to the absolute value of each negative $Z_x$, in which case $S = 0$,

$$K > 1$$

if the number of values of $Z_x$ greater than $+1$ and the number of values of $Z_x$ less than $-1$ are, together, less than the number of values of $Z_x$ between $-1$ and $+1$.

## Frequency Distributions

The numbers in a given set can be classified according to their values and the results of this classifying can be conveniently summarized in a *frequency distribution* which represents frequency as a function of the magnitude of $X$.

Consider a set of $N$ numbers in which the distinct or different values are

$$X_1, X_2, X_3, \ldots, X_r$$

and $f_1$ is the number of $X_1$'s, $f_2$ is the number of $X_2$'s, and so on. It is customary to say, in general, that $f$ is the " frequency of $X$." Note that

$$f_1 + f_2 + f_3 + \ldots + f_r = \Sigma f = N.$$

The frequency distribution of $X$ is shown in Table 4.1.

**Table 4.1**

**FREQUENCY DISTRIBUTION FOR A SET OF *N* NUMBERS**

| $X$ | $f$ |
|---|---|
| $X_1$ | $f_1$ |
| $X_2$ | $f_2$ |
| $X_3$ | $f_3$ |
| . | . |
| . | . |
| . | . |
| $X_r$ | $f_r$ |

$r$ = number of classes.
$f$ = frequency of $X$ in each class.
$\Sigma f = N$.

Notice that the notation has been altered. Earlier, each subscript identified one number in the set. Here, in the altered notation, each subscript identifies a class of numbers of the same value. A class may contain more than one number, or it may contain only one number, or it may not contain any, being empty or vacant.

One possible graphical representation of a frequency distribution is called a *histogram*. In a histogram, frequency is represented on the vertical axis and the scale of $X$ is placed on the horizontal axis. A rectangular column is erected over each value of $X$ with a height determined by the frequency in that class. With equal score intervals, the only case we shall consider, the area under the entire histogram is directly proportional to $N$, the total number of values in the set.

Table 4.2 presents a frequency distribution for a set of $N = 48$ numbers which range in value from 1 to 5. Figure 4.1 is a histogram which represents in graphical form the frequency distribution of Table 4.2.

**Table 4.2**

**A FREQUENCY DISTRIBUTION**

| $X$ | $f$ |
|---|---|
| 1 | 1 |
| 2 | 18 |
| 3 | 12 |
| 4 | 14 |
| 5 | 3 |

$$N = \Sigma f = 48.$$

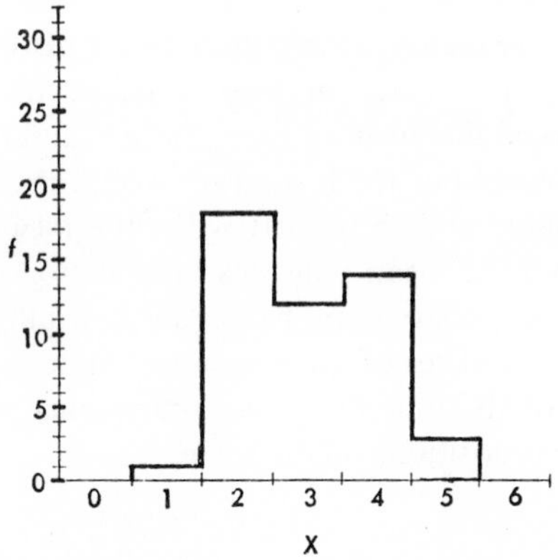


**Fig. 4.1** A histogram representing the frequency distribution of Table 4.2.

# Frequency Distributions and the Descriptive Moments

Formulas for the four descriptive moments can be written to take advantage of the classification provided by a frequency distribution. The sum of the $N$ numbers in a frequency distribution is

$$f_1X_1 + f_2X_2 + f_3X_3 + \dots + f_rX_r.$$

Therefore, the formula for the mean can be written

$$M_x = \frac{\overset{r}{\Sigma} fX}{N}.$$

The sum of squares of deviations for the $N$ numbers is

$$f_1x_1^2 + f_2x_2^2 + f_3x_3^2 + \dots + f_rx_r^2$$

and the variance can be written as

$$V_x = \frac{\overset{r}{\Sigma} fx^2}{N}.$$

This principle can be extended to the index of skewness to yield

$$S = \frac{\overset{r}{\Sigma} f Z_x^3}{N}$$

and to the index of kurtosis to yield

$$K = \frac{\overset{r}{\Sigma} f Z_x^4}{N}.$$

## LOCATION OF A DISTRIBUTION

With respect to a frequency distribution or its histogram, the mean is a measure of location. If we fixed or held constant all other moments of a distribution but allowed the mean to vary, the size and the form of the distribution would not change but the histogram would move to the right as the mean increased in value and to the left when the mean decreased in value. Therefore, we say that the mean indicates the location of the distribution.

Figure 4.2 shows two histograms based on distributions with equal total frequencies, variances, indices of skewness, and indices of kurtosis. Only the means of the two distributions differ, a circumstance which places the two histograms in different positions on the scale.

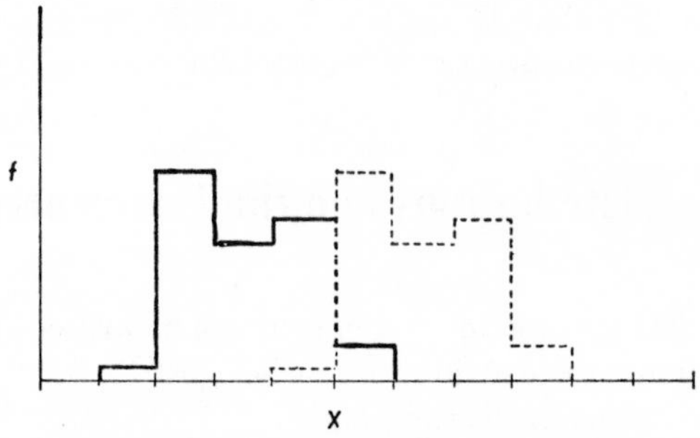


**Fig. 4.2** Two histograms based on distributions with unequal means, but equal total frequencies, variances, indices of skewness and indices of kurtosis. The histogram drawn with dotted lines represents the distribution with the larger mean.

## DISPERSION OF A DISTRIBUTION

The variance is said to be a measure of dispersion, spread, or scatter. If we held all moments constant except the variance, but allowed it to vary, the dispersion of the frequencies along the scale would increase as the variance increased and decrease as the variance decreased. Figure 4.3 shows two histograms with equal total frequencies, means, indices of skewness, and indices of kurtosis. The variances of the two distributions differ. Histogram A has a larger variance than histogram B.

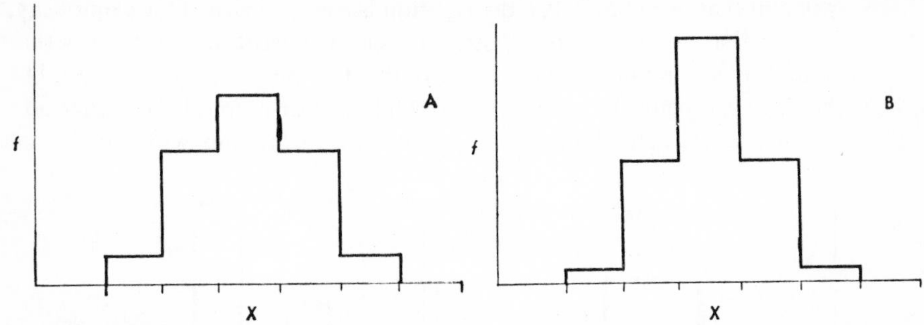


**Fig. 4.3** Two histograms based on distributions with unequal variances, but equal total frequencies, means, indices of skewness, and indices of kurtosis. Histogram A has a larger variance than histogram B.

## SKEWNESS OF A DISTRIBUTION

$S$ has been called an *index of skewness*. Skewness refers to the symmetry or asymmetry of a distribution or its histogram. A distribution which is symmetrical about the mean is called a symmetrical distribution. This implies that the histogram is to be divided into two parts by erecting a perpendicular at a point on the horizontal axis corresponding to the value of the mean. In a symmetrical figure, for any point in the part of the histogram above the mean, there is a corresponding point in the part below the mean. These corresponding points have the same ordinate and the absolute values of their abscissas are equal when the $X$'s have been transformed to deviations from the mean.

When the distribution is symmetrical, $S = 0$. When $S \neq 0$, a distribution is asymmetrical. When $S < 0$, we say the distribution is negatively skew. When $S > 0$, we say the distribution is positively skew.

In Figure 4.4 are two histograms for distributions with equal total

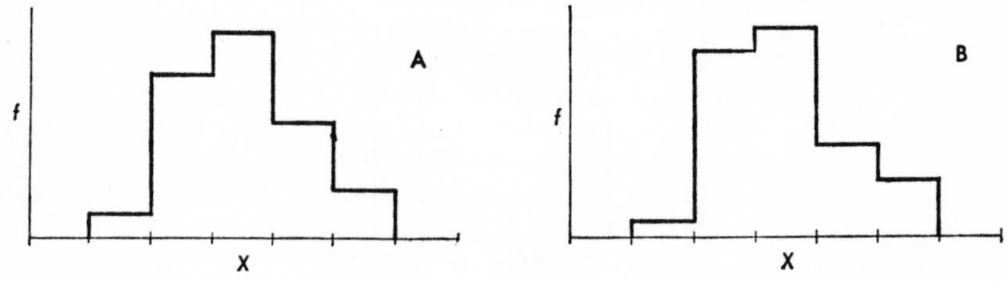


**Fig. 4.4** Histograms representing two distributions with equal total frequencies, means, variances, and indices of kurtosis, but unequal indices of skewness. The index of skewness for histogram A is 0.25; for B, it is 0.50.

frequencies, equal means, equal variances, and equal indices of kurtosis, but with unequal positive indices of skewness.

*Caution:* We have said above that, when a distribution is symmetrical,

$S = 0$, and that, when $S \neq 0$, a distribution is asymmetrical. One cannot say, in general, that, when $S = 0$, a distribution is symmetrical. One can say that when all the odd moments of $Z_x$ are zero, the distribution is symmetrical, but $S$, the third moment of $Z_x$, can be zero while one or more of the higher odd moments are not zero. Figure 4.5 presents two histograms with equal total

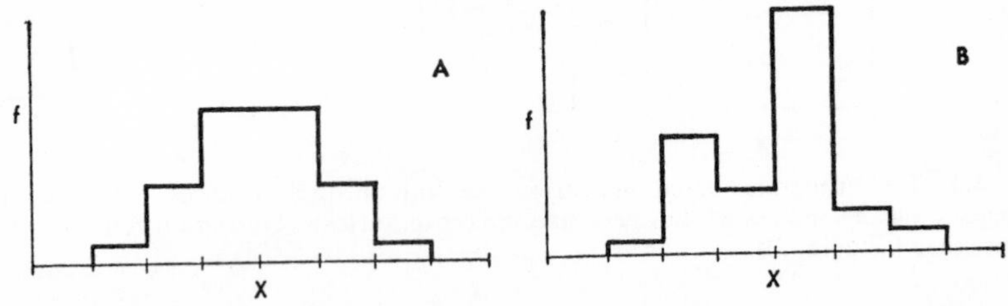


**Fig. 4.5** Histograms for distributions with equal total frequencies, means, variances, indices of skewness, and indices of kurtosis. $S = 0$ and $K = 2.6$ for both distributions. Histogram A is symmetrical, but B is not. They differ with respect to their fifth moments. The fifth moment of $Z_x$ for A is zero; for B, it is 0.50.

frequencies, equal means, equal variances, and equal indices of kurtosis, and with indices of skewness equal to zero. Histogram A is symmetrical; B is not.

## KURTOSIS OF A DISTRIBUTION

The index of kurtosis is said to reflect the flatness or peakedness of a histogram, but the appropriateness of these terms is not readily apparent in the case of distributions with extreme values of $K$. The index is also said to reflect the concentration of frequencies at or near the center of the distribution, relative to the concentration in the tails. Figure 4.6 shows a discrete

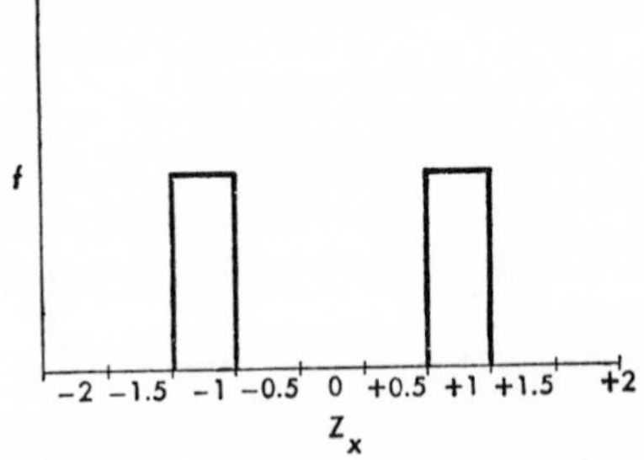


**Fig. 4.6** A frequency distribution of $Z_x$ for which $S = 0$ and $K = 1$.

distribution of $Z_x$ for which $K = 1$, the lower limit of the index. Notice the equal concentrations of frequencies at $-1$ and $+1$. In Figure 4.7 are two histograms which differ only with respect to kurtosis. Notice the difference between the two histograms with respect to the relative concentrations of

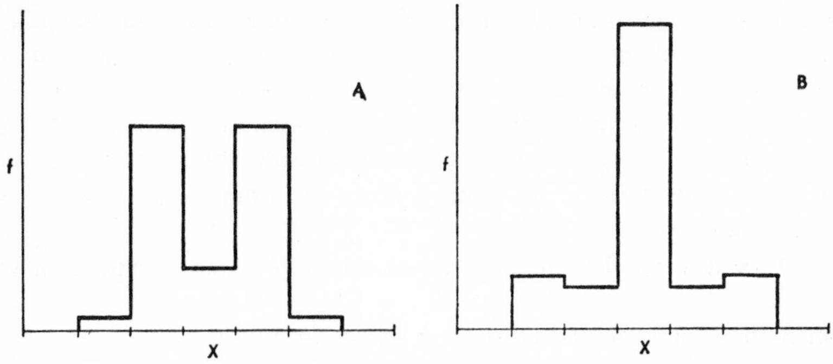


**Fig. 4.7** Histograms for two distributions which differ only with respect to their indices of kurtosis. $K$, for histogram A, is 1.5; the same moment for B is 3.5. For both histograms $S$ is zero.

frequencies in the middle interval and in the intervals at the extremes.

We have seen how moments can be computed from a frequency distribution. It is possible to reverse this process. There is a determining relation between the moments of a distribution and the frequencies in that distribution. It is in the nature of the relation that one can choose values for the moments and then compute the relative frequencies determined by the chosen values. (The computational procedure, which involves the solution of a set of simultaneous equations, will not be given here.) The number of moments required to fix the distribution depends on the number of distinct intervals in the range of the entire distribution. The zeroth moment can be counted as one of the required number. For example, five moments—the zeroth, first, second, third, and fourth—would be required to determine the frequency distribution of a set of numbers in which there occurred the five different values: 1, 2, 3, 4, and 5. The frequency distribution of a set of numbers whose range covered six intervals on the scale of $X$ is not fixed by five moments. In Figure 4.5 are two six-interval histograms with equal total frequencies, means, variances, indices of skewness, and indices of kurtosis. The two histograms differ with respect to their fifth moments. Histogram A has a fifth moment of $Z_x$ equal to zero; the same moment for B is 0.50. Both histograms have values of $S$ equal to zero, but A is symmetrical and B is obviously not symmetrical.

## Other Common Transformations

The numbers in a set may be transformed by the addition of a constant to each number, the subtraction of a constant from each number, the multiplication of each number by a constant, or the division of each number by a constant. The result of one of these operations, or a combination of them, is a new set of numbers. It will be instructive to examine the four descriptive moments of the new set in relation to those of the old set. When numbers are transformed in this way they are often said to be *coded.* These transformations are widely used and are of considerable importance.

First, we shall describe the consequences of adding a constant to each number in a set.

Let $X$ be any number in the original set of $N$ numbers and let $a$ be a constant.

Let $X'$ be a value computed from $X$ by the formula:

$$X' = X + a.$$

Then $X'$ is any number in a new set of $N$ numbers.

Let $M_{x'}$ be the mean of the new set. Then

$$M_{x'} = \frac{\Sigma X'}{N}.$$

We can substitute $(X + a)$ for $X'$ and obtain

$$M_{x'} = \frac{\Sigma(X + a)}{N} = \frac{\Sigma X + Na}{N} = M_x + a.$$

*Conclusion:* Coding by adding a constant adds the constant to the mean. By similar methods we could show that coding by subtracting a constant subtracts the constant from the mean.

Let $V_{x'}$ be the variance of the new set. Then

$$V_{x'} = \frac{\Sigma x'^2}{N} = \frac{\Sigma(X' - M_{x'})^2}{N}.$$

We can substitute $(X + a)$ for $X'$ and $(M_x + a)$ for $M_{x'}$ to obtain

$$V_{x'} = \frac{\Sigma[(X + a) - (M_x + a)]^2}{N},$$

which can be rewritten as

$$V_{x'} = \frac{\Sigma(X - M_x)^2}{N} = V_x$$

since the constants in the numerator cancel.

*Conclusion:* Coding by adding (or subtracting) a constant does not change the variance. Nor would the standard deviation be affected.

Let $S'$ be the index of skewness of the new set. Then

$$S' = \frac{\Sigma Z_x^3}{N} = \frac{\Sigma(x'^3/S_{x'}^3)}{N} = \frac{\Sigma x'^3}{NS_{x'}^3}.$$

Examine the numerator, $\Sigma x'^3$. By definition,

$$x' = (X' - M_{x'}).$$

We can substitute $(X + a)$ for $X'$ and $(M_x + a)$ for $M_{x'}$, to obtain

$$x' = (X + a) - (M_x + a) = X - M_x = x.$$

We have already found that $S_{x'} = S_x$, that is, coding by adding or subtracting a constant does not affect the standard deviation. Therefore, if we substitute $x$ for $x'$ and $S_x$ for $S_{x'}$, we find that

$$S' = \frac{\Sigma x^3}{NS_x^3} = S.$$

*Conclusion:* Coding by adding (or subtracting) a constant does not affect the index of skewness.

Let $K'$ be the index of kurtosis for the new set. Then

$$K' = \frac{\Sigma Z_{x'}^4}{N} = \frac{\Sigma(x'^4/S_{x'}^4)}{N} = \frac{\Sigma x'^4}{NS_{x'}^4},$$

but we have determined previously that $x' = x$ and $S_{x'} = S_x$. Therefore,

$$K' = \frac{\Sigma x^4}{NS_x^4} = K.$$

*Conclusion:* Coding by adding (or subtracting) a constant does not affect the index of kurtosis.

Next we shall consider the consequences of multiplying (or dividing) each number in a set by a constant.

Let $X'$ be a value computed from $X$ by the formula:

$$X' = aX.$$

Consider the mean of $X'$. By definition,

$$M_{x'} = \frac{\Sigma X'}{N}.$$

We can substitute $aX$ for $X'$ and obtain

$$M_{x'} = \frac{\Sigma aX}{N} = \frac{a\Sigma X}{N} = aM_x.$$

*Conclusion:* Coding by multiplying by a constant multiplies the mean by the constant. Since division can be expressed as equivalent multiplication, we also conclude that dividing by a constant divides the mean by the constant.

The variance of $X'$ is, by definition,

$$V_{x'} = \frac{\Sigma x'^2}{N} = \frac{\Sigma(X' - M_{x'})^2}{N}.$$

Substitution of $aX$ for $X'$ and $aM_x$ for $M_{x'}$ yields

$$V_{x'} = \frac{\Sigma(aX - aM_x)^2}{N} = \frac{\Sigma a^2(X - M_x)^2}{N} = \frac{a^2\Sigma(X - M_x)^2}{N} = a^2V_x.$$

*Conclusion:* Multiplying by a constant multiplies the variance by the square of the constant. Dividing by a constant divides the variance by the square of the constant.

Note that if

$$V_{x'} = a^2V_x,$$

then

$$\sqrt{V_{x'}} = S_{x'} = \sqrt{a^2V_x} = a\sqrt{V_x} = aS_x.$$

*Conclusion:* Multiplying by a constant multiplies the standard deviation by a constant. Dividing by a constant divides the standard deviation by a constant.

Consider next the index of skewness for the new set of numbers. We have already observed that

$$S' = \frac{\Sigma x'^3}{NS_{x'}^3}.$$

Let us examine $x'$ in the numerator, $\Sigma x'^3$. By definition,

$$x' = X' - M_{x'}$$

and, after substitution,

$$x' = aX - aM_x = a(X - M_x) = ax.$$

Then

$$S' = \frac{\Sigma a^3x^3}{NS_{x'}^3} = \frac{a^3\Sigma x^3}{NS_{x'}^3}.$$

Recall that $S_{x'} = aS_x$. After substituting, we find that

$$S' = \frac{a^3\Sigma x^3}{Na^3S_x^3} = \frac{\Sigma x^3}{NS_x^3} = S.$$

*Conclusion:* Since $S' = S$, coding by multiplying (or dividing) does not affect the index of skewness.

Finally, let us consider $K'$, the index of kurtosis for the new set of numbers. We have already established that

$$K' = \frac{\Sigma x'^4}{NV_{x'}^2},$$

that $x' = ax$, and that $V_{x'} = a^2V_x$. We can substitute $ax$ and $a^2V_x$ in the formula for $K'$ and obtain

$$K' = \frac{\Sigma a^4x^4}{Na^4V_x^2} = \frac{a^4\Sigma x^4}{Na^4V_x^2} = \frac{\Sigma x^4}{NV_x^2} = K.$$

*Conclusion:* Since $K' = K$, coding by multiplying (or dividing) by a constant does not change the index of kurtosis.

The effects of coding on the four descriptive moments and the standard deviation are summarized in Table 4.3.

**Table 4.3**

**EFFECTS OF CODING OPERATIONS ON THE DESCRIPTIVE MOMENTS**

| | | Operation | | |
|---|---|---|---|---|
| | | $X \pm a$ | $aX$ | $X/a$ |
| Moment | $M_{x'}$ | $M_x \pm a$ | $aM_x$ | $M_x/a$ |
| | $V_{x'}$ | $V_x$ | $a^2V_x$ | $V_x/a^2$ |
| | $S_{x'}$ | $S_x$ | $aS_x$ | $S_x/a$ |
| | $S'$ | $S$ | $S$ | $S$ |
| | $K'$ | $K$ | $K$ | $K$ |

The coding operations described above are often employed in computing. Traditional paper-and-pencil methods of computing means, variances, and standard deviations for numbers classified into score or class intervals in a frequency distribution have involved the following steps:

1. One chooses, as a new arbitrary origin, the midpoint of an interval, usually but not necessarily near the center of the distribution. (This new, arbitrary origin is often called an " assumed mean " or a " guessed mean.")

2. A " zero " is assigned to the interval containing the new origin. Then, working in both positive and negative directions from this interval, one assigns small whole numbers, with appropriate signs, to all other intervals.

3. The resulting, new scale values are employed in the computation of a mean, a variance, and a standard deviation.

Implicit in this procedure are the coding operations, subtracting a constant and dividing by a constant. The constant which is subtracted is the midpoint of the interval containing the assumed mean. The constant divisor is the size of the class interval. Moments computed from the coded values must, of course, be uncoded by the reverse operations. The variance must be multiplied by the square of the constant divisor; the mean must be multiplied by the constant divisor and that product must then be added to the constant which was subtracted.

Of more interest to us here than these paper-and-pencil methods are computational procedures for an automatic, desk calculator. It is often convenient, when one is working with large numbers, to subtract a constant from each as the numbers are entered in the calculator. For example, if one had a set of numbers ranging in value from 105 to 181, it would be a simple matter to drop the hundreds digit and compute with numbers ranging from 5 to 81. It is also convenient sometimes to ignore decimal points. Suppose the original numbers had values from 0.23 to 1.91. One could drop the decimal point, an action which is equivalent to multiplying each number by 100, and compute with numbers running from 23 to 191. Whenever numbers are coded to facilitate computation, one must, of course, take account of the effects of coding and, when it is necessary, uncode computed values to obtain final answers.

## Special Transformations

We shall mention and describe only briefly five transformations which are of some considerable importance in later work in statistics. We shall not attempt to show their specific effects on all of the descriptive moments.

1. *Squaring*. Let $X$ represent any number in an original set of numbers. Let $Y$ represent any number in a new set and, further, let $Y$ be defined by the formula:

$$Y = X^2.$$

*Example*. Consider the original set of numbers:

1, 2, 3, 4, and 5.

Squaring each produces a new set consisting of the numbers:

1, 4, 9, 16, and 25.

Notice that the original set is symmetrical ($S = 0$) and that the new set is not symmetrical ($S > 0$).

2. Extracting the square root. Let $Y$ be defined by the transformation formula:

$$Y = \sqrt{X}.$$

*Example*. Let the original set consist of the numbers:

4, 9, 16, 25, and 36.

Applying a square-root transformation produces the numbers:

2, 3, 4, 5, and 6.

The distribution of the original set is not symmetrical; that is, $S > 0$. The new distribution *is* symmetrical with $S = 0$.

3. Transforming to logarithms. Let $Y$ be defined by the formula:

$$Y = \log_{10} X.$$

*Example*. Given the set of numbers:

0.032, 0.320, and 3.200,

we can rewrite these three values as

$$0.320 \times 10^{-1},\ 0.320 \times 10^{0},\ \text{and } 0.320 \times 10^{1}.$$

We might find it convenient to code these numbers by dividing each by 0.320. After coding, the numbers would be

$$10^{-1},\ 10^{0},\ \text{and } 10^{1}.$$

The logarithmic transformation, applied to the coded values, would then yield

$$-1,\ 0,\ \text{and } +1.$$

We would undoubtedly find it more convenient to work with the transformed values than with the original values. Notice that the distribution of the transformed values is symmetrical whereas the original distribution was positively skew.

4. *The inverse sine transformation.* Let $p$ be any number in a set such that

$$0 \leqq p \leqq 1.$$

A transformation of $p$ to $\theta$, an angular measurement, is given by the formula:

$$\theta = \sin^{-1} \sqrt{p}.$$

The formula can be read: " Theta is an angle whose sine is equal to the square root of $p$." The transformation is effected by taking each value of $p$, obtaining its square root, and referring the root to a table of sines for the corresponding angle.

*Example.* Let the original values of $p$ consist of the numbers:

0.03, 0.12, 0.25, 0.41, and 0.59.

The angles whose sines are the square roots of these original values are, approximately,

$10°$, $20°$, $30°$, $40°$, and $50°$.

The original values are positively skew. The transformed values are symmetrical.

5. *The reciprocal transformation.* Let $X$ be any number in an original set of numbers. Then the reciprocal transformation to $Y$ is given by the formula:

$$Y = 1/X.$$

*Example.* It is evident that the asymmetry of the distribution of the numbers:

1, 1/2, 1/3, 1/4, and 1/5,

is eliminated when the values are transformed to their reciprocals, which are

1, 2, 3, 4, and 5.

## Substitution of Ranks

It is possible to substitute ranks for the original values in a set of numbers. We shall consider this substitution only for those sets of numbers for which the resulting ranks contain no ties. When there are no ties, the mean and the variance of the ranks can be expressed as a function of $N$. If $N$ numbers are ranked without ties, the sum of the $N$ ranks is the sum of the first $N$ positive integers. That is, the sum of ranks is given by the formula,

$$\Sigma R_x = \frac{N(N+1)}{2},$$

where $R_x$ is the rank assigned to $X$. Then the mean of ranks is

$$M_r = \frac{N+1}{2}.$$

The sum of squares of the $N$ ranks is given by the formula:

$$\Sigma R_x^2 = \frac{N(N+1)(2N+1)}{6}.$$

The variance is

$$V_r = \frac{\Sigma R_x^2 - \dfrac{(\Sigma R_x)^2}{N}}{N}$$

which, after substitution and appropriate changes, becomes

$$V_r = \frac{N^2 - 1}{12}$$

*Example.* Given the numbers:

2, 5, 6, 10, and 11,

the corresponding ranks are

5, 4, 3, 2, and 1.

In this example, $N = 5$ and the sum of ranks is

$$\frac{5(5+1)}{2} = 15.$$

The mean is $15/5 = 3$.

The sum of squares of the ranks is

$$\frac{5(5+1)(2 \times 5 + 1)}{6} = 55$$

and the variance is

$$\frac{5^2 - 1}{12} = 2.$$

# Summary

The discussion in the present chapter has consisted of a syntactical treatment of a class of values known as moments. The syntactical treatment dealt with the definitions of moments and the logical properties of the four descriptive moments—not including any properties which have to do with error. We shall leave syntactics for a time, but shall return to it in Chapter 7 where another class of values called *product moments* will be introduced. Having laid a groundwork of symbolism in Chapters 2, 3, and 4, we have chosen to take up, in Chapter 5, one of the major semantical problems—measurement. After we have discussed the nature of confirmation in psychological measurement, we will be ready to consider, in Chapter 6, the first topic in pragmatics: the use of moments in describing data.

**Table 4.4**

**FIVE SETS OF JOINTLY CLASSIFIED NUMBERS**

| | | Columns | | | | |
|---|---|---|---|---|---|---|
| | | *V* | *W* | *X* | *Y* | *Z* |
| | 1 | 11 | 42 | 3 | 12 | 101 |
| | 2 | 86 | 122 | 2 | 10 | 146 |
| | 3 | 39 | 77 | 3 | 9 | 129 |
| | 4 | 91 | 88 | 2 | 8 | 151 |
| | 5 | 16 | 62 | 4 | 13 | 136 |
| | 6 | 73 | 115 | 5 | 14 | 223 |
| | 7 | 30 | 45 | 4 | 12 | 150 |
| | 8 | 69 | 61 | 2 | 7 | 129 |
| | 9 | 27 | 57 | 2 | 10 | 87 |
| | 10 | 72 | 103 | 2 | 6 | 132 |
| | 11 | 37 | 57 | 4 | 15 | 157 |
| | 12 | 35 | 39 | 4 | 10 | 155 |
| Rows | 13 | 65 | 80 | 2 | 8 | 125 |
| | 14 | 71 | 74 | 2 | 6 | 131 |
| | 15 | 59 | 65 | 2 | 8 | 119 |
| | 16 | 82 | 103 | 3 | 8 | 172 |
| | 17 | 99 | 130 | 3 | 10 | 189 |
| | 18 | 11 | 42 | 3 | 11 | 101 |
| | 19 | 7 | 30 | 3 | 7 | 97 |
| | 20 | 24 | 62 | 4 | 14 | 144 |
| | 21 | 32 | 56 | 4 | 13 | 152 |
| | 22 | 88 | 107 | 4 | 13 | 208 |
| | 23 | 24 | 77 | 1 | 3 | 54 |
| | 24 | 19 | 29 | 4 | 10 | 139 |

**Exercise 4.1**

Compute $M_v$ and $V_v$, $M_w$ and $V_w$, $M_y$ and $V_y$, $M_z$ and $V_z$; in other words, compute the first and second descriptive moments for the variables: $V$, $W$, $Y$, and $Z$ in Table 4.4. For variable $X$, compute all four descriptive moments: $M_x$, $V_x$, $S$, and $K$.

Code variable $X$ by adding "one" and multiplying by "two." Then, for the coded values, compute the four descriptive moments: $M_{x'}$, $V_{x'}$, $S'$, and $K'$. Compare the moments for $X'$ with those for $X$. Could you have predicted what they would be?

Example of the use of computing formulas for the mean and variance of variable $V$. Formula (4.1) for the mean is

$$M_v = \frac{\Sigma V}{N}.$$

$\Sigma V = 1167$ and $N = 24$. Then

$$M_v = \frac{1167}{24} = 48.625.$$

Formula (4.2) for the sum of squares of deviations is

$$\Sigma V^2 - \frac{(\Sigma V)^2}{N}.$$

$\Sigma V = 1167$; $\Sigma V^2 = 76{,}795$; $N = 24$. Then the sum of squares of deviations is

$$76{,}795 - \frac{(1{,}167)^2}{24} = 20{,}049.625$$

and the variance is

$$V_v = \frac{20{,}049.625}{24} = 835.40.$$

**Exercise 4.2**

For each of the eight frequency distributions given in Table 4.5, compute the four descriptive moments: $M_x$, $V_x$, $S$, and $K$. You will find that the numbers are simple to work with and that an automatic desk calculator is not necessary.

**Table 4.5**

**EIGHT FREQUENCY DISTRIBUTIONS**

| (1) | | (2) | | (3) | | (4) | |
|---|---|---|---|---|---|---|---|
| $X$ | $f$ | $X$ | $f$ | $X$ | $f$ | $X$ | $f$ |
| 1 | 1 | 1 | 1 | 1 | 0 | 1 | 0 |
| 2 | 0 | 2 | 2 | 2 | 10 | 2 | 11 |
| 3 | 6 | 3 | 6 | 3 | 0 | 3 | 3 |
| 4 | 0 | 4 | 2 | 4 | 10 | 4 | 9 |
| 5 | 1 | 5 | 1 | 5 | 0 | 5 | 1 |

| (5) | | (6) | | (7) | | (8) | |
|---|---|---|---|---|---|---|---|
| $X$ | $f$ | $X$ | $f$ | $X$ | $f$ | $X$ | $f$ |
| 1 | 0 | 1 | 2 | 1 | 1 | 1 | 0 |
| 2 | 2 | 2 | 3 | 2 | 14 | 2 | 3 |
| 3 | 3 | 3 | 15 | 3 | 24 | 3 | 3 |
| 4 | 0 | 4 | 1 | 4 | 2 | 4 | 1 |
| 5 | 1 | 5 | 3 | 5 | 7 | 5 | 1 |

Obtain graph paper and draw a histogram for each frequency distribution. Enter beside each histogram the values you obtain for the four descriptive moments. Study the differences among the histograms and the corresponding differences among the moments.

Example of computation for distribution (1) of Table 4.5.

$\Sigma f = N = 8.$

$\Sigma fX = 1(1) + 0(2) + 6(3) + 0(4) + 1(5) = 24$

$$M_x = \frac{\Sigma fX}{N} = \frac{24}{8} = 3$$

The frequency distribution of $x$ is

| $x$ | $f$ |
|---|---|
| −2 | 1 |
| −1 | 0 |
| 0 | 6 |
| +1 | 0 |
| +2 | 1 |

$\Sigma fx^2 = 1(-2)^2 + 0(-1)^2 + 6(0)^2 + 0(1)^2 + 1(2)^2 = 8$

$$V_x = \frac{\Sigma fx^2}{N} = \frac{8}{8} = 1$$

$$S_x = \sqrt{V_x} = \sqrt{1} = 1$$

Since $Z_x = x/S_x$, the frequency distribution of $Z_x$ is

| $Z_x$ | $f$ |
|---|---|
| −2 | 1 |
| −1 | 0 |
| 0 | 6 |
| +1 | 0 |
| +2 | 1 |

$\Sigma fZ_x^3 = 1(-2)^3 + 0(-1)^3 + 6(0)^3 + 0(1)^3 + 1(2)^3 = 0$

$$S = \frac{\Sigma fZ_x^3}{N} = \frac{0}{8} = 0$$

$\Sigma fZ_x^4 = 1(-2)^4 + 0(-1)^4 + 6(0)^4 + 0(1)^4 + 1(2)^4 = 32$

$$K = \frac{\Sigma fZ_x^4}{N} = \frac{32}{8} = 4$$

# MEASUREMENT

## Semantics | 5

The totality of semantical issues and problems confronting the research psychologist is, without doubt, awesome. It would be ill-advised, to say the least, to attempt the resolution of all of these issues in the two chapters which are devoted to them in this text. Our goal is a modest one. In the present chapter there will be undertaken a preliminary and limited exploration of two specific questions about measurement. These questions are of concern to research psychologists and have special relevance to the study of statistical methods in psychological research. In Chapter 13, the problem of confirmation as it arises in statistical inference will be taken up.

The two questions to be considered in the present chapter are the following: (1) What is the nature of confirmation and disconfirmation with respect to the semantical designations of psychological measurement? (2) How do ideas, plans, and specifications for the preliminary tasks, operations, and materials originate in the initial period of test or scale development before confirmation is sought?

There is considerable agreement among psychologists regarding certain notions about measurement. Numbers have properties. Behavioral events and products have properties, too. When there is some kind or degree of correspondence between these two sets of properties, it is legitimate and worthwhile to assign the numbers to the events and products. When there is no correspondence between the two sets of properties, the assignment of numbers is, inevitably, a fruitless and wasted effort. (*Isomorphism* is a term that is often employed to refer to the one-to-one correspondence of numbers and objects or events.) Confirmation or disconfirmation involves demonstrating in some public and objective fashion that correspondence does or does not obtain in some given instance of attempted measurement.

When one goes beyond these basic notions about the nature of psychological measurement and its evaluation, one finds much less agreement. It is not possible and, even if it were, it would not be appropriate, to present here a complete historical and contemporary account of the various ideas psychologists and others have had about measurement and the requirements of measurement. It does seem reasonable and appropriate to describe here two approaches to the problem, both of which figure, in varying forms and to varying degrees, in current discussions of measurement.[1]

## The Structural Approach

If one takes for granted the desirability of correspondence between the properties of numbers and the properties of behavior, it is tempting to begin the quest for confirmation with a logical analysis of the properties of numbers. Having produced a list of the logically determined properties of numbers, one might then require a point-by-point demonstration of correspondence between these properties and the observable properties of the behavior. "Demonstration" and "observable" are key words here; the former implies that some kinds of operations, in which the objects or events being measured have a central role, must be performed by the investigator; the latter has the meaning one would expect an empirical scientist to give to it. For the empirical scientist, in general, measurement is quantified observation; it is his experience of the objects and events of the world, translated into the language of numbers. For the psychologist, measurement is the observation of behavior, given expression in the language of numbers.

If a point-by-point determination of the correspondence of the two sets of properties is necessary, how does one go about staging the demonstration? Let us consider an example involving a familiar kind of physical measurement, the measurement of length. Everyone is acquainted with the fact that numbers can be incorporated in statements like those listed below.

1. $X = Y$
2. $X > Y$
3. $X_1 - X_2 = Y_1 - Y_2$
4. $X_1X_2 = Y_1Y_2$

Let these four statements constitute our representation of at least some of the properties of numbers. So much for the numbers.

For the other half of the example, we shall use ropes of varying lengths, chosen to suit our purposes. Now two ropes, *A* and *B*, have the property, $A = B$, when they are of the same length. That they are of the same length can be determined, without reference to or use of numbers, by placing them

[1]No attempt will be made here to give an authoritative account of the views of particular individuals. In an area where the issues are so complex, it is probable that the views of any particular person could be given accurately only by that person. What follows is an attempt to formulate two representative positions. The student may, of course, readily identify certain elements of the present discussion as having derived from the work of persons other than the author.

side by side, stretching them reasonably taut, and observing that the ends of one coincide approximately with the ends of the other. In the same kind of situation, they have the property, $A > B$, when $A$ is longer than $B$, which, of course, is the case when one observes that the ropes coincide at one end but not at the other. Given four ropes—$A$, $B$, $C$, and $D$, they have the property, $A - B = C - D$, when the amount by which $A$ extends beyond $B$ can be shown to be equal to the amount by which $C$ extends beyond $D$. Understand that the set of relations can be demonstrated by arranging and observing the ropes. The demonstration would not require the use of numbers in any way.

To demonstrate the relation, $AB = CD$, requires a somewhat different set of operations. We would need a flat surface on which to mark off a rectangular area using rope $A$ for the one dimension and rope $B$ for the other. We would also mark off a rectangular area using ropes $C$ and $D$. By subdividing each area into some arbitrary unit area we could establish that the two rectangles enclosed the same amount of space.

The structural approach to confirmation does not require that, in every case, the demonstration of relations among properties of objects or events must necessarily be reduced to the specific operations with ropes which were described above. It is conceivable, although not necessarily true, that there are many other sets of operations which bear little or no resemblance to the physical manipulation of ropes, but which would be appropriate for the demonstrations.

What does seem to be clearly required by the structural approach is that the operations employed in demonstrating the properties of objects, as distinguished from the properties of numbers, are of a primitive type which does not involve the use of numbers and which does involve observation and the overt management of the observer. These primitive operations have the status of a criterion in that they constitute a procedure for confirming or disconfirming the designation.

Our reason for emphasizing the primitive character of the confirming operations and the important role of observation and management is that these are the features which guarantee the presence of the designatum in the evaluation of the sign-designatum relation. If one wished to evaluate a given method of psychological measurement and if there was not an obviously appropriate set of primitive operations available, one could make the mistake of confining his attention to the numbers themselves and forgetting the behavioral events. The numbers, of course, would prove to have the properties that numbers have. The mistake consists of leaving out of consideration the system of behavioral properties. One would have to be very clear and certain that both sets of properties had actually figured in the demonstration.

There are other pitfalls one must avoid in taking the structural approach. It is a mistake to try to find a substitute for the primitive operations, when they elude one's search. An improper substitution, to which psychologists have been known to resort, has its origin in a misinterpretation of the role of observation in measurement and in science. Many psychologists are familiar with and agree with some form or variation of the statement: Measurement always involves a human observer. It is easy to rearrange this sentence into one which may seem to be logically defensible, but certainly is not: The action of a human observer always results in measurement. There is an important area of psychological measurement which has to do with the judging of physical and behavioral stimuli; it is called *psychophysics*. In this area, it is understandable that, in the absence of an obviously relevant set of primitive operations, the judgments themselves might be mistakenly interpreted or viewed as constituting these operations. This amounts to rewriting the sentence about measurement and the human observer, given above, into the sentence: The judging of any attribute in a quantitative fashion always constitutes measurement. The concrete, manipulative operations which should be applied to the objects being measured have disappeared from the evaluation scene and the focus of attention is now on the act of observation.

To maintain that observing the relation between two ropes placed side by side is fundamentally the same as judging the pitch of two different tones presented successively, or judging the sourness of acid solutions of varying concentrations, is to deemphasize the role of the primitive operations in determining correspondence and to shift the burden of confirmation elsewhere. Perhaps that is just what should be done, but, if it is, we should recognize and acknowledge the fact. It may be that the important factor in confirmation is not the set of primitive operations, but is, rather, the quality of the observation itself. We shall not say what we mean by " quality " at this point or how it might be evaluated, since much of what will follow concerning the second approach will deal with these issues.

There is another kind of inappropriate substitute for the primitive operations—a logical analysis of the behavior in question. To try to solve the problem of confirmation by a logical analysis of numbers and a logical analysis of the behavior is to try to convert the problem from an empirical one to a theoretical one, or from a semantical problem to a syntactical problem. One might mistakenly resort to axioms, to *a priori* notions, or to theory—perhaps theory of a mathematical sort—in an effort to endow measures with the desired attributes by simply imputing these attributes to them. The syntax of the language in which the logical analysis of numbers and the logical analysis of behavior are reported might be perfect, but it would be devoid of empirical substance. The semantical question about confirmation would remain unanswered.

Before leaving the structural approach, we shall point to one more disturbing feature it possesses. It provides no way of assessing the consequences of failures in correspondence. The structural approach begins with a logical analysis of the properties of numbers. There is hardly any limit one can place on the number of abstract properties which might result from an exhaustive analysis. The analysis might cause our attention to be focused on properties which were irrelevant or superfluous to confirmation. What we need is some way of assessing the consequences of a failure in correspondence with respect to any given property, thereby assuring ourselves of its relevance. We could then establish a class of properties for which failure in correspondence had serious consequences and a class of properties for which failure had negligible consequences.

To date, there is very little evidence of success in using primitive operations to confirm or disconfirm the designations of psychological measurement. To say there has been little success does not mean that there can be none, or that there will be none. The possibility of breaking through this barrier in the future cannot be denied. In the meantime, however, psychologists who wish to take the structural approach to confirmation find themselves in a difficult and, perhaps, awkward situation. What happens if one wishes to seek confirmation for a given scale and cannot discover the primitive operations required in his case? Does he abandon his scale? Not likely, for to do so would mean, at this stage in the development of psychology, abandoning most, if not all, of psychological measurement.

## The Functional Approach

There is a sense in which one might say the structural approach is a molecular approach. That is, it requires an enumeration of individual properties and the checking of correspondence property by property. The structural approach requires a logical decomposition of the general features of the number system into quite specific attributes. There is neither *a priori* reason nor evidence which compels us to believe that confirmation or disconfirmation can only be achieved by means of a molecular approach. It may not be at all necessary to demonstrate point-by-point correspondence for a list of abstracted number properties. It is entirely possible that an approach, in which attention is directed to the general attributes of sets of numbers—a molar approach—can provide the evidence that is necessary and sufficient for confirmation or disconfirmation.

If the structural approach is a molecular one, then the functional approach is molar. Essentially, it requires examination of the correspondence or relation between two sets of paired numbers in each one of three kinds of situations. The three situations provide the basis for evaluating three important characteristics of a measurement variable: (1) its distribution, (2) its reproducibility, and (3) its predictiveness.

By *distribution* we mean that, under some, if not all, circumstances, measures of different objects or events should vary. That is to say, a given psychological test or scale, if it is to satisfy the distribution criterion, should, when it is administered to some group of subjects, produce varied scores. If that test or scale fails to produce variable scores, as it is applied to various groups of subjects, there is no evidence of confirmation with respect to distribution. There is an assumption here that on any single occasion people respond differently and that the test or scale should reflect these response differences.

A common way of exhibiting the variation in response, when it is detected, is to arrange the scores or measures in a frequency distribution which gives a pairing of each different measure of response and its frequency of occurrence in the group of subjects. Thus the characteristics of the relation between frequency and the magnitude of some measurement variable would be taken account of in evaluating the measurement with respect to the first criterion—distribution.

By *reproducibility* we mean that the results of repeated measurement of the same object or event should not vary much. In psychological measurement, this second requirement calls for two sets of measures on the same variable and the same subjects. The two sets of measures are paired, of course, as a consequence of measuring each subject twice. Assuming that the distribution requirement is met for both sets of measures, then the reproducibility requirement is met if there is a linear relation between the first set of measures and the second, and if the slope of the function is approximately unity. Saying there should be a linear relation does not imply that it should be perfect or that the plotted points must lie in a perfectly straight line. Some degree of irregularity can be tolerated. Just how this linear relation and the satisfactoriness of the regularity might be expressed will not be described here. It will be discussed in Chapter 9, which covers the descriptive uses of product moments. Notice that implicit in the evaluation is the ordering of subjects

**Table 5.1**

**TWO SETS OF MEASURES ON THE SAME SUBJECTS; AN ILLUSTRATION OF REPRODUCIBILITY**

| | | First Set | Second Set |
|---|---|---|---|
| Subjects | 1 | 17 | 18 |
| | 2 | 14 | 14 |
| | 3 | 25 | 26 |
| | 4 | 23 | 24 |
| | 5 | 11 | 12 |
| | 6 | 13 | 12 |
| | 7 | 24 | 24 |
| | 8 | 21 | 21 |
| | 9 | 15 | 16 |
| | 10 | 20 | 19 |

on each occasion and an examination of the equality or inequality of corresponding differences on the two sets of measures. If the relation is to be linear and the slope is to be unity, then the difference between two subjects on the first occasion must be equal to the difference between the same subjects on the second occasion.

As an illustration of a situation in which the reproducibility requirement is satisfied, two sets of measures are given in Table 5.1 and the plot of the two sets is given in Figure 5.1. A straight line has been drawn through the

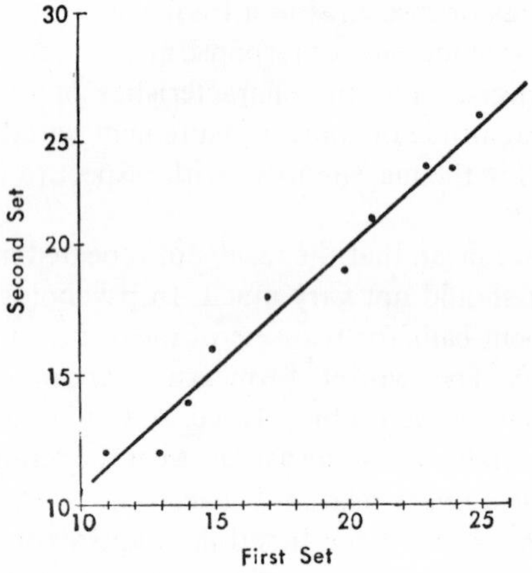


**Fig. 5.1** Plot of the two sets of measures in Table 5.1. Notice the distinct linear trend of the points. The plot indicates that the reproducibility of the measures is quite good.

configuration of points to show how close to linearity the relation is. The position of the line was determined by inspection. Its slope is approximately unity.

**Table 5.2**

**TWO SETS OF MEASURES ILLUSTRATING A LACK OF REPRODUCIBILITY**

| | | First Set | Second Set |
|---|---|---|---|
| Subjects | 1 | 15 | 19 |
| | 2 | 11 | 22 |
| | 3 | 13 | 14 |
| | 4 | 23 | 13 |
| | 5 | 21 | 21 |
| | 6 | 17 | 15 |
| | 7 | 19 | 20 |
| | 8 | 10 | 17 |
| | 9 | 14 | 11 |
| | 10 | 18 | 10 |

As an illustration of a situation in which the reproducibility requirement is not satisfied, two sets of measures are given in Table 5.2. Their plot appears in Figure 5.2. No line has been drawn through the points because the

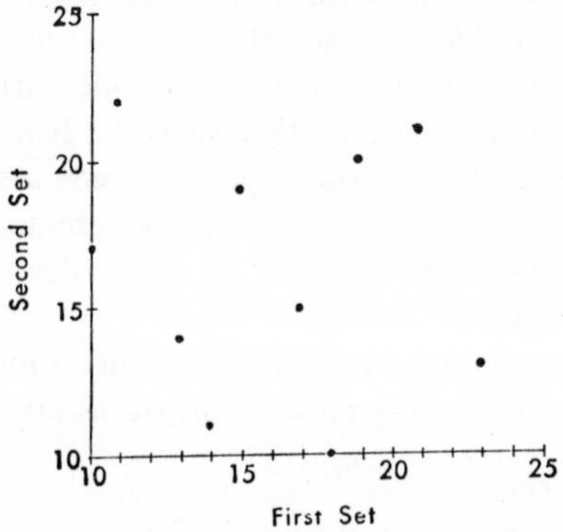


**Fig. 5.2** Plot of the two sets of measures in Table 5.2. There is no pronounced trend in the configuration of points. The plot indicates that the measures lack reproducibility.

**Table 5.3**

**MEASURES ON TWO VARIABLES; AN EXAMPLE OF A PREDICTIVE RELATION**

| | | Variables | |
|---|---|---|---|
| | | *X* | *Y* |
| Subjects | 1 | 22 | 47 |
| | 2 | 16 | 35 |
| | 3 | 11 | 6 |
| | 4 | 27 | 38 |
| | 5 | 21 | 46 |
| | 6 | 30 | 25 |
| | 7 | 24 | 45 |
| | 8 | 29 | 30 |
| | 9 | 12 | 13 |
| | 10 | 18 | 41 |
| | 11 | 26 | 41 |
| | 12 | 28 | 35 |
| | 13 | 13 | 20 |
| | 14 | 14 | 25 |
| | 15 | 23 | 46 |
| | 16 | 25 | 44 |
| | 17 | 20 | 45 |
| | 18 | 19 | 44 |
| | 19 | 15 | 30 |
| | 20 | 17 | 38 |

irregularity and inconsistency of corresponding differences are extreme and there is no suggestion of a linear relation.

The third requirement, in the functional approach to confirmation, is *predictiveness*. By predictiveness we mean that, given measures of the same objects or events on two *different* variables, the two sets of paired observations should be so related that, from a measure on one variable, one can predict the corresponding measure on the other variable. It is not required that the prediction be perfect and, consequently, one needs a standard for deciding when the requirement is met. The procedures commonly used for deciding the issue will be discussed in Chapter 9, which deals with the descriptive uses of product moments.

In Table 5.3 are presented measures on twenty subjects on two different variables, $X$ and $Y$. The twenty pairs of measures are plotted in Figure 5.3.

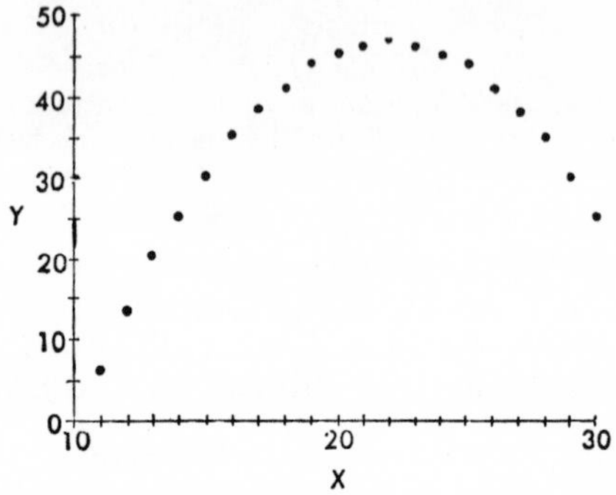


**Fig. 5.3** Plot of the paired measures from Table 5.3. Notice the highly predictive relation between $X$ and $Y$.

Notice that the pattern of points is distinctly curved indicating that the prediction from $X$ to $Y$ would be fairly accurate if one knew the equation for the curve which fits the configuration. The pattern could, of course, take many

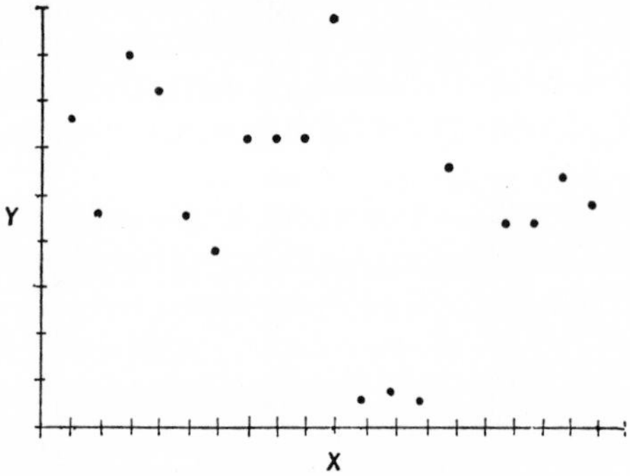


**Fig. 5.4** Plot of paired measures for variable $X$ and $Y$. There is no indication of a predictive relation between the two variables.

other forms, including that of a simple, linear trend. A highly irregular pattern, such as the one displayed in Figure 5.4, would be indicative of a failure in predictiveness for variable $X$ with respect to variable $Y$.

It has been our experience that many students of psychology possess a strong intuitive appreciation of certain scale properties which have to do with the equality or inequality of intervals, but that relatively few students perceive the relevance of a functional approach in investigating these properties. In some instances the problem of "equal intervals" is introduced into their discussions by vague references to the obvious equality of the standard units employed in the measurement of physical length and is then dismissed with an uneasy reference to the intervals on some psychological scale as being "probably not equal." This uncertain view of measurement is often accompanied by misgivings about the consequences of using nonlinear transformations of observations, such as square roots, logarithms, and reciprocals, because of the effect of these transformations on the scale intervals. An inadequacy is often revealed in the student's thinking by his apparent belief that the substitution of ranks can introduce a kind of regularity into his data which was not to be found in the original measures.

Implicit in this uncertain and sceptical view of psychological measurement are many issues which could, perhaps, be made explicit, but only with the investment of a great deal of time and effort in the analysis. It might be unprofitable, in the end, to make such an investment in the analysis of vague ideas and concerns. It could be more worthwhile to spend our time here in developing an adequate approach to measurement than in trying to cope with an inadequate one. We propose that the only appropriate questions one can ask about the intervals of a given scale are the following: Is there any regularity to be discerned in the relation between observed differences on that scale and observed differences on some other scale? Can this regularity, if it does exist, be expressed by means of a mathematical function or equation?

The nature of the intervals on a given scale may be difficult or impossible to determine in any absolute sense, but the regularities (or irregularities) of intervals on that scale in relation to the intervals of another scale can be determined and expressed. The procedure is not difficult. Furthermore, it is never impossible. That is to say, one can always examine measures on one scale as a function of measures on another. The procedure is a familiar and standard practice in many fields. It is readily available and widely applicable. To our knowledge, it is the only procedure that can be adopted as a standard practice and used routinely by the research psychologist. It may even be true that there is no meaningful way of discussing the properties of intervals on a scale, except as those intervals are related to intervals on another scale. The student's tendency to put the problem in terms of physical magnitudes, such as length, and in terms of concrete objects, such as meter bars, may even be considered a resort to a primitive type of expression of functional relations.

There is one final point to be considered—the relation between the structural approach and the functional approach. As appealing as the structural approach may be to a theoretically oriented research psychologist, he cannot afford to disregard the requirements of the functional approach. That is, even if he could achieve confirmation by demonstrating point-by-point correspondence, which as we have indicated is difficult, uncertain, and perhaps impossible, he could not take distribution, reproducibility, and predictiveness for granted. He would surely be very much interested in studying these characteristics of his scale and in achieving them. On the other hand, the practical-minded research psychologist may turn his attention directly to the requirements of the functional approach, assuming that if he can meet those requirements, then the requirements of the structural approach are not binding on him.

## Summary

The important semantical question as to the nature of confirmation is a difficult one. Two representative positions with respect to the question's answer have been described briefly and in somewhat general and elementary terms. It is probably apparent to the student that the present author takes a position supporting the functional approach. There is little doubt that discussion of these and other positions will continue for a long time before anything resembling complete agreement or unanimity of thought is realized by research psychologists.

## Devising New Scales

Before one can seek confirmation, one must have devised a provisional method of measurement. There must be a task or a set of tasks. Standard procedures, which almost always include a set of instructions for the subject, the investigator, or both, must be adopted. Materials or instrumentation may have to be devised. Arrangements have to be made for recording observations. Out of this integrated system of tasks, procedures, and materials will come a record of the subject's behavior to which numbers either already are or soon will be assigned. The quantified record represents a provisional set of measures, whose quality is unknown. An attempt at confirmation of the designations is usually the next step. But we have discussed confirmation; let us turn our attention now to the origins of the scale.

From what source do the ideas, plans, and specifications for the provisional system come? It will be worthwhile to intensify our awareness and sharpen our perception of the source. Perhaps we should say " sources," for there are at least three principal ones. First, the psychologist imitates the work of others and often the imitation is built upon other imitations and is far removed in time from the work of the originator. Second, he acts upon hunches and intuitions, which arise not only out of his professional and research experience but also out of his everyday experience of living. Third, he develops theories and from a particular theory he may deduce hypotheses about the quantification of behavior, which lend themselves to translation into provisional methods of measurement. Whatever the source—imitation, intuition, or theory—he obtains from it no more than a provisional scale. The attempt at confirmation must follow.

Most of the scales employed currently in psychological research are basically imitations of other scales. As we shall see later, it is appropriate that this should be so. Although the multitude of scales now being employed could be classified according to a variety of schemes, for purposes of our brief discussion, which is intended to provide the student with an overview of current practices, a simple classification scheme will be employed. The classification scheme involves five categories, each category being identified by a manifest and salient feature of the system which results in the assigning of numbers.

The first category contains physical measures of response. The distance an athlete can put the shot, the height he can jump, his time in running a distance of a mile, and many other assignments of numbers similar to these qualify as provisional measures of response. The length of a human figure drawn by a child, the time which elapses between the presentation of an interview question and the response of the interviewee, the quantity of water drunk by a dog, the pressure a subject exerts on a control lever in a stressful situation, and the change in conductivity of the skin surface in the palm of a subject's hand are also potential physical measures of behavior. Many others could be listed in this category. Some of them, of course, are of less current interest to psychologists than are others.

The second category consists of methods of measurement which require the counting of responses. To count in any meaningful fashion requires, of course, that the response to be counted must be identifiable. Frequency counts of responses constitute a major type of measurement in psychology and some of the best psychological measurement occurs in this area. The number of revolutions of an activity wheel produced by a rat in some standard period of time, the number of food pellets consumed by a rat, the number of bar pressings performed by a rat, the number of arithmetic problems a child solves correctly on a test, the number of goals a basketball player makes in a game, the number of pins a subject transfers and places correctly in a dexterity test, the number of questions answered " Yes " on a personality inventory, the number of parts assembled by a factory worker in a day, the number of accidents in which a truck driver is involved, the number of times a housewife expresses a preference for one brand of soap in comparing it with nine other brands, the number of activities a high-school student checks as his interests, the number of self-references in a client's protocol from a therapy session, the number of occasions on which a student signs out a particular reference book in the library, and the number of nonsense syllables recalled from a list which had been learned previously to some standard—these and countless others make up the class of psychological measures which require that responses be identified and counted.

In the third category are the measurements of classical psychophysics. The psychologist records a physical measure of a stimulus under standard conditions for counting the responses of a subject who must respond to the stimulus with a discrimination of some sort.[2] The discriminatory response of the subject may be detecting the presence of a stimulus or detecting a difference between two stimuli. It has been known for a long time that a stimulus or a difference between stimuli of any given magnitude within a broad range of values on a physical dimension, will sometimes be detected and sometimes not. Thus in a large number of judgments of a given stimulus magnitude or a given difference, the proportion of correct judgments can be determined. Since any stimulus within a considerable range will sometimes be detected and sometimes not, there is no value which obviously qualifies as the threshold, that is, as the lowest detectable value or the smallest detectable difference. The general practice is to define a threshold as a physical measure of the stimulus which is correctly detected in some specified proportion of trials. The procedure in determining a threshold value is to specify the proportion of correct judgments which will be taken as defining the threshold. The psychologist must then determine by systematic testing procedures, of which there are more than can be described adequately here, the value of the stimulus associated with the specified proportion. If the task is to detect the presence of a stimulus, the value so determined is called an *absolute* threshold. If the task is to detect a difference between stimuli, the value is called a *differential* threshold.

The intensity of a tone of specified frequency, the difference in frequency of two tones of specified intensity, the separation in millimeters between two black lines in a test of visual acuity, the voltage employed in the projection of taboo words on a screen, the concentration of sugar in a solution which is tasted repeatedly by a subject, the concentration of monosodium glutamate in a solution for taste testing, the ratio of the major axis of an ellipse to the minor axis in a visual test, the difference in temperature between two water baths in which the subject immerses his hands, and the angle of tilt of a chair

[2]The specific psychophysical methods implied by this statement are the "constant methods." The method of adjustment and the method of limits require physical measurement and repeated judgments but the data are handled differently.

in which the subject is seated—these physical measures of stimuli are typical of a vast array of psychophysical measurement variables.

In the fourth category are measures derived from the judgments of one or more persons but not based on physically measured attributes of the objects or events judged. In the method of absolute judgment, the stimulus object or event is presented to the judge who responds by giving a numerical rating. The rating may be recorded by the judge with the help of some simple graphic device or it may be recorded directly as a number. The ratings given by two or more judges in response to the same stimulus are often averaged. In the method of comparative judgment, two or more stimulus objects are presented to a judge who expresses a preference for one of the objects, orders the objects on some assumed dimension, or judges the relation(s) between the objects. The responses of a group of judges are then tabulated and given expression as placing the objects in positions on one or more quantitative scales. The judging operations vary from one research problem to another, and, for any given judging operation, there may be different procedures for converting the observed judgments into scale values. Some conversion systems are relatively simple, as is the case when the objects are ordered according to the proportion of preferences expressed for each. Other conversion systems are somewhat complex. An example of a complex system is Thurstone's law of comparative judgment.

Listed below are examples of ratings which have been applied to behavioral events: job efficiency, ability to do independent study, potential capacity for research or other creative acivity, social acceptance, interest in military assignment, resourcefulness, emotional control, speed and accuracy of judgment, agility, daring, stamina, initiative, social awareness, teamwork, organizing ability, conformity, reasonableness, leadership, integrity, altruism, reliability, sportsmanship, creativity, egotism, friendliness, courage, effort, conduct, citizenship, cooperation, adjustment, flexibility, originality, enthusiasm, supervising ability, adaptability, executive influence, eagerness, foresight, leadership, stinginess, obstinacy, disorderliness, bashfulness, sociability, emotional stability, and dominance.

Three examples of methods of obtaining comparative judgments are given below.

1. A manufacturer of perfumes desires information concerning the preferences of female college students for four new scents produced by his firm. A representative of the manufacturer interviews each one of a large number of young college women and obtains her preferences. In each interview the subject is given the opportunity to react to each possible pair of scents and to express a preference for one member of the pair. Since there are six different pairings possible for four objects, each subject indicates six preferences. The preferences of all subjects are pooled and used to derive values for the four scents on a quantitative scale.

2. In a study of verbal associations, a psychologist develops a list of ten words and forms all possible groups of three, numbering 120 in all. His subjects are instructed to examine each triad and to choose the two words closest together in meaning. Data for 100 subjects are combined, the relative frequency with which each word is associated with every other word is computed, and the pattern of relations among the words is studied. The result is that the ten words are assigned positions on each one of several hypothetical scales.

3. In developing a criterion of performance for enlisted men, a personnel psychologist had supervising officers rank their men on technical competence. Each officer was presented with a list of twenty enlisted men whom he had supervised and was instructed to order them in terms of competence, using for ranks the first twenty integers and giving the most competent man a rank of one and the least competent man a rank of twenty.

In the attempts to quantify absolute and comparative judgments, where no relevant physical measure of the stimulus is available, a great deal of research effort has been invested in devising scoring and weighting systems. An account of these varied systems would necessarily involve an extensive discussion of particular scaling theories and would go far beyond the proper scope of the present treatment.

The fifth and last category into which we have attempted to classify psychological measures is not as large as the other four categories, but does contain a distinctive set of measures. Two basic procedures can be distinguished in this fifth category. An example will be given below illustrating each procedure.

1. A clinical psychologist who specializes in marriage counseling wishes to assess the similarity of interest patterns of husband and wife for each one of a large number of married couples. He compiles a list of twenty of the most frequently reported leisure-time activities and asks each subject to rank these twenty activities in terms of their interest to him (or her). After the rankings are completed, the similarity of interest patterns for a couple can be assessed by evaluating the relation between the husband's ranks and his wife's ranks. When each of the twenty activities has the same rank for both husband and wife, there is maximum similarity. The ranks can, of course, be assigned with so little consistency that there is little or no similarity. The extent of the relation can be perceived if one plots the wife's ranks against the husband's. When the ranks are assigned in exactly the same way by both parties, the points of the plot will lie in a straight line. When there is considerable inconsistency, the points will scatter and will not define a trend. Similarity of response can be measured and represented by a single index number, a coefficient of correlation computed from the two sets of ranks. (The computation of this index will be described later.)

2. A counseling psychologist wishes to measure the congruence between

a student's description of himself with respect to social competence and his description of the person he would, ideally, like to be. The psychologist collects an appropriate set of thirty-two statements, each of which can be employed for self description in regard to social competence. The statements are typed separately on thirty-two cards. In an interview with each of his student clients, he instructs the client to sort the thirty-two cards into six categories on a scale running from most descriptive of himself to least descriptive. The first and sixth categories are to contain one statement in each; the second and fifth categories are to contain five statements; the third and fourth categories are to contain ten statements. After the sorting is completed, the psychologist records the placement of each statement and then has the client repeat the task, sorting on this second occasion into six categories running from most descriptive to least descriptive of the person he would, ideally, like to be. Again the thirty-two placements are recorded. Each statement now has two placements. If every statement is given the same placement on both occasions, there is no discrepancy between the subject's two descriptions and congruence is maximal. On the other hand, much inconsistency in the placements indicates that the two descriptions are quite discrepant and that congruence is low. Again, as in the two previous examples, the placements from the first sorting can be plotted against the placements from the second. If the placements in the two sortings are identical, then all thirty-two points will be located on a straight line, the discrepancy will be zero and the congruence will be perfect. A considerable degree of scatter in the points would indicate a considerable degree of discrepancy in the two descriptions and very low congruence. Congruence, or the lack of discrepancy, can be measured by computing a coefficient of correlation for the two sets of placements.

We have now completed our account of psychological measurement. The purpose of this account was to provide the student with a brief review of past and present measurement practices. It is hoped that the review will give him a general idea of the nature and scope of the background from which the psychologist can obtain ideas for measures which he can employ in his research. Confronted with the need for a scale, he can, and perhaps should, scan the whole field of psychological measurement. Is there a possibility that some physical measure of response would be appropriate? Can one arrange the task of the subject so that a threshold measure can be obtained? Could one specify a class of responses which can be identified and counted? Can judgments be employed to any advantage? Do sorting tasks offer any good possibilities?

Suggesting that a psychologist should deliberately survey the entire measurement scene when he is undertaking research on a given problem is merely to emphasize that he should consider the full range of possibilities, that he should take advantage of what has already been done, and that he should try to relate his work to the work of others. If he does so, he will sometimes simply adopt the specific measuring devices which someone else has employed. Frequently he will find it necessary to modify or adapt the techniques or instruments of others and may, in this way, make an original contribution to the field of measurement. Occasionally his survey may yield him nothing suitable for his purposes and he may have to engage in extensive research on the measurement problem itself.

What we have called imitation is the largest source of ideas for measurement in research, but it is not the only one. There is always the possibility that some essentially new way of measuring behavior will be invented or discovered, will be investigated and confirmed, and will then take its place in the body of available measurement practices. We have already mentioned the two sources of new ideas. They are intuition and theory.

Naming intuition as a source of ideas for new measures is simply recognizing the fact that the source of original ideas, whatever they may concern, can seldom, if ever, be determined in an objective fashion or with any degree of certainty. A man reads widely on some topic or problem, discusses it with learned colleagues, thinks about it intensely over a long period of time, and suddenly begins to talk about it as no one else has. Is his idea really new and entirely original? That is doubtful, but it may be so regarded. Thus it is that the invention of calculus is credited to Newton—and to Leibniz. In psychology, it may very well be that everyday experience, as well as study and research, plays a significant part in the conception of new ideas about measurement.

Finally, the important place of theory in psychological measurement must be given proper recognition and emphasis. Substantial bodies of theory have been formulated in at least four areas of measurement: the testing of achievement, ability, and aptitude; the assessing of attitudes; the determination of thresholds in psychophysics; and the scaling of absolute and comparative judgments. Detailed accounts of particular theories in these or other areas are not germane to the purpose of the present discussion. What is relevant to that purpose is a consideration, in general terms, of the nature of theory and its relation to confirmation.

A measurement theory is an attempt to give an explanatory account or a systematic view of the quantification of observations of some characteristic of behavior. The theory is given expression in a statement of general and abstract principles, but there is, almost always, a body of facts on which the principles have been based. It may be possible to deduce hypotheses from the theory and to test these hypotheses by devising tasks for subjects to perform, methods of observing the subjects' behavior, and rules for quantifying the observations. There are two principal points of difficulty in this process: the deduction of hypotheses and the devising of tasks. In its highest form, the deductive process is mathematical and therefore absolutely rigorous.

In its lowest form, it might be no more than a loose sequence of plausible statements, in which case it is lacking in rigor and is usually the cause of disagreement, argument, and controversy. Translating the terms of hypotheses and theory into the concrete operations of measurement is always accompanied by some degree of awkwardness and uncertainty. It is seldom, if ever, obvious as to just how this translation can be properly effected. The gap between the terms of the theory and the corresponding operations of measurement is disturbingly large.

Theory is, of course, very important as a vehicle for original thinking about measurement and as a source of inventions, discoveries, new approaches, modifications, and elaborations, but one point, concerning what theory cannot in itself accomplish, should be clear: *Theorizing does not itself constitute confirmation.* Theorizing before or during the process of scale construction may make confirmation more likely when confirmation is attempted, but there is no law that says it will do so in every endeavor. Everything depends on the quality of the theorizing and, ultimately, its relevance to the behavior in question. There are no guarantees of either quality or relevance.

## Summary

Two approaches to confirmation were described. The structural approach requires the demonstration of correspondence, point by point, between properties of numbers and properties of behavior. The functional approach requires the demonstration of distribution, reproducibility, and predictiveness. Measurement theory has its place in the devising of new scales, but theorizing does not itself constitute confirmation. Confirmation is empirical; it requires demonstration and observation; it cannot be deduced.

# DESCRIBING DATA BY MEANS OF MOMENTS

## Pragmatics | 6

Psychological data may, on occasion, take the simple form of a single set of measures which exhibit variability. The set may consist of repeated observations of the behavior of one subject, or it may consist of measures on a group of subjects, each of whom has been measured on one occasion.

The psychologist may wish to describe the set of observations; that is, he may wish to communicate to his colleagues, his employer, the public, or his students, information concerning the nature of his observations. He can, of course, provide a very complete and exact description by simply listing all of the measures. While this kind of description is complete and, in a sense, exact, it suffers from certain definite limitations. Although it might be quite satisfactory to list the measures if there were only a few, it would not be at all satisfactory to do so if there were many. If the number of observations was large, it would be difficult or impossible for the investigator's audience or reader to form an adequate impression concerning any of their characteristics and the salient features of the set of observations might not be apparent at all. Regularities in the data might be completely obscured by the mass of data and their irregularities.

To provide the student with some experience of the difficulties inherent in trying to grasp the main features of a fairly large number of observations, we have listed in Table 6.1 scores on a test. How many scores are there? What are the highest and lowest values? Can you determine from an inspection any other characteristics of the data?

Instead of listing all of the observations, the psychologist might classify them in a frequency distribution and represent the distribution graphically by means of a histogram. The frequency distribution and the histogram together provide an exact representation of the data in a form, some features of which are quickly and easily comprehended by the viewer. The person

**Table 6.1**

**A LISTING OF TEST SCORES**

| | | | | | | | | | | | | | | | |
|---|---|---|---|---|---|---|---|---|---|---|---|---|---|---|---|
| 12 | 9 | 15 | 10 | 13 | 12 | 8 | 10 | 11 | 11 | 9 | 12 | 11 | 13 | 10 | 13 |
| 12 | 14 | 8 | 13 | 11 | 12 | 11 | 14 | 10 | 10 | 9 | 11 | 13 | 14 | 10 | 12 |
| 10 | 12 | 11 | 11 | 10 | 9 | 13 | 12 | 12 | 11 | 10 | 11 | 10 | 13 | 12 | 12 |
| 12 | 11 | 11 | 12 | 9 | 14 | 15 | 13 | 13 | 12 | 10 | 11 | 11 | 12 | 9 | 8 |
| 10 | 10 | 9 | 10 | 11 | 12 | 12 | 10 | 13 | 7 | 9 | 11 | 10 | 13 | 12 | 13 |
| 9 | 11 | 11 | 9 | 11 | 10 | 10 | 10 | 11 | 10 | 12 | 13 | 12 | 12 | 13 | 11 |
| 12 | 14 | 13 | 11 | 11 | 10 | 10 | 13 | 10 | 10 | 12 | 13 | 10 | 11 | 11 | 11 |
| 11 | 11 | 10 | 12 | 11 | 11 | 10 | 10 | 10 | 9 | 13 | 14 | 11 | 11 | 10 | 12 |
| 10 | 12 | 10 | 10 | 12 | 13 | 11 | 11 | 11 | 9 | 11 | 11 | 10 | 12 | 11 | 11 |
| 9 | 11 | 10 | 11 | 10 | 11 | 11 | 10 | 12 | 12 | 12 | 13 | 11 | 9 | 14 | 11 |
| 12 | 9 | 10 | 11 | 11 | 10 | 9 | 12 | 12 | 11 | 13 | 14 | 13 | 12 | 12 | 11 |
| 11 | 12 | 11 | 11 | 10 | 10 | 10 | 11 | 10 | 11 | 12 | 13 | 9 | 10 | 11 | 10 |
| 10 | 11 | 9 | 9 | 10 | 11 | 10 | 10 | 11 | 13 | 13 | 12 | 11 | 10 | 11 | 11 |
| 11 | 11 | 10 | 12 | 14 | 13 | 13 | 9 | 11 | 11 | 10 | 10 | 11 | 12 | 13 | 13 |
| 12 | 13 | 9 | 13 | 11 | 11 | 11 | 10 | 12 | 14 | 13 | 11 | 11 | 11 | 10 | 10 |
| 8 | 8 | 13 | 13 | 12 | 11 | 11 | 12 | 10 | 10 | 12 | 9 | 10 | 10 | 10 | 10 |
| 12 | 9 | 10 | 10 | 11 | 9 | 14 | 12 | 12 | 12 | 10 | 11 | 11 | 11 | 12 | 12 |
| 11 | 12 | 9 | 12 | 11 | 11 | 10 | 11 | 10 | 12 | 12 | 10 | 11 | 11 | 10 | 10 |
| 9 | 14 | 15 | 12 | 11 | 10 | 11 | 10 | 11 | 12 | 13 | 9 | 9 | 11 | 11 | 11 |
| 12 | 9 | 9 | 10 | 11 | 9 | 10 | 11 | 11 | 12 | 12 | 9 | 12 | 12 | 11 | 10 |
| 9 | 11 | 9 | 11 | 10 | 11 | 8 | 8 | 11 | 9 | 8 | 12 | 12 | 11 | 11 | 11 |
| 10 | 14 | 8 | 12 | 12 | 10 | 9 | 10 | 10 | 11 | 11 | 12 | 10 | 10 | 12 | 12 |
| 10 | 12 | 12 | 10 | 9 | 9 | 12 | 10 | 10 | 14 | 13 | 11 | 10 | 9 | 12 | 12 |
| 13 | 8 | 9 | 10 | 10 | 11 | 11 | 9 | 9 | 13 | 12 | 12 | 12 | 11 | 11 | 10 |

*Note:* Columns and rows have no classificatory significance in the table; they represent simply an arbitrary arrangement of the data.

examining the distribution and its histogram can readily determine the highest and lowest values and the points of heavy and light concentrations of values; he can also form an impression of the shape of the distribution: its symmetry or lack of symmetry, and its flatness or peakedness. Table 6.2 contains a frequency distribution for the test scores in Table 6.1. Figure 6.1 is a histogram for that frequency distribution.

In theory, there is another way of providing a complete and exact description of a set of measures, but, in practice, it is almost always either very difficult or impossible. A complete description of the data might be given in terms of moments. The difficulty is that a large number of moments might be required. When the set of measures covers, in its range, $r$ distinct score intervals, then $r$ moments are required for a complete description. The $r$ moments may include the zeroth and all others up to the $(r - 1)^{\text{th}}$ moment.

**Table 6.2**

**A FREQUENCY DISTRIBUTION OF TEST SCORES FROM TABLE 6.1**

| $X$ | $f$ |
|---|---|
| 7 | 1 |
| 8 | 10 |
| 9 | 42 |
| 10 | 90 |
| 11 | 108 |
| 12 | 78 |
| 13 | 38 |
| 14 | 14 |
| 15 | 3 |

$N = 384 =$ total number of scores.

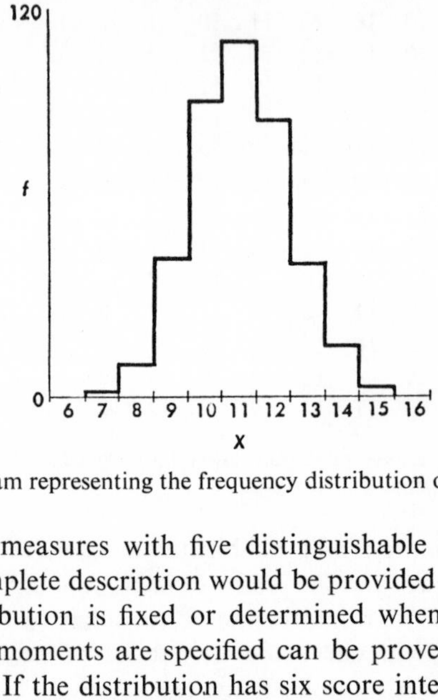


**Fig. 6.1** A histogram representing the frequency distribution of test scores in Table 6.2.

Given a set of measures with five distinguishable score intervals in its entire range, a complete description would be provided by $N$, $M_x$, $V_x$, $S$, and $K$. That the distribution is fixed or determined when there are five score intervals and five moments are specified can be proved, but the proof will not be given here. If the distribution has six score intervals, these same five values will not completely describe it. That is to say, there are many different six-interval distributions having the same values for the four descriptive moments and $N$. The example of skewness when $S = 0$, which was given in Figure 4.5, is explained by this fact.

The frequency distribution of Table 6.2 and the histogram of Figure 6.1 have nine score-intervals. The value of $N$ and eight moments would be required for complete description of the test scores on which the histogram and the frequency distribution were based. It would be quite impractical to compute the higher moments, which would involve the fifth, sixth, seventh, and eighth powers of the variable.

Since complete description is often either not desirable or not practical, it is reasonable to consider the possibilities of partial description or summarization. The summarizing of data can be accomplished so that it provides information concerning, and directs attention to, the salient features of a collection of measures. Summarizing is computationally feasible and economical. It may satisfy the requirements and the obligations of the investigator to provide a limited summary, in which case the information communicated may be no more than a crude approximation to the total information contained in the data, or an extensive summary, in which case the information communicated may be, for all practical purposes, a very good approximation.

Partial description or summarizing requires that the interpreter of data make a choice of a few moments out of a larger number, a number which could in fact be very large. The interpreter's choices are almost always limited to the first four descriptive moments, on which our attention was focused in Chapter 4. The choices are limited to these four moments not only because of the computational difficulty and cost in using the higher moments, but also because our understanding of, and familiarity with, the higher moments have not developed very far. The availability of high-speed, electronic computers will, perhaps, change this situation and, in the future, the higher moments may be used more extensively.

Limiting one's choice of moments to the first four does not solve all of the problems connected with that choice. As a matter of fact, the difficult features of the problem of choosing descriptive moments remain to be considered. The difficult features of the problem have to do with the relation between the logical properties of a particular moment and the interpretation intended by the investigator. Developing an understanding of the relevance of particular moments to particular practical questions or notions is an extremely difficult task for the student. It is important to cultivate this understanding and not to rely on imitation, even the imitation of recognized authorities. Imitation without understanding is often based on superficialities and often leads to incorrect use of statistics.

It is our opinion that an adequate working conceptualization with respect to a particular moment requires a thorough familiarity with, and a kind of synthesis of, the logical properties of that moment, in ready association with a class of practical situations and problems, which vary but have certain features in common.

We propose discussing below, in somewhat general terms, the various kinds of situations and problems commonly encountered by the psychologist and the appropriate choices of one or more moments for purposes of description. Before beginning the discussion, however, we must emphasize one point: At present we will not give consideration to error or random variation as they are defined statistically. We will be discussing values which are properly classified as *d*-statistics and not *i*-statistics. In Chapter 12, consideration will be given to *i*-statistics and logical properties having to do with error will be the focus of attention.

If a very limited description of a set of measures is to be given in the form of a single *d*-statistic, the choice will probably, but not necessarily, be the mean. The mean conveys information about the magnitude of the measures, but, of course, only in a general sense. The recipient of the information should know that the measures vary around the mean and that they lie in a region of the scale roughly indicated or approximated by the value of the mean. He should also realize that knowing only the mean leaves him without any other information. An assumption regarding other characteristics of the data would be risky. For example, he knows nothing of the magnitude of differences among the measures.

The mean of the test scores in Table 6.1 and the distribution in Table 6.2 is 11. Reflect, for a moment, on the fact that the mean is 11, and consider how much, or how little, one knows about the scores. Examine again the distribution in Table 6.2 and try to specify some of the properties of the distribution not revealed by the value of the mean.

Somewhat more completeness of description is achieved when two moments, the mean and the variance (or the standard deviation) are computed. The mean gives the general level of performance; the variance indicates the general magnitude of differences among the measures. It is a commonplace now to present the mean and variance of a distribution of observations and, in the use of moments, this practice occurs with far greater frequency than any other.

The variance of the distribution of scores in Table 6.2 is 2. Then $S_x = \sqrt{2}$. We have already indicated that the mean is 11. Recall that the variance is the average of the squares of deviations from the mean. It follows that, for the squared deviations, the variance is an interjacent value. That is, there are some squared deviations greater than 2 and some less than 2, if they vary at all. We also know that some of the original deviations were positive and some, negative. Knowing the mean and the variance gives one some crude notion of the general magnitude and the dispersion of the scores, but certainly does not give a clear or exact picture.

Computation of the four descriptive moments is probably the most complete description which may, at the present time, be said to be practical. It should be understood, however, that the distribution is not fixed in all respects by determination of the four values: $M_x$, $V_x$, $S$, and $K$. Although a number of moments equal to the number of score intervals would be required for a complete description, it is our opinion that distributions of psychological measures are quite adequately described by the first four moments and that variation in features not fixed by these values can, in practice, be disregarded. In other words, we are saying that the first four moments will take account of the important regularities or salient features in psychological data and that the irregularities or details not taken account of can be ignored. This opinion should not be mistaken for a statement of fact. In the future, experience may indicate the desirability and even the necessity for going on to additional, higher moments.

The index of skewness for the distribution in Table 6.2 is +0.177. The index of kurtosis is 2.875. Thus the first four descriptive moments can be summarized as follows:

$$\begin{aligned} M_x &= 11, \\ V_x &= 2, \\ S &= 0.177, \\ K &= 2.875. \end{aligned}$$

The distribution is positively skew, but only moderately so. In the range of values for $K$ commonly encountered in practice, the obtained value is not extreme; it lies well within the range of moderate values of $K$.

Description of the distribution in Table 6.2 in terms of four moments is

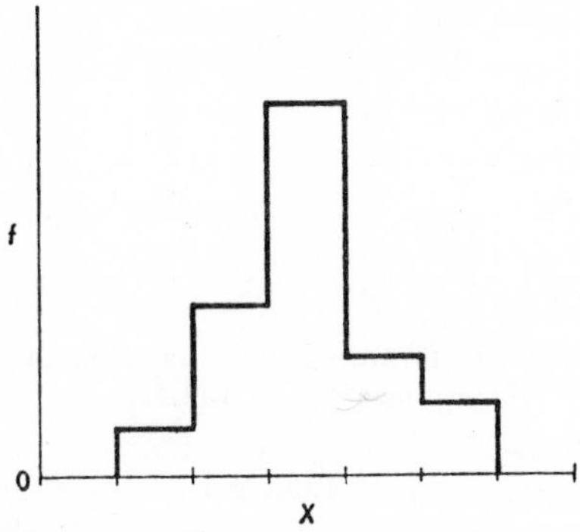


**Fig. 6.2** A five-interval histogram for a distribution completely described by the four descriptive moments: $M_x = 11$, $V_x = 2$, $S = 0.177$, and $K = 2.875$. N = 384.

only approximate; it is not complete, as would be a description based on nine moments. This approximate description might, however, be conceptualized in terms of a distribution which had fewer intervals, but could be described exactly by four moments. For example, the regularities of the original nine-interval distribution of Table 6.2, as these regularities are portrayed by the four descriptive moments, might be thought of as the characteristics of a five-interval distribution which is completely described by those moments and the zeroth moment or $N$. The original, nine-interval distribution of Table 6.2 has the following moments and total frequency: $M_x = 11$, $V_x = 2$, $S = 0.177$, $K = 2.875$, and $N = 384$. These values describe the original distribution inexactly, but they provide an exact description of the distribution represented by the histogram in Figure 6.2. One might, therefore, conceptualize this description of Figure 6.1 in terms of Figure 6.2.

## Measures on a Single Subject

In the preceding section, a distribution of test scores for 384 subjects was described through the use of moments. We shall consider next an example involving the description of 48 measures on a single subject.

A psychologist measured the reaction time of a single subject on presentation of an auditory stimulus on 48 trials. Measures were recorded in twenty-fifths of a second. The 48 measures are listed in Table 6.3. The frequency distribution is given in Table 6.4. The histogram is shown in Figure 6.3.

**Table 6.3**

**MEASURES OF REACTION TIME FOR A SINGLE SUBJECT**

| | | | | | |
|---|---|---|---|---|---|
| 4 | 5 | 5 | 4 | 6 | 6 |
| 3 | 4 | 4 | 5 | 5 | 5 |
| 7 | 7 | 5 | 6 | 4 | 4 |
| 5 | 5 | 7 | 6 | 5 | 5 |
| 4 | 4 | 5 | 7 | 6 | 5 |
| 6 | 4 | 4 | 4 | 5 | 7 |
| 4 | 5 | 5 | 6 | 4 | 4 |
| 5 | 6 | 5 | 5 | 4 | 4 |

Each observation is expressed in twenty-fifths of a second. Columns and rows have no classificatory significance; the arrangement is arbitrary.

**Table 6.4**

**A FREQUENCY DISTRIBUTION OF MEASURES OF REACTION TIME**

| $X$ | $f$ |
|---|---|
| 3 | 1 |
| 4 | 16 |
| 5 | 18 |
| 6 | 8 |
| 7 | 5 |

Original data given in Table 6.3. $X$ = Measure of reaction time in twenty-fifths of a second.

The four descriptive moments have been computed and have the following values:

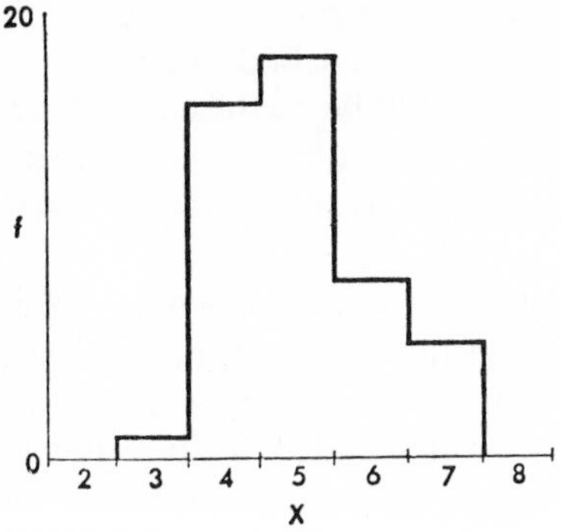


**Fig. 6.3** A histogram representing the frequency distribution of reaction time measures in Table 6.4. $M_x = 5$, $V_x = 1$, $S = 0.50$, and $K = 2.5$. $X$ = reaction time measured in twenty-fifths of a second.

$$M_x = 5,$$
$$V_x = 1,$$
$$S = 0.50,$$
$$K = 2.50.$$

It is not surprising that the distribution is positively skew, since one would expect the existence of a lower limit on reaction time, a limit imposed possibly by physiological and neurological factors.

## Some Issues in Description

In characterizing a single subject or a group of subjects, by presenting the mean, or in comparing one subject with another or one group with another by presenting the difference between two means, interest is often directed to one end of the scale or the other. The investigator may wish to point out that the individual or group is high or low on the scale, as the case may be. When he is making a comparison, he may wish to point out that one individual or one group is higher or lower than another individual or group. There are occasions, however, when interest is directed to the relation between the mean and some important reference point. For example, the measures might be positive and negative in value, representing deviations above and below some true value or known standard.

The choice of the mean as the only descriptive value to be presented is sometimes justified; sometimes, it is not. When the variation around the mean is judged to be the result of measurement errors or momentary and transitory fluctuations in response, as might well be the case in certain kinds of repeated measurements on a single subject, then computing a mean may be looked upon as eliminating error, that is, as removing variability which only obscures the true nature of the performance and which properly should be removed. An example would be establishing a threshold for visual acuity by repeated determinations under the same conditions. Variation in the values obtained might be considered error and might, therefore, be eliminated by computing a mean.

When individuals or groups are known to have approximately equal variances and higher moments, the presentation of means may be all that is required for a comparison. Since, under these conditions, the individuals or groups being compared would be alike in all respects save the one on which the comparison is to be made, the interpretation could be made straightforward and unambiguous. Any difference resulting from the comparison would be properly characterized as having to do with this single attribute as represented by mean values and with no other attributes.

In choosing the mean as a descriptive value over other values, it is possible, of course, to take an arbitrary position by saying that one's interest in the evaluation is defined as having to do with means. The inadequacy of this arbitrary position may be revealed, however, when an interpretation is made which implies the need for more information than is contained in the means. Here are two examples of inadequate interpretations resulting from the use of means alone.

1. Two men are tested repeatedly and then compared with respect to their aptitude for handling certain heavy construction equipment. One individual has a higher mean score than the other, thereby appearing to be the more skillful of the two, but further examination of the data reveals that this individual is much more varied in his performances than is the other and that some of his scores are low enough to imply serious consequences for his safety and the safety of others in the real-life situation. An intelligent choice between the two individuals could not be made without information as to the variability of their performances.

2. The freshman class of each of two large universities was administered a standard college admissions test. The two means were computed and compared. The report was circulated that the one class was superior to the other, thereby leaving the impression that the one university had a distinctly better freshman class than did the other. Further examination of the data would have revealed that the difference between the two means was very small when one considered the variability within each class. The overlap in the two distributions was quite large and, in the light of this fact, the small difference between means could reasonably be considered unimportant.

Before leaving the discussion of the mean, we should point out that the sum from which the mean is computed is often as useful as the mean itself in indicating the general magnitude of a set of measures. Means have the advantage over sums in that the former can be compared when the number of observations on which they are based varies. Sums can only be compared when the numbers of observations are equal, since a sum is directly a function of the number of values as well as their magnitude.

When variances may be unequal but means and the higher moments are equal, it is defensible to limit the comparison of individuals or groups to a comparison of variances. A larger variance indicates greater differences among the responses of an individual or the responses of a group than the differences for the other individual or group. It is interesting to note that, instead of variances, sums of squares of deviations might be used for comparison when $N$'s are equal. As was the case with means in relation to sums, variances can be compared when $N$'s are not equal whereas sums of squares of deviations cannot be compared.

In comparing individuals or groups with respect to both means and variances, a variety of interpretations is possible depending on the particular combination of values and the practical situation. When means are equal and variances are equal, or judged to be approximately so, the comparison offers no difficulties of interpretation. The conclusion that the individuals or the groups are alike is defensible unless there is some reason to believe that they differ with respect to higher moments. As has already been indicated, when means are unequal and variances as well as the higher moments are equal, it is reasonable to base one's interpretation on a comparison of means; when variances are unequal but means as well as the higher moments are equal, variances may be compared and interpreted. Values for means and variances may, on occasion, suggest that there is little or no overlap in the two sets of measures and that there is, consequently, a fairly substantial basis for the interpretation that one set of performances is superior to the other. The question of overlap can, of course, be answered much more conclusively by examination of the two frequency distributions or their histograms, and their overlap.

With certain combinations of unequal means and unequal variances, an interpretation which goes beyond the statement of the several values may be unwarranted. Students should be aware that only those interpretations whose appropriateness is obvious, or very nearly so, or which can be reduced to terms in which they become obvious and command assent, are worthwhile. When an interpretation cannot be stated so that its correctness is obvious, persisting in that interpretation only provokes unfruitful debate and argument.

## Test Construction

The descriptive moments are employed extensively in the construction and revision of psychological tests. A distribution of test scores can be given a partial description by computation of its mean, variance, index of skewness, and index of kurtosis. It is possible to express each of these moments in terms of certain characteristics of the items in the test so that it becomes theoretically possible to select items to produce a test whose score distribution will have the desired moments. What we are suggesting is that the distribution of test scores can be modified and determined through the selection of items for the test. On occasion we may wish to produce any one of a large number of distributions of varied form.

We may wish to produce a binomial distribution for which the number of score intervals is $(n + 1)$ and the frequencies are given by the successive terms in the expansion of $(1 + 1)^n$, where $2^n = N$. A distribution of this type is symmetrical and unimodal, with smaller frequencies in the tails than in the center. As $n$ becomes larger, the value of the index of kurtosis for the binomial distribution approaches three and the function approaches the normal curve, an important continuous function which will be discussed in some detail, later. Three examples of binomial distributions are given in Table 6.5.

**Table 6.5**

**EXAMPLES OF BINOMIAL DISTRIBUTIONS**

| $X$ | $f$ |
|---|---|
| $\binom{n = 2;}{N = 4}$ | |
| 0 | 1 |
| 1 | 2 |
| 2 | 1 |

| $X$ | $f$ |
|---|---|
| $\binom{n = 4;}{N = 16}$ | |
| 0 | 1 |
| 1 | 4 |
| 2 | 6 |
| 3 | 4 |
| 4 | 1 |

| $X$ | $f$ |
|---|---|
| $\binom{n = 10;}{N = 1{,}024}$ | |
| 0 | 1 |
| 1 | 10 |
| 2 | 45 |
| 3 | 120 |
| 4 | 210 |
| 5 | 252 |
| 6 | 210 |
| 7 | 120 |
| 8 | 45 |
| 9 | 10 |
| 10 | 1 |

It is conceivable that we might sometime wish to produce a test which distributed respondents uniformly, or approximately so, over the score intervals as in a rectangular distribution, or one which differentiated between two parts of the distribution. Table 6.6. gives two examples: a rectangular distribution and a distribution in which the upper 15 per cent of respondents is clearly differentiated from the lower 85 per cent.

In psychological testing, it is a common practice to assign a score of zero to the failing of a single test item and a score of one to the passing of a single item. Consequently, scores of a group of individuals on a single item may

**Table 6.6**

**DISTRIBUTIONS PROVIDING TWO KINDS OF DIFFERENTIATION**

| $X$ | $f$ ($N = 50$) | | $X$ | $f$ ($N = 48$) |
|---|---|---|---|---|
| 0 | 10 | | 0 | 3 |
| 1 | 10 | | 1 | 8 |
| 2 | 10 | | 2 | 30 |
| 3 | 10 | | 3 | 0 |
| 4 | 10 | | 4 | 7 |

vary, taking on values of zero and one. Two moments only, the zeroth and the first, are required to describe completely a distribution of item scores. An example of a distribution of item scores is given below.

| $I$ | $f$ |
|---|---|
| 0 | 60 |
| 1 | 40 |

In the example, $N = 100$ and the mean, $M_i = \Sigma fI/N = (60 \times 0 + 40 \times 1)/100 = 0.40$. Notice that $M_i$ turns out to be $p$, the proportion of subjects passing the item. $V_i$, the item variance, can be computed from the mean by the formula:

$$V_i = M_i(1 - M_i).$$

Of course, $S_i = \sqrt{V_i}$.

If we let $M_i = p =$ the proportion of subjects passing the item, and $(1 - M_i) = q =$ the proportion failing the item, then

$$V_i = pq$$

and

$$S_i = \sqrt{pq}.$$

## Describing Populations

As we shall see later on, in the discussion of statistical inference and sampling distributions, the four descriptive moments are also employed in characterizing what are called *population* distributions. Population distributions are the parent distributions from which random samples are obtained. We shall defer further comment on this topic.

## The Limitations of Description

Even when a complete description of the data at hand is possible, research psychologists are seldom satisfied with this kind of analysis and evaluation. In describing data, one ignores error but must admit that the original measures and any values computed from them were subject to uncontrolled influences or biases, which one would like to take account of, in a more rigorous fashion. If there was any selection of subjects, if the occasions of measurement were chosen in some arbitrary manner, if there were any environmental influences not intended by the investigator and not strictly controlled by him—and these conditions are almost inevitable in any psychological study—then the presence of error and the possibility of bias in the data can be taken for granted.

Because of the presence of biasing errors in his research, a psychologist prefers to analyze his data by methods which make it possible to estimate the magnitude of errors. It is conceivable that he could, on the basis of his own prior experience and the reported experience of others, make a judgment as to the size of errors and the possible size of the bias, and could reach conclusions which, even though the steps in the judging process cannot be made explicit, and even though the process is private and lacking in standardization, would be correct and could be defended in the scientific community. Nevertheless, there are far better methods and techniques available for estimating error and bias, and for making decisions about research data. We are referring to the procedures of statistical inference.

In saying that statistical inference provides the best methods for taking account of error and bias, we must add a crucial qualification. Statistical inference, when it is correctly and appropriately applied, is superior to description or any other kind of evaluation, but when it is incorrectly and inappropriately used, it is inferior to a descriptive evaluation which has been supplemented by good judgment. That is to say, there are situations in which statistical inference ought not to be used and in which the best choice for an evaluation is simple, straightforward description. The consequence of an indiscriminate application of statistical inference is a failure in the attempted inference and a misrepresentation on the part of the researcher. Far too frequently, students come to believe that making a choice between inference and description is no more than exercising a preference for a sophisticated method over an unsophisticated one. Their position implies that no knowledgeable researcher would ever limit himself to description. We cannot agree with a position which results, as it so clearly does in much of the published literature, in the misuse of statistical inference. There is no rigor in statistical inference when it is misapplied and, what is worse, the reader of a research report may be misled as to the nature and quality of the data behind the report by the presence of these elegant inferential techniques.

It is our viewpoint that research should be planned, whenever it is possible to do so, to permit an analysis and an evaluation by the very best methods, which are undoubtedly those of statistical inference. It is also our viewpoint that certain kinds of research data which are available to psychologists and educators are important and should be reported in their journals, but are suitable only for description plus an interpretation based on experienced judgment. To sum up, humble data deserve an unpretentious analysis and a simple, honest report.

Statistical inference will be discussed at length in Chapters 11, 12, 13, and 14.

# PRODUCT MOMENTS

## Syntactics 7

Product moments constitute a class of values which can be computed from two or more sets of numbers when the following conditions are satisfied: there are $N$ numbers in each set; there are $N$ classes or categories consisting of one number from each set. The product moments of interest to us here are those computed from *two* sets of *paired* numbers.

We let $X_i$ be the $i^{\text{th}}$ number in one set and $Y_i$ be the $i^{\text{th}}$ number in a second set, where $i = 1, 2, 3, \ldots, N$. The pairing of two values, one from each set, is indicated by the common subscript, $i$. The $(2N)$ numbers can be classified in the rectangular arrangement shown in Table 7.1. Each column in the Table represents a set of numbers; each row is a pair of values.

**Table 7.1**

**PAIRED VALUES OF X AND Y**

| | | Columns | |
|---|---|---|---|
| | | $X$ | $Y$ |
| | 1 | $X_1$ | $Y_1$ |
| | 2 | $X_2$ | $Y_2$ |
| | 3 | $X_3$ | $Y_3$ |
| Rows | . | . | . |
| | $i$ | $X_i$ | $Y_i$ |
| | . | . | . |
| | $N$ | $X_N$ | $Y_N$ |

To compute a product moment for $X$ and $Y$, we raise each $X$ value to some power and each $Y$ value to the same or a different power, obtain the product of the two powers for each pair of numbers, sum these $N$ products, and divide the sum by $N$. A particular product moment is identified by the two exponents employed, that is, by the power of $X$ and the power of $Y$. The general formula for a product moment of $X_i$ and $Y_i$—let us call it the $m^{\text{th}}$ and $n^{\text{th}}$ product moment—can be written as

$$\frac{\Sigma X_i^m Y_i^n}{N}.$$

It will be convenient to dispense with the subscripts and write simply

$$\frac{\Sigma X^m Y^n}{N}.$$

## The Product Moment of First Powers of $X$ and $Y$

We shall be concerned here with the special case of product moments in which $m = n = 1$. When both exponents are " one," the general formula becomes

$$\frac{\Sigma XY}{N}.$$

Computation of the product moment of first powers of $X$ and $Y$ involves summing the products of $X$ and $Y$, and dividing the resulting sum by $N$. It may be helpful to refer these operations to the paired values of $X$ and $Y$ in Table 7.1.

As a matter of convenience, we shall use the term " product moment " to refer to the special case involving first powers of two variables, but it should be understood that the term has a more general definition.

## The Product Moment of $x$ and $y$

Let us transform $X$ to $x$ by the formula, $x = X - M_x$, and $Y$ to $y$ by the formula, $y = Y - M_y$. The product moment of $x$ and $y$ is called the *covariance*. It will be represented by the symbol, $V_{xy}$. That is,

$$V_{xy} = \frac{\Sigma xy}{N}. \qquad (7.1)$$

## The Product Moment of $Z_x$ and $Z_y$

Consider $x$ transformed to $Z_x$ by the formula, $Z_x = x/S_x$, and $y$ transformed to $Z_y$ by the formula, $Z_y = y/S_y$. The product moment of $Z_x$ and $Z_y$ is an important value, the product-moment coefficient of correlation or $r_{xy}$. The formula is

$$r_{xy} = \frac{\Sigma Z_x Z_y}{N}. \tag{7.2}$$

The product moment of first powers of $X$ and $Y$ appears in certain computing formulas, but has no particularly important properties. The logical properties of the covariance, $V_{xy}$, and the coefficient of correlation, $r_{xy}$, will be discussed next. In this initial discussion, no attention will be given to properties having to do with error or random variation.

## Logical Properties of the Covariance

By definition,

$$V_{xy} = \frac{\Sigma xy}{N}.$$

The numerator can be written to make explicit the contributions of the four possible combinations of positive and negative deviations of $x$ and $y$. If we let

$x_+$ = positive $X$ deviation,
$x_-$ = negative $X$ deviation,
$y_+$ = positive $Y$ deviation,
$y_-$ = negative $Y$ deviation,
$f_{++}$ = frequency of pairings of positive deviations of $X$ and positive deviations of $Y$,
$f_{+-}$ = frequency of pairings of positive $X$ deviations and negative $Y$ deviations,
$f_{-+}$ = frequency of pairings of negative $X$ deviations and positive $Y$ deviations, and
$f_{--}$ = frequency of pairings of negative $X$ deviations and negative $Y$ deviations, then the numerator, $\Sigma xy$, in which there are $N$ terms, can be written

$$\Sigma xy = \Sigma x_+ y_+ + \Sigma x_+ y_- + \Sigma x_- y_+ + \Sigma x_- y_-.$$

The number of terms in each of the four sums on the right is equal to the frequency with which those particular pairings of deviations occur. The first and fourth sums on the right will always be positive or zero. The second and third sums will always be negative or zero. Thus $\Sigma xy$ and $V_{xy}$ will be positive when the absolute value of the sum of the positive products is greater than the absolute value of the sum of negative products; that is, when

$$|(\Sigma x_+ y_+ + \Sigma x_- y_-)| > |(\Sigma x_+ y_- + \Sigma x_- y_+)|.$$

$\Sigma xy$ and $V_{xy}$ will be negative when

$$|(\Sigma x_+y_+ + \Sigma x^-y^-)| < |(\Sigma x_+y_- + \Sigma x_-y_+)|,$$

that is, when the absolute value of the sum of positive products is less than the absolute value of the sum of negative products. $\Sigma xy$ and $V_{xy}$ will be zero when the absolute values of the two sums are equal, that is, when

$$|(\Sigma x_+y_+ + \Sigma x_-y_-)| = |(\Sigma x_+y_- + \Sigma x_-y_+)|.$$

Notice that the absolute values depend not only on the magnitudes of deviations, but on the frequency with which the pairings occur as well.

## Bivariate Frequency Distributions

Given two sets of paired numbers, $X_i$ and $Y_i$, the pairs can be doubly classified according to their values as shown in Table 7.2. The rectangular classification is called a bivariate frequency distribution.

**Table 7.2**

**A BIVARIATE FREQUENCY DISTRIBUTION**

| | $X_1$ | $X_2$ | $X_3$ | . | $X_k$ | . | $X_c$ |
|---|---|---|---|---|---|---|---|
| $Y_1$ | $f_{11}$ | $f_{12}$ | $f_{13}$ | . | $f_{1k}$ | . | $f_{10}$ |
| $Y_2$ | $f_{21}$ | $f_{22}$ | $f_{23}$ | . | $f_{2k}$ | . | $f_{2c}$ |
| $Y_3$ | $f_{31}$ | $f_{32}$ | $f_{33}$ | . | $f_{3k}$ | . | $f_{3c}$ |
| . | . | . | . | . | . | . | . |
| $Y_j$ | $f_{j1}$ | $f_{j2}$ | $f_{j3}$ | . | $f_{jk}$ | . | $f_{jc}$ |
| . | . | . | . | . | . | . | . |
| $Y_r$ | $f_{r1}$ | $f_{r2}$ | $f_{r3}$ | . | $f_{rk}$ | . | $f_{rc}$ |

A graphical representation of a bivariate frequency distribution might be achieved by means of a three-dimensional figure having two horizontal axes, one for $X$ and one for $Y$, and a single vertical axis for frequency. Instead of the two-dimensional rectangles employed in a histogram, we would have three-dimensional rectangular solids whose height would represent frequency.

Although three dimensions are implied by bivariate frequency distributions, it is usually more convenient to confine the figure to two dimensions. To do so, one takes the pair of $X$ and $Y$ values as the coordinates of a point in the two-dimensional space and plots all $N$ points. The points may form any one of a great variety of configurations, but are often scattered throughout the space, a circumstance which accounts for the designation of the figure as a *scatter plot*.

Original values of $X$ and $Y$ can be used for plotting purposes, but it is instructive to transform each variable to deviations and to plot pairs of deviations, $x$ and $y$. In Table 7.3 are 10 pairs of values of $x$ and $y$. These deviations have been used as coordinates for the plotting of the 10 points in Figure 7.1.

**Table 7.3**

**VALUES OF X AND Y TRANSFORMED TO DEVIATIONS**

(First Example)

| | | $x$ | $y$ |
|---|---|---|---|
| Pairs | 1 | 3 | 4 |
| | 2 | 1 | 0 |
| | 3 | 3 | 3 |
| | 4 | 2 | 1 |
| | 5 | −3 | −3 |
| | 6 | 0 | 2 |
| | 7 | −4 | −3 |
| | 8 | −3 | −2 |
| | 9 | −1 | −2 |
| | 10 | 2 | 0 |

The covariance, $V_{xy}$, is computed from the deviations in Table 7.3 by summing their products and dividing by $N = 10$. Thus

$$V_{xy} = \frac{\Sigma xy}{N} = \frac{52}{10} = 5.2.$$

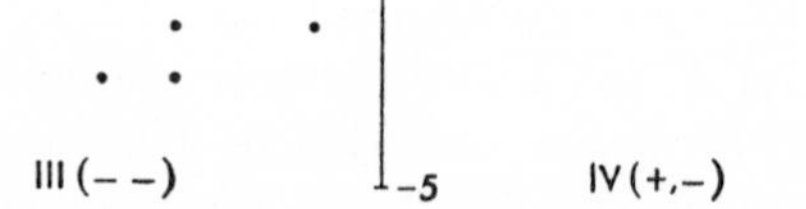

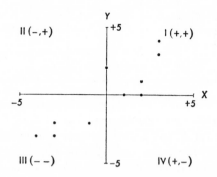


**Fig. 7.1** Plot of points whose coordinates are the paired deviations in Table 7.3.

The coordinate axes of Figure 7.1 define four quadrants which have been labeled in conventional fashion with Roman numerals. Beside each Roman numeral is the sign combination characteristic of the coordinates of points in that quadrant. In the preceding section on logical properties of the covariance, $f_{++}$, $f_{+-}$, $f_{-+}$, and $f_{--}$ were the frequencies for the four possible sign combinations arising from the pairing of $x$ and $y$ deviations. These four frequencies can be referred to Figure 7.1 and interpreted as the number of points plotted in each quadrant. In this particular example, there are no combinations of positive $x$'s and negative $y$'s, and no combinations of negative $x$'s and positive $y$'s. Consequently, although the points scatter somewhat, all of the points lie within or on the bounds of the first and third quadrants, and the trend is unmistakable.

Another bivariate distribution is given in Table 7.4 and the points for the paired deviations are plotted in Figure 7.2. Examination of the distribution will reveal that the $x$ and $y$ deviations of Table 7.4 are the same as those of Table 7.3. Although the deviations are the same, the pairing is different. Consequently, the covariance is different and the plot of Figure 7.2 is different from that of Figure 7.1. $V_{xy}$ for Table 7.4 is zero.

**Table 7.4**

**VALUES OF *X* AND *Y* TRANSFORMED TO DEVIATIONS**

(Second Example)

| | | $x$ | $y$ |
|---|---|---|---|
| Pairs | 1 | 3 | 0 |
| | 2 | 1 | 3 |
| | 3 | 3 | −2 |
| | 4 | 2 | 4 |
| | 5 | −3 | 2 |
| | 6 | 0 | −3 |
| | 7 | −4 | −2 |
| | 8 | −3 | 0 |
| | 9 | −1 | 1 |
| | 10 | 2 | −3 |

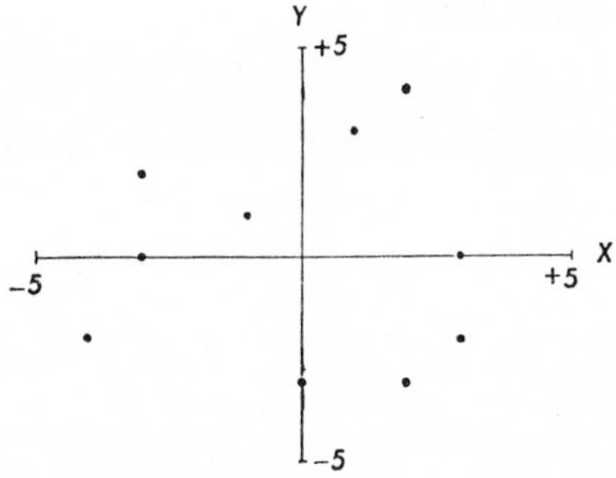


**Fig. 7.2** Plot of points whose coordinates are the paired deviations in Table 7.4.

## A Computing Formula for the Covariance

It is, of course, possible to compute $V_{xy}$ by transforming all the original $X$ and $Y$ values to deviations from the mean, obtaining the sum of the products, and dividing by $N$. It is usually more convenient, however, to employ a formula expressing $V_{xy}$ in terms of original values, $X$ and $Y$. The derivation of such a formula is given below.

By definition,

$$V_{xy} = \frac{\Sigma xy}{N}.$$

Consider the numerator, $\Sigma xy$. By definition,

$$\Sigma xy = \Sigma(X - M_x)(Y - M_y).$$

Multiplication of the two binomials yields

$$\Sigma xy = \Sigma(XY - M_x Y - M_y X + M_x M_y).$$

Simplification produces

$$\Sigma xy = \Sigma XY - M_x \Sigma Y - M_y \Sigma X + N M_x M_y.$$

Substitution of $\Sigma X/N$ for $M_x$ and $\Sigma Y/N$ for $M_y$ gives

$$\Sigma xy = \Sigma XY - \frac{\Sigma X \Sigma Y}{N} - \frac{\Sigma X \Sigma Y}{N} + \frac{\Sigma X \Sigma Y}{N}.$$

Combining terms on the right yields the final computing formula,

$$\Sigma xy = \Sigma XY - \frac{\Sigma X \Sigma Y}{N}. \tag{7.3}$$

Formula (7.3) is convenient for computing $\Sigma xy$, the sum of products of deviations, from which $V_{xy}$, the covariance, can be obtained by dividing by $N$.

## Prediction Coefficients

We shall define two *coefficients of prediction* or *prediction constants*, $b_{yx}$ and $b_{xy}$, as follows:

$$b_{yx} = \frac{V_{xy}}{V_x} \tag{7.4}$$

and

$$b_{xy} = \frac{V_{xy}}{V_y}. \tag{7.5}$$

These values are also called *regression coefficients*.

Notice that each prediction coefficient is the ratio of the covariance to one of the variances. A prediction coefficient is a constant value which can be employed, in an equation, to predict variability in one set of numbers from variability in the other.

The constant, $b_{yx}$, is derived, as follows: Given paired values of $x$ and $y$, we wish to find a value for the constant, $b_{yx}$, such that we can compute a value, $y'$, for each value of $x$ by the formula,

$$y' = b_{yx}x.$$

The computed value, $y'$, is called a *predicted deviation.* We wish to make the best possible predictions, that is, we intend that the values of $y'$ will, in some sense, be as nearly equal to the actual values of $y$ as we can manage to have them be. With some sets of paired numbers, the value of the desired constant might be determined quickly, by inspection, as in the example in Table 7.5, where it is apparent that, when $b_{yx} = 3$, the predicted values, $y' = 3x$, are identical with the actual values of $y$. That is, $y' = y$ in each prediction.

**Table 7.5**

**PAIRED DEVIATIONS WHICH PERMIT PERFECT PREDICTION**

| | | $x$ | $y$ | $y' = 3x$ |
|---|---|---|---|---|
| | 1 | −3 | −9 | −9 |
| | 2 | −1 | −3 | −3 |
| Pairs | 3 | 0 | 0 | 0 |
| | 4 | 2 | 6 | 6 |
| | 5 | 2 | 6 | 6 |

*Note* that $b_{yx} = 3$.

Usually the value of the constant cannot be chosen so easily and with such perfection in the predictions. Examine the paired values of Table 7.3 and also those of Table 7.4. It should be apparent that there is no value for $b_{yx}$ which will permit the computation of predicted values exactly equal to the given values of $y$. No matter what value is assigned to $b_{yx}$, there will be errors in the predictions. We shall define an error of prediction as the difference between $y$ and $y'$; that is, as

$$(y - y') = (y - b_{yx}x).$$

Keep in mind that we wish to choose a value for $b_{yx}$, which will make the " best " prediction. We have not said, exactly, in what sense prediction can be the best. A criterion commonly invoked to define " best " is that the sum of squares of errors of prediction shall be a minimum. In applying the criterion, it is the quantity,

$$\Sigma(y - y')^2 = \Sigma(y - b_{yx}x)^2,$$

which is to be minimized. The expression can be written as

$$\Sigma(y^2 - 2b_{yx}xy + b_{yx}^2x^2) = \Sigma y^2 - 2b_{yx}\Sigma xy + b_{yx}^2\Sigma x^2.$$

Reordering the three terms on the right gives

$$b_{yx}^2\Sigma x^2 - 2b_{yx}\Sigma xy + \Sigma y^2.$$

If we multiply the expression by $\Sigma x^2$ and then indicate division by $\Sigma x^2$, we obtain

$$\frac{b_{yx}^2(\Sigma x^2)^2 - 2b_{yx}\Sigma xy\Sigma x^2 + \Sigma x^2\Sigma y^2}{\Sigma x^2},$$

which has the same value as the original expression. We can also add and subtract the same quantity, $(\Sigma xy)^2$, in the numerator without changing the value of the expression. Adding and subtracting $(\Sigma xy)^2$ yields

$$\frac{b_{yx}^2(\Sigma x^2)^2 - 2b_{yx}\Sigma xy\Sigma x^2 + (\Sigma xy)^2 - (\Sigma xy)^2 + \Sigma x^2\Sigma y^2}{\Sigma x^2}.$$

The first three terms of the numerator constitute the square of a binomial and the numerator can be rewritten making the binomial explicit as indicated in

$$\frac{(b_{yx}\Sigma x^2 - \Sigma xy)^2 - (\Sigma xy)^2 + \Sigma x^2\Sigma y^2}{\Sigma x^2}.$$

Now the value of the function, as it depends on the choice of a value for $b_{yx}$, is determined by the expression,[1]

$$(b_{yx}\Sigma x^2 - \Sigma xy)^2,$$

which, since it is a square, must be equal to or greater than zero. The function will be a minimum when

$$(b_{yx}\Sigma x^2 - \Sigma xy)^2 = 0,$$

in which case

$$b_{yx}\Sigma x^2 - \Sigma xy = 0$$

and

$$b_{yx} = \frac{\Sigma xy}{\Sigma x^2}. \tag{7.6}$$

Thus it can be said that

$$\Sigma(y - b_{yx}x)^2 < \Sigma(y - ax)^2$$

when $a \neq b_{yx}$.

If we divide the numerator and the denominator of the fraction in formula (7.6) by $N$, we obtain

$$b_{yx} = \frac{\Sigma xy/N}{\Sigma x^2/N} = \frac{V_{xy}}{V_x}.$$

[1]The student may wish to review an earlier use of this method, in Chapter 4, to show that $\Sigma(X - M_x)^2 < \Sigma(X - a)^2$ where $a \neq M_x$.

Formula (7.6) is a convenient computing formula for $b_{yx}$ if one first obtains $\Sigma xy$ by formula (7.3),

$$\Sigma xy = \Sigma XY - \frac{\Sigma X \Sigma Y}{N},$$

and $\Sigma x^2$ by formula (4.2),

$$\Sigma x^2 = \Sigma X^2 - \frac{(\Sigma X)^2}{N}.$$

By similar procedures we could show that $b_{xy}$, the constant for predicting $x$ from $y$, is given by the formula,

$$b_{xy} = \frac{\Sigma xy}{\Sigma y^2}, \tag{7.7}$$

and that

$$b_{xy} = \frac{V_{xy}}{V_y}.$$

## Another Criterion for Prediction

Consider again the prediction of $y$ from $x$. We can write two covariances: one involving the actual deviations of $x$ and $y$,

$$V_{xy} = \frac{\Sigma xy}{N},$$

and another involving the actual deviations of $x$ and the predicted deviations,

$$V_{xy'} = \frac{\Sigma xy'}{N}.$$

If we impose the condition that these two covariances are to be equal, we can solve for $b_{yx}$ to satisfy this criterion. We write

$$V_{xy'} = V_{xy}$$

from which it follows that

$$\frac{\Sigma xy'}{N} = \frac{\Sigma xy}{N}$$

and

$$\Sigma xy' = \Sigma xy.$$

Since $y' = b_{yx}x$, we can substitute for $y'$ and obtain

$$\Sigma x b_{yx} x = \Sigma xy.$$

The constant, $b_{yx}$, can now be written before the summation sign and both sides of the equation can be divided by $\Sigma x^2$ to yield

$$b_{yx} = \frac{\Sigma xy}{\Sigma x^2}.$$

We observe that the same value for $b_{yx}$ satisfies both criteria. It makes the sum of squares of errors of prediction a minimum and the two covariances, $V_{xy}$ and $V_{xy'}$, equal.

## Summary

The prediction coefficient,

$$b_{yx} = \frac{\Sigma xy}{\Sigma x^2},$$

is the constant in the prediction equation,

$$y' = b_{yx}x.$$

We may substitute given or actual values of $x$ in the equation and compute predicted values of $y'$, which have the property that the sum of squares of errors of prediction,

$$\Sigma(y - y')^2,$$

is a minimum.

The equation for predicting $y$ from $x$ can be written in terms of original values, $X$ and $Y$. If we let $y' = Y' - M_y$ and $x = X - M_x$, then the equation,

$$y' = b_{yx}x,$$

becomes, after substitution for $y'$ and $x$,

$$Y' - M_y = b_{yx}(X - M_x).$$

Then

$$Y' = b_{yx}X - b_{yx}M_x + M_y$$

and

$$Y' = b_{yx}X + (M_y - b_{yx}M_x). \tag{7.8}$$

Notice that formula (7.8) has the form of the general linear equation,

$$Y = bX + a.$$

Attempting the prediction of $y$ from $x$ by means of a linear equation is equivalent to attempting the expression of $y$ as a linear function of $x$. The word " attempting " is used advisedly for the irregularities in the paired values often do not permit anything better than a crude approximation in the prediction or in the expression of the relation.

As regards $b_{xy}$, the constant in the equation,

$$x' = b_{xy}y,$$

substituting actual values of $y$ permits computation of predicted values of $x'$, which have the property that the sum of squares of errors in predicting $x$,

$$\Sigma(x - x')^2,$$

is a minimum. The equation can be written

$$X' = b_{xy}Y + (M_x - b_{xy}M_y). \tag{7.9}$$

Formula (7.9) represents an approximation in expressing the relation between $X$ and $Y$ as a linear function.

## Graphical Representation of Prediction Constants

After $b_{yx}$ has been computed for given paired values, the equation,

$$y' = b_{yx}x,$$

can be plotted by assigning two or more values to $x$, computing corresponding values of $y'$, and treating these pairs of values, $x$ and $y'$, as the coordinates of points located in the scatter-plot of $x$ and $y$. A straight line drawn through the points, $(x, y')$, is called the *best fitting line* or the *line of prediction.* The coordinates of any point on the line give a value of $x$ and the corresponding predicted value of $y'$. The line always passes through the point, $(x = 0, y' = 0)$.

The prediction coefficient, $b_{yx}$, is computed below for the paired values in Table 7.3.

$$\Sigma xy = 52,$$
$$\Sigma x^2 = 62,$$

and

$$b_{yx} = \frac{52}{62} = 0.84.$$

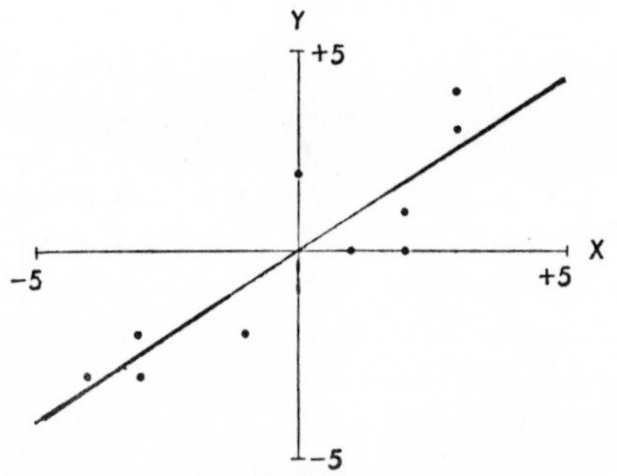


**Fig. 7.3** Plot of the best fitting straight line for the scatter-plot of Fig. 7.1.

We shall assign values of $-4$, 0, and $+4$ to $x$, and compute the corresponding values of $y'$ by the formula:

$$y' = b_{yx}x.$$

The three resulting pairs of values, $(x, y')$, are $(-4, -3.36)$, $(0, 0)$, and $(+4, +3.36)$. In Figure 7.3, these three points have been plotted in a reproduction of the scatter-plot of Figure 7.1, and a straight line has been drawn through the three points. Notice that the points of the original scatter-plot do not fall on the line. If one draws a vertical line from any point to the line of prediction, that distance represents an error of prediction,

$$(y - y') = (y - b_{yx}x).$$

The constant, $b_{yx} = 0.84$, is the slope of the line of prediction. It indicates the vertical change per unit horizontal change in the line of prediction. Notice that the slope has a positive sign.

The prediction coefficient, $b_{yx}$, for the values in Table 7.4 is

$$b_{yx} = \frac{\Sigma xy}{\Sigma x^2} = \frac{0}{62} = 0.$$

Since $b_{yx} = 0$, all predicted values, $y'$, will be equal to zero and the line of prediction will be a horizontal line coinciding with the $x$-axis. It is interesting to note that, since $b_{yx} = 0$,

$$(y - b_{yx}x) = y$$

and

$$\Sigma(y - b_{yx}x)^2 = \Sigma y^2,$$

that is, the sum of squares of errors of prediction is equal to the sum of squares for the actual values of $y$.

Another set of paired values is presented in Table 7.6 and plotted in

**Table 7.6**

**PAIRED VALUES OF $x$ AND $y$**

(Third Example)

| | | $x$ | $y$ |
|---|---|---|---|
| Pairs | 1 | $-1$ | 2 |
| | 2 | 0 | $-2$ |
| | 3 | 4 | $-3$ |
| | 4 | 2 | $-2$ |
| | 5 | $-3$ | 3 |
| | 6 | $-2$ | 2 |

Figure 7.4. The covariance is

$$V_{xy} = \frac{\Sigma xy}{N} = \frac{-31}{6} = -5.17.$$

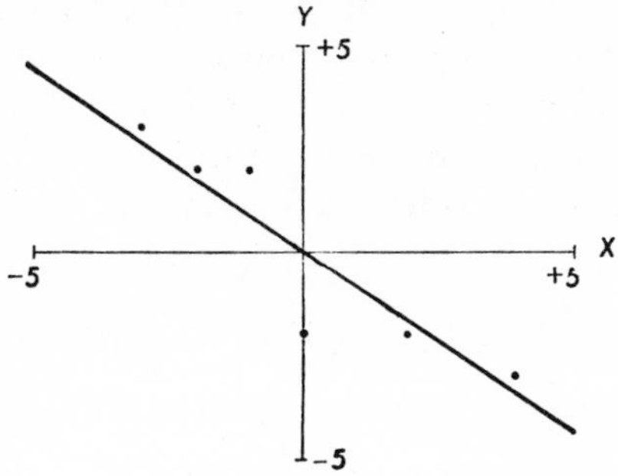


**Fig. 7.4** Scatter-plot and line of prediction for the paired values in Table 7.6.

The prediction coefficient, $b_{yx}$, is

$$b_{yx} = \frac{\Sigma xy}{\Sigma x^2} = \frac{-31}{34} = -0.91.$$

The line of prediction has been drawn in Figure 7.4 through the coordinates: (−4, +3.64), (0, 0), and (+4, −3.64).

Notice that the points of the scatter-plot of Figure 7.4 lie predominantly in the second and fourth quadrants, that the covariance is negative, and that the slope of the line of prediction is negative.

# Logical Properties of the Correlation Coefficient

By definition,

$$r_{xy} = \frac{\Sigma Z_x Z_y}{N},$$

the product moment of $Z_x$ and $Z_y$. If we substitute $x/S_x$ for $Z_x$ and $y/S_y$ for $Z_y$, we obtain

$$r_{xy} = \frac{\sum \frac{x}{S_x}\frac{y}{S_y}}{N},$$

which can be written as

$$r_{xy} = \frac{\Sigma xy}{NS_xS_y} = \frac{\Sigma xy/N}{S_xS_y}$$

and finally as

$$r_{xy} = \frac{V_{xy}}{\sqrt{V_xV_y}} \qquad (7.10)$$

Formula (7.10) gives the first property of the product-moment coefficient of correlation: The product-moment correlation coefficient is the ratio of the covariance to the square root of the product of the variances. Since the $n^{th}$ root of the product of $n$ numbers is the geometric mean of the $n$ numbers, $\sqrt{V_x V_y}$ is the geometric mean of the two variances.

Formula (7.10) can be rewritten, as follows:

$$r_{xy} = \frac{V_{xy}}{\sqrt{V_x V_y}} = \frac{\Sigma xy/N}{\sqrt{V_x V_y}} = \frac{\Sigma xy}{\sqrt{NV_x NV_y}}.$$

Since $NV_x = \Sigma x^2$ and $NV_y = \Sigma y^2$,

$$r_{xy} = \frac{\Sigma xy}{\sqrt{\Sigma x^2 \Sigma y^2}}. \tag{7.11}$$

Formula (7.11) is a convenient computing formula for $r_{xy}$. The sum of products in the numerator, $\Sigma xy$, can be obtained by formula (7.3). The two sums of squares in the denominator, $\Sigma x^2$ and $\Sigma y^2$, can be computed by formula (4.2).

Let us consider a second property of $r_{xy}$. Imagine that we had two sets of paired values, $X_i$ and $Y_i$, that we wished to predict variability in one set from variability in the other, but that we formulated the prediction problem in terms of $Z_x$ and $Z_y$ obtained by transformation from $X_i$ and $Y_i$. If we let

$Z_x$ = an actual $Z$-score for variable $X_i$;
$Z_y$ = an actual $Z$-score for variable $Y_i$;
$\beta_{yx}$ = the constant for predicting $Z_y$ from $Z_x$; and
$Z'_y$ = a predicted $Z$-score for variable $Y_i$;

then the prediction equation is

$$Z_y = \beta_{yx} Z_x.$$

An error of prediction is

$$(Z_y - Z'_y) = (Z_y - \beta_{yx} Z_x).$$

The sum of squares of errors of prediction, the quantity which we wish to minimize, is

$$\Sigma(Z_y - Z'_y)^2 = \Sigma(Z_y - \beta_{yx} Z_x)^2.$$

If we apply the least squares criterion in solving for the value of $\beta_{yx}$, just as we did in solving for $b_{yx}$, we find that

$$\beta_{yx} = \frac{\Sigma Z_x Z_y}{N} = r_{xy}.$$

Thus it turns out that the product-moment correlation coefficient is the prediction constant in the equation,

$$Z'_y = \beta_{yx} Z_x,$$

and also in the equation for predicting $Z_x$ from $Z_y$,

$$Z'_x = \beta_{xy} Z_y.$$

A third property of $r_{xy}$ is given by the equality,

$$r_{xy} = \sqrt{b_{yx}b_{xy}},$$

which can be expressed, as follows: The product-moment correlation coefficient is the geometric mean of the two prediction constants, $b_{yx}$ and $b_{xy}$. This relation can be proved by substituting $\Sigma xy/\Sigma x^2$ for $b_{yx}$ and $\Sigma xy/\Sigma y^2$ for $b_{xy}$ in the equality stated above. The substitutions yield

$$r_{xy} = \sqrt{\frac{\Sigma xy}{\Sigma x^2}\frac{\Sigma xy}{\Sigma y^2}} = \frac{\sqrt{(\Sigma xy)^2}}{\sqrt{\Sigma x^2 \Sigma y^2}} = \frac{\Sigma xy}{\sqrt{\Sigma x^2 \Sigma y^2}}$$

which is computing formula (7.11) derived earlier.

A fourth property of $r_{xy}$ is indicated in the following equality statement,

$$r_{xy} = r_{yy'} = r_{xx'},$$

which is to be interpreted, as follows: The coefficient, $r_{xy}$, is the correlation between actual and predicted values of either variable. Consider $r_{yy'}$. We can write

$$r_{yy'} = \frac{\Sigma yy'}{\sqrt{\Sigma y^2 \Sigma y'^2}}.$$

Substituting $b_{yx}x$ for $y'$ and simplifying yield

$$r_{yy'} = \frac{\Sigma y b_{yx}x}{\sqrt{\Sigma y^2 \Sigma b_{yx}^2 x^2}} = \frac{b_{yx}\Sigma xy}{\sqrt{b_{yx}^2 \Sigma x^2 \Sigma y^2}} = \frac{\Sigma xy}{\sqrt{\Sigma x^2 \Sigma y^2}} = r_{xy}.$$

A similar proof could be given showing that

$$r_{xx'} = r_{xy}.$$

The fifth property of $r_{xy}$ has to do with two standard deviations: the standard deviation of actual values and the standard deviation of predicted values for either variable. In discussing the prediction constants, $b_{yx}$ and $b_{xy}$, we defined $y'$ and $x'$ as predicted deviations. Predicted deviations exhibit variability which can be measured in terms of a variance and a standard deviation. The variance of predicted values of $y$ is

$$V_{y'} = \frac{\Sigma y'^2}{N}.$$

The standard deviation of values of $y'$ is, of course,

$$S_{y'} = \sqrt{V_{y'}}.$$

The product-moment correlation coefficient is the ratio of the standard deviation of predicted values to the standard deviation of actual values of $Y$. That is,

$$r_{xy} = \frac{S_{y'}}{S_y},$$

which statement can be proved, as follows:

$$r_{xy} = \frac{S_{y'}}{S_y} = \frac{\sqrt{V_{y'}}}{\sqrt{V_y}} = \frac{\sqrt{\Sigma y'^2/N}}{\sqrt{\Sigma y^2/N}} = \frac{\sqrt{\Sigma y'^2}}{\sqrt{\Sigma y^2}}.$$

Since $y' = b_{yx}x$, we can substitute and obtain

$$r_{xy} = \frac{\sqrt{\Sigma b_{yx}^2 x^2}}{\sqrt{\Sigma y^2}} = \frac{\sqrt{b_{yx}\Sigma x^2}}{\sqrt{\Sigma y^2}} = \frac{b_{yx}\sqrt{\Sigma x^2}}{\sqrt{\Sigma y^2}}.$$

Substitution of $\Sigma xy/\Sigma x^2$ for $b_{yx}$ gives

$$r_{xy} = \frac{\Sigma xy\sqrt{\Sigma x^2}}{\Sigma x^2\sqrt{\Sigma y^2}} = \frac{\Sigma xy}{\sqrt{\Sigma x^2 \Sigma y^2}}.$$

The proof is concluded. A similar proof could be given that

$$r_{xy} = \frac{S_{x'}}{S_x}.$$

The sixth property of $r_{xy}$ concerns the relation between $\Sigma y^2$ (the actual variability in $Y$), $\Sigma y'^2$ (the predicted variability), and $\Sigma(y - y')^2$ (the variability of errors of prediction). The first step in determining the relation involves writing the identity:

$$y = y' + (y - y').$$

Squaring both members of the identity gives

$$y^2 = y'^2 + 2y'(y - y') + (y - y')^2.$$

Summing $N$ terms, on the left and on the right, and simplifying produce

$$\Sigma y^2 = \Sigma y'^2 + \Sigma 2y'(y - y') + \Sigma(y - y')^2.$$

Examine the second sum on the right. We can remove the " 2 ", substitute $b_{yx}x$ for $y'$, and obtain

$$+\ 2\Sigma b_{yx}x(y - b_{yx}x)$$

which is equal to

$$2\Sigma b_{yx}xy - 2\Sigma b_{yx}^2 x^2 = 2b_{yx}\Sigma xy - 2b_{yx}^2\Sigma x^2.$$

The quantity, $\Sigma xy/\Sigma x^2$, can be substituted for $b_{yx}$, producing

$$\frac{2(\Sigma xy)^2}{\Sigma x^2} - \frac{2(\Sigma xy)^2\Sigma x^2}{(\Sigma x^2)^2} = \frac{2(\Sigma xy)^2}{\Sigma x^2} - \frac{2(\Sigma xy)^2}{\Sigma x^2} = 0.$$

Thus the second term in the right member of the original identity can be eliminated, yielding the equality:

$$\Sigma y^2 = \Sigma y'^2 + \Sigma(y - y')^2.$$

Dividing by $N$, we obtain

$$V_y = V_{y'} + V_{y-y'}.$$

Thus it can be said that the variability in $Y$ can be analyzed into two additive components: the variability which can be predicted from $X$ and the variability which cannot be predicted from $X$. A similar statement could be made regarding the prediction of $X$ from $Y$.

In the discussion of the fifth property of $r_{xy}$, it was shown that

$$r_{xy} = \frac{S_{y'}}{S_y} = \frac{\sqrt{V_{y'}}}{\sqrt{V_y}}.$$

Squaring reveals that

$$r_{xy}^2 = \frac{V_{y'}}{V_y}.$$

If we take the equality,

$$V_y = V_{y'} + V_{y-y'},$$

and divide both members by $V_y$, we obtain

$$1 = \frac{V_{y'}}{V_y} + \frac{V_{y-y'}}{V_y},$$

an equality statement which can be interpreted as saying that the whole of the variability in $Y$ consists of two proportions: the proportion that can be predicted and the proportion that cannot be predicted. Furthermore, since $r_{xy}^2 = V_{y'}/V_y$, we can say that the square of the product-moment correlation coefficient is the proportion of variability in one set of numbers that can be predicted by a linear equation from variability in another set. (The quantity, $r_{xy}^2$, is sometimes called the *coefficient of determination*.)

Since $r_{xy}^2 = V_{y'}/V_y$, we can write

$$1 = r_{xy}^2 + \frac{V_{y-y'}}{V_y}$$

and

$$1 - r_{xy}^2 = \frac{V_{y-y'}}{V_y}.$$

We observe that $(1 - r_{xy}^2)$ is the proportion of variability not predicted. (The value, $(1 - r_{xy}^2)$, is sometimes called the *coefficient of nondetermination*.)

The seventh property has to do with the limits of $r_{xy}$. It was shown above that

$$1 - r_{xy}^2 = \frac{V_{y-y'}}{V_y},$$

from which it follows that

$$V_{y-y'} = V_y(1 - r_{xy}^2).$$

Since variances are positive (or zero), $V_{y-y'}$, and $V_y$ will be positive (or zero). Then $(1 - r_{xy}^2)$ must be positive (or zero). That is,

$$(1 - r_{xy}^2) \geqq 0.$$

Then

$$1 \geqq r_{xy}^2$$

and

$$1 \geqq |r_{xy}|.$$

It follows that

$$-1 \leqq r_{xy} \leqq +1.$$

The product-moment coefficient of correlation is a dimensionless number having a value of $-1$, $+1$, or some value between these two limits.

The eighth property of $r_{xy}$ is that the coefficient can be expressed as a function of the pair differences, $X - Y$. Given two sets of numbers with a certain amount of variability in each set, then the smaller the variability of the pair differences, the greater $r_{xy}$ will be. The greater the variability of the pair differences, the smaller $r_{xy}$ will be, algebraically. The proof follows.

Consider the identities:

$$\Sigma(x - y)^2 = \Sigma(x^2 - 2xy + y^2)$$

and

$$\Sigma(x - y)^2 = \Sigma x^2 - 2\Sigma xy + \Sigma y^2.$$

Transposing terms in the second identity gives

$$2\Sigma xy = \Sigma x^2 + \Sigma y^2 - \Sigma(x - y)^2.$$

Dividing by two yields

$$\Sigma xy = \frac{\Sigma x^2 + \Sigma y^2 - \Sigma(x - y)^2}{2}.$$

Examine the quantity, $\Sigma(x - y)^2$, in the numerator. It is the sum of squares of differences between deviations. It can be shown to be equal to the sum of squares of deviations of differences, $X - Y$, from the mean difference, $\Sigma(X - Y)/N$.

By definition, $x = X - M_x$ and $y = Y - M_y$. Then

$$\Sigma(x - y)^2 = \Sigma[(X - M_x) - (Y - M_y)]^2 = \Sigma[(X - Y) - (M_x - M_y)]^2.$$

Let $(X - Y) = D$, a difference. Then the mean difference, $M_d$, can be expressed, as follows:

$$M_d = \frac{\Sigma D}{N} = \frac{\Sigma(X - Y)}{N} = \frac{\Sigma X - \Sigma Y}{N} = \frac{\Sigma X}{N} - \frac{\Sigma Y}{N} = M_x - M_y.$$

After substitution of $D$ for $(X - Y)$ and $M_d$ for $(M_x - M_y)$, we observe that

$$\Sigma(x - y)^2 = \Sigma(D - M_d)^2 = \Sigma d^2,$$

where $d = D - M_d$. Substituting $\Sigma d^2$ for $\Sigma(x - y)^2$ in

$$\Sigma xy = \frac{\Sigma x^2 + \Sigma y^2 - \Sigma(x - y)^2}{2}$$

yields

$$\Sigma xy = \frac{\Sigma x^2 + \Sigma y^2 - \Sigma d^2}{2}.$$

We divide by $N$ on both sides to obtain

$$V_{xy} = \frac{V_x + V_y - V_d}{2}.$$

Dividing on both sides by $\sqrt{V_x V_y}$ yields

$$\frac{V_{xy}}{\sqrt{V_x V_y}} = \frac{V_x + V_y - V_d}{2\sqrt{V_x V_y}} = r_{xy}.$$

If we consider $V_x$ and $V_y$ fixed and $V_d$ allowed to vary, then it is evident that $r_{xy}$ becomes smaller in algebraic value as $V_d$ becomes larger, and that $r_{xy}$ becomes larger in algebraic value as $V_d$ becomes smaller.

## Coding and Its Effect on Product-Moment Correlation

Consider first adding (or subtracting) a constant. Let

$$X' = X + a.$$

We wish to examine the relation between $r_{xy}$ and $r_{x'y}$. We can write

$$r_{x'y} = \frac{\Sigma x'y}{\sqrt{\Sigma x'^2 \Sigma y^2}}.$$

When $X' = X + a$, $M_{x'} = M_x + a$, and

$$x' = X' - M_{x'} = (X + a) - (M_x + a) = X - M_x = x.$$

Therefore,

$$r_{x'y} = \frac{\Sigma xy}{\sqrt{\Sigma x^2 \Sigma y^2}} = r_{xy}$$

and we conclude that adding (or subtracting) a constant does not affect the product-moment correlation.

Consider next coding by multiplying (or dividing) by a constant. Let

$$X' = aX.$$

Again we wish to examine the relation between $r_{xy}$ and $r_{x'y}$. We begin by writing

$$r_{x'y} = \frac{\Sigma x'y}{\sqrt{\Sigma x'^2 \Sigma y^2}}.$$

When $X' = aX$, $M_{x'} = aM_x$, and

$$x' = X' - M_{x'} = aX - aM_x = a(X - M_x) = ax.$$

Then

$$r_{x'y} = \frac{\Sigma axy}{\sqrt{\Sigma a^2x^2 \Sigma y^2}} = \frac{a\Sigma xy}{a\sqrt{\Sigma x^2 \Sigma y^2}} = \frac{\Sigma xy}{\sqrt{\Sigma x^2 \Sigma y^2}} = r_{xy}.$$

We conclude that multiplying (or dividing) by a constant does not affect the product-moment correlation.

## Special Formulas for Product-Moment Correlation

A special computing formula can be derived for the correlation between two variables, $X$ and $Y$, when one of them is dichotomous. Consider the formula,

$$r_{xy} = \frac{\Sigma xy}{\sqrt{\Sigma x^2 \Sigma y^2}}$$

where

$$\Sigma xy = \Sigma XY - \frac{\Sigma X \Sigma Y}{N},$$

$$\Sigma x^2 = \Sigma X^2 - \frac{(\Sigma X)^2}{N},$$

and

$$\Sigma y^2 = \Sigma Y^2 - \frac{(\Sigma Y)^2}{N}.$$

Let the variable $X$ have only two distinct values, $X_1$ and $X_2$. Let $Y$ have $r$ distinct values, $Y_1, Y_2, Y_3, \ldots, Y_j, \ldots$, and $Y_r$. Then the bivariate frequency distribution will have the form given in Table 7.7.

The derivation of a special formula is based on the fact that a dichotomous variable can always be coded to values of 0 and 1. Let $X_1'$ be the coded value of $X_1$ and $X_2'$, the coded value of $X_2$. The coding required involves subtraction of $X_1$ and division by $(X_2 - X_1)$, as follows:

$$X_1' = \frac{X_1 - X_1}{X_2 - X_1} = 0;$$

$$X_2' = \frac{X_2 - X_1}{X_2 - X_1} = 1.$$

After the two values of $X$ are coded, the bivariate distribution can still be represented by Table 7.7 except that $X_1$ should be changed to $X'_1 = 0$ and $X_2$ should be changed to $X'_2 = 1$.

**Table 7.7**

**A BIVARIATE FREQUENCY DISTRIBUTION WHEN ONE VARIABLE IS DICHOTOMOUS**

| | $X_1$ | $X_2$ | |
|---|---|---|---|
| $Y_1$ | $f_{11}$ | $f_{12}$ | |
| $Y_2$ | $f_{21}$ | $f_{22}$ | |
| $Y_3$ | $f_{31}$ | $f_{32}$ | |
| . | . | . | |
| $Y_j$ | $f_{j1}$ | $f_{j2}$ | |
| . | . | . | |
| $Y_r$ | $f_{r1}$ | $f_{r2}$ | |
| | $f_{.1}$ | $f_{.2}$ | Sums |

*Note:* $f_{.1} + f_{.2} = N$.

Recall that it was established earlier that the coding operations performed on the dichotomous variable have no effect on the correlation between the two variables. That is, $r_{x'y} = r_{xy}$. To see the changes which can be effected in the formula for the product-moment correlation between $X'$ and $Y$,

$$r_{x'y} = \frac{\Sigma x'y}{\sqrt{\Sigma x'^2 \Sigma y^2}},$$

let us examine the quantities: $\Sigma X'$, $\Sigma X'^2$, and $\Sigma X'Y$, in

$$\Sigma x'y = \Sigma X'Y - \frac{\Sigma X' \Sigma Y}{N}$$

and

$$\Sigma x'^2 = \Sigma X'^2 - \frac{(\Sigma X')^2}{N}.$$

Since $X'_1 = 0$ and $X'_2 = 1$, the sum of $X'$ will be simply the frequency of $X'_2$, which is the sum of the frequencies in the second column of Table 7.7. In symbols,

$$\sum_1^N X' = \sum_j^r f_{j1}X'_1 + \sum_j^r f_{j2}X'_2 = \sum_j^r f_{j1}(0) + \sum_j^r f_{j2}(1) = \sum_j^r f_{j2}.$$

Let us call the sum of the frequencies in the second column, $f_{.2}$. Then

$$\sum_{1}^{N} X' = \sum_{j}^{r} f_{j2} = f_{.2}.$$

The sum of squares of coded values, $\Sigma X'^2$, will also be equal to the frequency of $X'_2$, which is the sum of the frequencies in the second column of Table 7.7. Thus

$$\sum_{1}^{N} X'^2 = \sum_{j}^{r} f_{j1}X_1'^2 + \sum_{j}^{r} f_{j2}X_2'^2 = \sum_{j}^{r} f_{j1}(0)^2 + \sum_{j}^{r} f_{j2}(1)^2 = \sum_{j}^{r} f_{j2} = f_{.2}.$$

$\Sigma X'Y$, the sum of products of $X'$ and $Y$, is equal to the sum of the values of $Y$ which are paired with $X'_2$. This quantity—let us call it $Q_y$—is the sum of products of the frequencies in the second column and the $Y$ values along the left margin of Table 7.7. That is,

$$Q_y = \overset{N}{\Sigma} X'Y = \sum_{j}^{r} f_{j1}X'_1Y_j + \sum_{j}^{r} f_{j2}X'_2Y_j,$$

but $X'_1 = 0$ and $X'_2 = 1$, therefore

$$Q_y = \overset{N}{\Sigma} X'Y = \sum_{j}^{r} f_{j2}Y_j.$$

We can now substitute $f_{.2}$ for $\Sigma X'$, $f_{.2}$ for $\Sigma X'^2$, and $Q_y$ for $\Sigma X'Y$ in the formulas for $\Sigma x'y$ and $\Sigma x'^2$. After these substitutions, the formulas become

$$\Sigma x'y = Q_y - \frac{f_{.2}\Sigma Y}{N}$$

and

$$\Sigma x'^2 = f_{.2} - \frac{(f_{.2})^2}{N}.$$

Then the computing formula for $r_{x'y}$, when $X'$ is a dichotomous variable which has been coded to have values of 0 and 1, can be written

$$r_{x'y} = \frac{Q_y - f_{.2}\Sigma Y/N}{\sqrt{(f_{.2} - f_{.2}^2/N)\Sigma y^2}}$$

or as

$$r_{x'y} = \frac{NQ_y - f_{.2}\Sigma Y}{\sqrt{(N^2 f_{.2} - Nf_{.2}^2)\Sigma y^2}}. \tag{7.12}$$

To compute $r_{x'y}$ by means of formula (7.12), the following values are needed:

$\Sigma Y$ = the sum of the $N$ values of $Y$,
$\Sigma y^2$ = the sum of squares of deviations for the $N$ values of $Y$,
$Q_y$ = the sum of the $f_{.2}$ values of $Y$ which are paired with $X'_2$, and
$f_{.2}$ = the number of values of $X'_2$.

A product-moment coefficient of correlation computed by formula (7.12) is often called a *point-biserial* correlation coefficient.

There is also a special formula for the correlation between two variables, $X$ and $Y$, when both variables are dichotomous. Let the variable $X$ have two distinct values, $X_1$ and $X_2$. Let the variable $Y$ also have two distinct values, $Y_1$ and $Y_2$. Then the bivariate frequency distribution will have the form of distribution A in Table 7.8.

Both variables can be coded to values of zero and one as indicated below.

$X'_1 = (X_1 - X_1)/(X_2 - X_1) = 0$; $X'_2 = (X_2 - X_1)/(X_2 - X_1) = 1$.

$Y'_1 = (Y_1 - Y_1)/(Y_2 - Y_1) = 0$; $Y'_2 = (Y_2 - Y_1)/(Y_2 - Y_1) = 1$.

Since coding does not affect correlation, $r_{x'y'} = r_{xy}$.

After the coding of both variables, the bivariate frequency distribution can be represented as distribution B in Table 7.8.

To compute $r_{x'y'}$ we need the quantities: $\Sigma X'$, $\Sigma X'^2$, $\Sigma X'Y'$, $\Sigma Y'$, and $\Sigma Y'^2$. Since $X'_1 = 0$, $X'_2 = 1$, $Y'_1 = 0$, and $Y'_2 = 1$,

$\Sigma X' = f_{.1}X'_1 + f_{.2}X'_2 = f_{.1}(0) + f_{.2}(1) = f_{.2}$, the frequency of values of $X'_2$,

$\Sigma X'^2 = f_{.1}X'^2_1 + f_{.2}X'^2_2 = f_{.1}(0)^2 + f_{.2}(1)^2 = f_{.2}$,

$\Sigma Y' = f_{2.}$, and

$\Sigma Y'^2 = f_{2.}$.

**Table 7.8**

**A BIVARIATE FREQUENCY DISTRIBUTION FOR TWO DICHOTOMOUS VARIABLES**

A

| | $X_1$ | $X_2$ | |
|---|---|---|---|
| $Y_1$ | $f_{11}$ | $f_{12}$ | $f_{1.}$ |
| $Y_2$ | $f_{21}$ | $f_{22}$ | $f_{2.}$ |
| | $f_{.1}$ | $f_{.2}$ | |

$N = f_{11} + f_{12} + f_{21} + f_{22}$

B

| | $X'_1$ 0 | $X'_2$ 1 | |
|---|---|---|---|
| $Y'_1$ 0 | $f_{11}$ | $f_{12}$ | $f_{1.}$ |
| $Y'_2$ 1 | $f_{21}$ | $f_{22}$ | $f_{2.}$ |
| | $f_{.1}$ | $f_{.2}$ | |

$N = f_{11} + f_{12} + f_{21} + f_{22}$

Consider next the sum of products of the coded variables. We observe that $\Sigma X'Y' = f_{11}X'_1Y'_1 + f_{21}X'_1Y'_2 + f_{12}X'_2Y'_1 + f_{22}X'_2Y'_2 = 0 + 0 + 0 + f_{22}$. The sum of products, $\Sigma X'Y'$, is equal to $f_{22}$, the frequency with which values of $X'_2$ are paired with values of $Y'_2$.

Substituting $f_{.2}$ for $\Sigma X'$ and $\Sigma X'^2$, $f_{2.}$ for $\Sigma Y'$ and $\Sigma Y'^2$, and $f_{22}$ for $\Sigma X'Y'$ in the formulas for sums of squares and products of deviations yields

$$\Sigma x'^2 = f_{.2} - \frac{f_{.2}^2}{N},$$

$$\Sigma y'^2 = f_{2.} - \frac{f_{2.}^2}{N},$$

and

$$\Sigma x'y' = f_{22} - \frac{f_{.2}f_{2.}}{N}.$$

When these values are substituted in formula (7.11), the formula for $r_{x'y'}$ becomes

$$r_{x'y'} = \frac{f_{22} - f_{.2}f_{2.}/N}{\sqrt{(f_{.2} - f_{.2}^2/N)(f_{2.} - f_{2.}^2/N)}}$$

or

$$r_{x'y'} = \frac{Nf_{22} - f_{.2}f_{2.}}{\sqrt{(Nf_{.2} - f_{.2}^2)(Nf_{2.} - f_{2.}^2)}} \tag{7.13}$$

By substituting $(f_{11} + f_{12} + f_{21} + f_{22})$ for $N$, $(f_{12} + f_{22})$ for $f_{.2}$, and $(f_{21} + f_{22})$ for $f_{2.}$ in the numerator of formula (7.13), $(f_{.1} + f_{.2})$ for $N$ in the one factor and $(f_{1.} + f_{2.})$ for $N$ in the other factor of the denominator, and by carrying out the multiplication and combining of terms, we can obtain a computing formula,

$$r_{x'y'} = \frac{f_{11}f_{22} - f_{12}f_{21}}{\sqrt{f_{.1}f_{.2}f_{1.}f_{2.}}}. \tag{7.14}$$

Inspection of formula (7.14) will reveal that, when both variables are dichotomous, the computation of the product-moment correlation coefficient requires only the frequencies for the four possible combinations of values, $f_{11}$, $f_{22}$, $f_{12}$, and $f_{21}$, and the frequencies for each variable: $f_{.1}$ and $f_{.2}$ for $X$; $f_{1.}$ and $f_{2.}$ for $Y$.

## Other Transformations; Their Effect on Correlation

A nonlinear transformation of $X$, such as

$$Y = X^2,$$

may, on occasion, improve the prediction of a variable, $Z$. Given the paired values of $X$ and $Z$ shown in Table 7.9, the product-moment correlation coefficient, $r_{xz}$, is 0.985. If $X$ is transformed to $Y$ by the equation, $Y = X^2$, then the paired values for $Y$ and $Z$ are those shown in Table 7.10. The correlation coefficient, $r_{yz}$, is 1.00. The explanation of the improvement in prediction is that the relation between $X$ and $Z$ is not linear and the transformation has the effect of producing a linear relation between $Y$ and $Z$. That the

**Table 7.9**

**PAIRED VALUES ILLUSTRATING A NONLINEAR RELATION**

| | $X$ | $Z$ |
|---|---|---|
| 1 | .20 | .20 |
| 2 | .30 | .30 |
| 3 | .40 | .44 |
| 4 | .50 | .62 |
| 5 | .60 | .84 |
| 6 | .70 | 1.10 |
| 7 | .80 | 1.40 |

**Table 7.10**

**PAIRED VALUES FROM TABLE 7.9 AFTER TRANSFORMATION**

| | $Y = X^2$ | $Z$ |
|---|---|---|
| 1 | .04 | .20 |
| 2 | .09 | .30 |
| 3 | .16 | .44 |
| 4 | .25 | .62 |
| 5 | .36 | .84 |
| 6 | .49 | 1.10 |
| 7 | .64 | 1.40 |

trend in the scatter-plot is rectified is apparent from an inspection of the plot of $X$ and $Z$ before transformation and the plot of $Y$ and $Z$ after transformation. The plots are shown in Figure 7.5 and Figure 7.6.

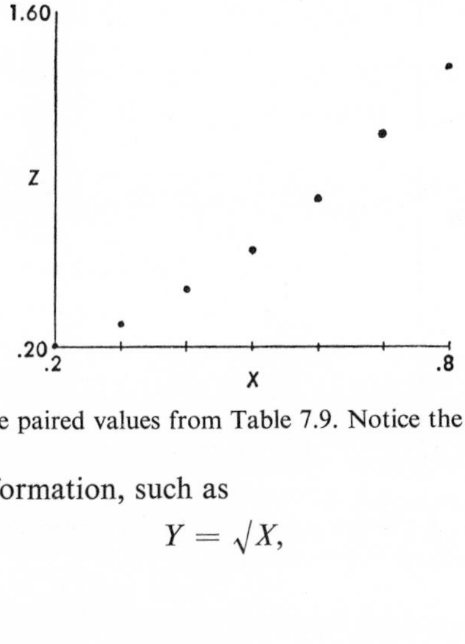


**Fig. 7.5** Plot of the paired values from Table 7.9. Notice the curvilinear trend.

A nonlinear transformation, such as

$$Y = \sqrt{X},$$

will also sometimes rectify a nonlinear trend and improve the prediction

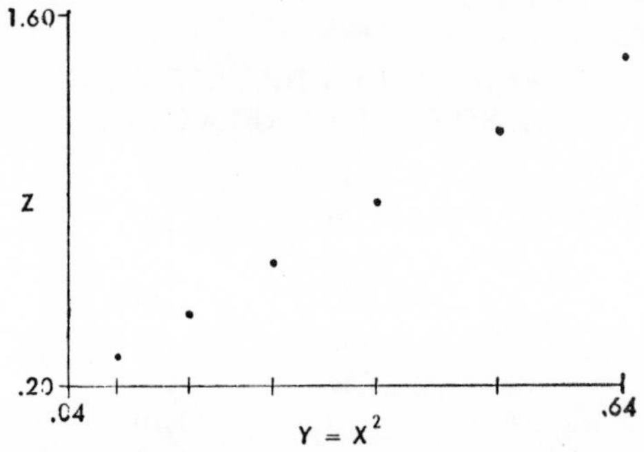


**Fig. 7.6** Plot of the paired values from Table 7.10. Notice the trend is linear after transformation.

involving a simple linear equation. Given the paired values of $W$ and $X$ shown in Table 7.11, for which the correlation is 0.987, the transformation,

**Table 7.11**

**PAIRED VALUES BEFORE AND AFTER TRANSFORMATION OF ONE VARIABLE**

| | $W$ | $X$ | $Y=\sqrt{X}$ |
|---|---|---|---|
| 1 | 2 | 4 | 2 |
| 2 | 3 | 9 | 3 |
| 3 | 4 | 16 | 4 |
| 4 | 5 | 25 | 5 |
| 5 | 6 | 36 | 6 |
| 6 | 7 | 49 | 7 |

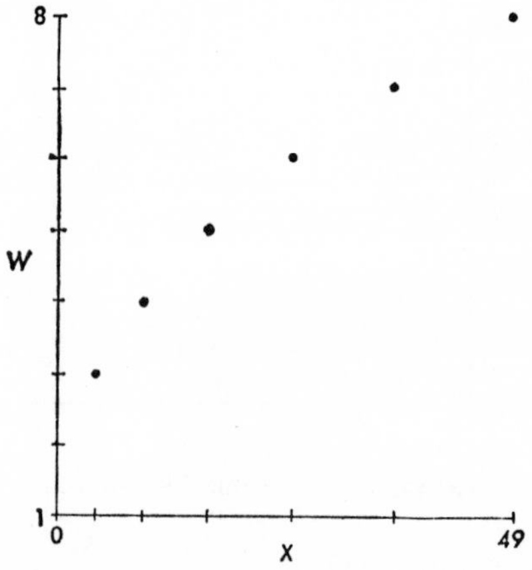


**Fig. 7.7** Plot of $W$ and $X$ for the values in Table 7.11. Note that the trend is curvilinear.

$Y = \sqrt{X}$, yields values of $Y$ which are linearly related to $W$ with a correlation of 1.00. Values of $Y$ are also shown in Table 7.11. The plot of $W$ and $X$ before transformation is given in Figure 7.7; the plot of $W$ and $Y$ after transformation of $X$ is given in Figure 7.8.

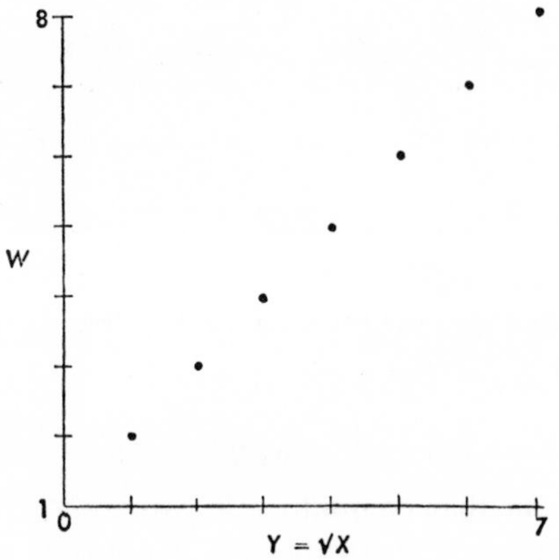


**Fig. 7.8** Plot of $W$ and $Y$ for the values in Table 7.11. Note that the trend, after transformation of $X$ to $Y$, is linear.

## Substitution of Ranks

A special formula can be used for computing the product-moment coefficient after ranks have been substituted for the original values of the two variables, $X$ and $Y$. Given $N$ pairs of values with $N$ distinct values of $X$ and $N$ distinct values of $Y$, the first $N$ ranks will be required in the substitution for each variable. It follows that the variance of the ranks will be the same for both variables and will be the variance of the first $N$ integers.

In Chapter 4 it was stated that the first $N$ integers have a mean of $(N + 1)/2$ and a variance of $(N^2 - 1)/12$. The formula for the product-moment coefficient computed from differences was earlier found to be

$$r_{xy} = \frac{V_x + V_y - V_d}{2\sqrt{V_x V_y}}.$$

If we let $R_{xy}$ be the product-moment correlation between two sets of ranks, $V_R$ be the variance of the first $N$ integers, and $V_D$ be the variance of the difference between paired ranks, then

$$R_{xy} = \frac{2V_R - V_D}{2V_R} = 1 - \frac{V_D}{2V_R} = 1 - \frac{V_D}{2(N^2 - 1)/12} = 1 - \frac{6V_D}{N^2 - 1}.$$

If we let $D = R_x - R_y$, a difference between the two ranks in any pair, then the variance of the differences, $V_D$, will be defined as

$$\frac{\Sigma(D - M_D)^2}{N}$$

where $M_D$ is the mean difference. Then

$$M_D = \frac{\Sigma(R_x - R_y)}{N} = \frac{\Sigma R_x}{N} - \frac{\Sigma R_y}{N} = 0,$$

since the means of the two sets of ranks are equal. $V_D$, which was defined above, now becomes

$$\frac{\Sigma D^2}{N}.$$

Substituting $\Sigma D^2/N$ for $V_D$ in the formula for $R_{xy}$ above yields the computing formula in final form:

$$R_{xy} = 1 - \frac{6\Sigma D^2}{N(N^2 - 1)}. \tag{7.15}$$

It should be apparent that computing $R_{xy}$ for two sets of paired ranks, when there are no ties in rank, is exactly equivalent to computing the product-moment correlation coefficient from the paired ranks. $R_{xy}$ is no more than a convenient computing formula for product-moment correlation involving two sets of ranks with no ties.

## Restrictions on the Magnitude of $r_{xy}$

If the number of distinct values of $X$ is not equal to the number of distinct values of $Y$, then

$$-1 < r_{xy} < +1$$

and $r_{xy}$ cannot equal either $-1$ or $+1$. That this restriction must obtain becomes apparent when one considers the predictions and their accuracy. If the number of distinct values of $X$ is less than the number of distinct values of $Y$, then predictions from at least one value of $X$ must be in error, for at least two different values of $Y$ will be associated with that one value of $X$.

An example is given in Table 7.12. The number of distinct values of $X$ is 4 and the number of distinct values of $Y$ is 8. Although a plot of the points would show a marked linear trend and although no other pairing of $X$ and $Y$ values could produce a larger covariance, the correlation is not perfect. It is, of course, very high, being 0.976.

When both variables are dichotomous, $r_{xy}$ can be computed from formula (7.14) which was derived earlier,

$$r_{x'y'} = \frac{f_{11}f_{22} - f_{12}f_{21}}{\sqrt{f_{.1}f_{.2}f_{1.}f_{2.}}}.$$

The magnitude of $r_{xy}$ is restricted when $f_{.2} \neq f_{2.}$, in which case it will also be true that $f_{.1} \neq f_{1.}$, since

$$f_{.1} + f_{.2} = N = f_{1.} + f_{2.} \,.$$

**Table 7.12**

**PAIRED VALUES ILLUSTRATING A RESTRICTION ON $r_{xy}$**

| | $X$ | $Y$ |
|---|---|---|
| 1 | 1 | 1 |
| 2 | 1 | 2 |
| 3 | 2 | 3 |
| 4 | 2 | 4 |
| 5 | 3 | 5 |
| 6 | 3 | 6 |
| 7 | 4 | 7 |
| 8 | 4 | 8 |

$r_{xy} = 0.976$

Examination of the 2 × 2 tables in Table 7.8 will reveal certain interesting relations among the frequencies. When $f_{.2} < f_{2.}$, then the largest value possible for $f_{22}$, the value which will make $r_{x'y'}$ as large a positive value as possible, is $f_{.2}$, in which case $f_{12} = 0$ and $f_{1.} = f_{11}$. Formula (7.14) can then be written

$$r_{x'y'} = \frac{f_{1.}f_{.2}}{\sqrt{f_{.1}f_{.2}f_{1.}f_{2.}}} = \frac{\sqrt{f_{1.}f_{.2}}}{\sqrt{f_{.1}f_{2.}}} \,. \tag{7.16}$$

Formula (7.16) gives the maximum positive value of $r_{x'y'}$ when $f_{.2} < f_{2.}$.

**Exercise 7.1**

1. Compute the 10 possible covariances for the five variables given in Exercise 4.1.

*Example:*

$\Sigma V \quad = 1{,}167$
$\Sigma W \quad = 1{,}723$
$\Sigma VW = 100{,}712$

$$\Sigma vw = \Sigma VW - \frac{\Sigma V \Sigma W}{N} = 100{,}712 - \frac{(1{,}167)(1{,}723)}{24} = 16{,}931.125.$$

$$V_{vw} = \frac{\Sigma vw}{N} = 705.46$$

2. Compute $b_{zv}$, $b_{zw}$, $b_{zx}$, and $b_{zy}$. Plot the equation for predicting $Z$ from each of the other four variables.

*Example:*

$V_{vw} = 705.46$ (from above)
$V_v \;= 835.40$ (from the example in Exercise 4.1)

$$b_{wv} = \frac{V_{vw}}{V_v} = \frac{705.46}{835.40} = 0.844$$

The prediction equation in terms of original values is

$$W' = b_{wv}V + (M_w - b_{wv}M_v).$$

The prediction equation written in terms of original values was derived earlier and presented as formula (7.8). To plot the equation, one selects three values for $V$ and computes the corresponding values of $W'$. The resulting three pairs of values are then used as the coordinates of three points which can be plotted. A straight line can then be drawn through the three points.

We shall use, as three values for $V$, 10, 50, and 90. $M_v$ is equal to 48.62; $M_w$ is equal to 71.79. The prediction constant, $b_{wv}$, is equal to 0.844. By substituting these values in the prediction equation given above, we obtain the three values of $W'$: 39.19, 72.95, and 106.71. Thus the coordinates of the three points are (10, 39.19), (50, 72.95), and (90, 106.71). The points have been plotted in Figure 7.9.

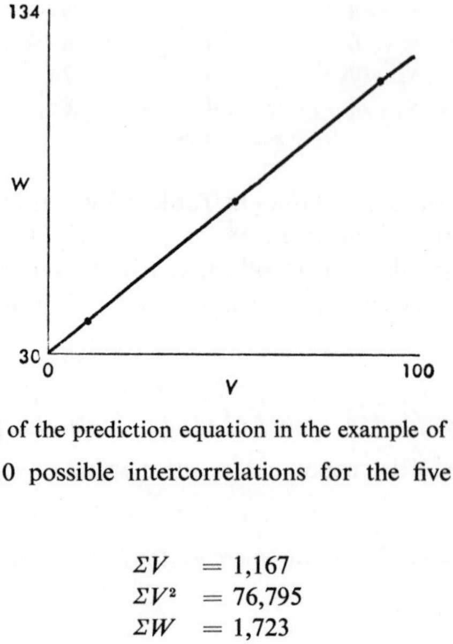


**Fig. 7.9** Plot of the prediction equation in the example of Exercise 7.1.

3. Compute the 10 possible intercorrelations for the five variables given in Exercise 4.1.

*Example:*

$$\Sigma V = 1{,}167$$
$$\Sigma V^2 = 76{,}795$$
$$\Sigma W = 1{,}723$$
$$\Sigma W^2 = 143{,}237$$
$$\Sigma VW = 100{,}712$$
$$N = 24$$

Formula (7.11) is

$$r_{vw} = \frac{\Sigma vw}{\sqrt{\Sigma v^2 \, \Sigma w^2}} \, .$$

$$\Sigma v^2 = \Sigma V^2 - \frac{(\Sigma V)^2}{N} = 76{,}795 - \frac{(1{,}167)^2}{24} = 20{,}049.62.$$

$$\Sigma w^2 = \Sigma W^2 - \frac{(\Sigma W)^2}{N} = 143{,}237 - \frac{(1{,}723)^2}{24} = 19{,}539.96.$$

$$\Sigma vw = \Sigma VW - \frac{\Sigma V \, \Sigma W}{N} = 100{,}712 - \frac{(1{,}167)(1{,}723)}{24} = 16{,}931.12.$$

Then

$$r_{vw} = \frac{16{,}931.12}{\sqrt{(20{,}049.62)(19{,}539.96)}} = 0.855.$$

# A Look Ahead

In the present chapter, product moments were introduced and certain special values, including the prediction constants and the coefficient of correlation, were discussed. The effects of coding on correlation were examined and some special formulas for product-moment coefficients were presented. Throughout the entire discussion of the present chapter, in every consideration of the predictive relation or of correlation, only two variables were involved. In Chapter 8, which is next, the methods of prediction and correlation are extended to more complex relations involving three or more variables. The three major topics of Chapter 8 are partial correlation, multiple prediction, and multiple correlation.

# PARTIAL AND MULTIPLE CORRELATION

## Syntactics 8

A partial correlation coefficient is the product-moment correlation of two sets of paired errors of prediction. For example, one might have the classification of values shown in Table 8.1 and carry out two sets of predictions: the

**Table 8.1**

**A CLASSIFICATION OF VALUES IN $N$ ROWS AND THREE COLUMNS**

| | | Columns | | |
|---|---|---|---|---|
| | | $W$ | $X$ | $Y$ |
| | 1 | $W_1$ | $X_1$ | $Y_1$ |
| | 2 | $W_2$ | $X_2$ | $Y_2$ |
| | 3 | $W_3$ | $X_3$ | $Y_3$ |
| Rows | . | . | . | . |
| | $i$ | $W_i$ | $X_i$ | $Y_i$ |
| | . | . | . | . |
| | $N$ | $W_N$ | $X_N$ | $Y_N$ |

prediction of $Y$ from $W$ and the prediction of $X$ from $W$. These two attempts at prediction would result in two sets of paired errors of prediction: the errors, $(y - b_{yw}w)$, in predicting $Y$ from $W$, and the errors, $(x - b_{xw}w)$, in predicting $X$ from $W$. There would be $N$ errors of prediction in each set and these errors would be paired because two predictions would be made from each of the $N$ values of $W$ and consequently two errors would be associated with each value of $W$. The two sets of paired errors of prediction could be arranged as indicated in Table 8.2.

We may now ask to what extent these two sets of errors are correlated. If we let $r_{xy.w}$ be the product-moment coefficient for the two sets of errors of prediction, $(x - b_{xw}w)$ and $(y - b_{yw}w)$, the desired product-moment formula can be written

$$r_{xy.w} = \frac{\Sigma(x - b_{xw}w)(y - b_{yw}w)}{\sqrt{\Sigma(x - b_{xw}w)^2 \Sigma(y - b_{yw}w)^2}} .$$

The possibility of expanding the expressions in this formula, simplifying them, and then substituting for the constants should be apparent. The

**Table 8.2**

**A CLASSIFICATION OF TWO SETS OF ERRORS OF PREDICTION**

Columns

| | | Errors in predicting $X$ from $W$ | Errors in predicting $Y$ from $W$ |
|---|---|---|---|
| | 1 | $(x_1 - b_{xw}w_1)$ | $(y_1 - b_{yw}w_1)$ |
| | 2 | $(x_2 - b_{xw}w_2)$ | $(y_2 - b_{yw}w_2)$ |
| | 3 | $(x_3 - b_{xw}w_3)$ | $(y_3 - b_{yw}w_3)$ |
| Rows | . | . | . |
| | $i$ | $(x_i - b_{xw}w_i)$ | $(y_i - b_{yw}w_i)$ |
| | . | . | . |
| | $N$ | $(x_N - b_{xw}w_N)$ | $(y_N - b_{yw}w_N)$ |

derivation will not be given here but the convenient computing formula which results is

$$r_{xy.w} = \frac{r_{xy} - r_{xw}r_{yw}}{\sqrt{(1 - r_{xw}^2)(1 - r_{yw}^2)}}\,. \tag{8.1}$$

Notice that formula (8.1) contains three values which must be computed from the original data: the three product-moment correlation coefficients for $X$, $Y$, and $W$.

The partial correlation coefficient, $r_{xy.w}$, is the product-moment correlation between variability in $X$ not predictable from $W$ and variability in $Y$ not predictable from $W$. The symbol, $r_{xy.w}$, is often read "the correlation between $X$ and $Y$ independent of $W$."

## Multiple Prediction with Deviations

The simple linear prediction equation,

$$y' = b_{yx}x,$$

which was discussed in Chapter 7, involves only two variables: $Y$, the variable to be predicted and $X$, the variable from which predictions are to be made. The prediction constant, $b_{yx}$, is given a value, $\Sigma xy/\Sigma x^2$, which can be computed from the paired values of $X$ and $Y$, and which minimizes the quantity,

$$\Sigma(y - y')^2 = \Sigma(y - b_{yx}x)^2,$$

the sum of squares of errors of prediction.

Linear prediction equations can be formulated for more than two variables.

Suppose we were given a classification of the variables, $X$, $Y$, and $Z$, similar to the classification of Table 8.1, and wished to predict $Z$ from $X$ and $Y$, simultaneously. For convenience, let us call $Z$ the *criterion* variable, and $X$ and $Y$ the *predictor* variables. The prediction equation can be written

$$z' = b_x x + b_y y$$

where

$z'$ = a predicted deviation for the criterion variable $Z$,
$x$ = an actual deviation for predictor variable $X$,
$y$ = an actual deviation for predictor variable $Y$,
$b_x$ = the prediction constant for variable $X$, and
$b_y$ = the prediction constant for variable $Y$.

Then an error of prediction can be expressed as

$$(z - z') = (z - b_x x - b_y y)$$

and the sum of squares of errors of prediction can be expressed as

$$\Sigma(z - z')^2 = \Sigma(z - b_x x - b_y y)^2,$$

which is the quantity we will want to minimize by a proper choice of values for $b_x$ and $b_y$. The procedure involved in applying the least squares criterion here is analogous to, but more complicated than, the procedure in two earlier applications: the demonstration that the sum of squares of deviations from the mean is smaller than the sum of squares of deviations from any other value, and the demonstration that the sum of squares of errors in predicting $Y$ from $X$, when $b_{yx} = \Sigma xy/\Sigma x^2$, is smaller than the sum of squares of errors when $b_{yx}$ takes any other value.

Steps in applying the least squares criterion in the multiple prediction problem will not be given here in complete detail. In general terms, they involve showing that the magnitude of the sum of squares of errors of prediction,

$$\Sigma(z - b_x x - b_y y)^2,$$

depends on $b_x$ as indicated by the expression,

$$(b_x \Sigma x^2 - \Sigma xz + b_y \Sigma xy)^2,$$

which must be equal to or greater than zero. The sum of squares of errors will have its smallest value when

$$(b_x \Sigma x^2 - \Sigma xz + b_y \Sigma xy)^2 = 0,$$

in which case

$$b_x \Sigma x^2 - \Sigma xz + b_y \Sigma xy = 0$$

or

$$b_x \Sigma x^2 + b_y \Sigma xy = \Sigma xz. \tag{8.2}$$

Note that equation (8.2) contains the unknown constant $b_y$ in addition to $b_x$ and that consequently it cannot be solved.

The sum of squares of errors of prediction can also be written in a form which reveals its dependence on $b_y$, as indicated in the expression,

$$(b_y \Sigma y^2 - \Sigma yz + b_x \Sigma xy)^2,$$

which quantity must be equal to or greater than zero. The sum of squares of errors will, of course, be as small as possible when

$$(b_y \Sigma y^2 - \Sigma yz + b_x \Sigma xy)^2 = 0,$$

in which case

$$b_y \Sigma y^2 - \Sigma yz + b_x \Sigma xy = 0$$

or

$$b_x \Sigma xy + b_y \Sigma y^2 = \Sigma yz. \tag{8.3}$$

Note that equation (8.3) contains two unknowns, $b_x$ and $b_y$, as does equation (8.2).

Equations (8.2) and (8.3) are rewritten below as (a) and (b).

$$\text{(a)} \qquad b_x \Sigma x^2 + b_y \Sigma xy = \Sigma xz$$

$$\text{(b)} \qquad b_x \Sigma xy + b_y \Sigma y^2 = \Sigma yz$$

The quantities, $\Sigma x^2$, $\Sigma y^2$, $\Sigma xy$, $\Sigma xz$, and $\Sigma yz$, are values which can be computed from the original classification of the three sets of numbers. To obtain values for the constants, $b_x$ and $b_y$, this set of simultaneous equations in two unknowns must be solved. The student should examine a similar solution which was presented in Chapter 3.

The equations can be solved by eliminating $b_y$ and obtaining a single equation containing one unknown, $b_x$. The steps in the elimination are, as follows:

Multiply (a) by $\Sigma y^2$ to obtain

$$\text{(c)} \qquad b_x \Sigma x^2 \Sigma y^2 + b_y \Sigma xy \Sigma y^2 = \Sigma xz \Sigma y^2.$$

Multiply (b) by $\Sigma xy$ to obtain

$$\text{(d)} \qquad b_x (\Sigma xy)^2 + b_y \Sigma xy \Sigma y^2 = \Sigma xy \Sigma yz.$$

Subtract (d) from (c) to eliminate $b_y$ and produce

$$\text{(e)} \qquad b_x \Sigma x^2 \Sigma y^2 - b_x (\Sigma xy)^2 = \Sigma xz \Sigma y^2 - \Sigma xy \Sigma yz.$$

Factor the left member of (e).

$$b_x [\Sigma x^2 \Sigma y^2 - (\Sigma xy)^2] = \Sigma xz \Sigma y^2 - \Sigma xy \Sigma yz.$$

Solve for $b_x$.

$$b_x = \frac{\Sigma xz \Sigma y^2 - \Sigma xy \Sigma yz}{\Sigma x^2 \Sigma y^2 - (\Sigma xy)^2} \tag{8.4}$$

Formula (8.4) can be written

$$b_x = \frac{V_{xz} V_y - V_{xy} V_{yz}}{V_x V_y - V_{xy}^2}.$$

By means of a similar set of operations applied to equations (8.2) and (8.3), one can eliminate $b_x$ and show that

$$b_y = \frac{\Sigma yz \Sigma x^2 - \Sigma xy \Sigma xz}{\Sigma x^2 \Sigma y^2 - (\Sigma xy)^2} \tag{8.5}$$

or

$$b_y = \frac{V_{yz}V_x - V_{xy}V_{xz}}{V_xV_y - V_{xy}^2}.$$

Formulas (8.4) and (8.5) can be used for the computation of $b_x$ and $b_y$, the two prediction constants in the linear prediction equation,

$$z' = b_x x + b_y y.$$

## Multiple Prediction with Standard Scores

Consider the prediction of $Z$ from $X$ and $Y$ by means of the linear equation,

$$Z_z' = \beta_x Z_x + \beta_y Z_y.$$

Notice that the three variables have been transformed to standard scores and that the two prediction constants are now denoted by the Greek letter $\beta$ (" beta ") with appropriate subscript.

An error of prediction is written

$$(Z_z - Z_z') = (Z_z - \beta_x Z_x - \beta_y Z_y).$$

The sum of squares of errors of prediction is

$$\Sigma(Z_z - Z_z')^2 = \Sigma(Z_z - \beta_x Z_x - \beta_y Z_y)^2,$$

which is the quantity to be minimized. Applying the least squares criterion for obtaining values of $\beta_x$ and $\beta_y$ yields the set of simultaneous equations:

$$\beta_x \Sigma Z_x^2 + \beta_y \Sigma Z_x Z_y = \Sigma Z_x Z_z,$$

$$\beta_x \Sigma Z_x Z_y + \beta_y \Sigma Z_y^2 = \Sigma Z_y Z_z.$$

Dividing each equation by $N$ yields

$$\beta_x \Sigma Z_x^2/N + \beta_y \Sigma Z_x Z_y/N = \Sigma Z_x Z_z/N,$$

$$\beta_x \Sigma Z_x Z_y/N + \beta_y \Sigma Z_y^2/N = \Sigma Z_y Z_z/N.$$

Since $\Sigma Z_x^2/N = \Sigma Z_y^2/N = 1$, $\Sigma Z_x Z_y/N = r_{xy}$, $\Sigma Z_x Z_z/N = r_{xz}$, and $\Sigma Z_y Z_z/N = r_{yz}$, substitutions can be made and the equations can be written

$$\beta_x \quad + \beta_y r_{xy} = r_{xz},$$

$$\beta_x r_{xy} + \beta_y = r_{yz}.$$

The equations contain two unknowns: the prediction constants, $\beta_x$ and $\beta_y$. The known values in the equations are the product-moment coefficients: $r_{xy}$, $r_{xz}$, and $r_{yz}$, which, in any specific problem, would either be given or be computed from the original classification of the three sets of numbers.

One might solve for $\beta_x$ and $\beta_y$ by the same methods employed in the preceding section in solving for $b_x$ and $b_y$. The procedure for eliminating one unknown, $\beta_y$, and the resulting formula for the other unknown, $\beta_x$, are presented below.

Given the equations,

(a) $\beta_x + \beta_y r_{xy} = r_{xz}$, and

(b) $\beta_x r_{xy} + \beta_y = r_{yz}$,

the steps in eliminating $\beta_y$ and solving for $\beta_x$ are, as follows:

Multiply (b) by $r_{xy}$ to obtain

(c) $\beta_x r_{xy}^2 + \beta_y r_{xy} = r_{xy} r_{yz}$.

Subtract (c) from (a) and obtain

(d) $\beta_x - \beta_x r_{xy}^2 = r_{xz} - r_{xy} r_{yz}$.

Solve for $\beta_x$ by factoring on the left and dividing by the coefficient of $\beta_x$.

$$\beta_x(1 - r_{xy}^2) = r_{xz} - r_{xy} r_{yz}$$

$$\beta_x = \frac{r_{xz} - r_{xy} r_{yz}}{1 - r_{xy}^2} . \tag{8.6}$$

By similar operations we could show that

$$\beta_y = \frac{r_{yz} - r_{xy} r_{xz}}{1 - r_{xy}^2} . \tag{8.7}$$

Where only two predictor variables are involved and, consequently, only two prediction constants must be determined, then the elimination of one of the unknowns by appropriate arithmetic operations which produce a single equation in one unknown is not at all difficult. When the prediction equation involves three or more predictor variables and a corresponding number of prediction constants, these fundamental arithmetic procedures, being quite lengthy and tedious, are not usually employed and formulas for the constants are not generally available. When there are three or more unknowns, two other computational approaches are widely used.

In the older approach, which is appropriate for computation involving desk calculators, the detailed computing instructions devised in 1878 by Doolittle, an engineer with the United States Coast and Geodetic Survey, or modifications of his instructions, are employed. These detailed instructions cleverly take advantage of certain standard features of the simultaneous equations in multiple prediction problems. Repetition in notation is reduced to a minimum and the entire computation is condensed and given a compact tabular representation. Even with the routinization and condensations of these procedures, however, the solution for three or more unknowns is still burdensome. For this reason, the Doolittle instructions will not be reproduced here. The student who may require these detailed computing instructions for a multiple prediction problem involving three or more unknowns can find them in a number of texts including those by Guilford (**1**, 406–409), Johnson (**2**, 330–337), and Kenney and Keeping (**3**, 298–301).

In the newer approach, one formulates the fundamental solution in terms of matrix algebra and has the burdensome computation done on an electronic computer. To demonstrate the nature of the computer solution, we shall employ the simple problem involving two predictors and two unknown prediction constants. The student should understand that one would not put such a simple problem on a computer. The simple problem is used here simply for convenience in introducing the student to matrix notation.

## Matrix Notation

For purposes of discussing matrix notation, we shall choose the problem of predicting variable $Z$ from variables $X$ and $Y$, when all three have been transformed to standard scores, in which case the simultaneous equations involve product-moment correlations and the unknowns, $\beta_x$ and $\beta_y$. The application of matrix notation to the equations involving sums of squares and products, and the unknowns, $b_x$ and $b_y$, follows the same principles.

The simultaneous equations for the problem in which $Z_z$ is to be predicted from $Z_x$ and $Z_y$ have been shown to be

$$\beta_x \quad + \beta_y r_{xy} = r_{xz}, \text{ and}$$

$$\beta_x r_{xy} + \beta_y \quad = r_{yz}.$$

It is interesting to note that these various quantities can be separated and displayed in tables or matrices. The coefficients of $\beta_x$ and $\beta_y$ can be displayed in a matrix of two rows and two columns, a $2 \times 2$ matrix. Notice that the unit values in the diagonal cells are actually coefficients of $\beta_x$ and $\beta_y$. The prediction constants themselves can be placed in a $2 \times 1$ matrix and the correlations with the criterion variable $Z$ can be arranged in a third matrix of two rows and one column. The three matrices are shown below.

$$\begin{bmatrix} 1 & r_{xy} \\ r_{xy} & 1 \end{bmatrix} \qquad \begin{bmatrix} \beta_x \\ \beta_y \end{bmatrix} \qquad \begin{bmatrix} r_{xz} \\ r_{yz} \end{bmatrix}$$

Assuming that you were given the task of computing the correlations, $r_{xz}$ and $r_{yz}$ in the $2 \times 1$ matrix on the right, from the information in the other two matrices, what system would you use? One system, which has now become a standard procedure, is to take the entries from the tables and compute with them according to the instructions contained in the equations themselves. In the first equation,

$$\beta_x + \beta_y r_{xy} = r_{xz},$$

one is instructed to obtain the product, $\beta_x(1)$, and the product, $\beta_y r_{xy}$, and to sum these products, obtaining $r_{xz}$. In the second equation,

$$\beta_x r_{xy} + \beta_y = r_{yz},$$

one is instructed to obtain the product, $\beta_x r_{xy}$, and the product, $\beta_y(1)$, and to sum these products, obtaining $r_{yz}$.

Examine closely how the operation of summing products relates to the arrangement of entries in the tables. It amounts to pairing entries in a row of the matrix at the left with entries in the column of the middle matrix, obtaining the product for each pair, and summing these products to obtain an entry in the matrix at the right. This operation of summing products of row and column entries in two tables is called *matrix multiplication.* The operation is expressible in a very compact notation when there is no need to show the tables themselves and the values they contain. For example, if we call the matrix on the left, $P$, because it contains the correlation between the two predictor variables, and call the matrix in the middle, $B$, for the $\beta$-values in it, and call the matrix on the right, $C$, because it contains the correlations with the criterion variable $Z$, then the entire matrix multiplication can be represented as

$$PB = C.$$

The student may find himself at a loss, initially, to react to such abbreviated notation. It may help to suggest that, in looking at $PB = C$, he should say to himself, "$P$ is a table of numbers; $B$ is another table of numbers. I am instructed to pair the entries in each row of $P$ with the entries in each column of $B$, to obtain the product for each pair of values, and to sum these products. Carrying out this operation for a given row of $P$ and a given column of $B$ yields a sum of products which is one entry in a cell of table $C$."

All that we have done, up to this point, is explore, in a limited fashion, the matrix representation and notation for the simultaneous equations in the multiple prediction problem. We have shown that, given $P$ and $B$, we could obtain $C$, but finding $C$ is not the problem we ordinarily have to solve. The problem we actually have can be stated, as follows: Given the correlations, $r_{xy}$, $r_{xz}$, and $r_{yz}$, compute $\beta_x$ and $\beta_y$. That is, given $P$ and $C$, find $B$.

Let us examine the two formulas for $\beta_x$ and $\beta_y$, (8.6) and (8.7), and we shall see that, when these two equations are written in matrix form, the computation does then correspond to the problem we are interested in solving. Formulas (8.6) and (8.7) are given below, with the direction of the equality statement reversed.

$$\frac{r_{xz} - r_{xy}r_{yz}}{1 - r_{xy}^2} = \beta_x$$

$$\frac{-r_{xy}r_{xz} + r_{yz}}{1 - r_{xy}^2} = \beta_y$$

The two equations can be rewritten with two terms in the left member of each, both terms having a common denominator, as follows:

$$\frac{r_{xz}}{1 - r_{xy}^2} - \frac{r_{xy}r_{yz}}{1 - r_{xy}^2} = \beta_x,$$

$$-\frac{r_{xy}r_{xz}}{1 - r_{xy}^2} + \frac{r_{yz}}{1 - r_{xy}^2} = \beta_y.$$

The equations can be rewritten again to emphasize the entries for matrix $C$, $r_{xz}$ and $r_{yz}$, and the coefficients of these values, as follows:

$$\left[\frac{1}{1 - r_{xy}^2}\right] r_{xz} + \left[-\frac{r_{xy}}{1 - r_{xy}^2}\right] r_{yz} = \beta_x,$$

$$\left[-\frac{r_{xy}}{1 - r_{xy}^2}\right] r_{xz} + \left[\frac{1}{1 - r_{xy}^2}\right] r_{yz} = \beta_y.$$

These various quantities can be tabulated in the three matrices below.

$$\begin{bmatrix} \dfrac{1}{1 - r_{xy}^2} & -\dfrac{r_{xy}}{1 - r_{xy}^2} \\ -\dfrac{r_{xy}}{1 - r_{xy}^2} & \dfrac{1}{1 - r_{xy}^2} \end{bmatrix} \qquad \begin{bmatrix} r_{xz} \\ r_{yz} \end{bmatrix} \qquad \begin{bmatrix} \beta_x \\ \beta_y \end{bmatrix}$$

Given values for the entries in the matrix at the left and values for $r_{xz}$ and $r_{yz}$, the entries in the middle matrix, we could, by the process of matrix multiplication, compute $\beta_x$ and $\beta_y$, entries in the matrix at the right. The student should be able to identify the middle matrix as $C$ and the matrix on the right as $B$. The matrix on the left is obviously not $P$, as originally written, but does contain entries which can be computed from entries in $P$. The matrix on the left is called the *inverse* of $P$ and is conventionally denoted by the symbol, $P^{-1}$. Computing entries for $P^{-1}$ from entries in $P$ is called *matrix inversion.*[1]

[1]Unfortunately the student will probably not be able to generalize the computation of an inverse matrix from the simple example given here to larger problems. A discussion making this generalization possible is beyond the scope of the present text. The interested student will find an excellent general treatment of matrix inversion in F. E. Hohn, *Elementary Matrix Algebra* (New York: Macmillan, 1958).

The problem of solving for values of $\beta_x$ and $\beta_y$ can now be expressed in the matrix notation:

$$P^{-1}C = B.$$

In reacting to this symbolism, it is suggested that the student say to himself, " $P^{-1}$ ($P$ inverse) is a table of values computed from $P$, another table containing the correlation between the two predictor variables. $C$ is a table containing the correlations between the predictor variables and the criterion variable. I am instructed to pair the entries in a row of $P^{-1}$ with the entries in a column of $C$, to multiply the paired entries, and to sum these products obtaining a prediction constant to be entered in table $B$."

All that has been said above about the simple prediction problem involving a total of three variables holds for larger problems. Given a specific problem, the student would construct two matrices: $P$, a table of intercorrelations for the predictor variables, with 1's as the diagonal entries, and $C$, a table of correlations between the predictor variables and the criterion. He would take matrix $P$ to a computation center and ask to have the matrix inverted.[2] The computer service would return to him the inverse matrix, $P^{-1}$. The student could then perform the matrix multiplication,

$$P^{-1}C = B,$$

to obtain the $\beta$'s.[3]

## The Prediction Equations

If one computes $\beta_x$ and $\beta_y$, and wishes to employ prediction equations involving $b_x$ and $b_y$, the latter values are obtainable by the formulas:

$$b_x = \beta_x \frac{S_z}{S_x} \qquad (8.8)$$

and

$$b_y = \beta_y \frac{S_z}{S_y} \qquad (8.9)$$

The prediction equation for deviations,

$$z' = b_x x + b_y y,$$

can be written in terms of original values, $X$, $Y$, and $Z$, as follows:

$$(Z' - M_z) = b_x(X - M_x) + b_y(Y - M_y)$$

[2]Programs for matrix inversion are found in all computer libraries.

[3]It is possible, of course, to have the entire computation done by the computer service. Entries in the original matrix of intercorrelations for all variables, a combination of $P$ and $C$, could be obtained on the computer, and the final multiplication, $P^{-1}C$, could also be done on the computer. The procedure was presented above, broken down into its major phases, so that the student's understanding and appreciation of it might be increased.

or

$$Z' = b_x X + b_y Y - b_x M_x - b_y M_y + M_z.$$

## Multiple Correlation

The coefficient of multiple correlation, $R_{z.xy}$, is defined as $r_{zz'}$, the product-moment correlation between actual values of $Z$ and predicted values of $Z$. It is computed by the formula,

$$R_{z.xy} = \sqrt{\beta_x r_{xz} + \beta_y r_{yz}} \tag{8.10}$$

$R^2_{z.xy}$ is the proportion of variability in $Z$ predicted, simultaneously, from variability in $X$ and $Y$. The quantity, $(1 - R^2_{z.xy})$, is the proportion of variability in $Z$ not predicted from variability in $X$ and $Y$.

**Exercise 8.1**

1. Compute $r_{xy.w}$, the correlation between $X$ and $Y$ independent of $W$ for each of the correlation matrices given in Table 8.3. Use formula (8.1). Study the pattern of relations in each problem.

*Example:*

Given $r_{wx} = -0.50$, $r_{wy} = 0.50$, and $r_{xy} = 0.40$, then

$$r_{xy \cdot w} = \frac{r_{xy} - r_{wx}r_{wy}}{\sqrt{(1 - r^2_{wx})(1 - r^2_{wy})}} = \frac{.40 - (-.50)(.50)}{\sqrt{(1 - .25)(1 - .25)}} = 0.867.$$

2. Compute the multiple correlation coefficient, $R_{z.xy}$, for the data in Exercise 4.1. Use formulas (8.6) and (8.7) to compute the beta-coefficients, $\beta_x$ and $\beta_y$, and formula (8.10) to compute $R_{z.xy}$.

**Table 8.3**

**FOUR 3 × 3 CORRELATION MATRICES**

| | W | X | Y |
|---|---|---|---|
| W | — | .60 | .60 |
| X | | — | .36 |
| Y | | | — |

| | W | X | Y |
|---|---|---|---|
| W | — | .60 | .60 |
| X | | — | .60 |
| Y | | | — |

| | W | X | Y |
|---|---|---|---|
| W | — | .60 | .60 |
| X | | — | .00 |
| Y | | | — |

| | W | X | Y |
|---|---|---|---|
| W | — | .00 | .70 |
| X | | — | .40 |
| Y | | | — |

Compute the coefficients, $b_x$ and $b_y$, by means of formulas (8.8) and (8.9), and write the prediction equation involving the original values of $X$, $Y$, and $Z$, with computed values of $b_x$ and $b_y$ substituted in the equation.

*Example:*

Given $r_{xy} = 0.30$, $r_{xz} = 0.50$, and $r_{yz} = 0.60$; $M_x = 50$, $M_y = 60$, and $M_z = 100$; $S_x = 10$, $S_y = 10$, and $S_z = 20$, then

$$\beta_x = \frac{r_{xz} - r_{xy}r_{yz}}{1 - r_{xy}^2} = \frac{.50 - (.30)(.60)}{1 - .30^2} = 0.352,$$

$$\beta_y = \frac{r_{yz} - r_{xy}r_{xz}}{1 - r_{xy}^2} = \frac{.60 - (.30)(.50)}{1 - .30^2} = 0.494,$$

and

$$R_{z.xy} = \sqrt{\beta_x r_{xz} + \beta_y r_{yz}} = \sqrt{(.352)(.50) + (.494)(.60)} = 0.687.$$

The coefficients, $b_x$ and $b_y$, are computed, as follows:

$$b_x = \beta_x \frac{S_z}{S_x} = .352 \frac{20}{10} = 0.704,$$

and

$$b_y = \beta_y \frac{S_z}{S_y} = .494 \frac{20}{10} = 0.988.$$

**Table 8.4**

**MATRICES *P*, $P^{-1}$, AND *C* FOR VARIABLES IN TABLE 4.4**

*P*

| | *V* | *W* | *X* | *Y* |
|---|---|---|---|---|
| *V* | 1.000000 | 0.855403 | −0.232095 | −0.186350 |
| *W* | 0.855403 | 1.000000 | −0.170851 | −0.084012 |
| *X* | −0.232095 | −0.170851 | 1.000000 | 0.833802 |
| *Y* | −0.186350 | −0.084012 | 0.833802 | 1.000000 |

*C*

| | *Z* |
|---|---|
| *V* | 0.600960 |
| *W* | 0.536812 |
| *X* | 0.637972 |
| *Y* | 0.537620 |

$P^{-1}$

| | | | |
|---|---|---|---|
| 3.924057 | −3.330181 | −0.113690 | 0.546268 |
| −3.330181 | 3.868282 | 0.441149 | −0.663428 |
| −0.113690 | 0.441149 | 3.398407 | −2.817722 |
| 0.546268 | −0.663428 | −2.817722 | 3.395484 |

The prediction equation can then be written

$$Z' = b_x X + b_y Y - b_x M_x - b_y M_y + M_z$$

or

$$Z' = 0.704X + 0.988\,Y - (0.704)(50) - (0.988)(60) + 100$$

or

$$Z' = 0.704X + 0.988\,Y + 5.52.$$

3. Table 8.4 gives the $P$ matrix for variables $V$, $W$, $X$, and $Y$ in Table 4.4 of Exercise 4.1, and $P^{-1}$, the inverse of $P$. Both matrices were computed on the IBM 650 in the Computation Center of Pennsylvania State University. (Actual computation time for the inverse was less than one minute.) Matrix $C$, which contains the correlations with the criterion variable, $Z$, is also given in Table 8.4.

Perform the matrix multiplication,

$$P^{-1}C = B,$$

to obtain the matrix of coefficients: $\beta_v$, $\beta_w$, $\beta_x$, and $\beta_y$. Also compute $R_{z.vwxy}$, $b_v$, $b_w$, $b_x$, and $b_y$. Write the prediction equation using $V$, $W$, $X$, and $Y$, and the computed coefficients. The formula for $R_{z.vwxy}$ is

$$R_{z.vwxy} = \sqrt{\beta_v r_{vz} + \beta_w r_{wz} + \beta_x r_{xz} + \beta_y r_{yz}}\,.$$

## REFERENCES


1. Guilford, J. P. *Fundamental Statistics in Psychology and Education* (New York: McGraw-Hill, 1956, 3rd ed.).
2. Johnson, P. O. *Statistical Methods in Research* (New York: Prentice-Hall, 1949).
3. Kenney, J. F., and Keeping, E. S. *Mathematics of Statistics* (New York: Van Nostrand, 1951, 2nd ed.).

# PRODUCT MOMENTS IN DESCRIPTION

## Pragmatics | 9

The following discussion of product moments, and the various *d*-statistics computed from product moments, will be based on their logical properties, as these were presented in Chapters 7 and 8, and will not entail consideration of the error to which these values might be subject in any formal statistical sense. As stated earlier, it is our purpose to make and maintain the distinction between description and inference, as clearly as it is possible to do so. The descriptive role of product moments and values computed from them will be outlined in the present chapter. The error properties of certain *i*-statistics computed from product moments will be presented in a later chapter.

Although there is no operation of more fundamental importance in research analysis than the specification of a relation between two variables by means of an equation, the wide applicability and general desirability of this operation are seldom understood and appreciated by the beginning student in his typical approach to a research problem. Too often he fails to see the potential and the relevance of a function and will, as a consequence, try to assess his results by some crude and inferior method of his own devising. The beginner's own inventions are usually inadequate not only because they fail to capitalize on functional relations, but also because they often result in the discarding of valuable information. Two common practices which betray a lack of appreciation of the role of functions and an inadequate conceptualization of research hypotheses are dichotomization of variables and selection of extreme values from distributions. One of the student's first goals in preparing to become a researcher should be the development of an understanding and appreciation of the great variety of situations in which obtaining a function to represent a relation is not only possible, but also highly desirable, as a way of handling data. The student researcher's first though in planning and evaluating research should be concerned with the possibility of a functional analysis.

It should be clearly understood, at the outset, that a function can be established for the relation between two variables only when the observations on the two variables are paired. How observations become paired seems obvious to the experienced researcher, but is often a mystery to the beginning student. Competence in research depends to a considerable extent on the capacity of the researcher to detect or discern possibilities for obtaining paired observations. Of course, this pairing of observations is never the result of arbitrary decisions and arrangements on the part of the investigator. The pairing is dictated by the observational procedures of the research. To be more specific, the investigator obtains a pair of observations, one on each variable, for a single object or a single event. Thus data consisting of $N$ pairs of observations imply the measurement of $N$ objects or events on each of two variables. Consequently, this pairing, being the circumstance which makes the expression of a relation between variables meaningful, must be held inviolate.

To convey to the student some idea of the wide range of situations which yield paired observations and therefore offer possibilities for functional interpretation and representation, we shall list below six broad classes or types of variables which are of continuing interest to the research psychologist. Under each class a few specific examples of variables are named but these are not described in detail with respect to the particular operations which are necessary and appropriate for obtaining the observations. For operational details, the student should consult texts or articles specializing in the particular area in question. The listing is not exhaustive and the types are not to be taken as absolutes in any sense. Following the list of classes with examples will be a number of combinations of variables which could be the basis for paired observations and which could conceivably give rise to a meaningful relation expressible by means of an equation. These are not meant to be suggestions for original research. They are simply intended to enlarge the student's concept of functional interpretation and representation.

Classes of variables of interest to the psychologist:

1. Data on the physical or social environment of a subject, including atmospheric temperature, barometric pressure, humidity, rainfall, altitude, latitude, longitude, population of community, size of school, size of family, family income, and per capita expenditure for education in the state.

2. Biographical data, including age, grade in school, amount of education, salary, number of years married, and number of children.

3. Body measurements, including height, weight, size of waist, and size of foot.

4. Food, nutrient, and drug consumption, including caloric intake, amount of carbohydrate, amount of protein, amount of fat, amount of vitamin A, amount of iron, drug dosage, number of cups of coffee, and number of glasses of water.

5. Series, including successive time periods, trials, and ordinal positions of successive events.

6. Behavioral measures, including

a. physical measures of responses or products, such as length of standing broad jump, distance of discus throw, weight lifted, time required to run 100 yards, latency of response, and area covered by a drawing;

b. physical measures of a stimulus under standard conditions for counting discrimination responses, including intensity of a tone, voltage of a light source, concentration of salt in solution, frequency of a tone, and wave length of a light source;

c. frequency counts of responses, including number of correct items, number of self-references, number of favorable statements endorsed, and number of " liked " activities;

d. judgments of response attributes, including rank given by an expert judge and average rating given by three observers;

e. measures of agreement between two sets of rankings of a number of items by a single individual.

To facilitate the outlining of possibilities for functional representation, we shall consistently refer to the two variables in each example as $X$ and $Y$, and shall use $N$ as the number of pairs of observations. In every case, the $2N$ observations could be displayed in a measurement matrix of $N$ rows and two columns as shown in Table 9.1 and could be represented graphically by means

**Table 9.1**

**GENERAL FORM OF A MEASUREMENT MATRIX FOR TWO VARIABLES**

| | | Variables | |
|---|---|---|---|
| | | $X$ | $Y$ |
| | 1 | $X_1$ | $Y_1$ |
| | 2 | $X_2$ | $Y_2$ |
| | 3 | $X_3$ | $Y_3$ |
| Pairs of Observations | . | . | . |
| | $i$ | $X_i$ | $Y_i$ |
| | . | . | . |
| | $N$ | $X_N$ | $Y_N$ |

of a scatter-plot as indicated, in general form, by Figure 9.1. The coordinates of any point in the scatter-plot are the pair of values: $X_i$ and $Y_i$. Graphically, the function relating $X$ and $Y$ will be a straight line or a curve of best fit for the points in Figure 9.1.

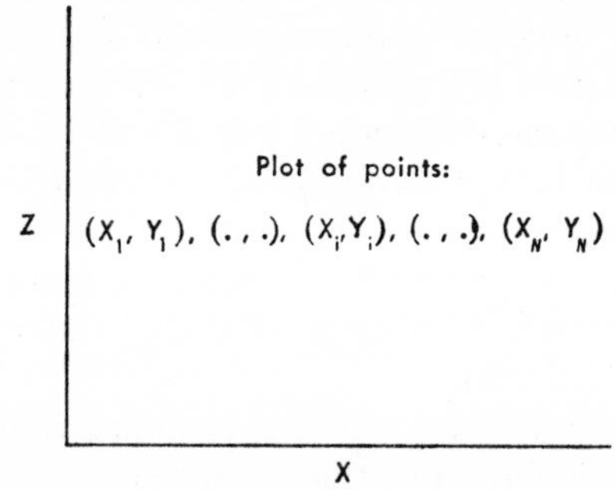


**Fig. 9.1** General form of the scatter-plot for the paired measures in Table 9.1. $N$ = number of pairs of measures = number of points in the plot.

Typical combinations of variables whose relation might be evaluated by a function given by a mathematical equation are listed below.

1. $X$ = score on a science interest inventory; $Y$ = score on a science achievement test; $N$ = number of subjects taking both tests.
2. $X$ = number of years of formal education; $Y$ = score on an attitude scale; $N$ = number of subjects with attitude scale scores.
3. $X$ = hours of food deprivation; $Y$ = amount of activity measured in terms of the number of revolutions of an activity wheel; $N$ = total number of successive hourly periods of food deprivation for a single animal.
4. $X$ = the ordinal number of a trial; $Y$ = latency of a running response; $N$ = total number of trials allowed an animal.
5. $X$ = the rank assigned to an item by a subject in describing his father; $Y$ = the rank assigned to an item by a subject in describing himself; $N$ = total number of items.
6. $X$ = physical measure of the intensity of a stimulus; $Y$ = percentage of correct discriminations; $N$ = number of different stimulus intensities used with a single subject.
7. $X$ = height of athlete; $Y$ = distance of running broad jump; $N$ = number of athletes.
8. $X$ = age of a salesman; $Y$ = amount of commissions for a specified period of time; $N$ = number of salesmen.
9. $X$ = a student's reported average amount of time per week spent in study; $Y$ = a student's final average college grade; $N$ = number of students.
10. $X$ = a teacher's rank in teaching ability as judged by an expert; $Y$ = a teacher's salary; $N$ = number of teachers.
11. $X$ = number of cups of coffee drunk daily; $Y$ = amount of carbohydrate in daily diet; $N$ = total number of days over which a single subject was observed.

## Choice of an Equation

In a strictly theoretical sense, the research psychologist has an unlimited number of different equations, from which he might choose one for the interpretation and representation of any given set of data. In practice, his choice most often turns out to be the simple, linear equation:

$$y' = b_{yx}x,$$

with its associated prediction constant, $b_{yx}$, and product-moment correlation coefficient, $r_{xy}$. The prediction constant, $b_{yx}$, indicates the number of units change in $Y$ per unit change in $X$ for the predicted values of $Y$, that is, change as a point moves along the best-fitting straight line. Since the units of many psychological variables are not invariant from one test or instrument to another, psychologists tend to report the results of their research more often in terms of the dimensionless correlation coefficients than in terms of prediction constants. Correlation coefficients are also employed when there is no desire on the part of the investigator to focus upon the direction of the predictive relation, as one does in using $b_{yx}$ or $b_{xy}$.

Three main factors appear to account for the psychologist's frequent choice of the simple, linear prediction equation. The first factor is the convenience which arises mainly from the ease and simplicity of computation, graphical representation, and communication. The second factor is the general background of experience in psychological research, known and shared by most active researchers, which background suggests that linear relations are to be found much more frequently than are nonlinear ones. The third factor is that linear functions are often useful approximations to a relation, even when the true function is curvilinear. It would be incorrect, of course, to convey the impression here that all relations between variables, in psychological research, are necessarily linear or even approximately so. The researcher must be ever on the alert for evidence of nonlinearity.[1] The student should also be reminded that, because all relations are not necessarily linear, it does not follow that they are necessarily curvilinear. The nature of the relation between two variables is, in the final analysis, a matter of empirical determination.

## Curvilinear Prediction and Correlation

There are countless nonlinear equations which might be employed for the

[1]The simplest check for nonlinearity is an inspection of the trend revealed in the scatterplot.

relation between two variables when a linear equation is not a sufficiently good approximation, but multiple-linear prediction and correlation, discussed in Chapter 8, provide the basis for a very practical solution to the problem.

To structure the problem and outline its solution, let us say that the criterion variable, $Z$, is to be predicted from predictor variable, $X$, but there is evidence of a moderate departure from linearity. To allow for this departure, we may manufacture a second predictor variable, $Y$, simply by transforming $X$, as indicated by the formula,

$$Y = X^2.$$

We now propose to predict $Z$ from $X$ and $Y$, simultaneously, in the equation,

$$z' = b_x x + b_y y,$$

where $x = (X - M_x) = X - \Sigma X/N$ and $y = (X^2 - M_{x^2}) = X^2 - \Sigma X^2/N$. Predicting from $X$ and $X^2$ amounts to solving for constants in a quadratic equation and to the fitting of a parabola to the scatter-plot for $Z$ and $X$. The $N \times 3$ measurement matrix is shown in Table 9.2. Keep in mind that

**Table 9.2**

**MEASUREMENT MATRIX FOR CURVILINEAR PREDICTION**

| | | $X$ | $Y = X^2$ | $Z$ |
|---|---|---|---|---|
| | 1 | $X_1$ | $Y_1$ | $Z_1$ |
| | 2 | $X_2$ | $Y_2$ | $Z_2$ |
| | 3 | $X_3$ | $Y_3$ | $Z_3$ |
| Subjects or | . | . | . | . |
| Occasions | $i$ | $X_i$ | $Y_i$ | $Z_i$ |
| | . | . | . | . |
| | $N$ | $X_N$ | $Y_N$ | $Z_N$ |

measures of $Z$ and $X$ are directly the result of observation, but that values in the $Y$ column are simply the computed squares of $X$. The form of the scatter-plot for $Z$ and $X$ is suggested in Figure 9.2. One could imagine a plot of points displaying a trend for which a curve, and not a straight line, gave the best fit. In the case of a simple, linear prediction equation, the coordinates of points lying on the line of prediction would be $(Z', X)$ where

$$Z' = b_x X - b_x M_x + M_z.$$

In the case of curvilinear prediction suggested above, the coordinates of points lying on the curve would be $(Z', X)$, where

$$Z' = b_x X + b_y Y - b_x M_x - b_y M_y + M_z.$$

Do not forget that $Y = X^2$ and $M_y = \Sigma X^2/N$.

To solve for $b_x$ and $b_y$, we might first solve for $\beta_x$ and $\beta_y$ following the procedures outlined in Chapter 8. The computation would involve obtaining

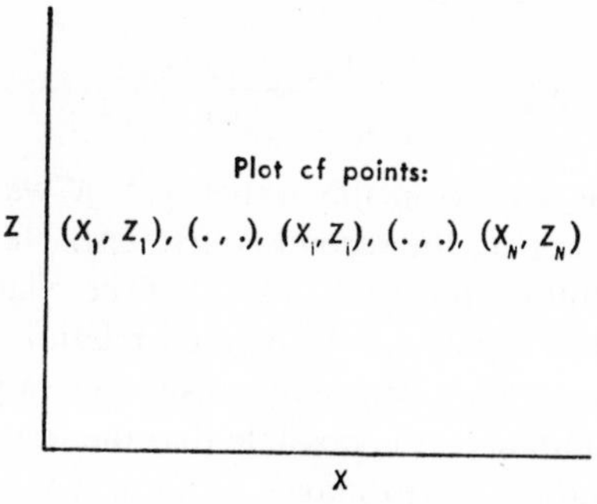


**Fig. 9.2** The scatter-plot for $Z$ and $X$ would consist of points whose coordinates were $(X_1, Z_1)$, $(.\ ,\ .)$, $(X_i, Z_i)$, $(.\ ,\ .)$, $(X_N, Z_N)$, pairs of values from Table 9.2. The coordinates of any point lying on the best-fitting curve would be $(X_i, Z_i')$ where

$$Z' = b_x X + b_y Y - b_x N_x - b_y M_y + M_z$$

and

$$Y = X^2.$$

$r_{xy}$, $r_{xz}$, $r_{yz}$, $S_x$, $S_y$, and $S_z$. Values could then be substituted in formulas (8.6) and (8.7) to compute $\beta_x$ and $\beta_y$. Formulas (8.8) and (8.9) could then be used to obtain $b_x$ and $b_y$. It would also be necessary to compute $M_x$, $M_y$, and $M_z$ for the prediction equation.

# Partial Correlation

Given two variables, $X$ and $Y$, having a substantial correlation, it is entirely possible that the observed relation between the two can be accounted for, wholly or in part, in terms of a third variable, $W$. That is to say, if we remove from $X$ and $Y$ the variability which can, in each case, be predicted from $W$, the correlation remaining between $X$ and $Y$ may be reduced considerably in magnitude. The correlation between $X$ and $Y$ after variability predicted from $W$ has been removed is the partial correlation coefficient, $r_{xy \cdot w}$. We have suggested that $r_{xy \cdot w}$ might be, but is not necessarily, less than $r_{xy}$. An example is given below.

An instructor of an introductory psychology class found the correlation between two successive course tests to be 0.70. He suspected that this consistency of performance in the course could be accounted for by differences in the ability of students as it could be measured by a precourse test of verbal ability. He decided to compute the partial correlation coefficient for the course tests independent of the verbal ability test as a check on his explanation of the consistency in performance. The correlation between the verbal ability test and the first course test was 0.30. The correlation between verbal ability and the second course test was 0.40. He used formula (8.1),

$$r_{xy\cdot w} = \frac{r_{xy} - r_{wx}r_{wy}}{\sqrt{(1 - r_{wx}^2)(1 - r_{wy}^2)}},$$

where variable $W$ was scores on the verbal test, $X$ was scores on the first course test, and $Y$ scores on the second course test. He obtained a value of 0.66 for $r_{xy\cdot w}$. The result supported his idea that the relation between the two course tests was, in part, accounted for by their relations with the verbal test, but indicated that a fairly high degree of consistency in performance existed, independent of verbal ability. It is possible that the test of verbal ability was a poor predictor of course performance because it was a poor measure of verbal ability, but it is also possible that other factors such as differences in motivation and interest accounted for the consistent differences among students.

## Practical Prediction for Selection

Prediction equations are used widely in industry, education, government, and the military for the selection of personnel. The general procedure in a selection program involves the following steps: (1) choosing a criterion variable and one or more predictor variables; (2) measuring applicants or candidates on the predictor variable(s); (3) evaluating their performances on the criterion; (4) doing the computation required in establishing the prediction equation; (5) testing a new group of applicants or candidates on the predictors only; (6) applying the equation to the new group to predict its performances on the criterion; and (7) selecting applicants or candidates from the new group on the basis of their predicted criterion scores.

The criterion variable is usually a measure of achievement, proficiency, or productivity. The measure may be a grade, a test score, an index of some sort, or a rating by a supervisor. A predictor variable is usually a test score or a personal history item. Sometimes a single predictor variable is satisfactory, but often two or more predictors prove to be better than one. Seldom is there an advantage in having more than five predictors. The criterion measure may be obtained at the same time as the predictor variables, but it is often obtained later.

There is a major problem in this selection procedure. Notice that the prediction equation is established on one group and applied to another for prediction purposes. Data for the original group consist of measures on the predictor variables and the criterion variable. From these data, the constants for the prediction equation can be computed. Data for the new group consist only of measures on the predictors. The criterion performance of an individual in the new group is predicted by substituting his predictor score(s) in the equation. One of the uncertainties as to the success of practical prediction relates to the question of whether or not the equation applies to the new group. Judging from experience accumulated by psychologists, there is little doubt that it is sometimes applicable or appropriate, being more so on some occasions than on others. The appropriateness of the equation for the new group depends on the response similarity of that group to the original one on which the equation was developed.

Another problem having to do with the appropriateness of the equation arises from the selection which may have taken place in the original group. Very seldom does an industry, an educational institution, or a government agency employ or accept any and all applicants. In practice there is almost always some screening and some rejecting. It is evident then that the prediction equation is established on a group which has gone through selection. The new group, to which the equation is applied, however, is usually an unselected group. Ideally, the equation would be established on an unselected group. The effect of this departure from the ideal can be expected to be a reduction in the accuracy of prediction.

## Test Construction

Product-moment correlation has important applications in the work of constructing and revising psychological tests, scales, inventories, and questionnaires. The reliability and the validity of the psychologist's measures are often expressed in terms of product-moment coefficients. Item analysis and item selection procedures also involve extensive applications of product-moment correlation.

Determining reliability is the psychologist's way of assessing reproducibility. There are three methods in common usage. The psychologist may administer a test on two different occasions to the same group of subjects. The correlation between the first administration and the second is a measure of *test-retest* reliability. Having administered a test on one occasion to a group of subjects, he may divide the test into two halves. A score is determined for each subject on each half. The correlation of one half with the other is a measure of *split-half* reliability. Finally, he may construct two equivalent or parallel forms of a test and administer both forms to the same group of subjects. The correlation of one form with the other is a measure of *equivalent-forms* reliability.

It can be shown that a coefficient of reliability compares interindividual differences with intraindividual differences. If we express an individual's standing on a test as a deviation from the mean of his group, then his average standing for two administrations can be computed by adding the two deviations and dividing the sum by two. Differences among these average standings for the individuals in a group might be called interindividual differences. If we measure the variability of the individual's two standings around his average standing and combine these measures for all subjects, the result might be called a measure of intraindividual differences. When intraindividual differences are small, one can say that the measures are reproducible. When intraindividual differences are large, the measures are lacking in reproducibility. Of course, these differences are " small " or " large " relative to some standard. In expressing reliability by means of a correlation coefficient, the psychologist compares the two kinds of differences.[2] Thus intraindividual differences are small or large by comparison with interindividual differences. Small, when the reliability coefficient is large. Large, when the reliability coefficient is small.

Validity has a number of different meanings for the psychologist. Here we shall use the term to refer to concurrent validity and predictive validity, both of which are often assessed by correlating a predictor variable and a criterion variable. Concurrent validity involves criterion measures obtained at the same time as the predictor measures. Predictive validity involves criterion measures obtained some time after the predictor measures. Computing the product-moment coefficient of correlation for a test and a criterion is the most common method of demonstrating the predictiveness of the test.

The student should review the discussion of the functional approach to confirmation in Chapter 5 and integrate that discussion with the comments on reliability and validity made above.

Many psychological tests and scales consist of items which are scored as dichotomous variables. Subjects' responses to an item can be classified into two categories, such as correct and incorrect, favorable and unfavorable, affirmative and negative, true and false, and so on. An individual's responses in one category are counted while those in the other category are not counted. Thus an individual's score is often simply a frequency count of items. It is possible to treat scores for a given item as a dichotomous variable and to correlate them with scores for another item, with scores on the test containing the item, and with measures on some criterion. The complex of issues surrounding item selection based on these correlations is beyond the scope of the present text. We would like only to point out that formula (7.12) could be employed to advantage in computing an item-test correlation or an item-criterion correlation, and that formula (7.13) could be used to compute the correlation between two items.

[2]The logical property of product-moment correlation, which supports this interpretation, is given in Chapter 10.

## Closing Comment

In the frequent practical use of prediction equations and in the common listing of correlation coefficients in research reports, there are implicit two fundamental notions which deserve considerable emphasis in the training of students. The first is that prediction and correlation actually constitute a functional interpretation of relations among variables. The concept of a function is central to the entire development. The second notion is that functional interpretation through prediction and correlation involves the fitting of lines and curves to data which often display much irregularity. Even though the irregularity makes fitting necessary, the function concept is still there. It is fundamental.

# THE ANALYSIS OF VARIABILITY

## Syntactics | 10

Classification procedures play an important part in statistical analysis. Two kinds of classifications can be distinguished. One kind, the frequency classification, includes univariate frequency distributions and bivariate frequency distributions, which have been discussed in earlier chapters. In a univariate frequency distribution, a set of numbers is represented by categories which correspond to intervals on a quantitative scale and by frequencies which indicate how many numbers in the set fall into each category on the scale. In a bivariate frequency distribution, two sets of paired numbers are represented by categories on two scales and by frequencies which indicate how many pairs of numbers are in each possible combination of categories, one from each scale. Later, frequency classifications in which the categories are qualitatively distinguishable will be considered.

The second kind of classification does not require the use of frequencies. Numbers in a set are classified according to the categories to which they belong. The categories are sometimes designated qualitatively, sometimes quantitatively. In either case, the variability of the numbers can be analyzed into components. Classifications of this second kind vary in complexity. We shall consider only two, fairly simple classifications and the analysis of variability appropriate to each one.

## Classification by Columns

Numbers in a set can be classified into subsets and the variability of the entire set can be analyzed into two components.

Let

$n$ = number of values per subset, a constant;
$c$ = number of subsets;
$N = cn$ = total number of values in the set;
$Y_{ik}$ = the $i^{\text{th}}$ value in the $k^{\text{th}}$ subset.

If we let a subset be indicated by a column in a rectangular arrangement of the $N$ numbers, the general form of the arrangement is that of Table 10.1.

**Table 10.1**

**NUMBERS CLASSIFIED BY COLUMNS**

Columns

| 1 | 2 | 3 | . | $k$ | . | $c$ |
|---|---|---|---|---|---|---|
| $Y_{11}$ | $Y_{12}$ | $Y_{13}$ | . | $Y_{1k}$ | . | $Y_{1c}$ |
| $Y_{21}$ | $Y_{22}$ | $Y_{23}$ | . | $Y_{2k}$ | . | $Y_{2c}$ |
| $Y_{31}$ | $Y_{32}$ | $Y_{33}$ | . | $Y_{3k}$ | . | $Y_{3c}$ |
| . | . | . | . | . | . | . |
| $Y_{i1}$ | $Y_{i2}$ | $Y_{i3}$ | . | $Y_{ik}$ | . | $Y_{ic}$ |
| . | . | . | . | . | . | . |
| $Y_{n1}$ | $Y_{n2}$ | $Y_{n3}$ | . | $Y_{nk}$ | . | $Y_{nc}$ |

*Note:* There are no rows in the table and the numbers are not, therefore, classified by rows.

The sum of the $n$ values in the $k^{\text{th}}$ subset or column can be written

$$\sum_{i}^{n} Y_{ik}.$$

Notiee that the index, $i$, governs the summation, which involves terms from "1" to "$n$" within any column.

$\bar{Y}_{.k}$, the mean of the $n$ numbers in the $k^{\text{th}}$ column, is given by the formula,

$$\bar{Y}_{.k} = \frac{\sum_{i}^{n} Y_{ik}}{n}.$$

The sum of all $N$ values can be written as the sum of the $c$ column sums,

$$\sum_{k}^{c} \sum_{i}^{n} Y_{ik}.$$

The purpose of the double subscript should now be apparent. The index, $i$, governs the inner sum which is restricted to the values within a column. The index, $k$, governs the outer sum which contains the $c$ column sums. It will be convenient to use the symbol $T_y$ for the sum of all $N$ values. Then

$$T_y = \text{the sum of the column sums} = \sum_{k}^{c} \sum_{i}^{n} Y_{ik}.$$

Let $M_y$ = the mean of all $N$ values. Then

$$M_y = \frac{T_y}{N}.$$

The variability in the entire set of numbers can be measured by the sum of squares of deviations from the total mean, $M_y$. The sum of squares of deviations from $M_y$ for the numbers in the $k^{\text{th}}$ column is

$$\sum_i^n (Y_{ik} - M_y)^2.$$

Then the sum of squares of deviations from $M_y$ for all $c$ columns is

$$\sum_k^c \sum_i^n (Y_{ik} - M_y)^2,$$

which quantity will be called the total sum of squares or the total variability. If we expand and simplify this expression, making appropriate substitutions as well, a computing formula can be obtained. The formula is

$$\sum_k^c \sum_i^n Y_{ik}^2 - \frac{T_y^2}{N}.$$

Let $C_y = T_y^2/N$. Then the formula for the total sum of squares can be written

$$\sum_k^c \sum_i^n Y_{ik}^2 - C_y. \tag{10.1}$$

*Example:*

In Table 10.2 are 15 numbers classified into three subsets, each subset consisting of five numbers. The column sums, means, and sums of squares are given at the bottom of the rectangular arrangement.

**Table 10.2**

**AN EXAMPLE OF NUMBERS CLASSIFIED BY COLUMNS**

| | Columns 1 | 2 | 3 |
|---|---|---|---|
| | 4 | 10 | 15 |
| | 9 | 8 | 10 |
| | 8 | 6 | 12 |
| | 7 | 7 | 13 |
| | 7 | 9 | 10 |
| Sums | 35 | 40 | 60 |
| Means | 7 | 8 | 12 |
| Sums of squares | 259 | 330 | 738 |

Computation of the total sum of squares requires the sum of the $N$ values and the sum of their squares. We find that

$$T_y = 135$$

and

$$\sum_k^c \sum_i^n Y_{ik}^2 = 1{,}327.$$

Having found $T_y$, we can compute $C_y$, the second term in formula (10.1), as follows:

$$C_y = \frac{T_y^2}{N} = \frac{135^2}{15} = 1{,}215.$$

The total sum of squares of deviations is found by the subtraction,

$$1{,}327 - 1{,}215 = 112.$$

The total sum of squares can be subdivided into two additive components. The first of these components we shall call the combined within-column sum of squares. We proceed below with the definition and computation of this component.

Consider the $k^{\text{th}}$ column. The sum of squares of deviations from the mean of the $k^{\text{th}}$ column is

$$\sum_i^n (Y_{ik} - \bar{Y}_{.k})^2,$$

a measure of the variability within that column. Formula (4.2), which was derived earlier for computing the sum of squares of deviations from the mean for a set of numbers, can be rewritten for a column sum of squares, with some slight modifications in the symbolism, as follows:

$$\sum_i^n Y_{ik}^2 - \frac{(\sum_i^n Y_{ik})^2}{n}.$$

*Example:*

The sum of squares of deviations for the first column of Table 10.2 is computed, as follows:

$$259 - \frac{35^2}{5} = 14.$$

The sum of squares for the second column is

$$330 - \frac{40^2}{5} = 10.$$

For the third column, it is

$$738 - \frac{60^2}{5} = 18.$$

Each of the three quantities computed above is a measure of the variability within a particular column. The three values can be added, yielding the combined within-column sum of squares, an overall measure of the within-column variability, as indicated by the expression,

$$\sum_{k}^{c} \sum_{i}^{n} (Y_{ik} - \bar{Y}_{.k})^2,$$

and by the computation,

$$14 + 10 + 18 = 42.$$

Observe that the combined within-column sum of squares, which is 42, is less than the total sum of squares, which is 112. Measurement of the variability within columns has not taken account of all of the variability in the entire set. We proceed now with the definition and computation of another component of the total variability.

The variability within any column can be eliminated by substituting the mean of the column for each of the $n$ values within that column. It will be instructive to do so. Table 10.3 shows the results of substituting the mean of each of the three columns of Table 10.2 for each of the five values in a column. Examination of the values in Table 10.3 reveals that the variability

**Table 10.3**

**VARIABILITY REMAINING AFTER ELIMINATION OF WITHIN-COLUMN VARIABILITY IN TABLE 10.2**

Columns

| 1 | 2 | 3 |
|---|---|---|
| 7 | 8 | 12 |
| 7 | 8 | 12 |
| 7 | 8 | 12 |
| 7 | 8 | 12 |
| 7 | 8 | 12 |

has indeed been eliminated within each column, but that some variability does remain. It seems appropriate to call the remaining differences in Table 10.3, *between-column* variability. The between-column variability can be measured by a sum of squares computed from the values in Table 10.3. The mean of the 15 values in the table is $M_y = 9$, the mean of the original values in Table 10.2. A deviation from $M_y$ for a value in the first column of Table 10.3 is

$$(7 - 9).$$

The square of this deviation is

$$(7 - 9)^2.$$

Observe that all five squared deviations for values in the first column are the same. Therefore, for the first column, the sum of squares of deviations from $M_y$ can be written as the product,

$$5(7 - 9)^2.$$

For the second column, the sum of squares of deviations from $M_y$ is

$$5(8 - 9)^2.$$

For the third column, it is

$$5(12 - 9)^2.$$

Combining these three quantities as a measure of the between-column variability yields

$$5(7 - 9)^2 + 5(8 - 9)^2 + 5(12 - 9)^2 = 70.$$

These numerical expressions, which combine to yield the between-column sum of squares, can be written symbolically, as follows:

$$n(\overline{Y}_{.1} - M_y)^2 + n(\overline{Y}_{.2} - M_y)^2 + n(\overline{Y}_{.3} - M_y)^2$$

or

$$\sum_k^c n(\overline{Y}_{.k} - M_y)^2$$

or

$$n \sum_k^c (\overline{Y}_{.k} - M_y)^2.$$

If this expression for the between-column sum of squares is expanded and simplified, with appropriate substitutions, the result is a convenient computing formula:

$$\frac{\sum_k^c (\sum_i^n Y_{ik})^2}{n} - C_y . \qquad (10.2)$$

Formula (10.2), representing the between-column sum of squares, can be translated into verbal instructions, as follows: Find the sum of each column. Square each column sum. Sum the squared column sums and divide the result by $n$, the number of values per column. Compute $C_y = T_y^2/N$, where $T_y$ is the sum of all $N$ values. Subtract $C_y$ from the quotient obtained just previously.

The derivation of formula (10.2) is based on the assumption that $n$, the number of values per column, is a constant. When $n$ varies, the instructions are modified in the following respects: Each squared column sum is divided by the number of values in that column. The $c$ quotients which result are then summed. Finally, the correction term, $C_y$ is subtracted.

The between-column sum of squares for the numbers in Table 10.2 was computed from the numbers in Table 10.3 and found to be equal to 70. We shall demonstrate the use of formula (10.2) in computing the same quantity. The column sums from Table 10.2 are 35, 40, and 60; $n$ is 5; $C_y$ is 1,215. Substituting these values in formula (10.2), we obtain

$$\frac{35^2 + 40^2 + 60^2}{5} - 1{,}215 = 70.$$

## Summary

Having been given a set of numbers classified by columns, we set out to analyze the total variability into two components. We found the total sum of squares of deviations from $M_y$ to be 112. For each column, we computed the sum of squares of deviations from its mean. We then combined the three values, 14, 10, and 18, to obtain a measure of the combined within-column variability, a sum of squares equal to 42. Finally, we eliminated the within-column variability by substituting the mean of a column for each value in that column. The remaining variability was called between-column variability. For these substituted values, the sum of squares of deviations from $M_y$ was found to be 70.

Notice the relation between the total sum of squares and the two components: the between-column sum of squares and the within-column sum of squares. In the example,

$$112 = 70 + 42.$$

That is to say, the total variability is equal to the between-column variability plus the within-column variability. This relation holds true in general. The example given above does not establish the generality of the relation, but it can be established. The proof will not be given here.

## On Classifications

Let $C_k$ be the $k^{\text{th}}$ category in a set of $c$ categories into whieh a set of $N$ numbers can be classified with $n_k$ numbers per category. In the classification scheme of the preceding section, the categories corresponded to columns in the rectangular tabulation. A classification involving one set of categories is sometimes called a *single* classification. There is nothing to prevent our classifying the same set of $N$ numbers into another set of categories.

Let $R_j$ be the $j^{\text{th}}$ category in the second set of $r$ categories. Classifying the $N$ numbers simultaneously into both sets of categories will be defined here as distributing them into new categories specified by the symbol combination,

$$R_jC_k.$$

That is, a number is classified into a new category because it belongs to the $j^{th}$ category in the $R$ set and the $k^{th}$ category in the $C$ set. The number of new categories is the number of possible combinations of $R_j$ and $C_k$, which is $(r \times c)$. The simultaneous classification can be represented by a rectangle of $r$ rows, $c$ columns, and $(r \times c)$ cells. The category $R_jC_k$ is the cell defined by the intersection of the $j^{th}$ row and the $k^{th}$ column. It is sometimes convenient to refer to such a classification as a double classification or as an $(r \times c)$ classification.

Table 10.4 illustrates the principle of doubly classifying numbers. Columns

**Table 10.4**

**SIMULTANEOUS CLASSIFICATION ON TWO SETS OF CATEGORIES**

| | | First Set | | | | | | |
|---|---|---|---|---|---|---|---|---|
| | | $C_1$ | $C_2$ | $C_3$ | . | $C_k$ | . | $C_c$ |
| | $R_1$ | $R_1C_1$ | $R_1C_2$ | $R_1C_3$ | . | $R_1C_k$ | . | $R_1C_c$ |
| | $R_2$ | $R_2C_1$ | $R_2C_2$ | $R_2C_3$ | . | $R_2C_k$ | . | $R_2C_c$ |
| | $R_3$ | $R_3C_1$ | $R_3C_2$ | $R_3C_3$ | . | $R_3C_k$ | . | $R_3C_c$ |
| Second Set | . | . | . | . | . | . | . | . |
| | $R_j$ | $R_jC_1$ | $R_jC_2$ | $R_jC_3$ | . | $R_jC_k$ | . | $R_jC_c$ |
| | . | . | . | . | . | . | . | . |
| | $R_r$ | $R_rC_1$ | $R_rC_2$ | $R_rC_3$ | . | $R_rC_k$ | . | $R_rC_c$ |

and rows of the table are appropriately labeled. Each cell contains a combination of symbols indicating the combination of categories represented by that cell. Symbols in the cells of Table 10.4 are not to be interpreted as numbers. The symbols identify the new categories. The table only serves the purpose of making explicit the way in which numbers can be classified simultaneously with respect to two sets of categories.

## Variability in a Double Classification

When numbers in a set are classified in two different ways simultaneously, as shown in Table 10.5, the variability of the entire set can be analyzed into three components.

**Table 10.5**

**SCHEME FOR DOUBLY CLASSIFYING NUMBERS WITH ONE NUMBER PER CELL**

Columns

| Rows | 1 | 2 | 3 | . | $k$ | . | $c$ |
|---|---|---|---|---|---|---|---|
| 1 | $Y_{11}$ | $Y_{12}$ | $Y_{13}$ | . | $Y_{1k}$ | . | $Y_{1c}$ |
| 2 | $Y_{21}$ | $Y_{22}$ | $Y_{23}$ | . | $Y_{2k}$ | . | $Y_{2c}$ |
| 3 | $Y_{31}$ | $Y_{32}$ | $Y_{33}$ | . | $Y_{3k}$ | . | $Y_{3c}$ |
| . | . | . | . | . | . | . | . |
| $j$ | $Y_{j1}$ | $Y_{j2}$ | $Y_{j3}$ | . | $Y_{jk}$ | . | $Y_{jc}$ |
| . | . | . | . | . | . | . | . |
| $r$ | $Y_{r1}$ | $Y_{r2}$ | $Y_{r3}$ | . | $Y_{rk}$ | . | $Y_{rc}$ |

Let $N$ = total number of values in the entire set; $c$ = number of columns = number of subsets or categories in the first way of classifying; $r$ = number of rows = number of subsets or categories in the second way of classifying. Then $(r \times c)$ = number of cells = number of combinations in the simultaneous classification.

Let $n$ = number of values per cell = number of values in each new category = 1.[1]

If we let $Y_{jk}$ be the value in the $j^{\text{th}}$ row and the $k^{\text{th}}$ column, then the sum of the $r$ values in the $k^{\text{th}}$ column can be written

$$\sum_{j}^{r} Y_{jk}.$$

The mean of the $r$ values in the $k^{\text{th}}$ column is

$$\overline{Y}_{.k} = \frac{\sum_{j}^{r} Y_{jk}}{r}.$$

$T_y$, the sum of all $N$ values, can be written as the sum of the $c$ column sums.

[1]Double classifications in which $n > 1$ will not be discussed here.

That is,

$$T_y = \sum_k^c \sum_j^r Y_{jk}.$$

The mean of all $N$ values is

$$M_y = \frac{T_y}{N} = \frac{T_y}{rc}.$$

The sum of the $c$ values in the $j^{\text{th}}$ row can be written

$$\sum_k^c Y_{jk}.$$

The mean of the $c$ values in the $j^{\text{th}}$ row is

$$\bar{Y}_{j.} = \frac{\sum_k^c Y_{jk}}{c}.$$

The sum of all $N$ values was written above as the sum of column sums. It can be written as the sum of row sums, as follows:

$$T_y = \sum_j^r \sum_k^c Y_{jk}.$$

The total variability exhibited by the $N$ numbers is defined by either of two equivalent expressions:

$$\sum_k^c \sum_j^r (Y_{jk} - M_y)^2$$

or

$$\sum_j^r \sum_k^c (Y_{jk} - M_y)^2$$

Thus in defining the total sum of squares it makes no difference whether one sums the $r$ squared deviations in each column and combines these $c$ quantities, or sums the $c$ squared deviations in each row and combines the $r$ resulting quantities. One obtains the same result for the total sum of squares by both methods.

Either one of these expressions for the total sum of squares can be expanded and simplified. If appropriate substitutions are then made, a convenient computing formula results:

$$\sum_k^c \sum_j^r Y_{jk}^2 - C_y \tag{10.3}$$

or

$$\sum^r \sum_k^c Y_{jk}^2 - C_y$$

where $C_y = T_y^2/N$.

*Example:*

Table 10.6 contains a 3 × 4 classification of numbers with one number per

**Table 10.6**

**EXAMPLE OF A DOUBLE CLASSIFICATION OF NUMBERS**

| | | Columns 1 | 2 | 3 | 4 | Row Sums | Row Means |
|---|---|---|---|---|---|---|---|
| Rows | 1 | 7 | 10 | 6 | 5 | 28 | 7 |
| | 2 | 9 | 8 | 8 | 7 | 32 | 8 |
| | 3 | 2 | 6 | 1 | 3 | 12 | 3 |
| Column Sums | | 18 | 24 | 15 | 15 | | |
| Column Means | | 6 | 8 | 5 | 5 | | |
| Sums of Squares of Original Values | | 134 | 200 | 101 | 83 | | |

cell. Thus $r = 3$; $c = 4$; and $N = r \times c = 12$. The sums and means of rows and columns are arranged on the margins of the table. The sum of squares of the values in each column is also given below the column.

Computation of the total sum of squares of deviations by means of formula (10.3) requires the sum of squares of all $N$ original values and the quantity, $C_y$. The sum of squares of the original values is

$$134 + 200 + 101 + 83 = 518.$$

The other required value, $C_y = T_y^2/N$, is computed, as follows:

$$C_y = \frac{72^2}{12} = 432.$$

Substitution of these values in formula (10.3) yields

$$518 - 432 = 86,$$

which quantity is the total sum of squares of deviations from $M_y$.

The variability within each column of Table 10.6 can be eliminated by substituting the mean of a column for each value in the column. Likewise, the variability within each row of the table can be eliminated by substituting row means. The results of both of these substitution procedures are shown in Table 10.7. The variability remaining after the within-column variability has been eliminated can be seen in arrangement A. We shall refer to what remains as between-column variability. The between-column sum of squares of deviations is defined by the expression,

$$\sum_k^c r(\overline{Y}_{\cdot k} - M_y)^2,$$

**Table 10.7**

**ELIMINATION OF WITHIN-COLUMN AND WITHIN-ROW VARIABILITY IN TABLE 10.6**

A. Results of substituting column means:

| | | | |
|---|---|---|---|
| 6 | 8 | 5 | 5 |
| 6 | 8 | 5 | 5 |
| 6 | 8 | 5 | 5 |

B. Results of substituting row means:

| | | | |
|---|---|---|---|
| 7 | 7 | 7 | 7 |
| 8 | 8 | 8 | 8 |
| 3 | 3 | 3 | 3 |

from which can be derived a convenient formula,

$$\frac{\sum_{k}^{c}(\sum_{j}^{r} Y_{jk})^2}{r} - C_y. \qquad (10.4)$$

Formula (10.4) should be compared with formula (10.2). The former is simply an adaptation of the latter. Formula (10.4) can be translated into verbal instructions, as follows: Find the sum of each column; square each column sum; combine the squared sums and divide by $r$, the number of rows; subtract $C_y = T_y^2/N$ from the resulting quotient.

*Example:*

The computation of the between-column sum of squares for the numbers in Table 10.6 (or for those in arrangement A of Table 10.7) requires the substitution of column sums, a value for $C_y$, and a value for $r$ in formula (10.4), as follows:

$$\frac{18^2 + 24^2 + 15^2 + 15^2}{3} - 432 = 18.$$

The variability remaining in Table 10.6 after the within-row variability has been eliminated can be observed in arrangement B of Table 10.7. We shall refer to this remaining variability as between-row variability. The between-row sum of squares of deviations is defined by the expression,

$$\sum_{j}^{r} c(\overline{Y}_j . - M_y)^2,$$

from which can be derived a convenient computing formula,

$$\frac{\sum_{j}^{r}(\sum_{k}^{c} Y_{jk})^2}{c} - C_y. \tag{10.5}$$

Formula (10.5) should be compared with formulas (10.4) and (10.2). The common features of the three formulas should be apparent. Formula (10.5) can be interpreted as giving the following instructions: Find each row sum; square each row sum; combine these squared sums and divide by $c$, the number of columns; subtract $C_y = T_y^2/N$ from the quotient.

*Example:*

To compute the between-row sum of squares for the numbers in Table 10.6 (or for those in arrangement B of Table 10.7), one substitutes values for the row sums, $C_y$, and $c$ in formula (10.5), as follows:

$$\frac{28^2 + 32^2 + 12^2}{4} - 432 = 56.$$

With respect to the numbers in Table 10.6, we have established that the total sum of squares is 86, the between-column sum of squares is 18, and the between-row sum of squares is 56. Observe that the sum of the two components is less than the total. There is some remaining variability, for which we have not yet accounted. What remains is called the *residual* variability.

The residual sum of squares is defined, as follows: Let $r_{jk}$ be a residual deviation for the cell in the $j^{\text{th}}$ row and the $k^{\text{th}}$ column. Then the sum of squares of the $N$ residuals is

$$\sum_{k}^{c}\sum_{j}^{r} r_{jk}^2.$$

A residual deviation, $r_{jk}$, is defined as

$$(Y_{jk} - M_y) - (\overline{Y}_{j\cdot} - M_y) - (\overline{Y}_{\cdot k} - M_y).$$

That is, $r_{jk}$ is what remains of the deviation, $(Y_{jk} - M_y)$, after subtraction of the deviation, $(\overline{Y}_{j\cdot} - M_y)$, and the deviation, $(\overline{Y}_{\cdot k} - M_y)$.

When the terms in the defining expression are combined, one obtains

$$r_{jk} = Y_{jk} - \overline{Y}_{j\cdot} - \overline{Y}_{\cdot k} + M_y. \tag{10.6}$$

*Example:*

The residual deviations for the numbers in Table 10.6 are displayed in Table 10.8. The computation of four of the twelve residual deviations is given

**Table 10.8**

**RESIDUAL DEVIATIONS FOR NUMBERS IN TABLE 10.6**

| | | | |
|---|---|---|---|
| 0 | +1 | 0 | −1 |
| +1 | −2 | +1 | 0 |
| −1 | +1 | −1 | +1 |

below. In the computation, values from Table 10.6 were substituted in formula (10.6). The student should verify the computation of the other eight residuals.

$$\begin{aligned} r_{11} &= 7 - 7 - 6 + 6 = 0 \\ r_{21} &= 9 - 8 - 6 + 6 = +1 \\ r_{31} &= 2 - 3 - 6 + 6 = -1 \\ r_{12} &= 10 - 7 - 8 + 6 = +1 \end{aligned}$$

The residual sum of squares is the sum of squares of the twelve values in Table 10.8:

$$\sum_k^c \sum_j^r r_{jk}^2 = 12.$$

The total variability of the numbers in Table 10.6 has now been analyzed into three components. The total sum of squares is 86; the between-column sum of squares is 18; the between-row sum of squares is 56; the residual sum of squares is 12. Notice that the total is equal to the sum of the three components. That is,

$$86 = 18 + 56 + 12.$$

The additivity of these three components is an example of a relation whose generality will not be proved here. It can be shown that the total sum of squares is equal to the sum of the three components: the between-column sum of squares, the between-row sum of squares, and the residual sum of squares. The example itself does not, of course, constitute a proof of the generality of the relation.

## Summary

Two ways of analyzing the variability in a rectangular table of numbers have been described in the present chapter. The first method of analysis was applied to a single classification of numbers. The total sum of squares was subdivided into two components: the between-column sum of squares and the within-column sum of squares. It was observed that the two components were additive, that is, they combined to yield the total. The second method of analysis was applied to a double classification of numbers. The total sum of squares was subdivided into three components: the between-column sum of squares, the between-row sum of squares, and the residual sum of squares. The three components combined to give the total.

Two principles of analysis were stated. The first was that the total variability in a single classification of numbers can be analyzed into two additive components: the between-column sum of squares and the within-column sum of squares. The second was that the total variability in a double classification of numbers can be analyzed into three additive components: the between-column sum of squares, the between-row sum of squares, and the residual sum of squares.

## Double Classification and Correlation

Product-moment correlation was discussed in Chaptei 7 with reference to a double classification of numbers, although the tabulation was not so designated. Table 7.1 consisted of $N$ rows and two columns with one entry per cell. The columns corresponded to two sets of numbers, $X$ and $Y$. The rows corresponded to pairs of numbers, a pair consisting of one number from each set. In a table of $r$ rows and two columns, the correlation between the columns can be expressed in terms of the between-row variability, the residual variability, and the variability within the columns. A connection is thereby established between correlation and the analysis of variability for classifications of numbers.

To emphasize the connection between correlation as a measure of concomitance for paired values of $X$ and $Y$, and the analysis of variability for an $r \times 2$ classification of numbers, we shall employ two different systems of symbols for the same quantities.

Let $r_{12}$ = the correlation between the columns of an $r \times 2$ classification of numbers $= r_{xy} =$ the correlation between two sets of paired numbers, $X$ and $Y$.

Let $B$ = the between-row sum of squares for an $r \times 2$ classification = the between-pair sum of squares for variables $X$ and $Y$.

Let $R$ = the residual sum of squares for an $r \times 2$ classification = the residual sum of squares for the $N \times 2$ table of $X$ and $Y$.

Let $W_1$ = the sum of squares for the variability within the first column of the $r \times 2$ classification $= W_x =$ the sum of squares of deviations for $X$.

Let $W_2$ = the sum of squares for the variability within the second column of the $r \times 2$ classification $= W_y =$ the sum of squares of deviations for $Y$.

It can be shown that the sum of products of deviations for the arrays of either arrangement is equal to $(B - R)/2$, from which it follows that

$$r_{12} = \frac{B - R}{2\sqrt{W_1 W_2}} \tag{10.7}$$

and that

$$r_{xy} = \frac{B - R}{2\sqrt{W_x W_y}} \tag{10.8}$$

Formula (10.7) states that the correlation between the columns of an $r \times 2$ classification is a function of the between-row sum of squares, the residual sum of squares, and the variability within each column. Formula (10.8) states that the correlation between $X$ and $Y$ is a function of the between-pair sum of squares, the residual sum of squares for the $N \times 2$ table, and the sums of squares for $X$ and $Y$. Imagine that the $W$'s are fixed values in both formulas. It follows that $r_{12}$ and $r_{xy}$ will increase in algebraic value as $B$ increases and $R$ decreases. When

$$B > R,$$

the correlation is positive; when

$$B = R,$$

the correlation is zero; when

$$B < R,$$

the correlation is negative.

## Pragmatics and the Analysis of Variability

Although methods of analyzing variability into component sums of squares can be applied to any table of numbers having the specifications set forth early in the present chapter, these methods of analysis are seldom used for purely descriptive purposes. They are, however, widely used in statistical inference, especially in the analysis of experimental data. Since the descriptive uses of these methods are of little importance, no discussion of them will be undertaken in this text. The very important role of these methods of analysis in statistical inference, in connection with the evaluation of research data, will be treated in Chapter 15. At that time it will be necessary to take up the computation of variances from the component sums of squares.

There is one topic in descriptive statistics which merits comment at this point. In Chapter 9, the use of product-moment correlation as a measure of reliability was presented. In that connection, an allusion was made to an interpretation of the coefficient in terms of interindividual variability and intraindividual variability. It is this interpretation which deserves additional comment.

In the earlier discussion of Chapter 9, it was stated that the product-moment correlation coefficient compared interindividual variability, the differences among the average standings of the subjects tested on two occasions on the same test, with intraindividual variability, the difference in standings for each subject on the two occasions.[2] This comparison is made explicit by formula (10.8). $B$ stands for the between-pair sum of squares,

[2]An individual's " standing " was defined as the deviation of his score from the mean of the group on a given occasion.

which is a measure of differences among average standings. *R* stands for the residual sum of squares, which combines measures of the variability in the two standings for each one of the *N* persons tested. Because the correlation can be expressed in terms of the comparison of interindividual variability and intraindividual variability, psychologists often refer to a reliable test as one which reveals large individual differences, or as a very discriminating test, that is, one which discriminates among respondents.

# SAMPLING THEORY

## Syntactics | 11

The most important applications of statistics involve what is known as statistical inference. In evaluating research data by the methods of statistical inference, one attempts to go beyond the mere description of a particular set of data with its unique temporal and spatial context, to take account of error in the data and in values computed from the data, and to arrive at propositions of some more general and transcendental meaning. These statistical inferences from the particular to the general are not always correct, but, under certain conditions, they endow the evaluation with a rigor which has not yet been, and perhaps never will be, equaled by any other means.

Underlying the applications of statistical inference is a body of theory concerning error. The syntactical features of this body of theory should be made explicit before any attempt is made to use the theory. In the present chapter, we shall try to sketch the principal features of a basic part of this theory, a part which might be called *sampling theory*. In doing so, many detailed developments which would ordinarily be covered in a course in mathematical statistics will be omitted.[1] It is our intention here to attempt to convey to the student some understanding and appreciation of the nature of the theory of random errors, by means of a very general and quite elementary formulation.

In addition to the underlying theory of random errors, there are certain considerations which are important in supporting and guaranteeing the rigor of statistical inferences. This additional set of considerations is semantical in nature and has to do with (1) the adequacy of measurement, a topic which has already been discussed in Chapter 5, and (2) the adequacy of the operations by means of which an investigator tries to realize in practice the requirements of the theory with respect to the nature of errors.

[1]Students who wish to consult a standard, detailed text in mathematical statistics might examine R. V. Hogg and A. T. Craig, *Introduction to Mathematical Statistics* (New York: Macmillan, 1959).

Chapter 12 will present in summary form some of the major inferential statistics with definitions and brief descriptions of their logical properties with respect to error. In Chapter 13, the semantical issues of statistical inference will be discussed.

Let us begin our discussion of sampling theory with a frequency distribution for variable $X$. We shall refer to this frequency distribution as a population or parent distribution because we plan to form samples out of values chosen from the distribution. Let $X_j$ be the value of $X$ in the $j^{\text{th}}$ score interval of the population. Let $f_j$ be the frequency of occurrence of $X_j$ in the population. Further, let $r$ be the number of distinct and equal score intervals in the distribution. Finally, let $N$ equal $\Sigma f_j$, the total number of values in the distribution. The distribution is shown in Table 11.1.

**Table 11.1**

**A POPULATION DISTRIBUTION**

| $X$ | $f$ |
|---|---|
| $X_1$ | $f_1$ |
| $X_2$ | $f_2$ |
| $X_3$ | $f_3$ |
| . | . |
| $X_j$ | $f_j$ |
| . | . |
| $X_r$ | $f_r$ |

$r$ = number of distinct score intervals. $N = \Sigma f_j$ = total number of values.

We propose next to adopt a system for forming combinations of values taken from the parent distribution. Any combination of values resulting from the application of this system will be called a *random sample*. The system of forming combinations, although it may seem arbitrary and artificial to the student, makes possible extremely powerful deductive procedures. In the system, we shall follow the rule that, if we wish to form one or more combinations of values taken from the population distribution, there is no restriction on the repeated use of any one value.[2] For example, if we desire to form several combinations of two values, any one of the pairs of values in Table 11.2 is allowed by the system. We shall say that giving the particular values in a combination and the order of their selection identifies a way of choosing a combination. Thus the pairs listed in Table 11.2 are examples of different ways of choosing combinations of two values.

It is worth noting that all possible different ways of choosing two values are defined by the $(r \times c)$ square matrix of Table 11.3. In the matrix, $X_j$ is the first value chosen for the pair and $X_k$ is the second value. Note that the values of the parent distribution are arranged along both margins. In this instance,

[2]In another system the repeated use of any single value is not allowed.

$r = c$ and the matrix is square. In interpreting the matrix, we let the intersection of the $j^{\text{th}}$ row and the $k^{\text{th}}$ column represent a way of choosing two

**Table 11.2**

**EXAMPLES OF PAIRS OF VALUES ALLOWED BY THE SYSTEM FOR SELECTING FROM THE POPULATION IN TABLE 11.1**

| | First Choice | Second Choice |
|---|---|---|
| | $X_1$ | $X_2$ |
| | $X_2$ | $X_1$ |
| Pairs or | $X_1$ | $X_3$ |
| Ways of | $X_3$ | $X_1$ |
| Choosing | $X_3$ | $X_7$ |
| | $X_1$ | $X_1$ |
| | $X_4$ | $X_4$ |
| | $X_8$ | $X_5$ |

values, $X_j$ and $X_k$. In the diagonal cells running from the upper left corner to the lower right corner are combinations for which $j = k$ and $X_j = X_k$.

**Table 11.3**

**ALL POSSIBLE DIFFERENT WAYS OF CHOOSING TWO VALUES FROM THE POPULATION DISTRIBUTION IN TABLE 11.1**

| | | Second Choices | | | | | |
|---|---|---|---|---|---|---|---|
| | | $X_1$ | $X_2$ | $X_3$ | . | $X_k$ | . | $X_c$ |
| | $X_1$ | $X_1, X_1$ | $X_1, X_2$ | $X_1, X_3$ | . | $X_1, X_k$ | . | $X_1, X_c$ |
| | $X_2$ | $X_2, X_1$ | $X_2, X_2$ | $X_2, X_3$ | . | $X_2, X_k$ | . | $X_2, X_c$ |
| | $X_3$ | $X_3, X_1$ | $X_3, X_2$ | $X_3, X_3$ | . | $X_3, X_k$ | . | $X_3, X_c$ |
| First Choices | . | . | . | . | . | . | . | . |
| | $X_j$ | $X_j, X_1$ | $X_j, X_2$ | $X_j, X_3$ | . | $X_j, X_k$ | . | $X_j, X_c$ |
| | . | . | . | . | . | . | . | . |
| | $X_r$ | $X_r, X_1$ | $X_r, X_2$ | $X_r, X_3$ | . | $X_r, X_k$ | . | $X_r, X_c$ |

*Note:* In this instance, $r = c$ and the matrix is actually square.

The matrix is symmetrical around the diagonal in the sense that the combination for the second row and the third column involves the same values as the combination for the third row and the second column, but chosen in a different order. To represent all possible different ways of choosing combinations of three values, a figure of three dimensions, that is, a cube, would be required. For combinations of $n$ values, an $n$-dimensional arrangement would be needed.

The cells of the square in Table 11.3 define all possible different ways of choosing combinations of two values. A way of choosing two values is identified by listing the values in the order of their selection. When there are $r$ distinct values in the population, the number of different *ways of choosing* combinations of two is $r^2$.

There is an important distinction which should now be made. The distinction involves the number of *ways of choosing* and the total number of *possible combinations*. The total number of possible combinations of two values is $N^2$, a conclusion reached by observing that there are $N$ possible first choices and, for each of these, $N$ possible second choices.

To determine all possible combinations of two values, we must take account of the frequency in each interval of the scale of $X$. Consider the cell in the second row and third column of Table 11.3. It represents the combination, $X_2$ chosen first and $X_3$ chosen second. We have said that $X_2$ occurs with a frequency of $f_2$ and $X_3$ occurs with a frequency of $f_3$ in the population. The number of possible combinations of $X_2$ chosen first and $X_3$ chosen second is $(f_2 \times f_3)$. The reasoning which supports this conclusion is simple. There are $f_2$ possibilities in choosing $X_2$ first; for each of these, there are $f_3$ possibilities in choosing $X_3$ second. It follows that the total number of these combinations is $(f_2 \times f_3)$.

Table 11.4 gives the number of possible combinations for each way of choosing two values.

**Table 11.4**

**NUMBER OF POSSIBLE COMBINATIONS PER WAY OF CHOOSING TWO VALUES**

Second Choices

| First Choices | $f_1$ | $f_2$ | $f_3$ | . | $f_k$ | . | $f_c$ |
|---|---|---|---|---|---|---|---|
| $f_1$ | $f_1f_1$ | $f_1f_2$ | $f_1f_3$ | . | $f_1f_k$ | . | $f_1f_c$ |
| $f_2$ | $f_2f_1$ | $f_2f_2$ | $f_2f_3$ | . | $f_2f_k$ | . | $f_2f_c$ |
| $f_3$ | $f_3f_1$ | $f_3f_2$ | $f_3f_3$ | . | $f_3f_k$ | . | $f_3f_c$ |
| . | . | . | . | . | . | . | . |
| $f_j$ | $f_jf_1$ | $f_jf_2$ | $f_jf_3$ | . | $f_jf_k$ | . | $f_jf_c$ |
| . | . | . | . | . | . | . | . |
| $f_r$ | $f_rf_1$ | $f_rf_2$ | $f_rf_3$ | . | $f_rf_k$ | . | $f_rf_c$ |

*Note:* In this instance, $r = c$ and the matrix is square.

To summarize, the number of different ways of choosing two values is $r^2$; the number of possible combinations of two for any way of choosing is $f_j f_k$; the total number of possible combinations of two is $N^2$. In general, the number of different ways of choosing combinations of $n$ values is $r^n$; the number of possible combinations for any way of choosing is the product of $n$ marginal frequencies; and the total number of possible combinations is $N^n$.

The frequencies in the cells and on the margins of Table 11.4 are often expressed as relative frequencies. In the population and in each of the corresponding marginal distributions, $p_j$, the relative frequency for the $j^{\text{th}}$ interval, is defined as

$$p_j = \frac{f_j}{N}$$

and $p_k$, the relative frequency for the $k^{\text{th}}$ interval, is defined as

$$p_k = \frac{f_k}{N}.$$

In the square matrix of Table 11.4, the relative frequency for the cell in the $j^{\text{th}}$ row and the $k^{\text{th}}$ column is

$$p_{jk} = \frac{f_j f_k}{N^2} = \frac{f_j}{N}\frac{f_k}{N} = p_j p_k.$$

Observe that the relative frequency for a cell is equal to the product of the two relative frequencies on the margins. Observe also that

$$\sum_j^r p_j = 1,$$

$$\sum_k^c p_k = 1,$$

and

$$\sum_k^c \sum_j^r p_{jk} = 1.$$

In further discussions of the population distribution, the corresponding marginal distributions, and the distribution of combinations, we shall employ relative frequencies.

## Distribution of the Sample Mean

Any combination of $n$ values chosen from the population distribution in Table 11.1 according to the strictly logical system outlined above is, by definition, a *random sample*. Any value computed from the values in a random sample is an *i*-statistic. It is of very great importance that a frequency distribution can be deduced which will specify the values taken by a given *i*-statistic for all possible random samples of a particular size. The frequency distribution of values of a given *i*-statistic is called the *sampling distribution* of that *i*-statistic. Of course, many different *i*-statistics can be computed from the values in a sample. For demonstration purposes, the sample mean will do quite well and we shall use it to show the deductive process by means of which a sampling distribution can be established.

Let us again work with samples of two values. For any sample, the sum of the two values in that sample will be

$$X_j + X_k$$

and the sample mean will be

$$M_x = \frac{X_j + X_k}{2}.$$

Since $M_x$ is computed from the values in a random sample, it is an inferential statistic or an *i*-statistic.

We now propose to establish the sampling distribution of $M_x$. The sampling distribution is a relative frequency distribution for values of $M_x$ computed from all possible random samples of two values from a given population. To arrive at the sampling distribution of $M_x$, we first determine the values $M_x$ can take for all the different ways of choosing samples of two values. We next combine the relative frequencies for each different value of $M_x$. These combined relative frequencies can be displayed in a new distribution showing the relation between relative frequency and values of $M_x$.

An example may help in clarifying the procedure of establishing the sampling distribution of $M_x$. Table 11.5 contains a simple, three-interval

**Table 11.5**

**AN EXAMPLE OF A POPULATION**

| $X$ | $p$ |
|---|---|
| 0 | 0.50 |
| 1 | 0.20 |
| 2 | 0.30 |

frequency distribution which will constitute the population in our example. Although the distribution possesses only three score intervals, the values of $X$ are small, whole numbers, and the relative frequencies have the values shown in the table, it qualifies as a population and will be quite satisfactory for the example. Keep in mind that, syntactically speaking, a population is nothing more than a frequency distribution.

In the example, $r = 3$ and $r^2 = 9$. The nine different ways of choosing combinations of two values of $X$ are specified by the entries in the nine cells of Table 11.6. The first choice is placed on the left in each cell; the second choice is placed on the right. The relative frequency for each cell is the pro-

**Table 11.6**

**WAYS OF CHOOSING TWO VALUES FROM THE POPULATION OF TABLE 11.5**

| | | $X_k$ 0 | 1 | 2 |
|---|---|---|---|---|
| | 0 | 0,0 | 0,1 | 0,2 |
| $X_j$ | 1 | 1,0 | 1,1 | 1,2 |
| | 2 | 2,0 | 2,1 | 2,2 |

In each cell, the first choice is on the left, the second is on the right.

duct of the marginal relative frequencies. Relative frequencies for the margins and the cells are displayed in Table 11.7. The value of $M_x$ for the combination

**Table 11.7**

**RELATIVE FREQUENCIES FOR WAYS OF CHOOSING TWO VALUES**

| $X_j$ | $p_j$ | 0 | 1 | 2 | $X_k$ |
|---|---|---|---|---|---|
| | | .50 | .20 | .30 | $p_k$ |
| 0 | .50 | .25 | .10 | .15 | |
| 1 | .20 | .10 | .04 | .06 | |
| 2 | .30 | .15 | .06 | .09 | |

in each cell has been computed and is shown in arrangement A of Table 11.8. In arrangement B of the same table, cells containing the same value of $M_x$

**Table 11.8**

**MEANS OF SAMPLES OF TWO VALUES**

A

| | | $X_k$ 0 | 1 | 2 |
|---|---|---|---|---|
| | 0 | 0 | .5 | 1 |
| $X_j$ | 1 | .5 | 1 | 1.5 |
| | 2 | 1 | 1.5 | 2 |

B

| | | |
|---|---|---|
| *A* | *B* | *C* |
| *B* | *C* | *D* |
| *C* | *D* | *E* |

have been assigned a common label from the letters: *A*, *B*, *C*, *D*, and *E*. The combined relative frequency for each different value of $M_x$ is the sum of the relative frequencies in cells having a common label. If we let the labeling letters be variables representing relative frequencies, then for $M_x = 0$, the relative frequency is $A = .25$; for $M_x = .5$, the combined relative frequency is $\Sigma B = .10 + .10 = .20$; for $M_x = 1$, the combined relative frequency is $\Sigma C = .15 + .04 + .15 = .34$; for $M_x = 1.5$, the combined relative frequency is $\Sigma D = .06 + .06 = .12$; and finally, for $M_x = 2$, the relative frequency is $E = .09$.

If we let $P$ be the relative frequency of any value of $M_x$, then the sampling distribution of $M_x$ for samples of two values is the relative frequency distribution of Table 11.9. The sampling distribution of $M_x$ gives the distribution of all possible values of $M_x$ for samples of a specified size.

**Table 11.9**

**AN EXAMPLE OF A SAMPLING DISTRIBUTION**

| $M_x$ | $P$ |
|---|---|
| .0 | .25 |
| .5 | .20 |
| 1. | .34 |
| 1.5 | .12 |
| 2. | .09 |

$M_x$ computed from samples of two values from the population in Table 11.5.

The reasoning which entered into the determination of the distribution of $M_x$, given in Table 11.9, is a very simple example of deduction in sampling theory. Although the extensions and elaborations of deduction in sampling theory go far beyond this simple example and sometimes involve advanced and difficult mathematics, all theoretically deduced sampling distributions serve basically the same purpose. The sampling distribution of any *i*-statistic is simply a specification of the relative frequencies of the totality of possible values for the particular *i*-statistic.

The *i*-statistic in the example given above was a mean computed from a single sample. There are, of course, many other *i*-statistics. Sampling distributions have been established for values, other than the mean, computed from a single sample, for values computed from a single sample from a bivariate or multivariate distribution, for values computed from two or more samples, and for values computed from samples classified in a great variety of ways.

The deductive procedures employed in obtaining the sampling distribution in Table 11.9 are applicable to discrete population distributions. Discrete distributions are those having a finite number of score intervals. The deductive procedures of advanced work in sampling theory differ from those of the example in three respects. First, the population distribution is continuous; that is, $r$, the number of score intervals, is indefinitely large. Second, the relative frequencies of the population distribution are specified by an equation for a continuous function. Third, the relative frequencies of the sampling distribution are specified by an equation for a continuous function.

The general principle we have been trying to communicate is summarized in the following conceptual formula: A specified population distribution plus a standard deductive procedure yields the sampling distribution of an $i$-statistic.

None of the deductive procedures of advanced work in sampling theory will be given here because these topics are appropriate to courses in mathematical statistics. What are important to psychological statistics and to the use of statistics in psychological research are the results of the deductions, the sampling distributions. In Chapter 12, the sampling distributions of a number of the more important $i$-statistics will be identified and the general nature of the information we need about these sampling distributions will be described.

**Exercise 11.1**

Given in Table 11.10 is a discrete population distribution. Obtain the sampling

**Table 11.10**

**A POPULATION DISTRIBUTION**

| $X$ | $p$ |
|---|---|
| 0 | .20 |
| 1 | .50 |
| 2 | .20 |
| 3 | .10 |

distribution for the mean of random samples of two values. What steps would be necessary to extend the procedure to samples of three values?

# SAMPLING DISTRIBUTIONS

## Syntactics 12

In deducing the form of a sampling distribution, one must begin with a specification of the population distribution. A vast part of sampling theory is concerned with the drawing of random samples from a population distribution in which the relative frequency of $X$ is specified by a normal probability function or normal curve. Although there are many other functions or curves which could serve as population distributions, the family of normal curves has occupied a central position in statistical theory. Because of its central position, a number of *i*-statistics deriving from normal curve theory will be discussed in this chapter.

The equation for a normal curve is

$$p = \frac{1}{\sqrt{2\pi}} e^{-\frac{(X-\mu)^2}{2\sigma^2}}$$

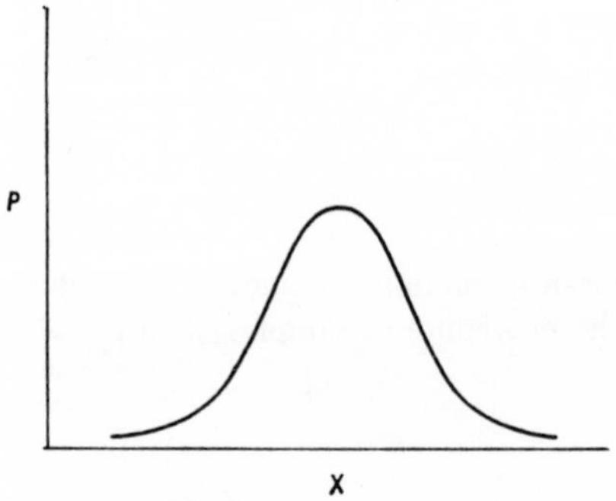

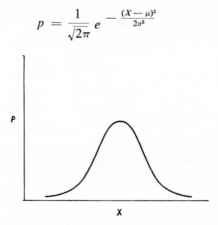

**Fig. 12.1** A normal probability function or normal curve. It is frequently employed to represent a population distribution in statistical inference. (The variance is $\sigma_x^2$.)

where $p$ is the relative frequency expressed as a function of $X$; $\mu$ is the mean of the population; $\sigma^2$ is the variance of the population; $e$ is a constant value of approximately 2.71828; and $\pi$ is a constant value of approximately 3.14159.

A normal curve is symmetrical and unimodal. Its branches approach, but do not reach, the horizontal axis no matter how far they are extended. $S$, the index of skewness, is 0 and $K$, the index of kurtosis, is 3. An example of a normal curve is given in Figure 12.1.

Imagine now that the function in Figure 12.1 is a population frequency distribution. Of interest to us here is the problem of forming all possible random samples, of some specified size, from this normally distributed population and determining the distribution of all possible values of some specified *i*-statistic computed from each random sample. The theoretical process of determining the sampling distribution of a specified *i*-statistic is one of mathematical deduction beginning with the equation for a normal curve and ending with another equation for the sampling distribution. Some of these sampling distributions are primarily of theoretical interest and importance; others are of great practical importance in the evaluation of research data.

# Sampling Distributions of Theoretical Interest

## THE MEAN OF A SAMPLE

$M_x$, the mean of a random sample of $n$ values, is itself normally distributed with mean equal to $\mu$, the population mean, and variance equal to $\sigma^2/n$, where $\sigma^2$ is the population variance. A normal curve representing a sampling distribution for $M_x$ is shown in Figure 12.2. That is to say, when the population

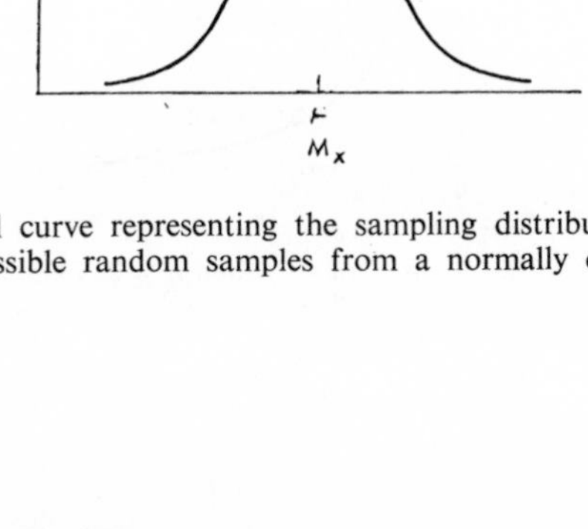

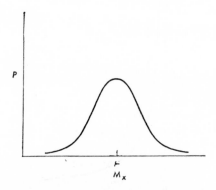


**Fig. 12.2** A normal curve representing the sampling distribution of values of $M_x$ computed from all possible random samples from a normally distributed population. (The variance is $\sigma_x^2/n$.)

is normally distributed, the totality of values for means of random samples of some fixed size is also normally distributed.

## THE VARIANCE OF A SAMPLE

$V_x$, the variance of a random sample of $n$ values, is seldom used as an $i$-statistic and its sampling distribution receives little attention. In place of $V_x$, the $i$-statistic, $V'_x$, is employed. $V'_x$ is defined as

$$V'_x = \frac{\Sigma x^2}{n - 1}.$$

Thus $V'_x$ is the sample variance computed by dividing the sum of squares of deviations by $(n - 1)$ instead of $n$. The divisor, $(n - 1)$, is usually called the *number of degrees of freedom.* $V'_x$ is sometimes referred to as the corrected value of the sample variance. The reason is that

$$V'_x = \frac{n}{n - 1} V_x.$$

Some additional implications of this correction will be discussed in connection with the estimation of population values.

$V'_x$, the sample variance computed with degrees of freedom, has a known sampling distribution whose equation will not be given here. That is to say, when the population distribution is normal, all possible values of $V'_x$ for

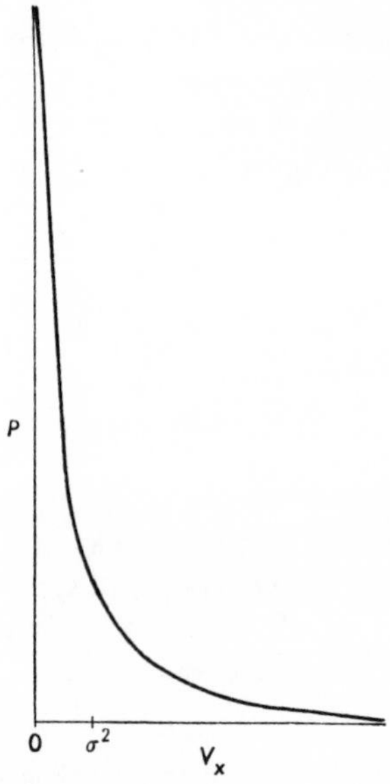


**Fig. 12.3** The sampling distribution of $V'_x$ when $n = 2$. (The mean of the distribution is $\sigma^2$.)

samples of some specified size from that population form a distribution exactly fitted by a known mathematical function. The mean of the sampling distribution of $V'_x$ is $\sigma^2$, the population variance. Figure 12.3 shows a distribution of $V'_x$ when $n = 2$. It is worth noting that a closely related variable, $(n - 1)V'_x/\sigma^2$, is distributed as chi square. That is, it has a sampling distribution specified by one of a family of functions called *chi square functions.* A particular chi square distribution is identified by its mean. The mean of a chi square distribution is equal to $(n - 1)$ the number of degrees of freedom employed in computing $V'_x$.

## THE DIFFERENCE BETWEEN TWO SAMPLE MEANS

Given all possible combinations of two random samples, each sample consisting of $n$ values from a normally distributed population, $D_x$, the difference between the means of two samples, is normally distributed. The mean of the sampling distribution is zero and the variance is equal to $2\sigma^2/n$. A sampling distribution of $D_x$ is displayed in Figure 12.4.

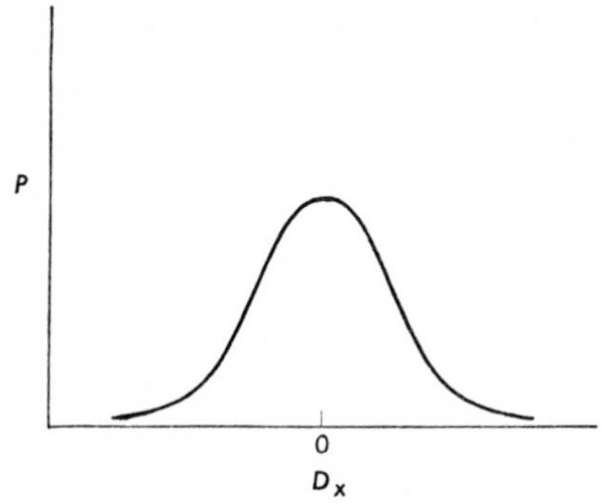


**Fig. 12.4** A normal curve representing the sampling distribution of $D_x$, the difference between means of two random samples of $n$ values. The mean of the sampling distribution is zero. (The variance is $2\sigma^2/n$.)

## BETWEEN-SAMPLE AND WITHIN-SAMPLE VARIANCES

In Chapter 10, it was shown that the total variability of numbers classified into subsets could be analyzed into additive components. Sampling provides one basis for classification. Numbers selected from a population distribution can be classified according to the sample in which they occur. For example, if we were given $c$ samples of $n$ values from a normally distributed population, we could classify the $(cn)$ values into $c$ subsets or columns corresponding to the $c$ samples. The total sum of squares for the $N = cn$ values could then be analyzed into two components: a between-column or between-sample sum of squares and a within-column or within-sample sum of squares. Variances can be computed from these two components. $V'_b$, the between-sample variance, is computed by dividing the between-sample sum of squares by a number of degrees of freedom equal to $(c - 1)$. In the case of two samples, of course,

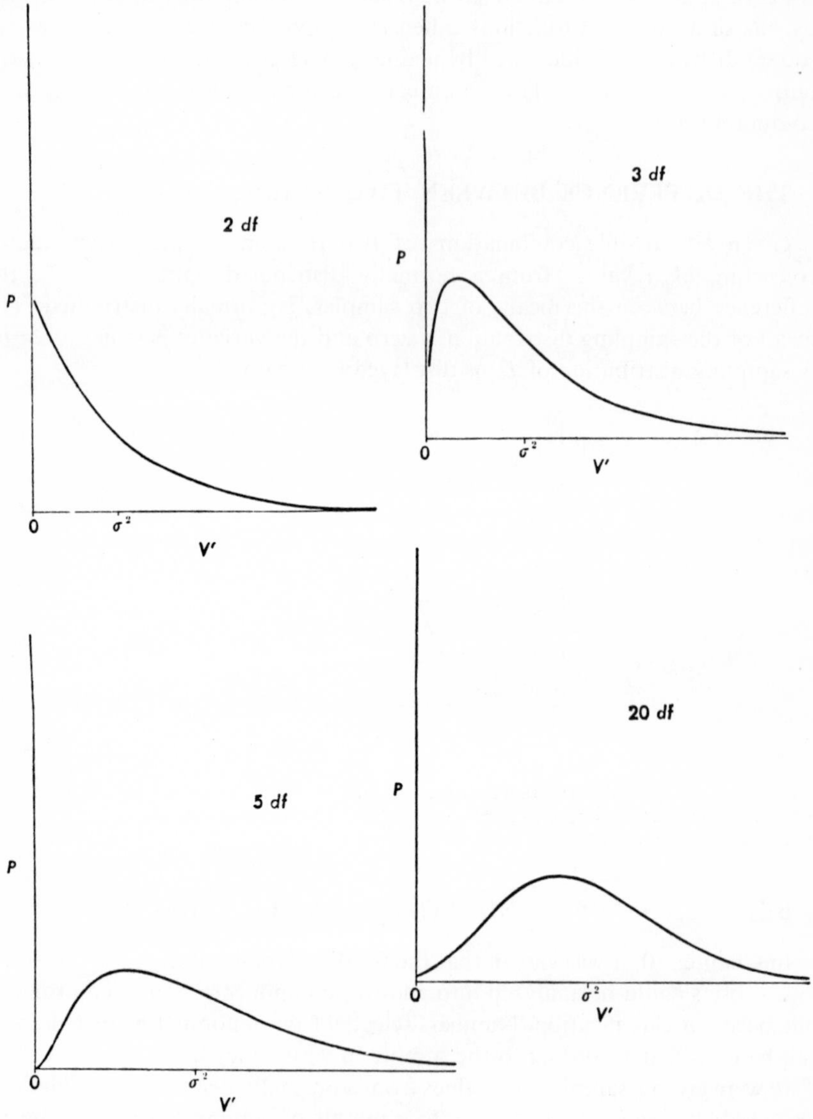


**Fig. 12.5** Functions representing the distributions of either $V'_b$ or $V'_w$. Each distribution is identified by the number of degrees of freedom used in computing the variance. Each distribution has a mean equal to $\sigma^2$.

$(c - 1) = 1$. $V'_w$, the combined within-sample variance, is computed by dividing the combined within-sample sum of squares by a number of degrees of freedom equal to $(N - c)$. In the case of two samples, $(N - c) = (N - 2)$.

$V'_b$, the between-sample variance, has a known sampling distribution, whose equation will not be given here. The mean of the sampling distribution is $\sigma^2$. $V'_w$, the within-sample variance, also has a known sampling distribution. Again the mean of the sampling distribution is $\sigma^2$. Figure 12.5 shows functions which can be viewed as representing distributions of either $V'_b$ or $V'_w$, depending on the number of degrees of freedom employed in computing the *i*-statistic. For example, the function labeled with two degrees of freedom could be the sampling distribution of $V'_b$ for three samples or of $V'_w$ for two samples of two values each. Notice that the number of degrees of freedom employed in computing $V'_b$ for three samples is two and that the number of degrees of freedom employed in computing $V'_w$ for two samples of two values each is two. The function labeled with three degrees of freedom could be the sampling distribution of $V'_b$ for four samples or for $V'_w$ for two samples, one of three values, the other of two. The function labeled with five degrees of freedom could be the sampling distribution of $V'_b$ for six samples or of $V'_w$ for samples of three and four values. The function labeled with twenty degrees of freedom could be the sampling distribution of $V'_w$ for four samples of six values each or for five samples of five values each. The student should figure out other combinations of $c$ and $n$ for which the sampling distributions of $V'_b$ or $V'_w$ would be represented by these functions.

# Sampling Distributions of Practical Importance

## THE DISTRIBUTION OF *t*

There is an important *i*-statistic which is designated $t$. A function which specifies the sampling distribution of $t$ is called a $t$ function. There is a family of $t$ functions, one for each particular number of degrees of freedom involved in the computation of $t$. Figure 12.6 shows $t$ functions for 1, 2, 5, and 30 degrees of freedom. A $t$ function is symmetrical and unimodal. Its branches approach but never reach the horizontal axis no matter how far they are extended. Its mean is zero. Its variance is $f/(f - 2)$ if $f > 2$, where $f$ is the number of degrees of freedom identifying the function. Its index of skewness is zero. Its index of kurtosis is greater than three. As the number of degrees of freedom increases, the distribution of $t$ approaches the normal form.

Values of $t$ can be computed from a variety of other *i*-statistics. Three cases are given below.

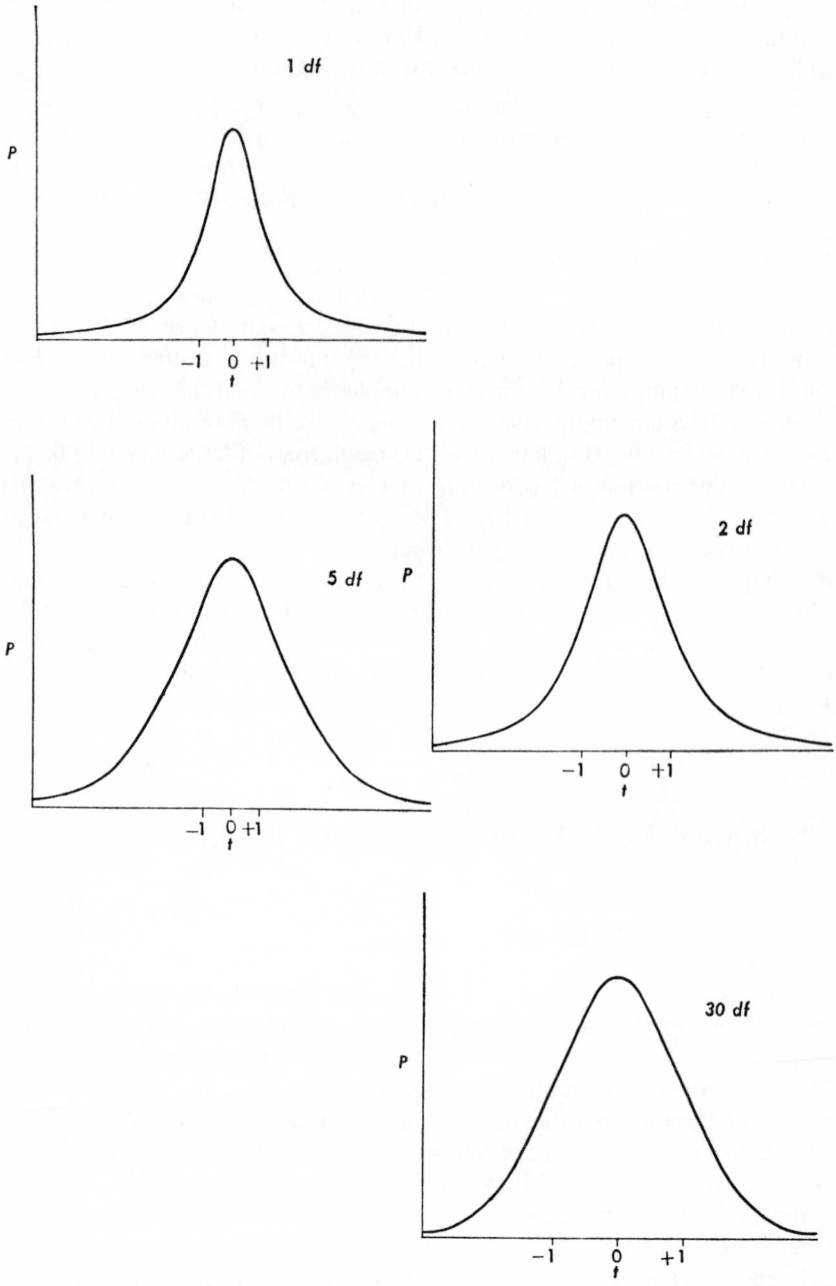


**Fig. 12.6** Functions for the sampling distribution of *t* for 1, 2, 5, and 30 degrees of freedom.

1. For a single random sample of $n$ values from a normally distributed population,

$$t = \frac{M_x - \mu}{\sqrt{V'_x/n}}. \tag{12.1}$$

Formula (12.1) can be interpreted as saying that the ratio on the right is distributed as $t$. The ratio compares the difference between $M_x$, the sample mean, and $\mu$, the population mean, with a value computed from $V'_x$, the sample variance computed with $(n - 1)$ degrees of freedom. The sampling distribution of $t$ computed by formula (12.1) is given, in Figure 12.6, by the $t$ function for one degree of freedom when $n = 2$, by the $t$ function for two degrees of freedom when $n = 3$, by the $t$ function for five degrees of freedom when $n = 6$, and by the $t$ function for thirty degrees of freedom when $n = 31$.

2. For two random samples from a normally distributed population distribution of $X$,

$$t = \frac{D_x}{\sqrt{2V'_w/n}}. \tag{12.2}$$

where $D_x$ is the difference between two sample means, $V'_w$ is the combined within-sample variance computed with $2(n - 1)$ degrees of freedom, and $n$ is the number of values per sample. Formula (12.2) can be interpreted as saying that the ratio on the right is distributed as $t$. The ratio compares the difference between two sample means with a value computed from the combined within-sample variance. The number of degrees of freedom is $2(n - 1)$. The sampling distribution of $t$ computed by formula (12.2) is given in Figure 12.6 by the $t$ function for two degrees of freedom when $n = 2$, and by the $t$ function for thirty degrees of freedom when $n = 16$.

3. For a single sample of paired values from a bivariate population distribution of $X$ and $Y$,

$$t = \frac{r_{xy}\sqrt{N - 2}}{\sqrt{1 - r_{xy}^2}}. \tag{12.3}$$

In formula (12.3), $r_{xy}$ is the product-moment correlation coefficient computed from a sample of $N$ pairs of values. In this case, the sampling distribution of $t$ contains values which could be computed from the totality of sample correlation coefficients based on all possible pairings of values of $Y$ with a given set of $N$ values of $X$. The deductions which establish that the ratio in formula (12.3) is distributed as $t$ require that the $Y$'s for any given $X$ are normally distributed and that $\rho$, the population correlation, is zero. The number of degrees of freedom is $(N - 2)$. The sampling distribution of $t$ computed by formula (12.3) is given in Fig. 12.6 by the $t$ function for two degrees of freedom when $N = 4$, and by the $t$ function for thirty degrees of freedom when $N = 32$.

## THE DISTRIBUTION OF *F*

Another important *i*-statistic, designated *F*, is the variance ratio. A function which describes the sampling distribution of *F* is called an *F* function. There is a family of *F* functions. A particular curve from the family is identified by a combination of degrees of freedom. The combination consists of the two numbers of degrees of freedom which enter into the computation of the two variances in the ratio. Figure 12.7 contains six *F* functions. Each of the six functions is labeled with two numbers giving the combination of degrees of freedom for that function.

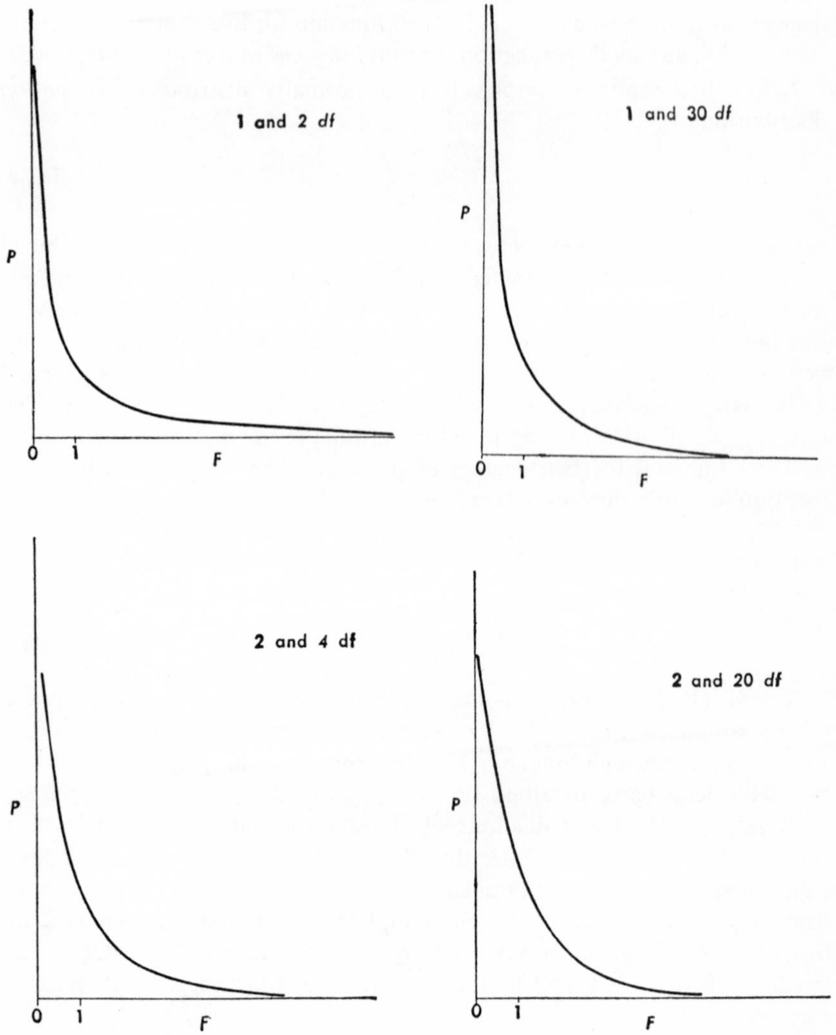

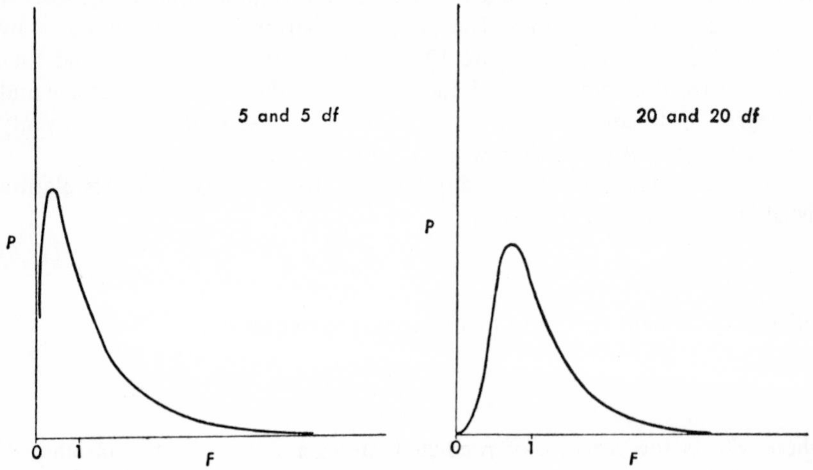


**Fig. 12.7** Functions for the sampling distribution of $F$ for six combinations of degrees of freedom.

$F$ is a ratio involving two variances. The ratio can be computed in a variety of ways, three of which are listed below.

1. For $c \geqq 2$ random samples from a normal population distribution,

$$F = \frac{V_b'}{V_w'}. \tag{12.4}$$

Let $n$ = the number of values per sample; let $N = cn$. $V_b'$ is the between-sample variance computed by dividing the between-sample sum of squares by $(c - 1)$ degrees of freedom. $V_w'$ is the combined within-sample variance computed by dividing the combined within-sample sum of squares by $(N - c)$ degrees of freedom. $F$ is the ratio of the between-sample variance to the within-sample variance. The sampling distribution of $F$ computed by formula (12.4) is given in Figure 12.7 by the $F$ function for one and two degrees of freedom when $c = 2$ and $n = 2$, and by the $F$ function for one and thirty degrees of freedom when $c = 2$ and $n = 16$. It is interesting to note that, when $c = 2$, $F$ computed by formula (12.4) is equal to $t^2$ when $t$ is computed by formula (12.2).

2. For two random samples from a normally distributed population,

$$F = \frac{V_1'}{V_2'}. \tag{12.5}$$

Let $n_1$ = the number of values in a first sample; let $n_2$ = the number of values in a second sample. Again $F$ is the ratio of two variances. In the numerator is the variance for a first sample computed by dividing the sample sum of squares by $(n_1 - 1)$ degrees of freedom. In the denominator is the variance for a second sample computed by dividing the sample sum of squares by $(n_2 - 1)$ degrees of freedom. The sampling distribution of $F$ computed by formula (12.5) is given in Figure 12.7 by the $F$ function for two and four degrees of freedom when $n_1 = 3$ and $n_2 = 5$, by the $F$ function for five and five degrees of freedom when $n_1 = n_2 = 6$, and by the $F$ function for twenty and twenty degrees of freedom when $n_1 = n_2 = 21$.

3. For a single sample of paired values from a bivariate population distribution of $X$ and $Y$,

$$F = \frac{r_{xy}^2(N - 2)}{1 - r_{xy}^2}, \tag{12.6}$$

which is equivalent to a ratio involving two variances,

$$\frac{V'_{y'}}{V'_{y-y'}},$$

where $V'_{y'}$, is the variance of predicted values and $V'_{y-y'}$ is the variance of errors of prediction. $V'_{y'}$ is computed by dividing $\Sigma y'^2$, the sum of squares of predicted values, by one degree of freedom. $V'_{y-y'}$ is computed by dividing $\Sigma(y - y')^2$, the sum of squares of errors of prediction, by $(N - 2)$ degrees of freedom. In formula (12.6), $r_{xy}$ is the product-moment correlation coefficient computed from a sample of $N$ pairs of values. In this case, the sampling distribution of $F$ contains values which could be computed from the totality of sample correlation coefficients resulting from all possible pairings of values of $Y$ with a given set of values of $X$. The deductions which establish that the ratio in formula (12.6) is distributed as $F$ require that the $Y$'s for any given $X$ are normally distributed and that $\rho$, the population correlation, is zero. The student should compare formula (12.3) and formula (12.6). $F$ computed by formula (12.6) is equal to $t^2$ when $t$ is computed by formula (12.3). The numbers of degrees of freedom for $F$ are 1 and $(N - 2)$. The sampling distribution of $F$ computed by formula (12.6) is given in Figure 12.7 by the $F$ function for one and two degrees of freedom when $N = 4$, and by the $F$ function for one and thirty degrees of freedom when $N = 32$.

## THE DISTRIBUTION OF δ

The standard normal deviate, an *i*-statistic which we shall designate as $\delta$, will be discussed next. The standard normal deviate, $\delta$, is a normally distributed variable. Its distribution has a mean of zero, a variance equal to one, an index of skewness equal to zero, and an index of kurtosis equal to three.

Only one way of computing $\delta$ will be given here and that way is only approximate, not exact. For two large, random samples from a bivariate population distribution, the ratio

$$\frac{Z'_1 - Z'_2}{\sqrt{2/(N - 3)}}$$

is distributed approximately as the standard normal deviate. Therefore, we write

$$\delta = \frac{Z_1' - Z_2'}{\sqrt{2/(N - 3)}}, \tag{12.7}$$

understanding that the equality holds only approximately. $Z_1'$ is computed from the product-moment correlation coefficient for the first sample, as follows:

$$Z_1' = \frac{1}{2}\log_e \frac{1 + r_{xy}}{1 - r_{xy}}.$$

$Z_2'$ is computed in the same way from the product-moment correlation coefficient for the second sample. $N$ is the number of pairs of values in each sample. Figure 12.8 shows a normal curve with zero mean and unit variance,

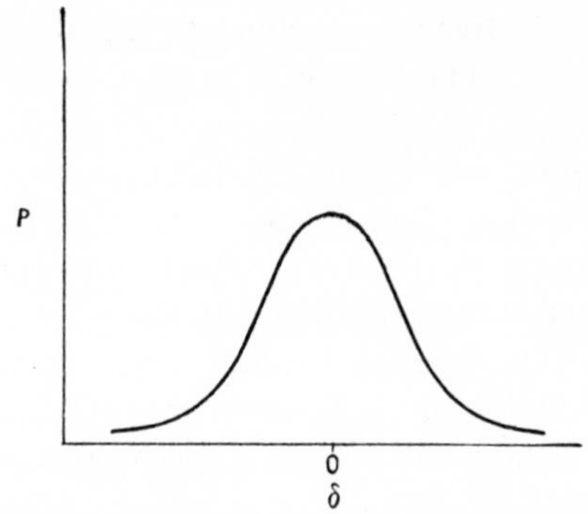


**Fig. 12.8** The sampling distribution of the standard normal deviate, $\delta$. The function is a normal probability function or normal curve with zero mean and unit variance.

the function for the sampling distribution of $\delta$. Notice that formula (12.7) involves the difference between $Z_1'$ and $Z_2'$. Since $Z_1'$ is a function of the magnitude of one sample correlation coefficient and $Z_2'$ is a function of the magnitude of the second sample correlation coefficient, $\delta$ indirectly compares the two sample correlation coefficients. In deducing the sampling distribution of $\delta$, there is no requirement that $\rho$, the population correlation coefficient, be zero, as there was for $t$ by formula (12.3) and $F$ by formula (12.6).

## The Tabled Functions

The distribution functions of $t$, $F$, and $\delta$ have been studied and information about them has been tabulated. In general terms, the tabulated information for a particular function consists of one or more values of the *i*-statistic, each of which is exceeded by a known proportion of all values in the sampling distribution. We shall comment on the tabled functions in the order: $t$, $F$, and $\delta$.

Table A in the Appendix presents information for 34 different $t$ functions, each one identified by a number of degrees of freedom. For each of these $t$ functions, a value of $t$ is given. Let us call this particular value $t_c$. It has two interpretations: one as a positive value, the other as a negative value. Interpreted as a positive value it is known to be exceeded by 0.025 of the totality of $t$ values in that sampling distribution. Interpreted as a negative value, it is known to exceed 0.025 of the totality of $t$ values in the distribution. Thus the proportion of values of $t$ exceeding the positive value of $t_c$ plus the proportion of values exceeded by the negative value of $t_c$ is equal to 0.05.

Examination of Table A reveals that, for two degrees of freedom, a value of $t_c$ equal to $+4.303$ is exceeded by 0.025 of all values of $t$ in that distribution and a value of $t_c$ equal to $-4.303$ exceeds 0.025 of all values in the distribution. For thirty degrees of freedom, a value of $t_c$ equal to $+2.042$ is exceeded by 0.025 of all values of $t$ and a value of $t_c$ equal to $-2.042$ exceeds the same proportion of values.

Interpreted with respect to the sampling distribution of $t$, the tabled values of $t_c$ provide a basis for classifying all values of $t$ in the distribution. We shall return later to this notion of classifying values of an $i$-statistic. It has great importance in the pragmatics of statistical inference.

Interpreted graphically, the tabled values locate points on the scale of $t$ which define areas under the curve. Consider the total area enclosed between the curve and the horizontal axis. If we erect perpendiculars to the horizontal

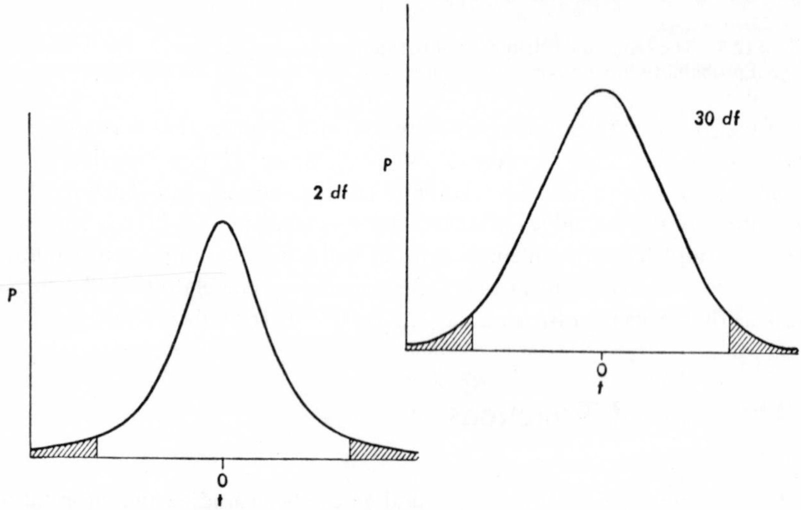


**Fig. 12.9** Two $t$ functions for two and thirty degrees of freedom. Perpendiculars have been erected at points defined by positive and negative values of $t_c$. The shaded area in each tail constitutes 0.025 of the total area under the curve.

axis at the points defined by positive and negative values of $t_c$, the area to the right of the positive value is 0.025 of the total area under the curve and the area to the left of the negative value is 0.025 of the total area. Together these two tail areas make up 0.05 of the total area. Figure 12.9 shows the $t$ functions for two and thirty degrees of freedom. Two perpendiculars have been erected for each curve. They were erected at +4.303 and −4.303 on the axis of the function for two degrees of freedom, and at +2.042 and −2.042 on the axis of the function for thirty degrees of freedom. The tail areas have been shaded.

Table $B_1$ in the Appendix gives information about 168 different $F$ functions, each one identified by two numbers of degrees of freedom. For each of these $F$ functions, a value of $F$ is given. Let us call this tabled value $F_c$. It is interpreted only as a positive value. It is known to be exceeded by 0.05 of the totality of $F$ values in the sampling distribution.

Examination of Table $B_1$ reveals that, for one degree of freedom in the numerator and four degrees of freedom in the denominator, a value of $F_c$, equal to 7.71 is exceeded by 0.05 of all values of $F$ in that distribution. For five degrees of freedom in the numerator and five degrees of freedom in the denominator, a value of $F_c$ equal to 5.05 is exceeded by 0.05 of the values of $F$ in the sampling distribution. (Table $B_2$ gives the value of $F_c$ exceeded by 0.025 of values in the distribution.)

The tabled values of $F_c$ provide a basis for classifying the totality of values in each sampling distribution. We shall have more to say about this classifying in a later discussion of pragmatics. Interpreted graphically, the tabled values

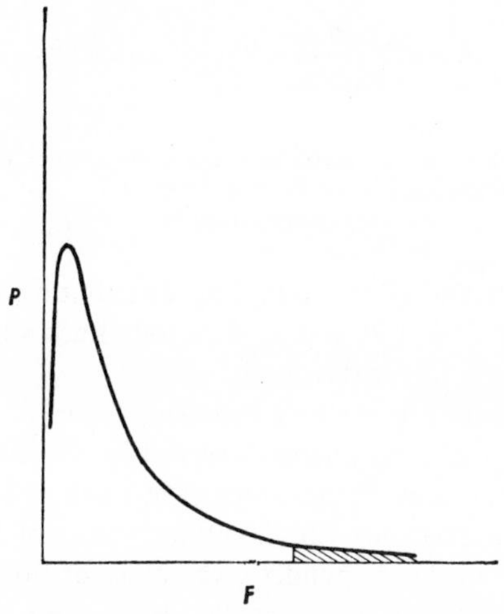


**Fig. 12.10** An $F$ function for five and five degrees of freedom. A perpendicular has been erected at a point on the horizontal axis such that the shaded tail area is 0.05 of the total area under the curve.

locate points on the scale of $F$. At each point a perpendicular can be erected to define areas under the curve. Figure 12.10 shows an $F$ function for five and five degrees of freedom. A perpendicular has been erected at the point on the horizontal axis, 5.05. The shaded tail area is 0.05 of the total area under the curve.

We have pointed out that there is a family of $t$ functions and a family of $F$ functions. Table A provides information about 34 $t$ functions selected from the entire family; Table $B_1$ provides information about 168 $F$ functions selected from the family; Table $B_2$ gives information about 100 $F$ functions. When the number of degrees of freedom is indefinitely large, $t$ is equal to $\delta$, the standard normal deviate. Therefore, the value of $\delta_c$ can be read from the last line of Table A. The value of $\delta_c$ has two interpretations: one as a positive value, the other as a negative value. Interpreted positively, the value of $\delta_c$ exceeded by 0.025 of the values in the sampling distribution is 1.96. Interpreted negatively, the value of $\delta_c$ which exceeds 0.025 of the values in the sampling distribution is $-1.96$. Figure 12.11 contains the normal curve in

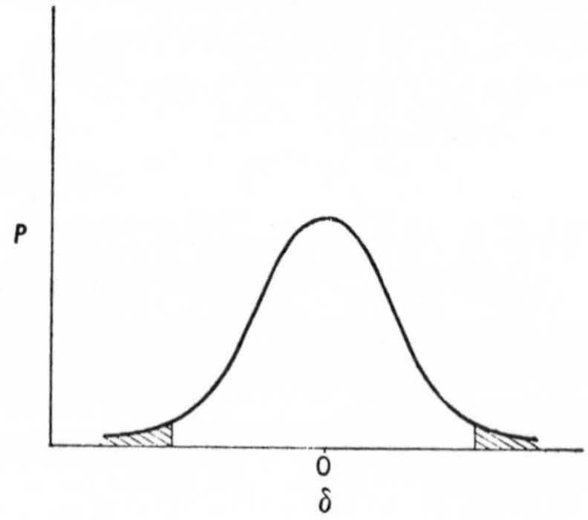


**Fig. 12.11** A normal curve with zero mean and unit variance representing the sampling distribution of $\delta$. Perpendiculars have been erected at $\delta = 1.96$ and $\delta = -1.96$. Each shaded area is 0.025 of the total area under the curve.

standard form representing the sampling distribution of $\delta$. Perpendiculars have been erected at $\delta_c = 1.96$ and $\delta_c = -1.96$. Each shaded area constitutes 0.025 of the total area under the curve.

Some statistical texts present very extensive tables of the standard normal deviate, but not for the same purposes served by the tables of $t$ and $F$. Since our interest in $\delta$ is the same as our interest in $t$ and $F$, we shall give only the information which is necessary for classifying values of $\delta$, as indicated above.

Tables of $t$ and $F$ in the Appendix give values of the $i$-statistics associated with the relative frequency 0.05. In the distribution of $t$, this relative frequency of 0.05 consists of the relative frequency 0.025 for extreme negative values and 0.025 for extreme positive values. In the distribution of $F$, the relative frequency 0.05 stands for extreme values in the positive direction only. Tables of $t$ and $F$ are available, which are more extensive than those given in the Appendix. These tables can be more extensive in two ways. They may exhibit greater variety in the numbers and combinations of degrees of freedom employed. They may present relative frequencies other than and in addition to 0.05. Values of an $i$-statistic are sometimes given for relative frequencies such as 0.10, 0.02, and 0.01 in addition to the values for the relative frequency 0.05. The limited tables presented in the Appendix have been found to be quite satisfactory for instructional purposes. The research psychologist would do well to have available the most complete tables. Two sources containing extensive tables are: R. A. Fisher, and F. Yates, *Statistical Tables for Biological, Medical, and Agricultural Research* (London and Edinburgh: Oliver and Boyd, 1948); and G. W. Snedecor, *Statistical Methods* (Ames, Iowa: Iowa State College Press, 1946).

## From Theory to Practice

Up to this point, the discussion has dealt only with the syntactical features of sampling error. The problem of realizing these features in practice is a problem of semantics, which remains to be considered. Practical random sampling, as distinguished from theoretical random sampling, will be considered in Chapter 13, which follows.

# PRACTICAL RANDOM SAMPLING

## Semantics | 13

There are two major semantical problems in psychological statistics. One of these, the problem of confirmation in psychological measurement, was discussed in Chapter 5. The other problem has to do with confirmation of the correspondence between random sampling theory and random sampling practice. The problem of confirmation in sampling theory and practice is the source of much misunderstanding, confusion, and incorrect usage in psychological research.

There are two principal ways in which the researcher can go wrong with respect to the problem of correspondence between sampling theory and practice. First, he may fail to recognize that the problem has to do not only with what he thinks, but also with what he does. For him, correspondence between theory and practice, or the lack of correspondence, is not a reality. He may look upon correspondence as nothing more than a conceptualization. He may adopt random sampling theory as no more than a sophisticated viewpoint, currently in vogue in the best research circles. If he does accept the reality of correspondence, he may err in thinking that its occurrence is fortuitous. He does not fully appreciate the fact that, within certain limits, he can actually make practice correspond to theory, and that his failure to do so leaves his work vulnerable to criticism and subject to rejection. He sees no connection between his choice of research operations and the statistical theory on which he will base his evaluation. He may advocate planning in advance so that a statistical evaluation is possible, but the demands of such an evaluation are not allowed to determine or limit the plans. If he worries at all about correspondence between theory and practice, he may attempt to rationalize his position or try to inveigle some person of statistical authority into doing so for him.

The person who fails to recognize the nature of the problem becomes undiscriminating in evaluating as well as in planning. He fails to coordinate his choice of a method of analysis with the character of his data. Critical features of his research operations may vary from one project to another, but this variation is not reflected in the kind of analysis he employs. The choice between description and inference is not determined by the nature of the operations which produce his data. It is often determined by nothing more than a preference for a sophisticated method over an unsophisticated one.

With respect to the correspondence between theory and practice, there are no standards, in an absolute sense, but there are standards in a relative sense. That is to say, correspondence is obviously better for some research operations and some evaluations than for others. It is sometimes possible to be discriminating in the choice of operations and thereby improve correspondence. When that is not possible, one can still be discriminating in his choice of a method of analysis. The discriminating researcher recognizes variation in the quality of research operations and is prepared to choose a type of evaluation which reflects this judgment and which is not likely to mislead his audience. Description and inference are the two kinds of analysis, between which a researcher can choose and thereby coordinate method of analysis and quality of operation.

The second way in which the researcher can go wrong relates to his misunderstanding of the consequences of various kinds of failure in correspondence between theory and practice. There is no way of assessing over-all correspondence. Practice may correspond to theory in one respect but not another. Furthermore, the degree of correspondence may vary. There is available substantial evidence as to the consequences of certain kinds and degrees of failure in correspondence. The consequences of one kind are known to be negligible. The consequences of another may be disastrous. All of this means that the psychologist must put the issues in a proper order; that is, he must put the more serious issues ahead of the less serious ones. He should, of course, try to satisfy all requirements perfectly, but if he falls short of the ideal, he should not become preoccupied with a trivial failure and ignore a serious one.

## Dimensions of Correspondence

We said above that there is no way of assessing over-all correspondence between random sampling theory and practice. Theoretical random sampling, as it was presented in Chapter 11, involved a known population distribution and a prescribed deductive system for obtaining the sampling distribution of some *i*-statistic. In Chapter 12, the population distribution was specified as a normal curve and the deduced sampling distributions were the *t* function, the *F* function, and the normal curve representing the standard normal deviate. (See formulas 12.1 to 12.7.) For convenience in discussion, let us divide the problem of correspondence into two parts: the characteristics of the population distribution and the system of obtaining samples.

A normal curve is a continuous function, unimodal and symmetrical. (See Figure 12.1.) Its index of skewness is zero. Its index of kurtosis is three. Suppose the population distribution is not a normal curve. Suppose there is, as we say, some departure from normality. What are the consequences? Are they serious?

Psychological measurements are always discrete variables, not continuous ones. The degree of discontinuity in the population may be great, as when the number of score intervals is two, or it may be small, as when the number of score intervals is one hundred. Whether the population discontinuity is great or small, the effect on a sampling distribution depends on the size of the sample. For any given number of score intervals, as sample size increases, the discontinuity of a sampling distribution diminishes. Furthermore, the effect will vary with the particular *i*-statistic under consideration. There is, of course, no absolute standard for deciding whether an effect is negligible or serious. Having surveyed the available evidence, we take the position here that the effect of discontinuity is negligible (1) when the number of values per sample is equal to or greater than twenty and the number of score intervals is equal to or greater than five; and (2) when the number of values per sample is equal to or greater than five and the number of score intervals is equal to or greater than twenty. The choice of these values is, to some extent, arbitrary. They are given simply as guides for the student who might be expected to form his own standards eventually after he accumulates more experience. There is evidence as to the specific effects of discontinuity on the sampling distributions of a variety of *i*-statistics, but presentation of that evidence would take us beyond the reasonable scope of this discussion.

Departures from normality with respect to the form or shape of the population distribution are usually given in terms of skewness and kurtosis. There is no question that the distributions of some psychological measures for some large groups of subjects do display nonnormal characteristics. Many distributions encountered in practice exhibit a slight to moderate degree of skewness and a slight to moderate degree of flatness. Only rarely does one encounter a so-called J-shaped or U-shaped distribution. The departure from normality in terms of skewness and kurtosis does affect the sampling distribution of those *i*-statistics presented in Chapter 12. Again this effect depends on the size of the sample. As sample size increases the effect becomes smaller. Furthermore, the effect of skewness and kurtosis varies depending on the *i*-statistic in question. There is no absolute standard for deciding how serious the effects are. After a considerable amount of independent research on this issue and an extensive study of the available evidence as to the effects of skewness and kurtosis, we have taken a position which can be summarized, as follows:

1. For the slight to moderate departures from normality ordinarily encountered in practice, the effect on the sampling distributions of $t$ and $F$, the multiple-sample $i$-statistics which compare sample means through formulas (12.2) and (12.4), is negligible when there are ten or more values per sample.

2. For the departures from normality encountered in practice, the effect on the sampling distribution of $t$, the single-sample $i$-statistic computed by formula (12.1), is more serious than the effect on the multiple-sample $t$ and $F$, but is negligible when there are thirty or more values in the sample.

3. The effect of moderate departures from normality on the sampling distribution of $F$, the ratio of two sample variances, as given by formula (12.5), is serious for very small samples, but is negligible for samples of fifty values or more.

4. The effect of moderate degrees of nonnormality on the sampling distribution of $t$, as in formula (12.3), or of $F$, as in formula (12.6), computed from a sample, product-moment coefficient of correlation, is negligible when the sample contains thirty or more values.

The arbitrary standards stated above obviously do not cover all situations. There is a vast amount of rational and empirical evidence concerning the effects of skewness and kurtosis on various sampling distributions, but we cannot do justice to the evidence here. While the standards suggested above are necessarily somewhat arbitrary, they have been adopted only after very serious study of the available evidence. There are some conspicuous gaps in the evidence on the effects of nonnormality. For example,we have not found evidence concerning the effect on the sampling distribution of $\delta$, as computed from two sample correlation coefficients by formula (12.7).

When we say that the sampling distribution of a given $i$-statistic is affected by nonnormality, we mean that the shaded areas in curves such as those of Figures 12.9, 12.10, and 12.11 may, under conditions of nonnormality in the population distribution, not be exactly what we expect them to be under the ideal, theoretical conditions represented by Tables A and B. When we say that the effects are negligible, we mean that the shaded areas, as a proportion of the total area, may deviate from 0.05, but will lie between 0.04 and 0.06. Again the student must be cautioned not to interpret these values as absolutes. In our judgment, the effect would be serious if the shaded areas constituted as much as 0.10 of the total area when the ideal, theoretical value was 0.05.

As it was described in Chapter 11, theoretical random sampling involved determining, by mathematical deduction, the nature of the sampling distribution of a given $i$-statistic. Notice that a random sample was defined as any logically possible set of $n$ values. It was not defined as a set of numbers consisting of typical values or as any particular combination of values. The sampling distribution of some given $i$-statistic is itself a frequency distribution of the values of that $i$-statistic computed for each one of all possible, logically determined samples. What, then, is random sampling in practice? Is there some set of concrete operations which deserve to be labeled as random sampling procedures and distinguished from other operations?

At the risk of seeming dogmatic, we shall define practical random sampling as selection by means of a tested mechanical system. The system involves concrete operations which are instituted and managed by the investigator. Before the system is ever used in research, it is tested to determine whether or not it will produce empirically, for a given *i*-statistic, a sampling distribution which corresponds to the mathematically deduced, theoretical sampling distribution. If there is substantial evidence of correspondence between the empirical sampling distribution and the theoretical sampling distribution, the mechanical system passes the test.

In real sampling, as distinguished from theoretical sampling, the selections are made from a population consisting of a large but finite number of existent and accessible units which can be measured. In psychological research, the unit of the population is a person, an animal, a behavioral event, or a behavioral product. The number of units selected is usually small relative to the number in the population. The population is real. That is, it exists and the units of the population are all equally accessible to the investigator doing the selecting.

## The Operations of Real Sampling

The mechanical system most widely used for selecting units from a population is one whose central feature is a so-called *table of random numbers*. A table of random numbers is a collection of digits with values from 0 to 9. The collection is usually generated, initially, by some mechanical device, such as a lottery, a die, or a roulette wheel, or by similar electronic equipment. The table is tested to determine whether it can be used to generate one or more appropriate sampling distributions. If repeated use of the table does produce an approximation to the desired distribution, then use of the table for sampling purposes is considered acceptable. That is, the correspondence between theoretical sampling and practical sampling is taken to be confirmed.

Broadly viewed, the system of real sampling has three phases: (1) units in the population are enumerated; (2) numbers are read from a table of random digits; and (3) units in the population are identified. The specific steps in these three phases are given below.

1. *Enumeration.* Assign ordinal numbers to the units of the population in any arbitrary fashion. For example, if the population consisted of 9,253 students listed in a university directory, each of the ordinal numbers from 0000 to 9,252 could be written beside the name of a student. Since the assignment may be arbitrary, the simplest procedure would be the best. Thus one

could begin at the beginning of the alphabetized directory and assign successive numbers to the names in alphabetical order.

2. *Reading*. Decide in advance the direction in which you will read numbers from the table of random digits and what you will do at the end of an array, at the end of a page, and at the end of the table. Choose a starting point in the table by some mechanical means. For example, a die could be used. The die could be thrown several times to indicate the starting page, row, and column. Next read groups of digits of a size appropriate to your needs. For example, if the population consists of 9,253 students enumerated from 0000 to 9,252, then you should read groups of four digits. It is usually advisable to record these groups in the order of their occurrence in the table. Read and record as many groups of digits as there are to be subjects in the sample. If the sample is to consist of 20 subjects, then it is necessary to read and record 20 groups of four digits from the table of random numbers. Numbers which recur and numbers which do not appear in the enumeration can be ignored.

3. *Identification and selection.* Take each group of digits and identify the unit bearing the same number in the enumerated population. Referring again to the population of 9,253 students, if one group of digits is 0389, look for the student whose name appears opposite that same ordinal number in the enumeration. He would be the $390^{th}$ in the listing of the directory. Thus each group of digits identifies a subject for the sample.

## A DEMONSTRATION OF REAL SAMPLING

Because of the importance of this system for obtaining samples and because students often have difficulty finding an account of the system, we shall go to some lengths to describe and discuss a demonstration of it.

We might demonstrate real sampling in any one of three ways:

1. Using a large group of real subjects as the population.

*Example:* Let the population consist of all male undergraduates listed in the student directory of University M. These students can be enumerated by writing ordinal numbers opposite their names. A sample of $n$ names can be obtained by means of a table of random digits. Students whose names are selected are measured on a response variable, $X$. An $i$-statistic is computed from the sample of real measures.

If it is desired, the sampling can be repeated many times. Each time, the value of the specified $i$-statistic can be computed. These values of the $i$-statistic can be arranged in a frequency distribution. This frequency distribution is actually an empirical sampling distribution for the specified $i$-statistic.

2. Using a frequency distribution of real measures as the population.

*Example:* Let the population consist of scores obtained from the files of the admissions office for students admitted to University M in September 1960. Ordinal numbers are assigned to these scores. A sample of $n$ scores is obtained by means of a table of random digits. An *i*-statistic is computed from the sample of $n$ scores.

If it was desired, the sampling could be repeated and an empirical sampling distribution for the *i*-statistic could be established.

3. Using an artificial frequency distribution of values as the population. The student should understand that we are concerned at this point with the possibility of demonstrating real sampling. It is entirely possible to do real sampling from an artificial population. Of course, sampling from an artificial population is only of interest as a demonstration, whereas sampling from a large group of real students might be an integral part of a serious research design. As a matter of convenience in providing a demonstration of real sampling in this text, we shall employ an artificial frequency distribution of values as the population.

*Example:* An artificial population distribution of 10,000 values is given in Table 13.1. The value of the variable $X$ is given in the first column. Score

**Table 13.1**

**AN ARTIFICIAL POPULATION OF 10,000 VALUES**

| $X$ | $f$ | Enumeration[a] |
|---|---|---|
| 9 | 30 | 0000–0029 |
| 8 | 150 | 0030–0179 |
| 7 | 630 | 0180–0809 |
| 6 | 1,610 | 0810–2,419 |
| 5 | 2,580 | 2,420–4,999 |
| 4 | 2,580 | 5,000–7,579 |
| 3 | 1,610 | 7,580–9,189 |
| 2 | 630 | 9,190–9,819 |
| 1 | 150 | 9,820–9,969 |
| 0 | 30 | 9,970–9,999 |

$N = \Sigma f = 10{,}000.$

[a]Ordinal numbers have been assigned to the values in each score interval.

intervals run from 0 to 9. The frequency for each of the 10 score intervals is given in the second column. The enumeration of these 10,000 values of $X$ has been carried out as indicated in the third column. Ordinal numbers from 0000 to 9,999 have been assigned to the values. Notice that the 30 values of $X = 9$ have been numbered from 0000 to 0029, that the 150 values of $X = 8$ have been numbered from 0030 to 0179, and so on.

To guide the selection of a sample from the artificial population distribution of Table 13.1, we need a table of random digits. One of the most extensive tables presently available has been published by the RAND Corporation (1). We recommend it to the student. It consists of 400 pages, each containing 2,500 digits arranged in 50 rows and 50 columns.

Before we choose a starting point in the RAND table, we must agree on a direction for reading. There are many legitimate ways of reading. On this occasion, we choose to read down a column. When we reach the bottom of a column, we shall go to the top of the next column to the right and again read down. When we reach the end of a page, we shall go to the top of the first column of the next page. If we should reach the end of the table, we shall go to the top of the first column of the first page.

**Table 13.2**

**PAGE 315 OF THE RAND TABLE OF RANDOM DIGITS**[a]

| | | | | | | | | | |
|---|---|---|---|---|---|---|---|---|---|
| 04053 | 17715 | 43400 | 34522 | 68089 | 30355 | 20322 | 52333 | 76076 | 91727 |
| 31727 | 22402 | 11241 | 61640 | 02827 | 50795 | 70134 | 16582 | 69014 | 55896 |
| 48972 | 14109 | 04845 | 34052 | 01783 | 00579 | 14707 | 56638 | 59995 | 56408 |
| 35099 | 31960 | 51506 | 59727 | 29550 | 88060 | 21648 | 23421 | 43386 | 41416 |
| 20483 | 88049 | 17811 | 70031 | 02221 | 30110 | 77697 | 63966 | 94679 | 10815 |
| 68653 | 97277 | 62431 | 72251 | 36814 | 43076 | 68312 | 89337 | 68758 | 54435 |
| 27371 | 05095 | 87439 | 71329 | 85939 | 64115 | 81106 | 90143 | 48199 | 60039 |
| 41026 | 60713 | 56004 | 82914 | 00715 | 83161 | 76961 | 58121 | 41355 | 06459 |
| 06875 | 44626 | 99143 | 25641 | 71349 | 14100 | 49379 | 13105 | 36046 | 28527 |
| 64218 | 57810 | 15692 | 15082 | 68878 | 08555 | 01203 | 61016 | 74250 | 64415 |
| 52402 | 60583 | 71761 | 33176 | 75982 | 16737 | 28581 | 99542 | 06190 | 33634 |
| 68304 | 38817 | 19251 | 13560 | 11777 | 05110 | 87031 | 23711 | 79992 | 13079 |
| 23596 | 97483 | 30567 | 48193 | 72614 | 02713 | 63404 | 56120 | 92247 | 65664 |
| 21925 | 00748 | 67909 | 76732 | 28409 | 60393 | 88008 | 24908 | 75505 | 25513 |
| 32992 | 15761 | 19539 | 37828 | 11066 | 07225 | 00852 | 57776 | 71082 | 43426 |
| 02937 | 37434 | 44330 | 47023 | 30645 | 72908 | 27689 | 81053 | 34433 | 23774 |
| 39030 | 04243 | 06733 | 98748 | 25280 | 27477 | 27120 | 59275 | 50174 | 10209 |
| 15868 | 20232 | 81938 | 86723 | 26893 | 36819 | 38430 | 68672 | 86559 | 73539 |
| 39142 | 09183 | 85563 | 42090 | 32553 | 61305 | 35799 | 06371 | 90528 | 03077 |
| 28809 | 31863 | 42937 | 34254 | 51279 | 72123 | 91317 | 44412 | 12396 | 07558 |
| 02722 | 89389 | 11279 | 04679 | 55813 | 59654 | 90215 | 45054 | 10847 | 62762 |
| 23515 | 35796 | 27400 | 21566 | 98177 | 23154 | 81545 | 43045 | 27143 | 44262 |
| 60828 | 50557 | 24130 | 41836 | 54027 | 38882 | 49655 | 14151 | 93316 | 92291 |
| 60223 | 38059 | 74420 | 83185 | 82692 | 73823 | 88512 | 65023 | 31227 | 68763 |
| 04236 | 07245 | 64062 | 05593 | 00297 | 98838 | 58142 | 72612 | 53560 | 53124 |
| 20550 | 94288 | 81185 | 97328 | 27471 | 78030 | 72060 | 02589 | 46817 | 24717 |
| 23894 | 78784 | 15002 | 92991 | 95177 | 36298 | 16537 | 88473 | 64426 | 50984 |
| 26911 | 68399 | 72830 | 98733 | 74928 | 01880 | 99084 | 20028 | 46629 | 62639 |
| 54723 | 39396 | 98377 | 28108 | 75949 | 73331 | 34178 | 46882 | 22794 | 30529 |
| 50238 | 83837 | 83753 | 27700 | 41183 | 93953 | 62126 | 78326 | 83809 | 69886 |

[a]Lines of the original RAND table are numbered. These numbers have been omitted from the table as it is reproduced above. Adapted with permission from the RAND Corporation, *A Million Random Digits* (Glencoe, Ill.: The Free Press, 1955), p. 315.

**Table 13.2**

**PAGE 315 OF THE RAND TABLE OF RANDOM DIGITS** (*continued*)

| | | | | | | | | | |
|---|---|---|---|---|---|---|---|---|---|
| 25618 | 40076 | 81223 | 34072 | 58189 | 09393 | 38528 | 09972 | 55984 | 77363 |
| 64302 | 92307 | 15246 | 15004 | 45925 | 65448 | 61462 | 38861 | 18612 | 90501 |
| 26803 | 58650 | 80410 | 04526 | 99352 | 25352 | 56848 | 25675 | 88086 | 89600 |
| 86214 | 24449 | 37100 | 30921 | 16325 | 65987 | 07534 | 24678 | 23150 | 20902 |
| 10817 | 66999 | 12056 | 22844 | 03847 | 33336 | 52092 | 24251 | 49702 | 24384 |
| 22677 | 51371 | 47284 | 22063 | 07727 | 31379 | 90462 | 65657 | 41798 | 00212 |
| 19193 | 79282 | 30388 | 60077 | 25370 | 03559 | 03151 | 61731 | 42763 | 24632 |
| 19052 | 65518 | 36005 | 78326 | 81155 | 97428 | 98679 | 15903 | 34641 | 51083 |
| 03231 | 80995 | 66618 | 13905 | 90549 | 29499 | 88947 | 66575 | 02525 | 08398 |
| 88063 | 16412 | 99869 | 38663 | 82026 | 06803 | 18966 | 78992 | 21280 | 29960 |
| 26529 | 35993 | 24584 | 00452 | 11108 | 75438 | 06078 | 98785 | 38040 | 93746 |
| 84241 | 57374 | 39160 | 27898 | 27412 | 35091 | 06716 | 78165 | 24196 | 12540 |
| 30581 | 12894 | 02779 | 03668 | 48223 | 88050 | 00591 | 07738 | 87437 | 60512 |
| 13719 | 64755 | 29962 | 32118 | 18738 | 30514 | 33012 | 89132 | 84340 | 97263 |
| 14983 | 13884 | 48457 | 81853 | 74278 | 33136 | 20349 | 71379 | 97447 | 42103 |
| 47762 | 02694 | 52343 | 62711 | 09088 | 35045 | 75288 | 00758 | 76053 | 60504 |
| 26793 | 37177 | 06115 | 74306 | 79880 | 93933 | 64200 | 06100 | 40161 | 08666 |
| 13144 | 61888 | 93496 | 34850 | 97094 | 50528 | 26382 | 64887 | 71587 | 21951 |
| 93754 | 22003 | 38235 | 87426 | 44051 | 03441 | 65669 | 16972 | 30122 | 16988 |
| 77437 | 95511 | 58403 | 56003 | 22978 | 30781 | 72495 | 67801 | 67423 | 20297 |

We now proceed with the selection of a starting point. There are 400 pages of random digits in the RAND table. We divide the 400 pages into five sections of 80 pages each, and throw a die to choose a section. We throw a " 4," thereby choosing the fourth section of 80 pages from page 241 to page 320. (If we had obtained a " 6 " on the first throw, we would have ignored it and thrown again.) We divide the 80 pages into five sections of 16 each and throw the die. This time we obtain a " 5," thereby choosing pages 305 to 320. We divide these 16 pages into four sections and throw the die. A " 3 " comes up and our choice has been narrowed to the four pages: 313, 314, 315, and 316. Another throw gives us a " 6 " which we ignore. Another throw yields " 3 " and page 315 is chosen for the starting point.

On page 315 of the RAND table there are 2,500 digits arranged in 50 rows and 50 columns. This arrangement is reproduced in our Table 13.2. Notice the grouping of rows and columns produced by the spacing. This grouping only serves the purpose of making the table easier to read. We shall take advantage of the grouping to locate our starting point. Five major columns can be distinguished. A throw of the die produces a " 1 " and puts us in the first major column of the page. The 10 major rows can be divided into five pairs. A throw of the die yields a " 3 " and puts us in the middle pair of the five pairs of major rows. Our choice has now been narrowed down to the arrangement of digits set apart by the rectangle of dotted lines in Table 13.2. There are two major columns in this arrangement. Let the left column be designated " odd " and the right column, " even." A throw of the die yields a " 2 " and we choose the right column. There are two major rows in the column. Let the upper row be " odd " and the lower row be " even." The die says " 3 " and we choose the upper row. There remains now a block of digits with five rows and five columns. A throw of the die for the column gives a " 3." Another throw for the row gives a " 2 " and the starting point is finally determined. The digit which serves as a starting point is a " 7 " in the twenty-second row and the eighth column of the $50 \times 50$ arrangement on page 315 of the RAND table.

Let us suppose that we want a sample of 10 values from the population of Table 13.1. We require 10 groups of four digits from the table of random digits, starting with the " 7." Reading down the column yields the following 10 groups: 7502, 2733, 8036, 4932, 5949, 3878, 6180, 5100, 6479, and 1218.

By means of these 10 numbers, we can now identify 10 values of $X$ in the population distribution of Table 13.1. The first number read from the table of random digits is 7502. In the distribution of Table 13.1, the value of $X$ numbered 7,502 is 4. The second number is 2733. The value of $X$ numbered 2,733 is 5. Thus we can determine 10 values of $X$ to which we were directed by the 10 groups of digits read from the table of random digits. Table 13.3

**Table 13.3**

**A RANDOM SAMPLE OF TEN VALUES FROM THE POPULATION IN TABLE 13.1**

| Random Numbers | Corresponding Values of $X$ |
|---|---|
| 7502 | 4 |
| 2733 | 5 |
| 8036 | 3 |
| 4932 | 5 |
| 5949 | 4 |
| 3878 | 5 |
| 6180 | 4 |
| 5100 | 4 |
| 6479 | 4 |
| 1218 | 6 |

gives the 10 groups of four digits from the table of random digits and the corresponding values of $X$ from the population in Table 13.1. The 10 values of $X$ constitute a real sample from the artificial population.

Having obtained a random sample of 10 values in this demonstration, we shall compute three *i*-statistics from those values. Among the *i*-statistics discussed in Chapter 12, there are three which can be computed from a single sample of values of $X$. The three possibilities include $M_x$, the sample mean; $V'_x$, the sample variance computed with degrees of freedom; and $t$, a ratio computed by formula (12.1). To complete the demonstration, we shall compute $t$. In the process of computing $t$, we shall have to compute the other two: $M_x$ and $V'_x$. Formula (12.1) is

$$t = \frac{M_x - \mu}{\sqrt{V'_x/n}}.$$

The required values can be computed, as follows:

$$M_x = \frac{\Sigma X}{n} = \frac{44}{10} = 4.4;$$

$$\Sigma x^2 = \Sigma X^2 - \frac{(\Sigma X)^2}{n} = 200 - \frac{44^2}{10} = 6.4;$$

$$V'_x = \frac{\Sigma x^2}{n-1} = \frac{6.4}{9} = 0.711; \text{ and}$$

$$\mu = 4.5.$$

Substituting these values in formula (12.1) yields the following result:

$$t = \frac{M_x - \mu}{\sqrt{V'_x/n}} = \frac{4.4 - 4.5}{\sqrt{0.711/10}} = -0.375.$$

The value of $t$ computed for a random sample from the population in Table 13.1 is $-0.375$. This completes the demonstration of the procedure for obtaining a single random sample.

If we wished to generate an empirical sampling distribution of $t$, we would repeat the selection of a sample many times and compute for each sample a value of $t$. The frequency distribution of a very large number of values of $t$, so obtained, would constitute an empirical sampling distribution, the counterpart of a theoretical $t$ function. We shall not attempt here to generate a complete sampling distribution but, to illustrate the results of repeated sampling on a limited scale, we have selected four additional samples of 10 values from the population in Table 13.1. Table 13.4 shows the numbers read from page 315 of the RAND table and the corresponding values of $X$ from the population. The student can verify that the random numbers for the four additional samples follow those of the first sample in the RAND table. Table 13.5 contains values of $M_x$, $V'_x$, and $t$ for each of the five samples. Figure 13.1 shows a frequency distribution of the five values of $t$ obtained from the five random samples. The student should verify the computation of the $t$ values from the four additional samples.

It is important to understand that each of the five sets of values discussed above qualify as random samples because of the method used in selecting the values and not because of any characteristics of the values themselves. Likewise, the variability of the $t$ values in Figure 13.1 is random variability because of the method used in selecting and not because of any characteristics of the

**Table 13.4**

**FOUR ADDITIONAL RANDOM SAMPLES**[a]

| Sample 2 | | Sample 3 | |
|---|---|---|---|
| Random Numbers | Corresponding Values of $X$ | Random Numbers | Corresponding Values of $X$ |
| 1846 | 6 | 2909 | 5 |
| 3438 | 5 | 7536 | 4 |
| 6895 | 4 | 0373 | 7 |
| 5488 | 4 | 8143 | 3 |
| 9937 | 1 | 2339 | 6 |
| 0549 | 7 | 6795 | 4 |
| 7819 | 3 | 8496 | 3 |
| 1979 | 6 | 7670 | 3 |
| 5897 | 4 | 9912 | 1 |
| 8015 | 3 | 8523 | 3 |

| Sample 4 | | Sample 5 | |
|---|---|---|---|
| Random Numbers | Corresponding Values of $X$ | Random Numbers | Corresponding Values of $X$ |
| 4454 | 5 | 1831 | 6 |
| 4783 | 5 | 4336 | 5 |
| 1410 | 6 | 9230 | 2 |
| 5168 | 4 | 2450 | 5 |
| 5917 | 4 | 9353 | 2 |
| 1361 | 6 | 1417 | 6 |
| 4088 | 5 | 2769 | 5 |
| 4122 | 5 | 5190 | 4 |
| 7681 | 3 | 7946 | 3 |
| 7988 | 3 | 1521 | 6 |

[a]Population in Table 13.1.

**Table 13.5**

**VALUES OF $M_x$, $V'_x$, AND $t$ FOR THE FIVE RANDOM SAMPLES**[a]

| | Sample 1 | 2 | 3 | 4 | 5 |
|---|---|---|---|---|---|
| $M_x$ | 4.4 | 4.3 | 3.9 | 4.6 | 4.4 |
| $V'_x$ | 0.711 | 3.122 | 2.989 | 1.156 | 2.489 |
| $t$ | −0.375 | −0.358 | −1.097 | 0.294 | −0.200 |

[a]Population in Table 13.1; sample values in Table 13.4.

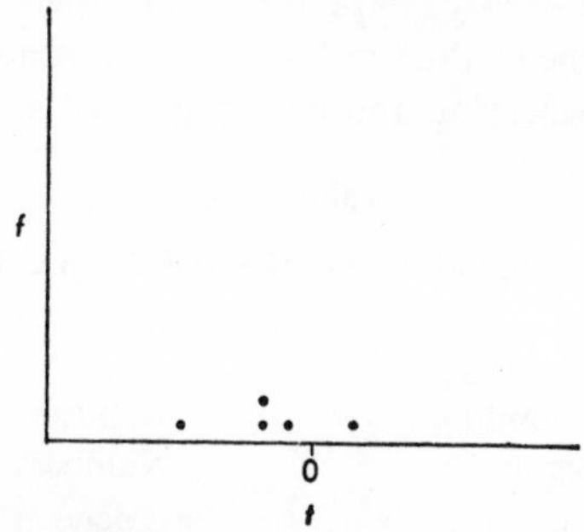


**Fig. 13.1** The distribution of *t* values computed from the five random samples in Tables 13.2 and 13.3. (Values have been grouped into intervals of 0.1.)

values themselves. Thus *i*-statistics, as values computed from random samples, can be expected to vary. As will be shown later, this circumstance constitutes the foundation or background for all uses of statistical inference. The particular operations devised by the research psychologist to answer a question, with the aid of statistical inference, are always superimposed on the operations which insure that error variability is randomly distributed and will affect the outcome in a random fashion. There is no pretending these procedures eliminate uncertainty in the evaluation of research results. The uncertainty is there in the form of random variation. At the same time, however, the fact that the uncertainty arises from random variation insures a kind of rigor for the evaluation in the sense that the distribution of outcomes strictly due to error is known. One might say that the nature of the uncertainty is well understood.

# Perspective

The purpose of the demonstration of the use of a table of random digits in sampling was to focus the student's attention on the concrete operations of real sampling. To do so, within this text, it seemed most convenient to use an artificial population—the frequency distribution of Table 13.1. This use of an artificial population in a demonstration of real sampling deserves comment. Beginning students are sometimes confused by demonstrations involving artificial elements or devices. They sometimes mistakenly conclude that sampling in psychological research must somehow involve an artificial distribution like the one in Table 13.1. The fact is that sampling in psychological research involves the selection procedures of the demonstration applied to a population of organisms, behavioral events, or behavioral products instead of the artificial population. They also sometimes mistakenly conclude that the purpose of a demonstration is simply to express and to dramatize an assumption. This is not true. We repeat that the purpose is to direct attention to and explain the use of a table of random digits in the set of concrete operations which should be employed for sampling in psychological research.

## The Random Interval Procedure

A table of random digits can be used correctly in a variety of ways, too numerous to list or discuss here. One variation in procedure deserves mention, however, because of its convenience in certain situations. One can sometimes avoid the burdensome task of actually enumerating the units of the population. For example, suppose one had a list of 5,000 voters and wanted a sample constituting 20 per cent of the total number. Taking every fifth name in the list would yield the desired number of subjects, but such a procedure is not acceptable because it cannot be subjected to a general test of randomness and, on any given occasion, it could be quite unsatisfactory. Instead of every fifth name, however, one might use a random interval, one determined by the succession of digits in a tested table.

The random interval procedure involves the following steps: Adopt a direction for reading and choose a starting point in the table of random digits. Agree to read the digit " 0 " as " 10." Read the first digit and count that number of names beginning with the first name in the list. The last name counted goes in the sample. Read the second digit and count again, starting with the next name in the list. The last name counted goes in the sample. Read the third digit from the table, count names, and so on. The number of names skipped will vary from 0 to 9, but, over a large number of selections, will average very close to four names, thus insuring that approximately one fifth of the names will be chosen. The procedure can be adapted to other population sizes and sample sizes by reading some combinations of digits and disregarding other combinations.

## Other Ways of Distributing Variability Randomly

There are two situations in which the investigator does not actually select a sample from a population but can and does insure the random distribution of certain kinds of variability over values he wishes to compute. When either of these two situations obtain, it is considered quite acceptable statistical practice to treat values computed from the collection of observations as *i*-statistics, that is, as values computed from random samples. The student will undoubtedly experience some difficulty in perceiving any equivalence in these several approaches. One reason is that the equivalence is not exact. Another reason is that the equivalence of the actual procedures cannot be deduced mathematically. Another is that the common acceptance and justification of the equivalence are, to some extent, based on experience. Finally, there is a certain exercise of common sense and argument here which the student will not likely be prepared to grasp immediately.

The first situation is one in which the investigator has a group of subjects which he wishes to divide into two (or more) subgroups so that the final difference between the subgroups constitutes a random event. He makes the division by sorting names into subgroups, with the sorting guided by a succession of numbers read from a table of random digits. If he wishes to sort into two subgroups, he may read digits as " odd " and " even," and sort successive names in the list into odd and even subgroups, as dictated by the succession of digits. If he wishes to sort into three subgroups, he may read single digits, ignoring all but 1's, 2's, and 3's, and sort successive names into groups numbered " 1," " 2," and " 3." Since there is nothing to do when all but one subgroup is filled but put the remaining names into that subgroup, it is necessary to randomize the original order in which names are listed. If the names are put on cards, then the cards could be well shuffled initially and then actually sorted into piles as dictated by the random digits.

When a group of subjects is divided randomly into subgroups, these subgroups are often treated as random samples and values computed from them are considered to be *i*-statistics. One may reasonably ask, What constitutes the population in this case? There is no population in the sense implied by the original definition of the word. There is a population, however, in the sense of a totality of logically possible arrangements of $N$ subjects into $c$ subgroups of $n$ subjects each. For example, if $N = 20$, $c = 2$, and $n = 10$, then the total number of logically possible arrangements is $20!/10!10! = 184{,}756$.[1] There has been some study of the relation between sampling distributions for *i*-statistics based on the theory of a normally distributed population and sampling distributions for *i*-statistics based on the theory of a population of arrangements. Under certain conditions, the relation is quite satisfactory and supports the practice just described.

Earlier, in connection with the discussion of selecting samples from a population, it was said that the population was real and accessible. The population of arrangements is obviously different. It is real, in the sense that any one arrangement can actually occur, but it is not accessible, in the sense that all arrangements are simultaneously available.

The second situation is one in which the investigator wishes to obtain observations on $n$ subjects in succession. There are, therefore, $n$ occasions of

[1]Factorial notation was briefly explained in Chapter 2. *Example:* $5! = 5 \times 4 \times 3 \times 2 \times 1 = 120$.

measurement, each of which is associated with an error of some unknown magnitude. It is the investigator's desire to distribute errors associated with occasions of measurement randomly over the subjects to be measured. To do so, he assigns ordinal numbers to the subjects arbitrarily and then determines the order of occurrence of these numbers in a table of random digits. Their order of occurrence is the order in which he measures the subjects. Usually the research requires at least one repetition of the whole procedure. Certain values computed from the entire collection of observations qualify as *i*-statistics. Here the population is the totality of orders into which $n$ objects can be placed. The number is $n!$ The population of orders is real in the sense that any one of them can occur, but it is not accessible, in the sense that all orders are simultaneously available.

## Incorrect Practice

When a tested mechanical device like a table of random digits is employed, random selection, random sorting, and random ordering, as well as combinations of these, constitute the admissible procedures for insuring semantical correspondence between theoretical sampling and practical sampling. What are the consequences of failure in this correspondence? When the procedure used has not been tested or when the investigator has done nothing to meet this requirement, then the consequences are unpredictable. Unintended and unwanted differences in the observations, and in the values computed from them, may be small or large, may operate in one direction or another, and may be consistent or inconsistent. One would not know what to expect. The shaded areas in the tails of the distributions of Figures 12.9, 12.10, and 12.11, and the form of those distributions, would be indeterminate. As a matter of fact, it would be more nearly correct to say these distributions do not then exist.

Because of the drastic consequences when there is a failure in the sampling aspect of the problem of correspondence, the investigator should place this issue first among his concerns. Since departures from normality in the distribution of errors may not be serious, if he can insure that the unintended variability in his observations is random, he has taken a giant step toward insuring correspondence between sampling theory and practice. If he can also insure that discontinuity and other departures from normality are negligible, so much the better. The frequent practice of ignoring the requirement that variability be distributed randomly and, at the same time, investing the problem of nonnormality with exaggerated importance cannot be defended.

We have something more to say about this problem of distributing variability randomly. We believe it is incorrect and indefensible for a psychologist to call a set of measures a random sample when he has done nothing to insure that the set of measures has the properties of a random sample. He may try to justify himself by saying that the set of measures can be thought of as a random sample from some hypothetical population. In doing so, he is referring to the particular values of the set and is considering them as typical of some imaginary population. He is mistaken in defining a random sample in terms of the values in it. He is completely disregarding the method of obtaining the values. Actually the populations which could give rise to a sample containing certain specified values are innumerable. A random sample, theoretical or practical, is defined by the procedures of selection. Calling a set of measures a random sample, when nothing has been done to insure that the set of measures has been selected as it should have been, is simply unrealistic.

## Transformations

Certain kinds and degrees of nonnormality can be reduced or eliminated by applying one of several transformations to the observations before *i*-statistics are computed. In Chapter 4, several examples were given of sets of numbers whose distributions were asymmetrical originally, but became symmetrical when the transformations were applied. The application of transformations to real measures cannot be expected to produce perfect symmetry as was true of the examples of Chapter 4. At best, the skewness of a distribution may only be reduced somewhat and the final distribution may only be approximately normal. Despite these limitations, one should be alert for indications that the departure from normality is such that a proper transformation will improve the distribution and bring about closer correspondence between theory and practice.

## Summary

As regards sampling theory and practice, the problem of correspondence has two parts: the nature of the population distribution and the properties of the method of selecting samples from that population. With respect to the first part of the problem, sampling distributions of *i*-statistics are affected by departures from normality such as discontinuity, skewness, and kurtosis. The effects are much less serious for certain *i*-statistics than for others. The effects become less serious as the size of the sample(s) increases. Our conclusion is that, under many conditions encountered in actual practice, failure in the requirement of a normal distribution is not so serious as to preclude the use of sampling theory in the evaluation of research. With respect to the second part of the problem, sampling distributions do not exist when there are no operations which insure that variability is randomly distributed. Our conclusion is that sampling theory does not apply when there is a failure in the requirement that variability be randomly distributed.

### REFERENCE

1. The RAND Corporation, *A Million Random Digits* (Glencoe, Ill.: The Free Press, 1955).

# STATISTICAL INFERENCE AND RESEARCH

## Pragmatics | 14

The research psychologist can never be certain that his observations of behavior are uncontaminated by error. No matter how careful he may be in planning and conducting a study, a multitude of influences, unintended and unwanted by the researcher, produces in his data effects of unknown magnitude. These unintended differences or biases make interpretation of the results of research quite difficult and introduce into the interpretation a degree of uncertainty which cannot be eliminated.

Sources of error in psychological research can be logically classified into two categories: differences which arise from the selection of subjects, and extraneous influences which come to bear upon an observation at the particular time and place it is made. Because there is no way of insuring that these biases will be completely eliminated from the data, the results of any investigation are, strictly speaking, specific to that endeavor. The results depend on the particular subjects studied and the particular occasions on which observations were obtained. The research psychologist cannot, of course, be satisfied with this limitation. His goal is the acquisition of knowledge in the form of general principles and laws.

Inductive inference, in science, is the act of reasoning in a logical fashion from the individual event to the universal event. It begins with a particular set of observations of some natural phenomenon and concludes with a general proposition concerning that phenomenon or its class. It is the process whereby the scientist hopes to transcend the limitations of his data with respect to their specificity.

There is now wide acceptance, in the behavioral sciences, of the proposition that the process of induction should take place in a context of theory and practice provided by statistical inference. This does not mean that inductive inference cannot be accomplished except through statistical procedures. Physical scientists have not been dependent on statistics for the high order of the inductive inferences which have characterized their research. There is a great deal more to research and the acquisition of knowledge than statistical manipulation of data. There is little doubt, however, that, in the analysis of data and in certain formal aspects of research design, the methods of statistical inference represent the most rigorous logic men have yet been able to achieve in this connection.

It is, of course, in the very nature of inference that it is accompanied by uncertainty and that it is subject to error. Statistical inference shares these faults. There is a sense, however, in which statistical inference can be said to be rigorous. In any given investigation, the probability of an incorrect inference is known and stated.

Before we become involved in the specific applications of statistical inference in psychological research, it would be well to consider two distinctions which are extremely important for an understanding of these applications. We can distinguish two kinds of procedures in statistical inference: the testing of significance and the estimating of population values or parameters. We can also distinguish two kinds of research: experimental research and empirical research. These terms will be defined and discussed later at length. At the moment, it would be appropriate to examine the relation between the statistical procedures and the two kinds of research.

Since the two statistical procedures can be employed in the evaluation of either kind of research, the subject matter of statistical inference and its applications in research can be divided into four topics representing the four possible combinations of procedure and kind of research. These four topics are given by the following brief outline:

A. Experimental research
    1. Testing significance
    2. Estimating parameters
B. Empirical research
    1. Testing significance
    2. Estimating parameters

Although the relative importance of these four topics might be debated, it is our opinion that a careful survey of the actual research being done by psychologists and the kinds of statistical procedures being used in the evaluation of that research would reveal that testing significance occurs much more often than estimating parameters. There is a reasonable explanation for this one-sided emphasis on testing significance and some comment will be made by way of explanation of the situation in Chapter 16. Furthermore, although there is probably some general inclination for research psychologists to view experimental research as being more important than nonexperimental research, we take the position here that both are important and merit discussion, as long as they are clearly distinguished. Under the assumption that both kinds of research are important, but that testing of significance is generally of more interest to the research psychologist than estimating parameters, we shall emphasize the testing of significance in separate discussions of experimental and empirical research. Testing significance in experimental research will be taken up in Chapter 15; testing significance in empirical research will be considered in Chapter 16.

Although the testing of significance will be emphasized, we do believe that the student should be introduced to estimation procedures. Our choice of examples for an introduction to estimation places the discussion in Chapter 16, which deals with empirical research. As we have indicated, estimation has many applications in experimental research, but space does not permit us to pursue the topic that far. Consequently, nothing will be said about estimation in Chapter 15, which deals with experimental research.

In labeling the two kinds of research, " experimental " and " empirical," we do not mean to imply that experimental research is not empirical in nature. Acquisition of experience through careful observation is an important part of both kinds of research. According to our definition, empirical research is planned investigation with the following features: careful observation, classification or measurement, establishing relations between qualitative or quantitative variables, and prediction involving these variables. Experimental research is also planned investigation, with these features and something in addition. Experimental research has the scientist intervening in natural processes, not just observing them. He stages the events of the research. He introduces changes and observes the consequences of these changes. He manipulates one or more variables and observes the effect of the manipulation on another variable. He changes conditions around his subjects and measures the effect of the change on some aspect of their behavior.

We have reason for being particular regarding the use of these terms. There is no room for loose thought and language in research. Success in acquiring knowledge depends to a very large extent on reducing issues to the simplest terms possible. If a research issue can be expressed in terms which make obvious the nature of a correct resolution of that issue, one is then on firm ground. If a research issue remains vague in one's thought and expression, and if its resolution is largely a matter of conjecture, then there is little chance for success. Rigorous thought and language should be the immediate objective of the student who hopes to become a research psychologist.

There is much loose usage of the term " experiment." Some of the worst usage comes about when a would-be researcher adopts the term to lend prestige to something he has done or wants to do. The result is that every kind of study has, at some time and place, been referred to as an experiment.

If everything is an experiment, there is no need for the term. It becomes synonymous with " research." An important discrimination is thereby lost.

There is a line of thought which connects experimental research with the determination of causes. While this usage comes very close to the important distinction on which we have been insisting, it ultimately runs afoul of the problem of defining " cause " and the many philosophical issues which that problem entails. Consequently, the word " cause " becomes a liability rather than an asset in making explicit the difference between the two kinds of research.

The distinction between experimental and empirical research is actually a simple one and its importance is obvious when one takes a direct and straightforward view of the research situation. The research psychologist engages in one or the other of two clearly distinguishable kinds of operations. In the one kind of operation, he installs himself at some vantage point and observes the behavior of human or animal subjects in an environment whose characteristics he may also record. The information he acquires from observing may turn out to have broad generality and may be of great practical consequence. In the other kind of operation, he controls certain conditions, manipulates one or more others, and observes the effect of the manipulation on the behavior of his subjects. Again the information he acquires may possess generality and practical value. As we indicated earlier, the first operation characterizes empirical research; the second operation characterizes experimental research.

As long as the psychologist reports faithfully what he did and as long as his interpretation of his results is appropriate to what he did, there is no problem. The trouble begins when he engages in the first operation and tries to interpret his results as indicating what would be found out from the second operation. That is, he observes, and does nothing more than observe, but draws conclusions from his data as to what would happen if he intervened. Now it is obvious that the most certain knowledge about intervention is going to come from investigations in which intervention takes place. When the researcher does nothing more than observe, a conclusion about the effects of intervention can be a very bad guess. If he wishes to learn what effect some manipulation of conditions has on the behavior of subjects, he should perform exactly that manipulation. Even if he actually does manipulate conditions, the results will entail some degree of uncertainty because of error, but if he does not manipulate, the prospect is far worse.

The controversy over the connection between lung cancer and smoking is an excellent example of this issue. There seems to be little doubt that scientists have observed a relation between the incidence of lung cancer and smoking. What the nature of this relation is, remains quite uncertain. What they have not observed is the effect of manipulating smoking. To be exact, they have observed that the incidence of lung cancer is greater among smokers than among nonsmokers. They have not observed that the incidence of lung cancer increases among nonsmokers when they take up smoking. Nor have they observed that the incidence of lung cancer decreases among smokers when they quit smoking. They have not shown that young people could avoid lung cancer by not smoking and that the same young people would contract lung cancer if they did smoke. They have not shown that elimination of smoking would eliminate the lung cancer now known to be associated with it.

To sum up, the researcher may observe or he may manipulate and observe. Observation alone may yield valuable information. However, if he wishes to know the effect of manipulation, he must do it. He cannot claim to know the effect of manipulation until he does.

There is one further complication in the issue. Although one does not find out about manipulation by simply observing, it is entirely possible that an observed relation will be confirmed in experimental manipulation. Imagine that one has observed a relation between two variables—an environmental condition and some aspect of behavior. Is it possible that changing the condition would change the behavior? Yes, but the experimental demonstration remains to be done. Thus the observed relation could serve as a pretext for an experiment in which it is demonstrated that changing the condition does change the behavior.

Here is an example. Scientists observe that the incidence of tooth decay among children in communities having water supplies which contain natural fluorides is lower than the incidence in communities whose water supplies do not contain those chemicals. A relation is thus established between incidence of tooth decay and presence of fluorides in the water. Does this mean that they know that introducing fluorides into a water supply will reduce tooth decay? No, it does not. It is entirely possible that some other chemical associated with the natural fluorides provides the key to the situation. That such an action will have the desired effect remains to be established. To find out, these same scientists embark upon an extensive experimental project in which fluorides are introduced into water supplies and the effects are observed. The evidence indicates that the incidence of tooth decay is reduced by introducing fluorides into the water supply. Thus an observed relation may, but does not necessarily, suggest a manipulation which can be demonstrated to be effective.

We have chosen "empirical research" as the label for those investigations which are limited to observation and we shall reserve "experimental research" as the label for investigations in which the psychologist actually manipulates one or more variables and observes the effect of the manipulation.

It should be clear that the distinction between experimental and empirical research does not depend on the choice of an *i*-statistic for the analysis of data. Experimental research is distinguished from empirical research by the operations of the investigator, but not by his choice of *i*-statistics. It is not uncommon to encounter a student who expresses a preference for a particular *i*-statistic because, as he says, he wants his study to be an experiment. In thinking that the choice of a particular *i*-statistic can make his study an experiment, he has failed to understand the difference between an experiment and an empirical investigation. A given *i*-statistic may be appropriate for an evaluation of either kind of research. The beginning student would probably be astonished if we were to describe here all of the equivalent methods of analysis which can be applied equally well to experimental and empirical research data.

Although the choice of method of analysis does not determine whether the research is experimental, appearances might give the student the impression that it does. By appearances, we mean that there is some tendency for experimental data to be evaluated by certain methods while nonexperimental data are evaluated by other methods. There is some tendency for experiments to be evaluated by means of *i*-statistics, such as $t$ and $F$, computed from means and variances. There is some tendency for nonexperimental research to be evaulated by the same *i*-statistics computed from correlation coefficients and other measures of association. These tendencies reflect superficial, rather than necessary, correspondences.

The two major applications of statistical inference, testing significance and estimating parameters, will be discussed next, in general terms, before they are treated in detail in the following chapters.

## Testing Significance

Observation and measurement in research are always subject to unintended and undesired influences which scientists call error. Consequently, in announcing positive results, the investigator may be mistaken no matter how favorable those results may appear to be. While the researcher cannot avoid being misled by outcomes due to error, he can be selective or discriminating with respect to those outcomes in two ways. First, within the totality of strictly error outcomes, he can define a class of the most favorable outcomes, by which he is willing to be misled. Second, he can place any desired limit on the size of that class. His erroneous decisions to announce positive results will then occur with a relative frequency which is known and can be stated.

The evaluation of research data by application of a statistical test of significance requires computation of an *i*-statistic which embodies a comparison of interest to the investigator. The comparison is a difference, a ratio, or a combination of the two. To define a class of error outcomes about which he is willing to be mistaken and, further, to specify its size, the investigator must be able to deduce the nature of all possible outcomes for the comparison. That is, he must know the sampling distribution of an *i*-statistic whose logical properties are relevant to his purposes. Within this sampling distribution he can establish two classes of values: error results which appear least favorable, or those values of the *i*-statistic which are smaller than some criterion value; and error results which appear most favorable, or those values of the *i*-statistic which are larger than the criterion value. In evaluating his research data, he computes the *i*-statistic which embodies the comparison of interest to him and observes the class into which the obtained value falls. If it exceeds the criterion value, it belongs in the class of error outcomes about which he is willing to be mistaken and he announces positive results. If it is exceeded by the criterion value, it belongs in the class of error outcomes by which he is not willing to be misled and he acknowledges negative results.

The size of the class of error outcomes which appear most favorable and which will be the occasion for announcing positive results erroneously is arbitrarily determined, but it seems reasonable and consistent with the purpose of scientific research to make the size of the class small rather than large. The size of the class is expressed as a proportion of the totality of error outcomes. A proportion of 0.05 has gained wide acceptance as being small enough to afford the researcher, his colleagues, and his public a reasonable degree of protection from false announcements of positive results. Some researchers, who are more demanding of themselves, adopt a proportion of 0.01, thus reducing the size of the class of erroneous decisions considerably.

To further focus attention on the general characteristics of tests of significance, we shall give here an example in which the sampling distribution is identified but no details are given about the investigation itself. In the evaluation of a certain body of research data, the *i*-statistic computed was $F$, a variance ratio. The sampling distribution of $F$ for this particular set of data could be represented by the function in Figure 12.10. Bear in mind that the sampling distribution is a specification of all of the possible error outcomes for the investigation. The point on the horizontal axis which separates the unshaded area under the curve from the shaded area represents the criterion value, $F_c$. The shaded area represents the class of error outcomes about which the investigator is willing to be mistaken. The unshaded area represents the class of error outcomes about which he is not willing to be mistaken. Having computed $F$, the investigator determines in which class it belongs. He does so by consulting a table of $F$ such as Table $B_1$ or $B_2$ in the Appendix. If the obtained $F$ exceeds the criterion value given by the table, the investigator announces positive results. If it does not, he acknowledges negative results.

Classifying a given *i*-statistic as above or below some criterion value in the totality of error results is an action consistent with the viewpoint that the result is due to error, a viewpoint which is referred to formally as the *null hypothesis.* When the obtained *i*-statistic exceeds the criterion value and positive results are announced, the investigator is said to reject the null hypothesis. When the value fails to equal the criterion and negative results are acknowledged, the investigator is said to accept the null hypothesis. The proportion of error outcomes which are the occasions for announcing positive results or rejecting the null hypothesis is called the *level of significance.*

## Estimating Parameters

We have said that values computed from a population are called *parameters* and that values computed from one or more random samples are called "*i*-statistics." Some values computed from samples correspond to values computed from populations. For example, there is the mean of a sample and the mean of the population from which the sample was obtained. There is the variance of a sample and the variance of the population from which the sample was obtained. There is the product-moment correlation for a sample of paired values and the product-moment correlation for the population of paired values from which the sample was obtained. Population values or parameters are designated by Greek letters. Sample values or *i*-statistics are designated by Latin letters.

When a real population is too large to measure and describe, that is, when it is too large to permit the computation of parameters, it is often of interest to a researcher to obtain an estimate of one or more of the parameters. In general terms, an attempt is made to infer values of parameters from *i*-statistics.

Estimates of parameters are divided into two broad classes: point estimates and interval estimates.

A point estimate is a single value which is computed from one or more samples and which possesses certain properties which qualify it as an estimate of the corresponding parameter. We shall consider only point estimates which are unbiased or approximately so. An *i*-statistic is an unbiased estimate of a parameter when the mean of its sampling distribution is equal to the parameter. It has been our experience that the beginning student is usually not prepared for this definition. "Unbiased" usually has connotations for the student which go beyond the somewhat limited and arbitrary definition of the statistician. Examples of unbiased estimates will be given in Chapter 16.

An interval estimate consists of a pair of values called *limits,* which are computed from one or more samples. These limits, which establish an interval, have a sampling distribution. The interval has the property that it will sometimes encompass the parameter and will sometimes fail to do so. In the totality of such intervals, some known and stated proportion of intervals will fail. The size of this proportion can be fixed by the researcher and made as small as he desires. The size of the interval depends on the chosen proportion of failures. The smaller the proportion of failures, the larger the interval. Several interval estimates will be described in Chapter 16.

We shall comment here briefly on our reasons for emphasizing tests of significance. In testing significance, when an investigator rejects the null hypothesis and announces positive results, he is under no obligation to report the size of the obtained difference or ratio in terms of the original scale units. On the other hand, in establishing an estimate of a parameter, it is in the very nature of the procedure that the size of the computed value is indicated. When the estimate is expressed in terms of units on a psychological scale, its size may be difficult to interpret because of the unknown differences among scales, even those intended to measure the same characteristic of behavior. Consequently, psychologists are not prone to emphasize the magnitude of differences, ratios, or other values, expressed in terms of original scale units. Estimation is more likely to be used when the value of interest to the researcher is a pure or dimensionless number like a proportion, a percentage, or a correlation coefficient.

There is another reason for the emphasis on tests of significance in psychological research. Much of psychological research is exploratory; controls are often poor; measurement is frequently of dubious quality. To detect a replicable difference or ratio under these circumstances is itself no small accomplishment. Attempting the estimation of the size of a parameter is often not justified. Perhaps the day will come when measurement, prediction, and control in psychological research will improve to the point that the emphasis will shift from testing significance to estimating parameters.

## Summary

Applications of statistical inference in research can be placed in two broad classes: tests of significance and estimates of parameters. Research operations themselves can also be placed in two classes: experimental research and empirical research. It is possible to do tests of significance and estimates of parameters in both experimental and empirical research. In this text, testing significance will be emphasized. Only a brief introduction to estimation will be given. This introduction will be limited to applications of estimation in empirical research. Chapter 15 deals with tests of significance in experimental research. Chapter 16 deals with tests of significance and estimates of parameters in empirical research.

# EXPERIMENTAL INFERENCE

## Pragmatics 15

An experiment is a planned event in which the researcher manipulates one or more variables and determines the effects of this action by making observations on another variable. A manipulated variable is called an *independent* variable. The variable on which observation is made is called a *dependent* variable. Although either kind of variable, independent or dependent, may be qualitative or quantitative in nature, we shall limit our discussion to quantitative variables.

In psychological experimentation, the manipulation of an independent variable takes a characteristic form. The independent variable is the feature which varies in a set of conditions, often called *treatments*, and the manipulation is the actual imposition of these conditions on groups of subjects. A set of conditions may consist of a number of stimuli which vary along some specific dimension, a number of different levels of some characteristic of the environment which can be controlled by the experimenter, varied allowances of some consumable substance such as water, food, nutrients, or drugs, or variations in tasks and programs prescribed by the experimenter for his subjects. Listed below are four examples of independent variables described as sets of conditions.

1. Two auditory signals consisting of pure tones equal in intensity but differing in frequency.
2. Three levels of illumination for a testing room.
3. Three different concentrations of salt in solution in drinking water.
4. Two different amounts of practice: five trials and ten trials.

The dependent variable in a psychological experiment is a measure of response of the subjects in the experiment. The subjects may be human or animal. Typically, subjects differ in their responses, when they are measured under uniform conditions, and it is not uncommon for these differences to persist in repeated measurement. This is to say that pyschologists frequently encounter evidence of stable or reproducible differences among their subjects. Because subjects differ, the selection of subjects for the conditions of an experiment can bias the final comparisons. Thus differences among subjects constitute a major source of error in psychological experiments.

Subject differences are not the only errors by which experiments can be biased. A multitude of influences affect the experimenter's observation of a subject's response under a given condition at a specific time and place in the conduct of the experiment. The experimenter, of course, tries to control and hold constant as many of these influences as he can, and to whatever extent he can, so that unintended differences will be eliminated and only intended differences will occur in the data. Intended differences are those he is trying to produce by means of the varied conditions of the experiment. He can never be certain that these efforts to control extraneous influences and eliminate bias are completely successful.

The presence of error and bias in experimental data introduces uncertainty into the evaluation of the data. In announcing positive results for an experiment, the investigator can never be certain that he has not been deceived by error. The only kind of rigor he can achieve in his evaluation is the rigor of a test of significance in which the probability of an incorrect rejection of the null hypothesis is known and stated. Meaningful application of a test of significance requires, of course, that the distribution of errors have the attributes of random variation.

Three simple plans for conducting and evaluating experiments are described below. Plans for experiments are often called *experimental designs*.

## The Completely Randomized Design

Imagine an experiment in which we wish to determine the differential effect of two conditions, $A_1$ and $A_2$. Each of the two conditions is to be imposed on a group of subjects, after which the subjects are to be measured on a response variable, $Y$.

The selection of subjects and their assignment to the two conditions is a critical step in the conduct of the experiment. Subjects can be expected to vary prior to the experiment and the differences among them will act as errors which can bias the experimental comparison of conditions in many different ways, depending on the selection of subjects and on the particular arrangement of subjects into groups, produced by the assignment.

Imagine that we have selected $(2n)$ subjects from some large supply of subjects, that we have assigned them to two conditions with $n$ subjects per condition, and that we have imposed the conditions and obtained measures on the dependent variable. We recognize that the particular arrangement of subjects which results from the selection and the assignment is only one of many possible arrangements.

Table 15.1 shows the main features of the design and the way of recording

**Table 15.1**

**AN EXPERIMENTAL DESIGN WITH TWO CONDITIONS AND TWO RANDOM SAMPLES**

| Conditions | |
|---|---|
| $A_1$ First Sample | $A_2$ Second Sample |
| $Y_{11}$ | $Y_{12}$ |
| $Y_{21}$ | $Y_{22}$ |
| $Y_{31}$ | $Y_{32}$ |
| . | . |
| $Y_{i1}$ | $Y_{i2}$ |
| . | . |
| $Y_{n1}$ | $Y_{n2}$ |

the data which consist of $(2n)$ measures. Each column of the table corresponds to a sample and the condition which was imposed on the subjects in that sample. Notice there are no rows in the table. The double subscripts permit the identification of any measure in either column.

It is obvious that the total variability in the $(2n)$ observations will contain three different kinds of differences. It will contain differences due to the effects of the treatments, to the extent there are such effects. It will contain differences among subjects, to the extent that preexperimental inequalities of response have persisted into the experiment. Finally, it will contain unintended differences arising from extraneous influences which the experimenter has failed to eliminate. The intended differences are often called *treatment effects*. The unintended differences are often called *error*.

The total variability in the $(2n)$ observations can be analyzed into two components: the between-sample sum of squares and the combined within-sample sum of squares. It will be interesting to consider the relation between the two components produced by the arithmetic analysis of the total sum of squares and the two sources of variability described above as treatment effects and error. Under certain circumstances to be described below, the treatment effect will be contained in the between-sample variability and nothing but error will be contained in the within-sample variability.

Treatment effects can be divided logically into two classes: those effects which are constant and additive and those which are not. Let us consider the first possibility, the case of constant and additive effects. We shall return later to the other possibility. A treatment effect is constant and additive when all subjects in a particular condition of the experiment change with the same increment or decrement of response. When the effects of conditions $A_1$ and $A_2$ are constant and additive, but different, the differential treatment effect is contained in the between-sample variability and does not enter the within-sample variability.

The conclusion that the differential effects of treatments will not be contained in the within-sample sums of squares can be justified in the following manner. It was established in Chapter 4, in connection with the discussion of coding transformations, that adding a constant to, or subtracting a constant from, each number in a set does not change the variability of that set. A constant additive treatment effect can be conceptualized as a constant value added to, or subtracted from, the response of each subject in a sample. Consequently, the variability among the measures of response in a sample will not be different from what it would have been had there been no treatment. That is to say, the variability within a sample will not have changed during the experiment. Since the total variability consists only of two components, the between-sample variability and the within-sample variability, the effects of treatments must be contained in the between-sample variability.

The between-sample sum of squares measures differences among subjects who have been treated differently and, therefore, contains any differential constant and additive treatment effects, but that is not all. The between-sample sum of squares may also contain a bias resulting from the selection and assignment of subjects. Because of the random selection and assignment, the samples may not be exactly comparable at the start of the experiment. Thus we often say that the between-sample variability is the *apparent* treatment effect, by which we mean that it is the treatment effect plus some unknown bias.

The error effects in the experiment consist of preexperimental differences among subjects and differences arising from uncontrolled and unintended influences operating in the experiment. Let us focus our attention for the moment on that part of the error consisting of differences among subjects. Differences among subjects are errors which affect the comparison as a consequence of the selection of subjects and their assignment to the conditions of the experiment.

The combined within-sample sum of squares measures differences among subjects treated alike. Since constant additive treatment effects will not affect the variability of a sample, that variability provides a basis for gauging the size of errors. We often say that the within-sample variability provides an estimate of the bias to which the experiment is liable.

Let us review the equivalences of the terms and concepts introduced above to characterize this simple experiment involving two conditions and two random samples of subjects.

The total sum of squares is a measure of the variability in all of the data. It contains differential treatment effects, differences due to inequalities among subjects, and other errors. The total sum of squares can be analyzed into two components.

The between-sample sum of squares measures differences among subjects treated differently. It contains differential treatment effects and, possibly, a bias from errors. It is referred to as the apparent treatment effect.

The within-sample sum of squares measures differences among subjects treated alike. It contains subject inequalities and errors of other kinds. From the within-sample sum of squares we obtain an estimate of the size of errors affecting the experiment.

## THE GUARANTEES OF RANDOM ERROR

Two kinds of errors affect the comparisons in a psychological experiment. One kind consists of inequalities among subjects. These inequalities become errors, in the selecting and assigning of subjects with respect to the conditions of the experiment. The experimenter can insure that these errors are randomly distributed over the conditions by using a table of random numbers or some other tested device to make the selection and assignment. The other kind of errors consists of unintended differences produced by uncontrolled influences and associated with the particular occasion on which an observation is obtained. The experimenter can insure that errors associated with occasions of measurement are also random in their distribution over the conditions of the experiment. He can do so by arranging for the random conjunction of a subject, a treatment, and the occasion on which the subject is measured under that treatment in the experiment.

## THE EVALUATION

The random selection of subjects and the random assignment of subjects and conditions to occasions of measurement can produce any one of many different combinations of an apparent treatment effect and an estimate of error. That is, random selection and assignment can produce many different combinations of values for the between-sample variability and the within-sample variability. Just on appearances, the outcomes which are most favorable for the announcement of positive results are those which suggest large treatment effects and small errors. Even though it must be admitted that these most-favorable-appearing outcomes could actually be due to random error, if one must risk being misled, it is reasonable to take one's chances on them rather than on the outcomes which suggest small treatment effects and large errors.

The experimenter needs a systematic procedure for detecting outcomes which give the most favorable comparisons of apparent treatment effect and error. There are two *i*-statistics which provide the desired comparison. Either one employed in a test of significance provides the desired systematic procedure. One is $t$ as computed by formula (12.2), which is

$$t = \frac{D_y}{\sqrt{2V'_w/n}}\cdot$$

This ratio compares the apparent treatment effect, as measured by the difference between two sample means, with an estimate of error computed from the within-sample variability. The other *i*-statistic is $F$ as computed by formula (12.4), which is

$$F = \frac{V'_b}{V'_w}\cdot$$

This variance ratio compares the apparent treatment effect, as measured by the between-sample variability with the estimate of error, as given by the combined within-sample variability.

In the test of significance, the result of the comparison is classified as being larger or smaller than a predetermined criterion value. If the obtained value falls in the class of error outcomes by which the experimenter is willing to be misled, he rejects the null hypothesis; if it does not, he accepts the null hypothesis.

With two conditions and two samples, $t$ by formula (12.2) and $F$ by formula (12.4) give exactly the same result for the test of significance. As a matter of fact, $t^2 = F$ when $c$, the number of samples, is two. $F$ has the advantage that it can be used when the number of conditions is greater than two. When $F$ is employed, the evaluation is usually reported as an *analysis of variance*, and the results are commonly represented in the form of Table 15.2

**Table 15.2**

**GENERAL FORM OF THE ANALYSIS OF VARIANCE FOR A COMPLETELY RANDOMIZED DESIGN**

| Component of Variability | $SS$ | $df$ | $V$ | $F$ |
|---|---|---|---|---|
| Between samples or conditions | $B$ | $c - 1$ | $V'_b$ | $V'_b/V'_w$ |
| Within samples or conditions | $W$ | $N - c$ | $V'_w$ | |
| Total | $T$ | $N - 1$ | | |

$B$ = the between-sample sum of squares.
$W$ = the combined within-sample sum of squares.
$T$ = the total sum of squares.

## NONADDITIVE EFFECTS

Constant and additive treatment effects do not affect the estimate of error, which is computed from the combined within-sample sum of squares. Treatment effects which are not constant and additive may change the variability of a sample. When two or more samples of subjects are treated differently and the effects are not constant and additive, the result may be differences between the sample variances not solely due to error. There is a test of non-additivity for an experiment involving two conditions and two samples. The test of significance involves the comparison of one sample variance with another in an $F$ ratio, as given by formula (12.5),

$$F = \frac{V_1'}{V_2'} \cdot$$

The test is often called a test of homogeneity of sample variances. When the obtained $F$ is significant, we often say that we have found heterogeneous variances. There is also a test for the case of more than two samples. The student will find the test described by Edwards (**1**), Ray (**2**), Walker and Lev (**3**), and others.

## AN EXAMPLE

A psychologist obtains two random samples of rats of a particular strain. He administers a small, carefully measured amount of a common stimulant to the animals in one sample. He administers a carefully prepared placebo containing none of the stimulant to the other animals. He then observes the number of revolutions of an activity wheel each animal produces in the first hour after it has been fed to satiation. Table 15.3 gives the recorded observations. The psychologist proceeds to analyze the variability in the 20 observations, as follows.

**Table 15.3**

**ACTIVITY MEASURES FROM THE STIMULANT EXPERIMENT**

| Conditions | |
|---|---|
| Placebo Sample 1 | Stimulant Sample 2 |
| 7 | 4 |
| 13 | 43 |
| 42 | 30 |
| 17 | 47 |
| 9 | 23 |
| 20 | 31 |
| 20 | 32 |
| 15 | 34 |
| 14 | 15 |
| 22 | 43 |

$N = 20$ = number of animals.

Summary data for the entire set of 20 measures in Table 15.3:

$$\Sigma Y = 481$$
$$\Sigma Y^2 = 14{,}775$$
$$N = 20$$

$$C_y = \frac{(\Sigma Y)^2}{N} = \frac{481^2}{20} = 11{,}568.05.$$

*Computation of the total sum of squares:*

$$\Sigma Y^2 - C_y = 14{,}775 - 11{,}568.05 = 3{,}206.95$$

*Summary data for Sample 1:*

$$\Sigma Y = 179$$
$$\Sigma Y^2 = 4{,}057$$
$$n = 10$$

*Computation of the sum of squares for Sample 1:*

$$\Sigma Y^2 - \frac{(\Sigma Y)^2}{n} = 4{,}057 - \frac{179^2}{10} = 852.9$$

*Summary data for Sample 2:*

$$\Sigma Y = 302$$
$$\Sigma Y^2 = 10{,}718$$
$$n = 10$$

*Computation of the sum of squares for Sample 2:*

$$\Sigma Y^2 - \frac{(\Sigma Y)^2}{n} = 10{,}718 - \frac{302^2}{10} = 1{,}597.6$$

*Computation of the combined within-sample sum of squares:*

$$\sum\left[\Sigma Y^2 - \frac{(\Sigma Y)^2}{n}\right] = 852.9 + 1{,}597.6 = 2{,}450.5$$

*Computation of the between-sample sum of squares:*

$$\frac{\Sigma(\Sigma Y)^2}{n} - C_y = \frac{179^2 + 302^2}{10} - 11{,}568.05 = 756.45$$

The fact that the total sum of squares should be equal to the between-sample sum of squares plus the combined within-sample sum of squares provides a check on the computation.

$$3{,}206.95 = 756.45 + 2{,}450.5$$

The computation checks.

$V'_b$, the variance for the apparent treatment effect, is computed by dividing the between-sample sum of squares by $(c - 1) = 1$ degree of freedom.

$$V'_b = \frac{756.45}{1} = 756.45$$

$V'_w$, the variance for the estimate of error, is computed by dividing the combined within-sample sum of squares by $(N - c) = 18$ degrees of freedom.

$$V'_w = \frac{2{,}450.5}{18} = 136.14$$

The null hypothesis is that observed differences between conditions are due to error. Let the level of significance be 0.05. The test of significance involves computing $F$, the ratio of $V'_b$ to $V'_w$ or the ratio of the treatment variance to the error variance.

$$F = \frac{V'_b}{V'_w} = \frac{756.45}{136.14} = 5.56$$

$F_c$, the criterion value of $F$ for one and 18 degrees of freedom and the 0.05 level of significance, is 4.41. (See Table $B_1$ in the Appendix.) Since the obtained $F$ exceeds the criterion $F$, the psychologist rejects the null hypothesis and announces positive results. The results are summarized in conventional form in Table 15.4.

**Table 15.4**

**ANALYSIS OF VARIANCE FOR THE STIMULANT EXPERIMENT**[a]

| Component | *SS* | *df* | *V* | *F* |
|---|---|---|---|---|
| Apparent treatment effect | 756.45 | 1 | 756.45 | 5.56[b] |
| Estimate of error | 2,450.5 | 18 | 136.14 | |
| Total | 3,206.95 | 19 | | |

[a]Data in Table 15.3.
[b]Criterion value, $F_c$, is 4.41; null hypothesis is rejected.

A test for nonadditivity of treatment effects should also be applied. The test involving $F$ requires the computation of a variance for each sample. $V'_1$, the variance for the first sample, is obtained by dividing the sample sum of squares, 852.9 by $(n - 1) = 9$ degrees of freedom.

$$V'_1 = \frac{852.9}{9} = 94.77$$

$V'_2$, the variance for the second sample, is obtained by dividing 1,597.6 by $(n - 1) = 9$ degrees of freedom.

$$V'_2 = \frac{1{,}597.6}{9} = 177.51$$

Since tables of $F$ give ratios greater than one, we compute by dividing the larger sample variance by the smaller.

$$F = \frac{V'_2}{V'_1} = \frac{177.51}{94.77} = 1.87$$

Since this procedure of putting the larger sample variance over the smaller will double the number of ratios greater than one, we shall need to compensate by choosing a level of significance which when doubled will give us the desired value. We choose 0.025. The effective level of significance is then 0.05. The null hypothesis is that the observed difference between variances is due to error. $F_c$, the criterion value for nine and nine degrees of freedom, is 4.03. (See Table $B_2$.) The null hypothesis is accepted and the assumption of constant additive treatment effects is taken to be justified.

Even if significance is obtained in the test of homogeneity of sample variances, there is no reason to abandon the main analysis. The consequences of nonadditivity are not serious. It has been shown that heterogeneity of sample variances has the effect of making the true level of significance slightly larger than the chosen level.

## The Matched-Group Design

The completely randomized design is subject to large errors because differences among subjects are randomly distributed as errors over the conditions of the experiment. Differences among subjects on psychological variables are often large. A reduction of the size of errors influencing an experiment can be effected by matching subjects. In carrying out this matching, it is necessary to restrict the randomization in a particular way.

Imagine that we are to conduct an experiment with two conditions, $A_1$ and $A_2$, and a dependent variable, $Y$. If we choose two subjects as much alike as possible in their responses, impose one condition on each subject, and measure on $Y$, the comparison will be subject to a smaller error than if we made no attempt to match subjects. This single comparison on a matched pair cannot be evaluated, however, because it is still subject to a residual error, the size and direction of which are unknown.

Let us extend the matching procedure by constituting a number of matched pairs. Each pair is to consist of two subjects chosen to be as much alike as possible. We shall defer, for the moment, consideration of the actual matching procedure.

If we assign the members of each pair randomly, one to each condition, the residual errors, representing failures in matching, will be distributed randomly at the same time. If the treatment-subject combinations for each pair are assigned randomly to the two occasions on which observation is to take place, then the errors associated with occasions of measurement will also be randomly distributed over the conditions of the experiment.

Imagine that these randomization procedures have been carried out, that the conditions have been imposed, and that measures on the dependent variable have been obtained. The data can be tabulated in two columns, corresponding to conditions $A_1$ and $A_2$, and as many rows as there are pairs of subjects. The general plan for two conditions and $r$ matched pairs of subjects is shown in Table 15.5. Recall that the total sum of squares in a

**Table 15.5**

**GENERAL PLAN FOR A MATCHED-PAIR DESIGN**

| | Conditions $A_1$ | $A_2$ |
|---|---|---|
| 1 | $Y_{11}$ | $Y_{12}$ |
| 2 | $Y_{21}$ | $Y_{22}$ |
| 3 | $Y_{31}$ | $Y_{32}$ |
| Pairs . | . | . |
| $j$ | $Y_{j1}$ | $Y_{j2}$ |
| . | . | . |
| $r$ | $Y_{r1}$ | $Y_{r2}$ |

double classification can be analyzed into three components: the between-column sum of squares, the between-row sum of squares, and the residual sum of squares.

The magnitude of differences among pairs, relative to the total variability, will depend on the effectiveness of the matching procedure. If the matching is nearly perfect, errors will be very small and most of the intersubject variability will appear in the between-row component. If the matching is poor, errors will be large and much less of the intersubject variability will appear in the between-row component, on the average. Large or small, differences among pairs do not enter into the evaluation of the experiment. Since the experimental comparison can be made within each pair, only the failures in matching must be taken account of in the evaluation. The extent to which a given pair differs from any other pair is of no concern to us.

Differential, constant, additive treatment effects will enter the between-column component and will not affect the between-row variability or the residual variability. Since between-row variability consists of differences among pairs and between-column variability contains treatment effects, the residual variability must provide an estimate of error. That constant additive treatment effects do not affect the residual variability can be deduced, as follows.

Let $Y_{jk}$ be the measure on the dependent variable for the j[th] matched pair and the $k^{\text{th}}$ treatment. Now $Y_{jk}$ can be conceptualized as consisting of two parts: the level of response which would have been obtained without treatment and the increment (or decrement) of response produced by treatment.

If we let $L_{jk}$ be the level of response without treatment and $a_k$ be the increment or decrement produced by treatment, then

$$Y_{jk} = L_{jk} + a_k.$$

This equality statement should not be interpreted as meaning that the experimenter ever knows the values of $L_{jk}$ and $a_k$. If he actually knew the value of $a_k$, there would be no point in doing an experiment. We have introduced these symbols for deductive purposes only. They do not have to be given numerical values to serve our purposes. Notice that $a_k$ varies only from column to column, but that it is a constant from row to row, within any column.

The mean of the $j^{\text{th}}$ row can be written

$$\overline{Y}_{j.} = \overline{L}_{j.} + \bar{a}_{.},$$

where $\bar{a}_{.}$ is the average of the $c$ values of $a_k$ in any row. In comparing row means with one another, a process implicit in the computation of the between-row sum of squares, $\bar{a}_{.}$ will cancel. For example, the difference between the mean of the third row and the mean of the fifth row can be written

$$\overline{Y}_{3.} - \overline{Y}_{5.} = \overline{L}_{3.} - \overline{L}_{5.}.$$

Thus the between-row variability will be a measure of the differences between pairs and will be unaffected by the treatments.

The mean of the $k^{\text{th}}$ column can be written

$$\overline{Y}_{.k} = \overline{L}_{.k} + a_k.$$

In comparing column means, a process implicit in the computation of the between-column sum of squares, values of $a_k$ will not cancel. For example, the difference between the mean of the first column and the mean of the second column will be

$$\overline{Y}_{.1} - \overline{Y}_{.2} = (\overline{L}_{.1} + a_1) - (\overline{L}_{.2} + a_2).$$

Since the two treatment effects, $a_1$ and $a_2$, may differ, the between-column variability will contain this differential effect.

The residual deviation for the $j^{\text{th}}$ row and the $k^{\text{th}}$ column is

$$r_{jk} = Y_{jk} - \overline{Y}_{j.} - \overline{Y}_{.k} + M_y.$$

$M_y$, the total mean, is equal to the average row mean or the average column mean. In either case,

$$M_y = M_l + \bar{a}_{.}.$$

We have said that

$$Y_{jk} = L_{jk} + a_k,$$

and have shown that

$$\bar{Y}_{j.} = \bar{L}_{j.} + \bar{a}_{.}$$

and

$$\bar{Y}_{.k} = \bar{L}_{.k} + a_k.$$

Substituting for $Y_{jk}$, $\bar{Y}_{j.}$, $\bar{Y}_{.k}$, and $M_y$ in the formula for $r_{jk}$ yields

$$r_{jk} = (L_{jk} + a_k) - (\bar{L}_{j.} + \bar{a}_{.}) - (\bar{L}_{.k} + a_k) + (M_l + \bar{a}_{.}).$$

Removing parentheses and combining terms gives an expression for $r_{jk}$ in which $a_k$ and $\bar{a}_{.}$ do not appear:

$$r_{jk} = L_{jk} - \bar{L}_{j.} - \bar{L}_{.k} + M_l.$$

We conclude that the residual variability does not contain the constant, additive effects of treatments, that it reflects failures in matching which have been randomly distributed over conditions, and that it provides an estimate of error.

The variability in the data for a matched-group design can be analyzed into three components: the apparent treatment effect as measured by the between-column sum of squares, the differences among the matched groups as measured by the between-row sum of squares, and the error variability as measured by the residual sum of squares. The investigator evaluates the experiment by comparing the treatment variance to the error variance in a test of significance. He chooses a level of significance. The treatment variance, $V'_t$, is computed by dividing the between-column sum of squares by $(c - 1)$ degrees of freedom. The error variance, $V'_e$, is computed by dividing the residual sum of squares by $(r - 1)(c - 1)$ degrees of freedom. The comparison involves computation of an $F$ ratio,

$$F = \frac{V'_t}{V'_e}.$$

The investigator compares the obtained $F$ with $F_c$, the criterion value, and accepts or rejects the null hypothesis.

The general form of the conventional presentation of the results of an analysis of variance, applied to a matched-group design, is given in Table 15.6.

## THE MATCHING PROCEDURE

The first step in matching is the measurement of all subjects prior to the experiment and under uniform conditions on a variable $X$ which is known to be correlated with $Y$. The second step is the ranking of subjects according

**Table 15.6**

**THE ANALYSIS OF VARIANCE FOR A MATCHED-GROUP DESIGN**

| Component | *SS* | *df* | *V* | *F* |
|---|---|---|---|---|
| Treatments | $C$ | $c - 1$ | $V'_t$ | $V'_t/V'_e$ |
| Groups | $G$ | $r - 1$ | | |
| Error | $R$ | $(r - 1)(c - 1)$ | $V'_e$ | |
| Total | $T$ | $N - 1$ | | |

$C$ = between-column sum of squares.
$G$ = between-row sum of squares.
$R$ = residual sum of squares.
$T$ = total sum of squares.

to the magnitude of their measures on $X$. The third step is the pairing. The first and second subjects in the ranking are put in one pair; the third and fourth subjects are put in a second pair; the fifth and sixth are put in a third pair; and so on. Matching in this fashion on $X$ indirectly matches the members of each pair on $Y$. The effectiveness of the matching depends, of course, on the correlation between $X$ and $Y$.

The members of each matched group are assigned randomly to the conditions of the experiment. Each subject-treatment combination is then randomly assigned to an occasion of measurement.

When the number of conditions is greater than two, the matched groups must be correspondingly larger. Thus for an experiment involving three conditions, each matched group would consist of three subjects. Subjects would be ranked on the preexperimental variable, $X$. The first three subjects in the ranking would then be chosen for the first group; the next three subjects would be placed in the second group; and so on.

## AN EXAMPLE

A psychologist wishes to determine the effect of paying subjects for their participation in an experiment. He chooses a measure of visual acuity as the dependent variable. He obtains a sample of 20 male, freshman college students. He measures all of the student subjects on the test of visual acuity under standard conditions prior to the experiment. He next ranks the 20 subjects on this preliminary measure and then forms 10 matched pairs. The members of each pair are then assigned randomly to the two conditions: $A_1$, no payment for participation in the experiment; $A_2$, payment of one dollar per hour for participation. Subjects in condition $A_2$ are informed they will be paid. Subjects in $A_1$ are not told they will be paid. Measures of visual acuity are obtained on all subjects. To insure the maintenance of good public relations, subjects in $A_1$ are paid, after the experiment is over.

The data for the visual acuity experiment are given in Table 15.7. Measures are expressed in millimeters. The analysis and evaluation of the data are described below.

**Table 15.7**

**THE MATCHED-PAIR EXPERIMENT ON VISUAL ACUITY**

| | | Conditions $A_1$ | $A_2$ |
|---|---|---|---|
| | 1 | 19 | 18 |
| | 2 | 14 | 19 |
| | 3 | 15 | 16 |
| | 4 | 16 | 15 |
| Pairs of | 5 | 14 | 15 |
| Subjects | 6 | 12 | 15 |
| | 7 | 12 | 15 |
| | 8 | 12 | 13 |
| | 9 | 13 | 10 |
| | 10 | 10 | 11 |

*Summary data:*

Let $r$ be the number of rows; $c$, the number of columns; $N = (rc)$, the total number of observations.

Let $Y$ be the observation in any cell; $R$, the sum of any row; $C$, the sum of any column; $\Sigma Y$, the sum of all values; $\Sigma Y^2$, the sum of squares of all original values.

$$r = 10 \qquad c = 2 \qquad N = 20$$

$$\Sigma Y = 284 \qquad \Sigma Y^2 = 4{,}166$$

$$\Sigma R^2 = 8{,}274 \qquad \Sigma C^2 = 40{,}378$$

$$C_y = \frac{284^2}{20} = 4{,}032.8$$

*Computation of the total sum of squares:*

$$\Sigma Y^2 - C_y = 4{,}166 - 4{,}032.8 = 133.2$$

*Computation of the between-column sum of squares:*

$$\frac{\Sigma C^2}{r} - C_y = \frac{40{,}378}{10} - 4{,}032.8 = 5.0$$

*Computation of the between-row sum of squares:*

$$\frac{\Sigma R^2}{c} - C_y = \frac{8{,}274}{2} - 4{,}032.8 = 104.2$$

*Computation of the residual sum of squares:*
Let $r_{jk}$ be the residual deviation for the $j^{\text{th}}$ row and the $k^{\text{th}}$ column. Then

$$r_{jk} = Y_{jk} - \overline{Y}_{j.} - \overline{Y}_{.k} + M_y$$
$$r_{11} = 19 - 18.5 - 13.7 + 14.2 = +1$$
$$r_{21} = 14 - 16.5 - 13.7 + 14.2 = -2$$

| | | | |
|---|---|---|---|
| $r_{31}$ | $= 0$ | $r_{22}$ | $= +2$ |
| $r_{41}$ | $= +1$ | $r_{32}$ | $= 0$ |
| $r_{51}$ | $= 0$ | $r_{42}$ | $= -1$ |
| $r_{61}$ | $= -1$ | $r_{52}$ | $= 0$ |
| $r_{71}$ | $= -1$ | $r_{62}$ | $= +1$ |
| $r_{81}$ | $= 0$ | $r_{72}$ | $= +1$ |
| $r_{91}$ | $= +2$ | $r_{82}$ | $= 0$ |
| $r_{10\cdot 1}$ | $= 0$ | $r_{92}$ | $= -2$ |
| $r_{12}$ | $= -1$ | $r_{10\cdot 2}$ | $= 0$ |

$$\Sigma r_{jk}^2 = 24$$

The fact that the total sum of squares should equal the combination of the three components provides a check on the computation. We observe that

$$133.2 = 5 + 104.2 + 24.$$

The computation checks.

Table 15.8 shows the sums of squares, degrees of freedom, variances, and the $F$ ratio for the test of significance. The null hypothesis is that differences between conditions are due to random error. The criterion value for the 0.05 level of significance and one and nine degrees of freedom is 5.12. (See Table $B_1$ in the Appendix.) The obtained value of $F$, 1.87, is not significant. The null hypothesis is accepted. The researcher does not announce positive results; he may decide to abandon this line of research or to try to improve the experiment and repeat it.

**Table 15.8**

**ANALYSIS OF VARIANCE FOR THE MATCHED-PAIR DESIGN**[a]

| Component | *SS* | *df* | *V* | *F* |
|---|---|---|---|---|
| Treatments | 5.0 | 1 | 5.0 | 1.87[b] |
| Groups | 104.2 | 9 | | |
| Error | 24 | 9 | 2.67 | |
| Total | 133.2 | 19 | | |

[a]Data in Table 15.7.
[b]$F_c$, the criterion value for the 0.05 level of significance and one and nine degrees of freedom, is 5.12. The null hypothesis is accepted.

# A Design with a Correlational Adjustment

Given observations on a dependent variable, $Y$, for two random samples on which different conditions have been imposed, we can present the data as shown in Table 15.1. This table was used earlier in the discussion of the completely randomized design. We can use the table again as the starting point for our discussion of a design with a correlational adjustment.

We know that differences among the observations in Table 15.1 may be due in part to differences which existed among the subjects prior to the experiment and which persisted through the experiment. We could adjust the observations on $Y$, for the purpose of eliminating these initial differences, if we had available measures obtained on the subjects prior to the experiment. We could then eliminate that part of the variability in $Y$ which was accounted for by variability existing prior to the experiment as measured by $X$, a variable correlated with $Y$. By doing so, the size of the bias in the apparent treatment effect would be reduced, on the average, and the estimate of that bias would also be reduced a corresponding amount, on the average. The result would be an experiment subject to errors which were smaller than those of a completely randomized design.

To employ a correlational adjustment, the following operations are necessary. Obtain two random samples of subjects from a supply. Measure all subjects on $X$ under uniform conditions. Impose the two conditions, $A_1$ and $A_2$, one condition on each sample. Measure the subjects on $Y$, the dependent variable. Table 15.9 gives the general form in which the measures can be arranged.

**Table 15.9**

**GENERAL FORM OF THE DESIGN INVOLVING A CORRELATIONAL ADJUSTMENT**

| | Conditions | | | | | | | |
|---|---|---|---|---|---|---|---|---|
| | $A_1$ Sample 1 | | | | $A_2$ Sample 2 | | | |
| | 1 | $X_1$ | $Y_1$ | | 1 | $X_1$ | $Y_1$ |
| | 2 | $X_2$ | $Y_2$ | | 2 | $X_2$ | $Y_2$ |
| | 3 | $X_3$ | $Y_3$ | | 3 | $X_3$ | $Y_3$ |
| *Ss* | . | . | . | *Ss* | . | . | . |
| | $i$ | $X_i$ | $Y_i$ | | $i$ | $X_i$ | $Y_i$ |
| | . | . | . | | . | . | . |
| | $n$ | $X_n$ | $Y_n$ | | $n$ | $X_n$ | $Y_n$ |

*Ss* = Subjects.

Consider a new way of analyzing the variability in the two samples of paired measures represented in Table 15.9.

Let $r_t$ be the product-moment correlation between $X$ and $Y$ over the entire table, disregarding the classification by samples. Then $r_t^2$ is the proportion of $Y$ variability correlated with $X$, and $(1 - r_t^2)$ is the proportion not correlated with $X$.

Let $\Sigma y^2$ be the total variability in $Y$ as given by the sum of squares of deviations from $M_y$, the total mean. The total variability includes treatment effects, differences among subjects, and other errors.

Then $r_t^2 \Sigma y^2$ represents the predicted variability, a sum of squares reflecting differences among subjects to the extent that these differences can be predicted from $X$. Furthermore, $(1 - r_t^2)\Sigma y^2$ represents the unpredicted variability, a sum of squares containing treatment effects and errors other than the predictable differences among subjects. It will be convenient to represent this unpredicted sum of squares by the expression, $(T + E_t)$. $T$ stands for treatment effects; $E_t$ stands for error or bias in the unpredicted sum of squares when it is computed in this particular way. This expression is not meant to imply that values can be determined for $T$ and $E_t$ separately. If they could be, evaluation of the experiment would be very simple. The expression, $(T + E_t)$, stands for a single quantity which, we can deduce, contains the differential effect of treatment and the effect of errors in unknown amounts. The student may wonder how we can deduce the fact that treatment effects will be in the unpredicted sum of squares rather than in the predicted sum of squares. Assigning subjects to conditions randomly insures that $X$ is random with respect to the effects of the conditions. Therefore, the differential effects of the conditions will not be correlated with $X$ and will not be predicted from $X$, on the average over many experiments.

We enter upon a new phase in the analysis by defining another product-moment correlation coefficient which can be computed from the data. Let $r_w$ be the combined within-sample correlation between $X$ and $Y$. That is,

$$r_w = \frac{\Sigma \Sigma xy}{\sqrt{\Sigma \Sigma x^2 \Sigma \Sigma y^2}} .$$

To compute the numerator, we find the sum of products of deviations for each sample, separately, and then combine these quantities. To compute the double sum on the left in the denominator, we find the sum of squares of deviations in $X$ for each sample and then combine those sums. The double sum on the right in the denominator is computed in the same way. What we are doing is computing the correlation between $X$ and $Y$ after the between-sample variability has been eliminated. In other words, we are computing the correlation between $X$ and $Y$ using only the within-sample variability for each variable.

Then $r_w^2$ is the proportion of within-sample $Y$ variability correlated with the within-sample $X$ variability, and $(1 - r_w^2)$ is the proportion not correlated with $X$.

Note that $\Sigma\Sigma y^2$ is the combined within-sample variability in $Y$. It includes differences among subjects treated alike and other errors, but does not include treatment effects when they are constant and additive.

It follows that $r_w^2\Sigma\Sigma y^2$ is the within-sample predicted variability, a sum of squares measuring differences among subjects, to the extent that these differences can be predicted from $X$. Furthermore, $(1 - r_w^2)\Sigma\Sigma y^2$ is the within-sample unpredicted variability, the sum of squares which provides an estimate of error. Let $E_w$ be this error sum of squares. It can be computed and used to estimate $E_t$, the error component or bias in $(T + E_t)$.

By the subtraction,

$$(T + E_t) - E_w,$$

we obtain a quantity which we shall call $T_{\text{biased}}$, the apparent treatment effect. $T_{\text{biased}}$ is a sum of squares which measures the treatment effect as it may have been biased by error and we therefore call it the *apparent* treatment effect. We can evaluate $T_{\text{biased}}$ in a test of significance.

The analysis and evaluation are summarized in Table 15.10. This kind of

**Table 15.10**

**GENERAL FORM OF THE ANALYSIS OF COVARIANCE**

| Component | *SS* | *df* | *V* | *F* |
|---|---|---|---|---|
| Treatment effect | $T_{\text{biased}}$ | $c - 1$ | $V_t'$ | $V_t'/V_e'$ |
| Error | $E_w$ | $N - c - 1$ | $V_e'$ | |

$T_{\text{biased}}$ = sum of squares for apparent treatment effect.
$E_w$ = sum of squares for estimating error.

analysis, in which the original data for the dependent variable are adjusted with respect to preexperimental differences among subjects as measured by a variable $X$, is often referred to as an *analysis of covariance.*

It is appropriate to test the sample variances on $Y$ for evidence of nonadditivity of treatment effects. It is also appropriate to test the homogeneity of sample correlation coefficients as providing further evidence on the nonadditivity of treatment effects. These tests for nonadditivity will be illustrated in the example which follows.

The effectiveness of the covariance design in reducing the size of errors depends on the magnitude of the correlation between $X$ and $Y$. If this correlation is zero, there is no point in doing an analysis of covariance. When the correlation is zero, one discards the preexperimental measures and does a simple analysis of variance on the $Y$ measures. One's decision about the magnitude of the correlation is based on a test of significance of the within-sample predicted variability. A predicted variance, $V_p'$, can be computed from the within-sample predicted sum of squares, $r_w^2\Sigma\Sigma y^2$, by dividing it by one degree of freedom. $F$ is the ratio of $V_p'$ to $V_e'$, the error variance from the main analysis of Table 15.10.

## AN EXAMPLE

Table 15.11 contains experimental data which will be analyzed and evaluated by the analysis of covariance. The data were obtained from an experiment in which the psychologist wanted to determine the effect of practice on scores for a mechanical assembly test. The experimenter obtained

**Table 15.11**

**DATA FOR THE ASSEMBLY-TEST EXPERIMENT**

| | Conditions | | | | | |
|---|---|---|---|---|---|---|
| | $A_1$ Sample 1 | | | $A_2$ Sample 2 | | |
| | | $X$ | $Y$ | | $X$ | $Y$ |
| | 1 | 4 | 2 | 1 | 5 | 11 |
| | 2 | 3 | 7 | 2 | 5 | 11 |
| | 3 | 4 | 5 | 3 | 3 | 7 |
| | 4 | 3 | 7 | 4 | 3 | 8 |
| | 5 | 5 | 6 | 5 | 3 | 7 |
| *Ss* | 6 | 6 | 14 | *Ss* 6 | 4 | 12 |
| | 7 | 5 | 7 | 7 | 4 | 14 |
| | 8 | 3 | 5 | 8 | 4 | 5 |
| | 9 | 3 | 1 | 9 | 4 | 5 |
| | 10 | 3 | 5 | 10 | 5 | 9 |

*Ss* = subjects.
$X$ = preexperimental test score.
$Y$ = dependent variable test score.

two samples of subjects and measured all subjects on a different assembly test under uniform conditions prior to the experiment. He then imposed the practice conditions, which were one hour for the first sample and two hours for the second sample. Subjects practiced on the initial assembly test. He then administered the assembly test which yielded the scores on the dependent variable. A score on either test indicated the number of assemblies completed in a five-minute period.

*Summary data for the entire set of measures:*

$$\Sigma X = 79 \qquad \Sigma Y = 148$$
$$\Sigma X^2 = 329 \qquad \Sigma Y^2 = 1{,}334$$
$$\Sigma XY = 617$$
$$N = 20$$

*Computation of the total sums of squares and products:*

$$\Sigma x^2 = \Sigma X^2 - \frac{(\Sigma X)^2}{N} = 329 - \frac{79^2}{20} = 16.95$$

$$\Sigma y^2 = \Sigma Y^2 - \frac{(\Sigma Y)^2}{N} = 1{,}334 - \frac{148^2}{20} = 238.8$$

$$\Sigma xy = \Sigma XY - \frac{\Sigma X \Sigma Y}{N} = 617 - \frac{(79)(148)}{20} = 32.4$$

The adjustment of the total sum of squares, $\Sigma y^2$, to obtain $(T + E_t)$, the sum of squares of errors of prediction, is defined by the expression

$$(1 - r_t^2)\Sigma y^2$$

which can be written as

$$\Sigma y^2 - r_t^2 \Sigma y^2 = \Sigma y^2 - \frac{(\Sigma xy)^2}{\Sigma x^2} = 238.8 - \frac{32.4^2}{16.95} = 176.867.$$

$(T + E_t)$, the sum of squares of errors of prediction based on the total sums of squares and products, is 176.867.

*Summary data for Sample 1:*

$$\Sigma X = 39 \qquad \Sigma Y = 59$$
$$\Sigma X^2 = 163 \qquad \Sigma Y^2 = 459$$
$$\Sigma XY = 252$$
$$n = 10$$

*Computation of sums of squares and products for Sample 1:*

$$\Sigma x^2 = \Sigma X^2 - \frac{(\Sigma X)^2}{n} = 163 - \frac{39^2}{10} = 10.9$$

$$\Sigma y^2 = \Sigma Y^2 - \frac{(\Sigma Y)^2}{n} = 459 - \frac{59^2}{10} = 110.9$$

$$\Sigma xy = \Sigma XY - \frac{\Sigma X \Sigma Y}{n} = 252 - \frac{(39)(59)}{10} = 21.9$$

*Summary data for Sample 2:*

$$\Sigma X = 40 \qquad \Sigma Y = 89$$
$$\Sigma X^2 = 166 \qquad \Sigma Y^2 = 875$$
$$\Sigma XY = 365$$
$$n = 10$$

*Computation of sums of squares and products for Sample 2:*

$$\Sigma x^2 = \Sigma X^2 - \frac{(\Sigma X)^2}{n} = 166 - \frac{40^2}{10} = 6$$

$$\Sigma y^2 = \Sigma Y^2 - \frac{(\Sigma Y)^2}{n} = 875 - \frac{89^2}{10} = 82.9$$

$$\Sigma xy = \Sigma XY - \frac{\Sigma X \Sigma Y}{n} = 365 - \frac{(40)(89)}{10} = 9$$

*Combining of sums of squares and products for the two samples:*

$$\Sigma\Sigma x^2 = 10.9 + 6 = 16.9$$
$$\Sigma\Sigma y^2 = 110.9 + 82.9 = 193.8$$
$$\Sigma\Sigma xy = 21.9 + 9 = 30.9$$

The adjustment of the within-sample sum of squares, $\Sigma\Sigma y^2$, to obtain $E_w$, the sum of squares of errors of prediction based on the within-sample sums of squares and products, is defined by the expression,

$$(1 - r_w^2)\Sigma\Sigma y^2,$$

which can be written as

$$\Sigma\Sigma y^2 - r_w^2 \Sigma\Sigma y^2 = \Sigma\Sigma y^2 - \frac{(\Sigma\Sigma xy)^2}{\Sigma\Sigma x^2}.$$

$E_w$ is computed, as follows:

$$193.8 - \frac{30.9^2}{16.9} = 137.302$$

Thus $E_w$, the sum of squares of errors of prediction based on the within-sample sums of squares and products, is 137.302.

$T_{\text{biased}}$, the sum of squares for the apparent treatment effect, is the difference,

$$(T + E_t) - E_w = 176.867 - 137.302 = 39.565.$$

Table 15.12 gives $T_{\text{biased}}$, $E_w$, degrees of freedom, variances computed from the two sums of squares, and the $F$ ratio comparing the apparent treatment effect with the estimate of error. The null hypothesis is that the apparent treatment effect is due to error. $F_c$ for the 0.05 level of significance and one and 17 degrees of freedom is 4.45. (See Table $B_1$ in the Appendix.) Since the obtained value of $F$, 4.90, exceeds $F_c$, the null hypothesis is rejected and the investigator announces positive results.

**Table 15.12**

**ANALYSIS OF COVARIANCE FOR THE ASSEMBLY-TEST EXPERIMENT**[a]

| Component | *SS* | *df* | *V* | *F* |
|---|---|---|---|---|
| Treatment | 39.56 | 1 | 39.56 | 4.90[b] |
| Error | 137.30 | 17 | 8.08 | |

[a]Data in Table 15.11.
[b]$F_c$ for the 0.05 level of significance and one and 17 degrees of freedom is 4.45; the null hypothesis is rejected.

The main evaluation of the assembly-test experiment has been described above. The test of significance of the correlation between the dependent variable, $Y$, and the adjusting variable, $X$, will be described next. This order of events is followed here because of its convenience in explaining the analysis. In actual practice, the test of significance of the correlation between $X$ and $Y$ would precede the main evaluation. If the correlation proved to be nonsignificant, an analysis of covariance would not be used for the main evaluation.

The correlation to be tested is $r_w$, which is based on the within-sample sums of squares and products. A convenient way of performing the test is to compute the within-sample predicted sum of squares,

$$r_w^2 \Sigma\Sigma y^2,$$

which can be written

$$\frac{(\Sigma\Sigma xy)^2}{\Sigma\Sigma x^2}$$

and computed, as follows:

$$\frac{30.9^2}{16.9} = 56.50.$$

The predicted variance, $V'_p$, is computed by dividing the predicted sum of squares by one degree of freedom. Thus

$$V'_p = \frac{56.50}{1} = 56.50.$$

The test of significance requires the computation of $F$, the ratio of the predicted variance, $V'_p$, to the error variance, $V'_e$, from Table 15.12. That is,

$$F = \frac{V'_p}{V'_e} = \frac{56.50}{8.08} = 6.995.$$

The null hypothesis is that the observed correlation between $X$ and $Y$ is due to error. $F_c$ for the 0.05 level of significance and one and 17 degrees of freedom is 4.45. (See Table $B_1$ in the Appendix.) Since the obtained value exceeds the criterion value, the null hypothesis is rejected. The finding of a significant correlation between $X$ and $Y$ justifies the use of analysis of covariance in the main evaluation, which has already been described.

There are two tests for nonadditivity of treatment effects. The first involves the comparison of one sample variance with the other. The comparison of sample variances is carried out only for the dependent variable, since the treatments could not have had any effect on $X$. The variance for the first sample is

$$V_1 = \frac{110.9}{9} = 12.32.$$

The variance for the second sample is

$$V'_2 = \frac{82.9}{9} = 9.21.$$

The ratio of the larger variance to the smaller is

$$F = \frac{V'_1}{V'_2} = \frac{12.32}{9.21} \doteq 1.34.$$

Since we have compared the larger with the smaller, we must choose a value of $F_c$ which is exceeded by 0.025 of values in the sampling distribution to achieve an effective level of significance of 0.05. The null hypothesis is that the observed difference between the two sample variances is due to error. The criterion value, $F_c$, for nine and nine degrees of freedom is 4.03. (See Table $B_2$ in the Appendix.) Since $F$ is less than $F_c$, the null hypothesis is accepted.

The second test for nonadditivity is a test of the homogeneity of the sample correlations. We compute $E_1$, the sum of squares of errors of prediction for Sample 1, as follows:

$$E_1 = \Sigma y^2 - \frac{(\Sigma xy)^2}{\Sigma x^2} = 110.9 - \frac{21.9^2}{10.9} = 66.90.$$

For Sample 2, the sum of squares of errors of prediction is

$$E_2 = \Sigma y^2 - \frac{(\Sigma xy)^2}{\Sigma x^2} = 82.9 - \frac{9^2}{6} = 69.4.$$

$E_i$, the combined sum of squares of errors of prediction from the individual samples, is computed, as follows:

$$E_i = E_1 + E_2 = 66.90 + 69.4 = 136.30.$$

The difference,

$$E_w - E_i = 137.30 - 136.30 = 1.00,$$

is a measure of the heterogeneity of the sample correlations. It can be evaluated by comparing its variance, $V'_h$, computed with $(c - 1) = 1$ degree of freedom, with $V'_i$, a variance computed from $E_i$ with $N - 2c = 20 - 4 = 16$ degrees of freedom. Thus

$$V'_h = \frac{E_w - E_i}{c - 1} = \frac{1.00}{1} = 1,$$

$$V'_i = \frac{E_i}{N - 2c} = \frac{136.30}{16} = 8.52,$$

and

$$F = \frac{V'_h}{V'_i} = \frac{1.00}{8.52} = 0.12.$$

The null hypothesis is that the observed difference between sample correlations is due to error. $F_c$ for the 0.05 level of significance and one and 16 degrees of freedom is 4.49. (See Table $B_1$ in the Appendix.) The null hypothesis is accepted. Since sample variances and sample correlations were not found to differ significantly, the assumption of constant and additive treatment effects is taken to be justified.

## Summary

Three designs for simple experiments have been presented in the present chapter. The first design required that subjects be selected randomly, and that subjects and treatments be assigned randomly to occasions of measurement. There is no provision in this first design for reducing the size of errors to which the experiment is liable. Consequently, when subjects are heterogeneous and uncontrolled influences have large effects, this completely randomized design may yield data containing large biases. The second design required that subjects be measured, under uniform conditions prior to the experiment, on a variable related to the dependent variable. Subjects are ranked and formed into matched groups. Subjects within each matched group are then assigned randomly to conditions and to occasions of measurement. To the extent that the matching variable and the dependent variable are related, the matching will be successful and the errors will be small. The third design required the random selection of subjects and random assignment to conditions and occasions of measurement, with measurement prior to the experiment on a variable known to be correlated with the dependent variable. After the conditions are imposed on the random groups and after measures on the dependent variable have been obtained, the resulting data are adjusted by computational procedures which take advantage of the correlation between the two variables.

An example was given for each design. The examples involved only two conditions. The designs can, of course, be enlarged to incorporate any number of conditions. For examples in which the number of conditions is greater than two, the student might wish to consult a text on experimental design by Ray (2) or others.

In this discussion of experimental research, only tests of significance were considered. No attention was given to the estimation of parameters. It is possible to compute, from experimental data, estimates of means, variances, and differences between means, but the procedures of estimation are seldom used in psychological experimentation. One reason is the arbitrary nature of the units in many psychological scales. Another reason is that much of psychological experimentation is exploratory and detecting the differential effect of two or more treatments is itself quite an accomplishment.

### REFERENCES

1. Edwards, A. L., *Experimental Design in Psychological Research* (New York: Rinehart, 1950).
2. Ray, W. S., *An Introduction to Experimental Design* (New York: Macmillan, 1960).
3. Walker, H. M., and Lev, Joseph, *Statistical Inference* (New York: Holt, 1953).

# INFERENCE IN EMPIRICAL RESEARCH

## Pragmatics 16

In what we choose to call empirical research, the psychologist observes, establishes relations among variables, and makes predictions based on those relations. He does not deliberately interfere with or change natural processes for the purpose of determining the consequences of such action. Experimental research is, of course, a more ambitious undertaking than empirical research. Experimental knowledge bestows the power to control natural events. Because men in practical affairs place high value on experimental knowledge, empirical studies are often valued less highly than experiments. Nevertheless, empirical research can produce knowledge which makes it possible to predict natural events. It is often the only kind of research which the psychologist is permitted to undertake by society. In many areas of human behavior, experimentation is out of the question.

Statistical inference is employed in the evaluation of empirical research data in both of its major forms: testing significance and estimating parameters. It is not possible to present all of the specific applications of significance-testing and estimation in empirical research. We have chosen only a few of the more important tests and estimation procedures for discussion here.

## Tests of Significance

Three examples of tests of significance as they might be applied to data from empirical investigations are described below.

1. A psychologist wishes to know whether the student bodies of two large universities differ in verbal fluency. It is not practical to test all of the students so he obtains a random sample of 100 students from each university and administers the test to students in both samples under standard conditions.

He computes the mean of each sample, the difference between means, the combined within-sample sum of squares, and the combined within-sample variance. He then computes $t$ by formula (12.2),

$$t = \frac{D_x}{\sqrt{2V'_w/n}}.$$

In the formula, $D_x$ is the difference between sample means, $V'_w$ is the combined within-sample variance, and $n$ is the number of subjects per sample. $V'_w$ is computed by dividing the combined within-sample sum of squares by $(2n - 2)$ degrees of freedom. The null hypothesis is that any observed difference between means is due to random error. He sets the level of significance at 0.05 and then refers to a table of $t$ to classify his result. (See Table A in the Appendix.) If his obtained value of $t$ exceeds $t_c$, positive, or is exceeded by $t_c$, negative, he rejects the null hypothesis and announces positive results. If it neither exceeds nor is exceeded, he accepts the null hypothesis and acknowledges negative results.

2. The psychologist in the first example may also decide to compare the two sample variances. Doing so would serve two purposes. First, the test of the difference between means provided by formula (12.2), applied to two samples from *different* populations, requires that the populations have equal variances. If he compares the two sample variances in a test of significance, he will obtain evidence bearing on this requirement. In addition, he may actually be interested in comparing the dispersions of the two student bodies. Not all of the information one might desire in comparing two groups is necessarily contained in a comparison of means. To compare sample variances, he computes $F$ by formula (12.5),

$$F = \frac{V'_1}{V'_2}.$$

$V'_1$ is computed by dividing a sample sum of squares by $(n - 1)$ degrees of freedom. $V'_2$ is computed in the same way. The null hypothesis is that any observed difference between the two sample variances is due to error. Since tables of $F$ usually give only ratios greater than one, it is a general practice to place the larger variance in the numerator and the smaller in the denominator. The effect is to double the number of values of $F$ greater than $F_c$ for a given level of significance. To compensate and achieve a level of significance of 0.05, the psychologist chooses a value of $F_c$ exceeded by 0.025 of the values in the sampling distribution. (See Table $B_2$ in the Appendix.) He then compares the computed $F$ with $F_c$, and accepts or rejects the null hypothesis.

3. An educator has decided to investigate the relation between verbal ability and grades in the junior high schools of a large metropolitan area. He obtains a random sample of junior high-school students and tests them on

verbal ability. He also obtains their average grades for the preceding term. He computes the product-moment correlation coefficient for the sample and from that value computes $t$ by formula (12.3),

$$t = \frac{r_{xy}\sqrt{N - 2}}{\sqrt{1 - r_{xy}^2}}.$$

In the formula, $r_{xy}$ is the sample correlation; $N$ is the number of subjects in the sample. The null hypothesis is that any observed correlation is due to random error. He determines the criterion value of $t$ for the 0.05 level of significance and $(N - 2)$ degrees of freedom, and accepts or rejects the null hypothesis. (See Table A in the Appendix.)

## Estimating Parameters

Within the context of the present discussion, an *i*-statistic is a value computed from one or more random samples. A corresponding value computed from the population is called a *parameter*. When a population is too large to be measured and described, that is, when it is too large to permit the computation of parameters, it is often of interest to the researcher to obtain an estimate of one or more of the parameters. In general terms, an attempt is made to infer values of parameters from sample values.

Estimates are divided into two large classes: point estimates and interval estimates. They will be discussed in that order.

### POINT ESTIMATES

A point estimate is a single value computed from one or more samples. It possesses certain properties which qualify it as an estimate of the corresponding parameter. Although several different kinds of point estimates can be distinguished, we shall consider only point estimates which are unbiased or approximately so.

Consider any *i*-statistic, the corresponding parameter, and the sampling distribution of the *i*-statistic. When the mean of the sampling distribution is equal to the parameter, any obtained value of the *i*-statistic is said to be an unbiased estimate of the parameter. When the mean of the sampling distribution does not equal the parameter, the *i*-statistic is said to be a biased estimate.

Four examples of unbiased estimates are given below.

1. $M_x$, the sample mean, is an unbiased estimate of $\mu$, the population mean. That is, $\overline{M}_x$, the average of all possible sample means, is equal to the population mean, $\mu$.

2. $D_x$, the difference between the means of two samples from two populations, is an unbiased estimate of the difference between the two population means,

$$\mu_1 - \mu_2.$$

That is,

$$\overline{D}_x = \mu_1 - \mu_2.$$

In other words, the average of the totality of differences between sample means is equal to the difference between the two population means.

3. $V'_x$, the sample variance computed with $(n - 1)$ degrees of freedom is an unbiased estimate of the population variance, $\sigma^2$. That is,

$$\overline{V}'_x = \sigma^2$$

or, in words, the average of all possible sample variances, when each one is computed with $(n - 1)$ degrees of freedom, is equal to the population variance.

The student may be interested in knowing that $V_x$, the sample variance computed with $n$, is a biased estimate of the population variance, since the average of all such sample values is less than the population variance. In symbols,

$$\overline{V}_x < \sigma^2.$$

It can be shown that

$$\overline{V}_x = \frac{n - 1}{n} \sigma^2 < \sigma^2.$$

4. When $\rho_{xy}$, the population product-moment correlation coefficient is zero, then $r_{xy}$, the sample product-moment correlation coefficient, is an unbiased estimate of the parameter, since the mean of the sampling distribution of $r_{xy}$ is zero. Symbolically,

$$\bar{r}_{xy} = \rho_{xy} = 0.$$

When the population correlation is not zero, $r_{xy}$ is a biased estimate. An approximately unbiased estimate of $\rho_{xy}$, when it is not zero, is given by

$$r_{xy} + r_{xy} \frac{(1 - r_{xy}^2)}{2(N - 1)}.$$

## INTERVAL ESTIMATES

To obtain an interval estimate of a given parameter, one computes, from one or more samples, two values which are called *limits*. These limits establish an interval which is known to vary with sampling. That is to say, the end-points of the interval have a sampling distribution. The interval has the property that it will sometimes encompass or bracket the parameter and will sometimes fail to do so. The size of the interval can be established by the researcher so that, in the totality of such intervals, some known and stated proportion of them will fail to bracket the parameter. By his choice of the size of the interval, the researcher can make the proportion of failures as small as he desires. In any given attempt, of course, he has no way of knowing whether the interval has succeeded or failed. He anticipates that, in a large number of such attempts, the interval will fail to bracket the parameter with the relative frequency he has intended.

The logic of the procedure whereby one arrives at an interval estimate is illustrated below with an example involving the estimation of a population mean from the mean of a sample. As we indicated earlier in the discussion of formula (12.1), the *i*-statistic,

$$\frac{M_x - \mu}{\sqrt{V'_x/n}},$$

is distributed as $t$. It will be convenient to let $S_e = \sqrt{V'_x/n}$.

Then

$$t = \frac{M_x - \mu}{S_e}.$$

It follows that

$$tS_e = M_x - \mu.$$

The quantity, $(M_x - \mu)$, can be thought of as the distance of $M_x$ from $\mu$. Notice that $t$ is negative when $M_x < \mu$ and positive when $M_x > \mu$.

We shall choose a particular value of $t$ and designate it as $t_p$, where the subscript refers to the proportion, $P$. The value of $t_p$ is chosen so that $P/2$ of the values of $t$ in the sampling distribution are less than $t_p$ when it is negative, and $P/2$ of the values of $t$ in the sampling distribution are greater than $t_p$ when it is positive.

Consider now the relation between $tS_e$ and $t_pS_e$. In the sampling distribution of $tS_e$, $P/2$ of the values will be less than $t_pS_e$ when it is given a negative sign, and $P/2$ of the values will be greater than $t_pS_e$, when it is given a positive sign. That this relation holds can be verified by observing that

$$tS_e < t_pS_e$$

whenever

$$t < t_p$$

and that

$$tS_e > t_pS_e$$

whenever

$$t > t_p.$$

Recall that $tS_e = M_x - \mu =$ the distance of $M_x$ from $\mu$. We conclude that the distance of a sample mean from the population mean varies with sampling and that it relates to $t_pS_e$ just as does $tS_e$. This is to say that $P/2$ of the values of $(M_x - \mu)$ in the sampling distribution of such distances will be less than

$t_pS_e$, when it is taken to be negative, and $P/2$ of the values will be greater than $t_pS_e$, when it is taken to be positive. We can take account of both classes of values by saying that the absolute value of $(M_x - \mu)$ exceeds the absolute value of $t_pS_e$ in $P$ of the totality of sample values.

Now let $M_x$ represent any point on the scale of values for sample means. We can construct an interval on this scale around the point, $M_x$. The limits of the interval will be

$$M_x - t_pS_e$$

and

$$M_x + t_pS_e.$$

The interval will have the following characteristics. When $M_x < \mu$, the interval will fail to bracket or encompass $\mu$ for any sample whose mean is a distance from the population mean greater than $t_pS_e$, a circumstance which is true for $P/2$ of samples. When $M_x > \mu$, the interval will again fail to bracket $\mu$ for any sample whose mean is more distant from the population mean than $t_pS_e$, a characteristic of $P/2$ samples. Thus the interval,

$$M_x \pm t_pS_e,$$

will fail to bracket $\mu$ in $P$ of all samples. The interval is called an *interval estimate* of the population mean, $\mu$. The value, $M_x - t_pS_e$, is called the *lower limit* of the estimate. The value, $M_x + t_pS_e$, is called the *upper limit*. Considered together, the two values are called *confidence limits*. The value of $P$ is called the *level of confidence*.

Figure 16.1 shows graphically how interval estimates of the population

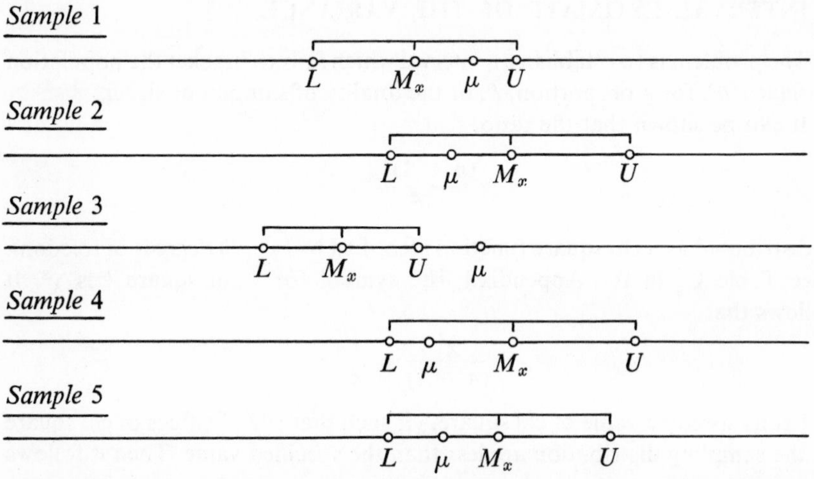


**Fig. 16.1** Interval estimates of the population mean, $\mu$, computed from five random samples from the same population. $M_x$ is the sample mean; $L$ is the lower limit of the interval; $U$ is the upper limit of the interval. Notice how the locations and the widths of the intervals vary from one sample to another.

mean can vary from one sample to another. In the figure, $\mu$ is the population mean, $M_x$ is the sample mean, $L$ is the lower limit of the interval, $U$ is the upper limit. Notice that the location of the interval and the width of the interval vary. The population mean does not vary. In one of the five examples of Figure 16.1, the estimate fails to bracket the population mean.

## AN EXAMPLE

An instructor in physical education wishes to determine the average pulse rate for college freshmen who have been enrolled in special gymnastics classes for a period of eight weeks. He obtains a sample of 50 students from a total enrollment of 2,300. The mean of the 50 determinations of pulse rate is 80. The variance, $V'_x$, is 4.5. $S_e$, which is equal to $\sqrt{V'_x/n}$, is 0.30. For 49 degrees of freedom and the 0.05 level of confidence, $t_p = 2.01$, a value obtained from Table A by linear interpolation. The lower limit for the interval estimate is

$$M_x - t_p S_e = 80 - (2.01)(.30) = 79.397.$$

The upper limit is

$$M_x + t_p S_e = 80 + (2.01)(.30) = 80.603.$$

Thus the estimate is the interval from 79.397 to 80.603. The instructor knows that 5 per cent of the totality of such estimates fail to bracket the parameter.

## INTERVAL ESTIMATE OF THE VARIANCE

The problem is to establish an interval which fails to bracket the population variance, $\sigma^2$, for a proportion, $P$, of the totality of samples of size $n$.

It can be shown that the ratio,

$$\frac{(n-1)V'_x}{\sigma^2},$$

is distributed as a chi square function identified by $(n-1)$ degrees of freedom. (See Table $C_2$ in the Appendix.) The symbol for "chi square" is $\chi^2$. It follows that

$$\frac{\chi^2}{(n-1)} = \frac{V'_x}{\sigma^2}.$$

Let us specify a value of chi square, $\chi_1^2$, such that $P/2$ of values of chi square in the sampling distribution are less than the specified value. Then it follows that

$$\frac{\chi^2}{(n-1)} < \frac{\chi_1^2}{(n-1)}$$

for $P/2$ values in the sampling distribution. Since the left member of this inequality is equal to the ratio, $V'_x/\sigma^2$, we can substitute the ratio and obtain

$$\frac{V'_x}{\sigma^2} < \frac{\chi_1^2}{(n-1)}$$

for $P/2$ values in the sampling distribution. By multiplication and division on both sides of the inequality, we obtain

$$\frac{(n-1)V'_x}{\chi_1^2} < \sigma^2$$

for $P/2$ values in the sampling distribution. Let us call the quantity on the left $U$ for it will be the upper limit in the interval estimate. Note that $U$ is less than $\sigma^2$ in $P/2$ samples.

Let us now specify a second value of chi square, $\chi_2^2$, such that $P/2$ values of $\chi^2$ in the sampling distribution are greater than the specified value. It follows that

$$\frac{\chi^2}{(n-1)} > \frac{\chi_2^2}{(n-1)}$$

for $P/2$ values in the distribution. Again we can substitute the ratio of $V'_x$ to $\sigma^2$ on the left and obtain

$$\frac{V'_x}{\sigma^2} > \frac{\chi_2^2}{(n-1)}$$

for $P/2$ values in the sampling distribution. By multiplication and division on both sides of the inequality, we obtain

$$\frac{(n-1)V'_x}{\chi_2^2} > \sigma^2$$

for $P/2$ values in the sampling distribution. We shall call the quantity on the left $L$ for it will be the lower limit of the interval estimate. Note that $L$ is greater than $\sigma^2$ in $P/2$ samples. Note also that $L < U$ because $\chi_1^2 < \chi_2^2$.

The two limits, $L$ and $U$, form an interval which will fail to bracket $\sigma^2$ in $P$ samples from the totality of samples of $n$ units from a population.

## AN EXAMPLE

Free association times to verbs as stimulus words were determined for a sample of 30 male adults. The mean of the 30 response times was 1.5 seconds. The unbiased estimate of the population variance was 0.04 seconds. The investigator proceeded to establish an interval estimate with a level of confidence of 0.05 by computing the following quantities:

$$U = \frac{(n-1)V'_x}{\chi_1^2} = \frac{(29)(0.04)}{16.0} = 0.072,$$

$$L = \frac{(n-1)V'_x}{\chi_2^2} = \frac{(29)(0.04)}{45.7} = 0.025.$$

Values of chi square were obtained from Table $C_2$ in the Appendix.

## AN INTERVAL ESTIMATE OF THE PRODUCT-MOMENT COEFFICIENT

Because a product-moment correlation coefficient is a dimensionless number not influenced by certain arbitrary scale differences, psychologists frequently use interval estimates of that coefficient. The problem is to obtain limits for an interval which will be computed from $r_{xy}$, the sample product-moment correlation coefficient, and used to estimate $\rho_{xy}$, the population coefficient.

When $\rho_{xy}$, the population correlation, is not zero, the distribution of $r_{xy}$ is skewed. Its distribution has been tabulated for sample sizes of 25 or less.[1] For larger samples, it has been shown that

$$Z_r = \frac{1}{2} \log_e \frac{1 + r_{xy}}{1 - r_{xy}}$$

is approximately normally distributed with variance, approximately $1/(N-3)$. The problem is to estimate $\zeta$, which is a function of $\rho_{xy}$, as indicated by

$$\zeta = \frac{1}{2} \log_e \frac{1 + \rho_{xy}}{1 - \rho_{xy}}.$$

We determine $\delta_p$, the standard normal deviate appropriate for the level of confidence, $P$. (See the last line of Table A in the Appendix.) Then the limits are found in the following manner: Compute the sample correlation coefficient, $r_{xy}$. Compute $Z_r$ by the transformation formula given above. Compute $S_z = 1/\sqrt{N-3}$. The lower limit is then given by the expression

$$Z_r - \delta_p S_z.$$

The upper limit is

$$Z_r + \delta_p S_z.$$

These confidence limits define an interval which will fail to bracket the parameter in approximately $P$ of the totality of estimates.

It is usually desired to express the limits in terms of correlation. Tables are available which permit one to read values of a correlation coefficient corresponding to the upper and lower limits on the scale of $Z_r$. These tables can also be used for the transformation of $r_{xy}$ to $Z_r$.[2]

[1]See F. N. David, *Tables of the Correlation Coefficient*, Biometrika Office, University College, London.

[2]See R. A. Fisher and Frank Yates, *Statistical Tables for Biological, Agricultural and Medical Research*, 3rd ed. (Edinburgh and London: Oliver and Boyd, 1948).

## AN EXAMPLE

A public opinion pollster obtains a sample correlation of 0.60 for the relation between income and favorableness of attitude toward a certain candidate for public office. $N$, the number of respondents in his sample, is 103. For a level of confidence equal to 0.05, $\delta_p$ is 1.96. The value of $Z_r$ corresponding to $r_{xy} = 0.60$ is 0.69. $S_z$ is 0.1. The lower limit for the interval estimate of $\zeta$ is

$$0.69 - (0.1)(1.96) = 0.49.$$

The upper limit is

$$0.69 + (0.1)(1.96) = 0.89.$$

Converted to the correlation scale, the confidence limits are 0.455 and 0.710, approximately.

# FREQUENCY CLASSIFICATIONS

# 17

Univariate and bivariate frequency distributions have figured prominently in the preceding chapters. A univariate distribution expresses the relation between frequency and the magnitude of a single variable. A bivariate distribution expresses the relation between frequency and the magnitudes of values for two variables. Another important kind of research data takes the form of frequencies in classes or categories which are distinguished qualitatively rather than quantitatively.

The simplest form of frequency classification involves one set of two categories. For example, a psychologist may obtain a sample of $N$ respondents in a public opinion survey. As one part of the interview conducted with each respondent, a question is asked and an answer of " Yes " or " No " is obtained. He computes the proportion, $p$ of those answering " Yes." The *i*-statistic, $p$, is an unbiased estimate of the population proportion.

## Interval Estimate of a Proportion

If the psychologist wishes to establish an interval estimate of the population proportion, he has a choice of three methods: computing exact limits, reading limits from a table, and computing approximate limits. Computing exact limits is somewhat difficult, unless the sample is quite small, and will not be described here. Tables by Clopper and Pearson (1), Fisher and Yates (3), and Mainland (4) are available. In these tables, one can locate the sample proportion and read directly the confidence limits for some specified level of confidence. The procedure for computing approximate limits will be given below.

The sample proportion, $p$, is computed and then transformed to an angle by the formula,

$$\theta = \sin^{-1}\sqrt{p}.$$

To compute $\theta$ by means of this formula, one obtains the square root of the proportion and reads from a table of trigonometric functions the value of the angle whose sine is the computed square root. The variance of the sampling distribution of $\theta$ is approximately equal to $821/N$. Values of $\theta$ are approximately normally distributed. The lower limit of the interval estimate of the parametric angle is

$$\theta - \delta_p \sqrt{\frac{821}{N}}$$

where $\delta_p$ is the standard normal deviate for the desired level of confidence. (See the last line of Table A in the Appendix.) The upper limit is

$$\theta + \delta_p \sqrt{\frac{821}{N}}\,.$$

The approximation resulting from use of the inverse sine transformation is considered very good when the parametric proportion lies between 0.05 and 0.95 and when $N \geqq 20$. Tables have been made available by Fisher and Yates (3) for converting proportions directly to angles and for converting angular limits to limits on the proportion scale.

## Single Set of More Than Two Categories

It may be that the psychologist obtains more than two responses to an interview question. For example, the subject may be asked to respond by answering "Yes," "No," or "Undecided." These responses, in effect, classify the $N$ subjects into three categories. It is possible to test the significance of the differences among the three categories in terms of the discrepancies between the three observed frequencies and the average of the three frequencies. The test of significance involves the *i*-statistic, chi square, which is computed, as follows.

The observed frequency, $f_o$, is determined for each of the three categories. The average frequency, $\bar{f}$, is given by $\Sigma f_o/c$, where $c$ is the number of categories and, in the example under consideration, is equal to 3. The average frequency is, of course, also given by $N/c$. A discrepancy, $(f_o - \bar{f})$, is computed for each category. Each of these discrepancies is squared. Finally, the sum of the $c$ squared deviations is computed. The *i*-statistic, chi square, is the sum of the squared deviations divided by the average frequency. That is,

$$\chi^2 = \frac{1}{\bar{f}}\, \Sigma(f_o - \bar{f})^2.$$

The null hypothesis is that variation in the observed frequencies is due to sampling.

The psychologist chooses a level of significance and consults a table of chi square to determine the criterion value of chi square for $(c - 1)$ degrees of freedom. (See Table $C_1$ in the Appendix.) If the obtained value exceeds the criterion value, he rejects the null hypothesis. If it does not, he accepts the null hypothesis.

## The Significance of a Difference Between Proportions

When the researcher has obtained two samples from different populations and has determined the proportion of subjects in each sample who respond in a specified way, he may wish to examine the difference between the two proportions and make an inference about the difference between the two populations. The procedure for the test of significance is described below.

A proportion is computed for each sample. Let us use $p_1$ for the first sample and $p_2$ for the second sample. The corresponding angles will be denoted $\theta_1$ and $\theta_2$. $\theta_1$ is determined by computing the square root of $p_1$ and referring the root to a table of trigonometric functions for the angle whose sine is that square root. $\theta_2$ is determined in the same way. The *i*-statistic used in the test of significance is a ratio involving the difference between the two angles and the value, $\sqrt{821/N_1 + 821/N_2}$, where $N_1$ and $N_2$ are sample sizes. The ratio is distributed approximately as $\delta$, the standard normal deviate. The formula for $\delta$ is

$$\delta = \frac{\theta_1 - \theta_2}{\sqrt{821/N_1 + 821/N_2}} \cdot$$

The null hypothesis is that any observed difference between the two proportions is due to sampling.

A level of significance is chosen and the criterion value of $\delta$ is obtained from a table of standard normal deviates. (See the last line of Table A in the Appendix.) If the absolute value of the obtained $\delta$ exceeds the criterion value, the null hypothesis is rejected.

## Joint Frequency Classifications

It is often of interest to a psychologist to determine how the units of some population are jointly classified by two sets of categories. Let the first set of categories be labeled $R_1, R_2, R_3, \ldots, R_j, \ldots, R_r$, and the second set, $C_1$,

$C_2, C_3, \ldots, C_k, \ldots, C_c$. Jointly classifying units of the population requires the $(rc)$ subcategories defined by forming all combinations of the type $R_jC_k$.

It is convenient to represent the joint classification, in general form, by a rectangular table of $r$ rows and $c$ columns, such as the one in Table 17.1.

**Table 17.1**

**CATEGORIES AND SUBCATEGORIES FOR A JOINT CLASSIFICATION**

| | | *C* Categories | | | | | | |
|---|---|---|---|---|---|---|---|---|
| | | $C_1$ | $C_2$ | $C_3$ | . | $C_k$ | . | $C_c$ |
| | $R_1$ | $R_1C_1$ | $R_1C_2$ | $R_1C_3$ | . | $R_1C_k$ | . | $R_1C_c$ |
| | $R_2$ | $R_2C_1$ | $R_2C_2$ | $R_2C_3$ | . | $R_2C_k$ | . | $R_2C_c$ |
| *R* | $R_3$ | $R_3C_1$ | $R_3C_2$ | $R_3C_3$ | . | $R_3C_k$ | . | $R_3C_c$ |
| Categories | . | . | . | . | . | . | . | . |
| | $R_j$ | $R_jC_1$ | $R_jC_2$ | $R_jC_3$ | . | $R_jC_k$ | . | $R_jC_c$ |
| | . | . | . | . | . | . | . | . |
| | $R_r$ | $R_rC_1$ | $R_rC_2$ | $R_rC_3$ | . | $R_rC_k$ | . | $R_rC_c$ |

Each cell of the table represents a subcategory formed by combining one category from each of the original sets given on the margins of the table. We shall assume for purposes of discussion that an entire population can be classified by the subcategories of Table 17.1.

The purpose of investigating the joint classification would be to ascertain whether or not there was a relation between the two ways of classifying. No relation between the two ways of classifying is taken to mean that the relative frequency distributions of all columns are the same and that the relative frequency distributions of all rows are the same. When these conditions obtain, we say that the two ways of classifying are independent. We mean simply that the relative frequency distributions of either classification do not vary. In still other words, the differences among column relative frequencies do not vary with rows.

If we let

$p_{.k}$ = the population relative frequency for category $C_k$,
$p_{j.}$ = the population relative frequency for category $R_j$, and
$p_{jk}$ = the population relative frequency for subcategory $R_jC_k$,

then the joint, relative frequency distribution for the population can be represented, in general form, by Table 17.2. When the two ways of classifying are independent, that is, when there is no relation between them,

$$p_{jk} = p_{j.}p_{.k}.$$

When this equality does not hold for all $(rc)$ cells for the population joint classification, we say that the two ways of classifying are not independent and that there is a relation between them.

**Table 17.2**

**THE JOINT RELATIVE FREQUENCY DISTRIBUTION FOR A POPULATION**

| | | Relative Frequencies for the $C$ Categories | | | | | | |
|---|---|---|---|---|---|---|---|---|
| | | $p_{.1}$ | $p_{.2}$ | $p_{.3}$ | . | $p_{.k}$ | . | $p_{.c}$ |
| | $p_{1.}$ | $p_{11}$ | $p_{12}$ | $p_{13}$ | . | $p_{1k}$ | . | $p_{1c}$ |
| Relative | $p_{2.}$ | $p_{21}$ | $p_{22}$ | $p_{23}$ | . | $p_{2k}$ | . | $p_{2c}$ |
| Frequencies | $p_{3.}$ | $p_{31}$ | $p_{32}$ | $p_{33}$ | . | $p_{3k}$ | . | $p_{3c}$ |
| for the $R$ | . | . | . | . | . | . | . | . |
| Categories | $p_{j.}$ | $p_{j1}$ | $p_{j2}$ | $p_{j3}$ | . | $p_{jk}$ | . | $p_{jc}$ |
| | . | . | . | . | . | . | . | . |
| | $p_{r.}$ | $p_{r1}$ | $p_{r2}$ | $p_{r3}$ | . | $p_{rk}$ | . | $p_{rc}$ |

When the population is too large to be classified in its entirety, the investigator may obtain a random sample of $N$ units from the population, classify the units in the sample into the subcategories of an $(r \times c)$ table, and make an inference from the sample to the population regarding the relation between the two ways of classifying.

The test of significance which can be applied to the sample frequency data requires the computation of chi square, as indicated by the formula:

$$\chi^2 = \sum \frac{(f_o - f_e)^2}{f_e},$$

where $f_o$ is the observed frequency in each subcategory and $f_e$, the so-called *expected* frequency, is computed from the marginal frequencies and the total frequency, as indicated by the expression, $f_j f_k / N$. The summation has $(rc)$ terms, consisting of one value from each cell. The number of degrees of freedom is $(r - 1)(c - 1)$.

One can imagine there is a totality of samples of size $N$ which could be formed from the population and there is, also, a corresponding totality of values of chi square. These chi square values could be thought of as forming a sampling distribution, but this is not the distribution employed in the test of significance. The observed marginal frequencies for the particular sample obtained by the investigator identify a subset of samples and a corresponding subset of values of chi square from the totality of such values. The values of chi square in the subset form the sampling distribution on which the test of significance is based.

## AN EXAMPLE

The example we shall give would be classified, in our system, as an empirical research study.

A psychologist is hired to determine whether political affiliation is related to position on a current issue, where the position of an individual subject is indicated by a response of " Yes " or " No " to an interview question. A random sample of 150 registered voters is obtained and they are jointly classified as being Democrat or Republican and as having answered " Yes " or " No " to the question. The joint classification for the sample is given in Table 17.3. The computation of the expected frequency for each cell is shown in the table.

**Table 17.3**

**JOINT CLASSIFICATION OF VOTERS**

| | Democrat | Republican | $f_{j.}$ |
|---|---|---|---|
| Yes | $f_o = 75$<br>$f_e = (100)(90)/150 = 60$ | $f_o = 25$<br>$f_e = (100)(60)/150 = 40$ | 100 |
| No | $f_o = 15$<br>$f_e = (50)(90)/150 = 30$ | $f_o = 35$<br>$f_e = (50)(60)/150 = 20$ | 50 |
| $f_{.k}$ | 90 | 60 | $N = 150$ |

$f_o$ = observed frequency.
$f_e$ = expected frequency.

The null hypothesis is that any discrepancies between observed and expected frequencies are due to sampling.

The *i*-statistic, chi square, is computed by finding the difference between the observed and expected frequency for each cell, squaring that difference, dividing the squared difference by the expected frequency, and summing these four quotients for the four cells of the 2 × 2 table. The computation is given below.

$$\chi^2 = \frac{(75\text{–}60)^2}{60} + \frac{(25\text{–}40)^2}{40} + \frac{(15\text{–}30)^2}{30} + \frac{(35\text{–}20)^2}{20} = 28.125$$

The criterion value of chi square for $(r - 1)(c - 1) = 1$ degree of freedom and the 0.05 level of significance is 3.841. (See Table $C_1$ in the Appendix.) The null hypothesis is rejected and the investigator announces the finding of a relation between political affiliation and position on the issue.

Since the chi square function is a continuous curve and the values computed from frequency data are always discrete values, the actual sampling distribution is only approximated by the continuous function. For large samples, the disparity between the two distributions is negligible. For small samples, the disparity can be serious. In 2 × 2 classifications, it is possible to improve the approximation by reducing the absolute value of each difference, $(f_o - f_e)$, by 0.5 before computing chi square. The effect of this correction is to reduce the size of chi square. If one wishes to avoid the problem of discontinuity, one should apply the exact test described by Fisher (2).

It is interesting to note that

$$\chi^2 = N\phi^2$$

where $\phi$ is the phi coefficient, the product-moment coefficient for two dichotomous variables, when each has been coded to or assigned values of 0 and 1.

## REFERENCES

1. Clopper, C. J., and Pearson, E. S., " The Use of Confidence or Fiducial Limits Illustrated in the Case of the Binomial," *Biometrika*, **26**: 404–13 (1934).
2. Fisher, R. A., *Statistical Methods for Research Workers*, 10th ed. (London and Edinburgh: Oliver and Boyd, 1948).
3. Fisher, R. A., and Yates, Frank, *Statistical Tables for Biological, Agricultural and Medical Research* (London and Edinburgh: Oliver and Boyd, 1943).
4. Mainland, D., " Statistical Methods in Medical Research: I. Qualitative Statistics," *Canadian Journal of Research*, **26**: 1–166 (1948).

# APPENDIX

## TABLE A[a]

Values of $t$ exceeded by 0.025 of values in the sampling distribution.

In testing the significance of a difference between two sample means, the number of degrees of freedom is $2(n - 1)$ where $n$ is the number of units per sample.

In testing the significance of a product-moment correlation coefficient, the number of degrees of freedom is $(N - 2)$ where $N$ is the number of pairs in the sample.

In computing an interval estimate of the population mean, the number of degrees of freedom is $(n - 1)$ where $n$ is the number of units in the sample.

When the number of degrees of freedom is indefinitely large, $t$ is equal to $\delta$, the standard normal deviate. Therefore, the value of $\delta$ exceeded by 0.025 of values in the sampling distribution is given in the last line of the table.

If values of $t$ and $\delta$ are given negative signs, then these values exceed 0.025 of values in their respective distributions.

| *df* | *t* |
|---|---|
| 1 | 12.706 |
| 2 | 4.303 |
| 3 | 3.182 |
| 4 | 2.776 |
| 5 | 2.571 |
| 6 | 2.447 |
| 7 | 2.365 |
| 8 | 2.306 |
| 9 | 2.262 |
| 10 | 2.228 |
| 11 | 2.201 |
| 12 | 2.179 |

[a]Table A is abridged from Table III for Fisher and Yates, *Statistical Tables for Biological, Agricultural and Medical Research*, published by Oliver & Boyd Ltd., Edinburgh, by permission of the authors and publishers.

**TABLE A** *continued*

| | |
|---|---|
| 13 | 2.160 |
| 14 | 2.145 |
| 15 | 2.131 |
| 16 | 2.120 |
| 17 | 2.110 |
| 18 | 2.101 |
| 19 | 2.093 |
| 20 | 2.086 |
| 21 | 2.080 |
| 22 | 2.074 |
| 23 | 2.069 |
| 24 | 2.064 |
| 25 | 2.060 |
| 26 | 2.056 |
| 27 | 2.052 |
| 28 | 2.048 |
| 29 | 2.045 |
| 30 | 2.042 |
| 40 | 2.021 |
| 60 | 2.000 |
| 120 | 1.980 |
| $\infty$ | 1.960[b] |

[b]Note that $t = \delta$, the standard normal deviate, when the number of degrees of freedom is indefinitely large.

TABLE $B_1$[a]

Values of $F$ exceeded by 0.05 of the values in the sampling distribution.

The table can be used, when the 0.05 level of significance is desired, in testing differences between means, correlation, and homogeneity of sample correlations in analysis of covariance.

| | | *df* for Variance in Numerator | | | | | | |
|---|---|---|---|---|---|---|---|---|
| | | 1 | 2 | 3 | 4 | 5 | 6 | 7 |
| | 4 | 7.71 | 6.94 | 6.59 | 6.39 | 6.26 | 6.16 | 6.09 |
| | 5 | 6.61 | 5.79 | 5.41 | 5.19 | 5.05 | 4.95 | 4.88 |
| | 6 | 5.99 | 5.14 | 4.76 | 4.53 | 4.39 | 4.28 | 4.21 |
| | 7 | 5.59 | 4.74 | 4.35 | 4.12 | 3.97 | 3.87 | 3.79 |
| | 8 | 5.32 | 4.46 | 4.07 | 3.84 | 3.69 | 3.58 | 3.50 |
| | 9 | 5.12 | 4.26 | 3.86 | 3.63 | 3.48 | 3.37 | 3.29 |
| | 10 | 4.96 | 4.10 | 3.71 | 3.48 | 3.33 | 3.22 | 3.14 |
| | 11 | 4.84 | 3.98 | 3.59 | 3.36 | 3.20 | 3.09 | 3.01 |
| | 12 | 4.75 | 3.89 | 3.49 | 3.26 | 3.11 | 3.00 | 2.91 |
| *df* | 13 | 4.67 | 3.81 | 3.41 | 3.18 | 3.03 | 2.92 | 2.83 |
| for | 14 | 4.60 | 3.74 | 3.34 | 3.11 | 2.96 | 2.85 | 2.76 |
| Variance | 15 | 4.54 | 3.68 | 3.29 | 3.06 | 2.90 | 2.79 | 2.71 |
| in | 16 | 4.49 | 3.63 | 3.24 | 3.01 | 2.85 | 2.74 | 2.66 |
| Denominator | 17 | 4.45 | 3.59 | 3.20 | 2.96 | 2.81 | 2.70 | 2.61 |
| | 18 | 4.41 | 3.55 | 3.16 | 2.93 | 2.77 | 2.66 | 2.58 |
| | 19 | 4.38 | 3.52 | 3.13 | 2.90 | 2.74 | 2.63 | 2.54 |
| | 20 | 4.35 | 3.49 | 3.10 | 2.87 | 2.71 | 2.60 | 2.51 |
| | 21 | 4.32 | 3.47 | 3.07 | 2.84 | 2.68 | 2.57 | 2.49 |
| | 22 | 4.30 | 3.44 | 3.05 | 2.82 | 2.66 | 2.55 | 2.46 |
| | 23 | 4.28 | 3.42 | 3.03 | 2.80 | 2.64 | 2.53 | 2.44 |
| | 24 | 4.26 | 3.40 | 3.01 | 2.78 | 2.62 | 2.51 | 2.42 |
| | 25 | 4.24 | 3.39 | 2.99 | 2.76 | 2.60 | 2.49 | 2.40 |
| | 30 | 4.17 | 3.32 | 2.92 | 2.69 | 2.53 | 2.42 | 2.33 |
| | 40 | 4.08 | 3.23 | 2.84 | 2.61 | 2.45 | 2.34 | 2.25 |

Interpolation may be performed using reciprocals of the degrees of freedom.

[a]This table is abridged from M. Merrington and C. M. Thompson, "Tables of Percentage Points of the Inverted Beta Distribution," *Biometrika*, **33**: 73 (1943). It is printed here with permission of the Trustees of *Biometrika*.

## TABLE B$_2$[a]

Values of $F$ exceeded by 0.025 of the values in the sampling distribution.

If, in testing the homogeneity of two sample variances, the larger variance is placed over the smaller, the number of ratios greater than any given value, equal to or greater than unity, is doubled. Therefore use of the values tabled below, in comparing two sample variances, will provide a 0.05 level of significance.

| | | *df* for Larger Variance (numerator) | | | | | | | | | |
|---|---|---|---|---|---|---|---|---|---|---|---|
| | | 4 | 5 | 6 | 7 | 8 | 9 | 10 | 12 | 15 | 20 |
| | 4 | 9.60 | 9.36 | 9.20 | 9.07 | 8.98 | 8.90 | 8.84 | 8.75 | 8.66 | 8.56 |
| | 5 | 7.39 | 7.15 | 6.98 | 6.85 | 6.76 | 6.68 | 6.62 | 6.52 | 6.43 | 6.33 |
| *df* | 6 | 6.23 | 5.99 | 5.82 | 5.70 | 5.60 | 5.52 | 5.46 | 5.37 | 5.27 | 5.17 |
| for | 7 | 5.52 | 5.29 | 5.12 | 4.99 | 4.90 | 4.82 | 4.76 | 4.67 | 4.57 | 4.47 |
| Smaller | 8 | 5.05 | 4.82 | 4.65 | 4.53 | 4.43 | 4.36 | 4.30 | 4.20 | 4.10 | 4.00 |
| Variance | 9 | 4.72 | 4.48 | 4.32 | 4.20 | 4.10 | 4.03 | 3.96 | 3.87 | 3.77 | 3.67 |
| (denomi- | 10 | 4.47 | 4.24 | 4.07 | 3.95 | 3.85 | 3.78 | 3.72 | 3.62 | 3.52 | 3.42 |
| nator) | 12 | 4.12 | 3.89 | 3.73 | 3.61 | 3.51 | 3.44 | 3.37 | 3.28 | 3.18 | 3.07 |
| | 15 | 3.80 | 3.58 | 3.41 | 3.29 | 3.20 | 3.12 | 3.06 | 2.96 | 2.86 | 2.76 |
| | 20 | 3.51 | 3.29 | 3.13 | 3.01 | 2.91 | 2.84 | 2.77 | 2.68 | 2.57 | 2.46 |

Interpolation may be performed using reciprocals of the degrees of freedom.

[a]This table is abridged from M. Merrington and C. M. Thompson, " Tables of Percentage Points of the Inverted Beta Distribution," *Biometrika*, **33**: 73 (1943). It is published here with permission of the Trustees of *Biometrika*.

## TABLE $C_1$[a]

Values of chi square exceeded by 0.05 of values in the sampling distribution. In using chi square for a test of significance on a single set of *c* categories, the number of degrees of freedom is $(c - 1)$. In using chi square for a test of significance on a joint classification of *r* rows and *c* columns, the number of degrees of freedom is $(r - 1)(c - 1)$.

| *df* | $\chi^2$ |
|---|---|
| 1 | 3.841 |
| 2 | 5.991 |
| 3 | 7.815 |
| 4 | 9.488 |
| 5 | 11.070 |
| 6 | 12.592 |
| 7 | 14.067 |
| 8 | 15.507 |
| 9 | 16.919 |
| 10 | 18.307 |
| 11 | 19.675 |
| 12 | 21.026 |
| 13 | 22.362 |
| 14 | 23.685 |
| 15 | 24.996 |
| 16 | 26.296 |

[a]Table $C_1$ is abridged from Table III of R. A. Fisher, *Statistical Methods for Research Workers*, published by Oliver & Boyd Ltd., 1946, Edinburgh, by permission of the author and publishers.

## TABLE $C_2$[a]

Two chi square values are given below for each number of degrees of freedom. The value in the left column, $\chi_1^2$, exceeds 0.025 of the values in the sampling distribution. The value in the right column, $\chi_2^2$, is exceeded by 0.025 of the values in the sampling distribution.

In using these values to establish an interval estimate of the population variance, the number of degrees of freedom is $(n - 1)$ where $n$ is the number of measures in a random sample.

| *df* | $\chi^2$ | $\chi_2^2$ |
|---|---|---|
| 4 | 0.484 | 11.1 |
| 5 | 0.831 | 12.8 |
| 6 | 1.24 | 14.4 |
| 7 | 1.69 | 16.0 |
| 8 | 2.18 | 17.5 |
| 9 | 2.70 | 19.0 |
| 10 | 3.25 | 20.5 |
| 11 | 3.82 | 21.9 |
| 12 | 4.40 | 23.3 |
| 13 | 5.01 | 24.7 |
| 14 | 5.63 | 26.1 |
| 15 | 6.26 | 27.5 |
| 16 | 6.91 | 28.8 |
| 17 | 7.56 | 30.2 |
| 18 | 8.23 | 31.5 |
| 19 | 8.91 | 32.9 |
| 20 | 9.59 | 34.2 |
| 21 | 10.3 | 35.5 |
| 22 | 11.0 | 36.8 |
| 23 | 11.7 | 38.1 |
| 24 | 12.4 | 39.4 |
| 25 | 13.1 | 40.6 |
| 26 | 13.8 | 41.9 |
| 27 | 14.6 | 43.2 |
| 28 | 15.3 | 44.5 |
| 29 | 16.0 | 45.7 |
| 30 | 16.8 | 47.0 |

[a]Table $C_2$ was abridged from C. M. Thompson, " Tables of Percentage Points of the Incomplete Beta Function and of the Chi Square Distribution," *Biometrika*, **32**: pp. 188-189 (1941). It is printed here with permission of the Trustees of *Biometrika*.

# INDEX